The Governor as Party Leader

Campaigning and Governing

SARAH McCALLY MOREHOUSE

Ann Arbor

THE UNIVERSITY OF MICHIGAN PRESS

Copyright © by the University of Michigan 1998
All rights reserved
Published in the United States of America by
The University of Michigan Press
Manufactured in the United States of America
⊚ Printed on acid-free paper

2001   2000   1999   1998   4   3   2   1

A CIP catalog record for this book is available from the British Library.

Library of Congress Cataloging-in-Publication Data

Morehouse, Sarah McCally.
    The governor as party leader : campaigning and governing / Sarah McCally Morehouse.
        p.   cm.
    Includes bibliographical references and index.
    ISBN 0-472-10848-4 (cloth : acid-free paper)
    1. Governors—United States.   2. Political parties—United States—States.   3. State governments—United States.   I. Title.
JK2447.M67   1997
324'.0973—dc21   97-21108
                                                                       CIP

To the memory of my daughter
Catherine Page McCally

Contents

Figures

Tables

Preface

Many years ago I sat at the feet of Louise Overacker during our senior seminar on Political Parties at Wellesley College. Under her guidance, I wrote my senior thesis entitled "Party Responsibility under the New Deal." At that time, Overacker was working on the famous report "Toward a More Responsible Two-Party System," which was published in 1950 by the American Political Science Association. Thus began my enthusiasm for political parties and their intimate connection with democracy.

This enthusiasm has lasted a lifetime and has driven my research on the structure and performance of political parties using the states as political laboratories. In 1956 my enthusiasm was buttressed by David Truman, who introduced me to the works of V. O. Key as I embarked on my graduate work at Yale. I believe I have carried out the research that Key indicated should be done, namely, testing the ability of political parties to carry out the requirements of democracy: electing and governing.

The research reported in this book was started in 1982 and has pervaded my time ever since, although I had to lay it aside for long periods as professional demands intervened. After I became an emerita ten years later, I joyously completed the project. Along the way some special mentors have been both critical and comforting. Ed Lindblom, my former professor, has maintained an interest in my thoughts. The late Aaron Wildavsky and Nelson Polsby lured me out to Berkeley to test my ideas in that crucible. Leon Epstein and Malcolm Jewell were always ready to provide wisdom and encouragement. Ruth Jones provides sage advice on politics and money and in 1992 invited me to Arizona State to present my research results on the governor as legislative leader. Closer to home at the University of Connecticut, David Repass kept the "Money versus Party Effort" project methodologically secure, and Howard Reiter did not let me forget that parties should be ideological as well as electoral.

Throughout the years of this research, the University of Connecticut has been exceedingly supportive, funding my travels for interviews in 1982, which launched the undertaking, and providing money for graduate assistance in 1989. A Russell Sage Foundation research grant in 1983 meant that I could spend a full year's sabbatical analyzing and interpreting the candidate interviews and convention proceedings. A Yale University visiting fellowship provided library privileges and faculty contacts. The research might have withered had it not been for a National Science Foundation Visiting Professorship for Women award in 1991, which funded a second sabbatical to gather and assume command over the multiple facets of the project, acquire needed graduate help, and write. During that sabbatical, I was a visiting scholar at the Institute for Governmental Studies, University of California, Berkeley, and enjoyed the community of scholars at the institute. During 1992–94, an appointment as visiting scholar at the University of Kentucky propelled the book toward completion. Research based on 1982 candidates and conventions needed to be updated, and a National Science Research Foundation travel grant awarded to Malcolm Jewell and me allowed for a revisit to the state party conventions in 1994 and the processing of fifteen hundred questionnaires to convention delegates.

The research has two parts, as the subtitle suggests: campaigning and governing. The first part, which examined the efforts of gubernatorial hopefuls to receive their party's nomination, is based on interviews with forty-three gubernatorial candidates during the summer of 1982. (The appendix lists the names of those interviewed and the date they were interviewed. Citations in the text include the interviewee's last name, the year, and, where applicable, the transcript page.) Many of these interviews were lengthy, and many required innovative timing such as recesses in state legislative sessions, airport interviews, Sunday afternoon invasions, political convention interludes, campaign headquarters coffee breaks, and for incumbents, time slots in administrative schedules. I thank all those candidates and their campaign managers, who are listed in the appendix. During my stay in Duluth to visit the Democratic Convention in 1982, Craig Grau provided transportation as well as lively anecdotes about Minnesota politics, and he has contributed more of the latter on several occasions. In chapter 6, I quantify party effort, and to do so, I asked faculty experts in thirty-one states to rank the gubernatorial candidates on the basis of leadership support. They are also listed in the appendix, and I owe them a great debt. In the spring of 1993, Don Jonas, graduate student at the University of Kentucky, analyzed the campaign finance reports of all forty-three candidates and organized them according to sources of contributions.

The second part of the research examines the governor as legislative leader. It tested the hypotheses that there is a correlation between state party electoral strength and legislative party loyalty on governor's program bills. This test involved thousands of hours obtaining administration bills, and roll call votes on them for fifteen hundred legislators in twenty legislative chambers in the ten states in my study. Electoral and socioeconomic data by legislative district were also obtained. Several people were unusually helpful in identifying administration bills in their governor's program: in California, Gene Lee of the Institute for Governmental Studies at Berkeley, Bob Williams, legislative consultant, and Stephen Ardetti of the Office of State Government Relations; in Colorado, Don Eberle, Governor Lamm's legislative aide; in Illinois, Paula Wolff, director of programs and policy for Governor Thompson; in Kansas, Michael Swanson, press secretary to Governor Carlin; in Minnesota, Frank Ongaro, aide to Governor Perpich; in Oregon, Dave Moss, legislative counsel to Governor Atiyeh; in Tennessee, Vickie Trull, Governor Alexander's legal assistant. The monumental task of recording roll call votes on the governors' program bills for each legislator in eight states was performed by Joe Lazzaro, graduate student in political science at the University of Connecticut. Legislators' voting in Connecticut and New York was tabulated by Marlene Seder and Steve Kitowitz, also graduate students.

Many of the electoral data used in the legislative district analysis were made available by the Inter-University Consortium for Political and Social Research at the University of Michigan. Socioeconomic data per legislative district in 1982 were difficult to obtain. I thank Elizabeth Gerber of the Division of Humanities and Social Sciences, California Institute of Technology, for providing data, and Dee Long, former speaker of the Minnesota House, for helping me obtain information.

I owe a great debt to David Hadwiger of the University of New Mexico, who performed many of the statistical manipulations for this research. For each legislator, all votes, electoral background variables, and socioeconomic data in some cases, were entered and subjected to correlation and regression analysis. I am also greatly indebted to Malcolm Jewell, professor emeritus, University of Kentucky, who continued the statistical program and provided assistance with the analysis of the results.

Two of the chapters in this book draw from previously published work. Chapter 6 is based on Sarah M. Morehouse, "Money versus Party Effort: Nominating for Governor," *American Journal of Political Science,* vol. 34 (1990): 706–24, reprinted by permission of the University of Wisconsin Press. Chapter 7 draws on some material from Sarah M. Morehouse, "Legislative Party Voting for the Governor's Program," *Legislative Studies Quarterly* vol. 21 (1996): 359–81, reprinted by permission of *Legislative Studies Quarterly.*

In addition to the friends and colleagues mentioned earlier who have read and commented on parts of my research in progress, I want to thank Ron Weber, professor, and Neil Cotter, professor emeritus, of the University of Wisconsin–Milwaukee, who have read various of my efforts and encouraged me to continue. Pat Patterson of Ohio University has labored through the entire manuscript and pronounced it worthy of publication. His comments came at a most opportune time, and I thank him deeply.

None of the mentors, colleagues, contacts, research assistants, or institutions mentioned here are responsible for the contents of this book. The University of Michigan Press people have assumed the responsibility for publishing it. Charles T. Myers, editor for political science, Michael Landauer, editorial assistant, Kevin M. Rennells, copyediting coordinator, and Jillian Downey, production coordinator, have my gratitude for accepting it and producing it.

My existence depends upon my family's support. Even though some live in faraway places, they have managed to have input into this eternal project. Suzan was able to organize my travels to nine states in 1982, even providing transportation from Duluth airport to the convention by truck driven by an aide of Governor Rudy Perpich. My three sons, Rick, John, and David, have asked politely about this research from time to time, confident that someday it would be done. Grandchildren have been loyal, but why would a grandmother want to write a book? There is one knight mentioned from time to time throughout this preface who deserves almost all the credit for bringing this book to completion. He started out as a mentor, became a colleague and then a husband, and in that role has now assumed the role of editorial assistant. Malcolm Jewell, dearest one, here's to your patience and belief in me. Without it I would have been too lonely to seek the needed 1994 update. It was such fun with the two of us. Thanks for trimming 12 percent off the manuscript when I couldn't bear to cut my precious prose. I wish my daughter Catherine could confirm how happy I am. I dedicate this book to her, whose life was far too short.

CHAPTER 1

Party Government: The American Model

Those who seek to become governor and those who move on to govern put flesh and blood on party theory. Models of political behavior must be personified to be tested. Men and women who pursue and win the most important political post in each of our fifty states offer in number and significance a measure of the political party as a coalition of those seeking to govern by winning elective office.

The ambition and effort of those who offer themselves to govern and who gather the resources to succeed or fail give us a test of the political party's health or weakness. This book portrays how governors emerge in our fifty states. It describes the rules and the money and the human effort that produce our modern governors. In 1982 and in 1994, thirty-six states elected governors, and their campaigns provided the candidates and the records for this enterprise. Forty-three of those who sought to become governor in 1982 in ten states, both large and small, are followed closely. A follow-up study in 1994 revisited five of these states (among others) to reexamine the rules and question the leaders and activists who make them work.

The Condition of the Parties in the 1980s and into the 1990s

The year 1982 was a good year to sample the condition of the parties and their most important political race—the race for governor. That time period reflected a decade of party response to the reforms that followed the intense political upheaval of the late 1960s. Most of the trends in political campaigning that have become familiar today were already under way in the early 1980s. In 1982 the gubernatorial elections were characterized by the "air wars" of telecommunications and the financing that was necessary to wage them. The campaign financing disclosures, available for the first time, revealed the capital-intensive efforts of the modern candidates for governor. By 1990, the costs of gubernatorial races had leveled off, with the exception of some large states where open seat races, challenges to an incumbent governor, or a rematch drove the price up (Beyle 1994, 39–41). The much higher costs of the 1994 elections (in 1994 dollars) in at least seventeen states may have reversed this trend. In 1992, one of the wizards of campaign finance argued that the American system of campaign financing had become increasingly stable and institutionalized during the preceding sixteen years. He claimed that we have reached an end to the growth of political action committees (PACs) and PAC spending that marked the late 1970s and early 1980s (Sorauf 1992).

In the early 1980s the courts had already begun to loosen some of the regulations that the states had imposed upon their political parties, as part of the Progressive reforms, because they violate freedom of political association guaranteed by the First and Fourteenth amendments. While there does not appear to be much organizational change that can be attributed to this freedom, parties have potential control over their own organization and operation, which argues for more, rather than less, organizational strength.

The most significant state regulation of the Progressive era required parties to nominate their candidates in direct primaries. Some states mandated preprimary endorsements at the time the laws were passed. Others allowed this practice. In 1982, parties in sixteen states had developed preprimary endorsement procedures, and these have changed very little since that time. Only the California Democrats, freed of regulation that forbade endorsing, have initiated the practice.

Preprimary endorsements play an important part in this analysis of how governors are selected and particularly how they are nominated. The study compares the nominating process in five states where one or usually both parties make preprimary endorsements and in five states where the parties do not. The operation of these party endorsing systems in 1982 is examined in detail to determine how they work and why the endorsed candidates are usually nominated. Most state parties that made endorsements in the early 1980s continue to do so today. In 1994 I studied ten state party endorsement systems in seven states, including all but one of the parties in the 1982 study, to determine how much continuity and how much change have occurred in the process and its effectiveness.

It is the pursuit of office that is so important, for from those who pursue are chosen those who govern. I examine in depth forty-three of those who sought to become governor in 1982 in ten states (populating 43 percent of the nation). Only ten of the forty-three candidates entered the governor's mansion, and of those, six reentered. A seventh, Governor Perpich of Minnesota, reclaimed office after four years. The three newly elected governors, in the three largest states, came from behind to attain the highest office the state could bestow. Thus, the election of 1982 returned six out of seven of our incumbents, somewhat above the predicted rate of success (Beyle 1991, 19). Yet the predictions were based on incumbency: those who were already successful. We know little about the challengers and those who try for open seats. We need to know more about the backgrounds, motivations, abilities, and governing potential of gubernatorial candidates.

Ambition for office is related to the opportunities that exist. The ten states chosen are competitive between the parties so that either could anticipate winning and hence attract candidates to make the race. Gubernatorial candidates must form coalitions in order to win their party's nomination. Doing so involves the people they ask to join their campaign for the nomination, the resources these people have, the strategies they use to win, and the results. This book describes the way American state governors and state political parties join in an effort to nominate, elect, and govern. In some states, this process works according to the classical model of party government. In others, neither the candidate for governor nor the party expects to form a joint coalition to organize the nomination and election and to enact policy. In these states, gubernatorial candidates capture the party label by building personal campaign organizations, and they face unfamiliar or unorganized—or even worse, organized and hostile— legislative parties. It is the assumption of this book that party organization matters, but how it matters needs to be determined.

This concern with the ability of the state's chief executive to build a party coalition to support his or her election and legislative program has national implications. Three of the last four presidents were former governors, and the character of their coalition building had an impact on the national nominating and policy-making process.

A good nominating system is one in which the traits that make a successful nominee match those of a successful officeholder. Concern continues over the effects of the state-by-state sequence of direct primaries for the selection of presidential candidates. The increased recourse to primaries to make the process more democratic has pushed the parties out of the nominating process, and, as a result, candidate organizations have evolved out of ad hoc groups. Professional scrutiny has been abolished.

A president's influence depends upon his or her electoral coalition. The groups that played an important part in the nomination stage play an important role in presidential policy-making and administration. The president chooses principal members of the White House staff and other key officials based on their participation in the campaign. President Clinton has discovered that his Arkansas staffers did not serve him well in Washington. If a president does not build coalitions for the nomination and election, he or she will not be able to govern once elected. President Clinton's reluctance to bring Congress into the process of formulating national health-care legislation contributed to its demise. Our presidential nominating process does not ensure that candidates must build potential governing coalitions in order to be elected.

For years, states as political laboratories have been experimenting with ways to increase the role of the political party in the nominating process despite the direct primary now operative in all of them. They have had more time to experience the effects of the primary since it became law in most of them several decades ago. Their experience as well as their efforts to strengthen the party in the gubernatorial selection process are relevant to the national parties.

Party as Coalition Building

Definition of Party as Coalition Building

Our gubernatorial candidates inherit state political parties that they will embrace, ignore, or reject. Their choice depends upon their own political experience and upon the type of party that exists. A party is defined in terms of effort: collective effort directed toward capturing public office and governing once that office is attained (Epstein 1986, 3; Downs 1957, 34; Schlesinger 1991, 6). Most definitions of political parties as organizations assume the electoral and the governing functions. Anthony Downs defined the party as "a team seeking to control the governing apparatus by gaining office in a duly constituted election," essentially the definition that is used here. Those who criticize it as too devoid of policy commitment do not recognize that his whole theory of parties is based on the distribution of voter preferences. Charles Lindblom argues that parties base their electoral activity on voter preferences and that this has been the common approach of party theorists (1957). Without the desire to win elections as a leading motive, candidates need not pay attention to the preferences of the people.

The concept of party that guides this book is the party coalition that organizes to elect and govern. It links two of the three parts of the traditional tripartite definition of the political party. The concept does not include the voters as part of the party organization, but as just explained, the preferences of the voters are the base of party organization. The voters are choosers among competing parties. Because they are less committed partisans than they were before does not mean that the parties as organizations are weaker. In fact, Schlesinger believes that the more flexible the electorate, the more the party must organize to win and govern (Schlesinger 1991, 192–99). Or, as Pomper states, parties are to be examined as "groups of people who seek power through the ballot box, not as voters who grant power through their ballots" (Pomper 1992, 5).

Party Coalitions and Responsible Party Government

The term *responsible parties* evokes professional passion as well as scholarly protest. I mean to use the term *party government* as a model of a perfectly plausible coalition of men and women that operates under a party label to nominate, elect, and govern. The degree to which this model is operative in our ten states will help us understand parties as they are rather than as we would wish them to be. First an explanation of the responsible party government model of the reformers will demonstrate what is more vision than reality.

Responsible Party Government of the Reformers

The advocates of responsible party government want to transcend the normal operation of American political parties and make them vehicles for policy-making in a manner uncharacteristic of our experience. Policy is to be determined by assessing the public interest and by consensus among party activists. Proponents of responsible party government say its most ideal form should work in the following manner: two well-disciplined parties, each with its own conception of what the voters want and a program designed to satisfy those wants, compete for the favor of the electorate. Each party attempts to convince the majority that its program is best. In the election, 50 percent or slightly more of the voters choose the party whose policies they favor. The party takes over the executive and legislative power of government and the entire responsibility for what government does. It then proceeds to put its program into effect. The opposition party seeks to control the government at a future time. This goal is reasonably well assured because of the evenness in electoral competition between the parties. By voting at the next election, the people decide whether or not they approve of the general direction the party in power has been taking—in short, whether their wants are being satisfied. If the answer is yes, they return that party to power; if the answer is no, they replace it with the opposition. The parties, therefore, are responsible to the electorate because they fear losing the next election. They are cohesive because they know that disunity may mean defeat. This is what is meant by "responsible party government" (Ranney 1962, 8–22).

According to the doctrine, responsible party government performs three indispensable functions in a truly democratic society. First, it clarifies the issues and enables people to express themselves effectively on those issues. Second, it accomplishes the important function of activating public opinion—responsible party government educates the public. Finally, parties establish popular control over government by making the group of rulers in power collectively responsible to the people. Needless to say, the proponents of responsible party government are not pleased with the operation of the American party system (APSA 1950, 22–23; Burnham 1967, 305–6).

Critics of this model of responsible party government see a danger in making parties policy driven. They fear any group determining in advance what the public interest is and binding party members to it. They see party as an agency for compromise. They see the public interest as "whatever emerges from the negotiations, adjustments and compromises made in fair fights or bargains among conflicting interest groups" (Polsby and Wildavsky 1991, 275). The critics want parties whose major focus is to win elections. This focus brings party attention to the electorate and creates the desire to bring many diverse interests together, leading to moderation in government.

The responsible parties model emphasizes the policy motivations of party elites who participate in politics to achieve policy or ideological goals, while the party coalition model emphasizes electoral incentives. In the responsible parties model, the party elites push the party away from the center in order to remain ideologically pure. In the party coalition model, the elites push the party toward the center in order to win. Which of these two models represents reality?

In *Statehouse Democracy,* Erikson, Wright, and McIver (1993) resolve the apparent conflict between the two models by examining the ideological preferences of two groups of elites within each political party: the activist elite and the electoral elite. For the activist elite (convention volunteers, contributors, convention delegates, party officials), maintaining ideological purity and distance from the opposite party is preferable. For the electoral elite, those who seek and are elected to office, appealing to the ideologically moderate center where more voters are, is strategically necessary. Hence each party is torn between these two ideological elites, and every election represents a compromise between elites that are ideologically driven and elites that are electorally driven.

Party Government as Action

It is the thesis of this book that party organization matters. It matters to the candidates for governor whether they can count on party resources to win the nomination. It matters if they contest in states where the party remains neutral until after the primary and they cannot count on its help in the nomination process. It matters whether legislators identify with the party and commit to the platform because they can be counted on to support it in the legislative session. These are minimal conditions for political parties to fulfill, and they are possible under our system.

Political practitioners do not read the doctrine of responsible party government. They go about their work of nominating, electing, and governing with another set of assumptions—primarily those of winning or of winning again. In contrast to the model of responsible party government that deduces the type of actions a party should take from some ethical principle about its proper function, my concept of political party is based on the office ambitions of men and women. Ambition is not as noble a motive as "responsibility," but it is a more accurate description of the propelling force behind political party organizations in the American states. Anthony Downs says that political parties formulate policies to win elections instead of winning elections to formulate policy (1957, 27–28). Self-interest is a more convincing explanation of political action than common good.

If ambition is the dominant motive in the political party, a party would logically contain many office-seeking factions or groups, each contesting for vacant offices to be filled at the state, county, and local level. Under what conditions would these factions and groups join a coalition to present one candidate for an office, and under what conditions would the same coalition present candidates for several offices? Office-seeking groups under the party label may combine forces to present one candidate for an office because they believe cohesion is their only chance of winning. They may also unite to control the nomination for more than one office in the party, for they may realize that a strong gubernatorial candidate, for instance, can bring others into office. In this case, the rudiments of a cohesive party structure begin to emerge (Schlesinger 1991, 151). If legislators support the governor's election because they see their own election chances bound up with those of the governor, the party has a measure of unity. For the governor, legislative cooperation is crucial to policy-making. Policies that please the electorate (or at least a majority of it) are crucial to the next election. As a result, in some states, a kind of symbiotic relationship develops between office-seeking groups.

To the extent that the governors and legislators find it to their advantage to run on the same policy record, we have the makings of party government. This party government has come about because office seekers must appeal to the electorate and believe that their next election depends on their performance in office. Jim Thompson, as a Republican candidate for governor in Illinois, a politically competitive industrial state, had to offer enough benefits to workers and Chicago dwellers to weaken their normal support for his Democratic opponent. He could not win the election by appealing to large farmers, industrialists, bankers, and business executives. There are not enough votes from those groups. After Thompson was elected, he had to present a program to the legislature to offer advantages to enough groups of voters to ensure reelection. The legislators will respond if they, in turn, believe that their next election depends on support for the governor's program.

A governor represents the totality of interests within the party. No single legislator or faction represents as wide a variety of interests. The governor's legislation is geared to please the statewide constituency and, depending largely on his or her degree of control over the party, is passed, modified, or rejected. The governor is head of both political party and state government. The two roles are intertwined; the more successful he or she is as party leader, the more successful as head of state. A governor's ability to capture the loyalty of party leaders to build winning coalitions within the legislature provides mastery over the decision-making process. This process allocates the burdens and benefits of the system. The governor's leadership can provide the link between the people and their problems and the extent and direction of resources that state government can allocate to these problems.

Figure 1.1 represents a governing coalition within a political party. The two elements of political party, the party in office (the governing party) and the party of groups and elites (the electoral party), are joined in a governing coalition. The governor is at the apex of both the electoral and governing parties. He or she must form winning coalitions both within and outside the government. The gubernatorial electoral coalition may be a permanent one based on traditional party loyalty, as in Minnesota, or it may be dominated by a powerful governor, such as Governor Cuomo of New York. Instead of the legislative party being an independent entity, it is subject to the direction and influence of the governor's coalition within the electoral organization. The essentials of party government exist if there is a leadership coalition with enough power to nominate the governor and to command enough votes in the legislature to pass executive requests.

Divided Government and Party Government

Our model of party government, unlike that of the original party responsibility model, does not require unified party control over the executive and legislative branches. The proportion of states having divided government has increased from under 30 percent fifty years ago to over half in the last few years. Fiorina (1992, 26–28) has shown that since the 1960s, a party's control of the governorship is statistically independent from its control of the legislature.

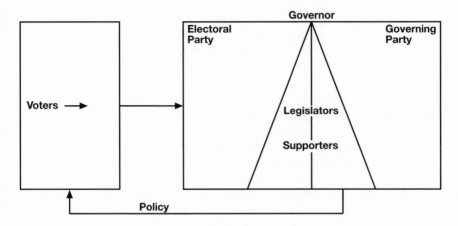

Fig. 1.1.   A governing coalition

Our model of party government would predict that a governor with a strong electoral coalition would gain strong support from his or her legislators even if in the minority. This support might be lessened because the governor has to negotiate compromises with the majority opposition party and hence alienate some of his or her own party members. We will anticipate this possibility in our party government model.

Party Government: American Style

This book tests the party government model of a strong party system. In this model, parties are composed of men and women who operate under a party label and recruit, nominate, and elect candidates for public office who are broadly representative of the party's voters and who, when elected, will present, enact, and implement programs that reflect the needs and demands of the same voters.

Most would agree that a strong state party involves the following activities:

1. It seeks to control the gubernatorial nomination through an endorsement process that produces candidates who are broadly in step with the program needs of the party's constituency.
2. During the election campaign, the gubernatorial candidate enunciates the program objectives of the party.

3. Once elected, the governor proposes a legislative program that is in agreement with the campaign promises.
4. The governor is able to enlist the support of all or most of his or her legislative party members to enact the program.

Based on this model, we would expect that in states where the governor's coalition is strong, as evidenced by nominating strength, the governor would be able to obtain loyalty from the legislators in the party. In states where the party is weak or divided, the governor will face a legislature in which sit remnants of the factions that opposed him or her in the nominating contest. Very little research has been done on the relationship between the political efforts of party leaders and gubernatorial candidates to capture the nomination and their success when in office to put the program into effect. The forty-three gubernatorial candidates who made a run for the nomination and the ten who became governor provide us with the human material to test this party government model.

Plan of Study

Selection of Ten States

In 1982, thirty-six states nominated and elected governors. I selected ten of them to test the coalition-building efforts of party leaders and candidates. In the first group of states, the gubernatorial candidate must put together his or her own coalition because the party leaders have little influence and the primary determines the outcome of the nominating process (California, Kansas, Oregon, Tennessee, and Texas). Candidates must raise a war chest, get themselves on the primary ballot, and proceed to campaign for the nomination. In some states party leaders back their favorite candidates, but they cannot deliver the money and support typically given the endorsee in the preprimary endorsement states. In these situations the candidate has to develop a personal coalition and try for early money in order to beat off other contenders. Incumbent governors are generally able to achieve renomination, as was true in Kansas, Oregon, Texas, and Tennessee, although they may be challenged in the primary, as were the first three governors.

In the second group of five, the possibility of a strong party coalition exists because gubernatorial candidates are endorsed in a convention or party gathering and party cohesion is traditionally strong (Colorado, Connecticut, Illinois, Minnesota, and New York). This situation offers the maximum potential for party control over the nominating process, for if the party is unified, the gubernatorial candidate will be endorsed and not seriously challenged in a primary. The leaders, on the other hand, have the chance to influence, if not control, the nomination of a candidate who will be supportive of the party as well as electable. In these states there is ordinarily a party favorite before the convention. After the convention the endorsee has the backing of party leaders and activists. Half the time that means that opponents do not contest the primary, as was true in Colorado, Connecticut, and Illinois. Incumbents in these states generally will win the endorsement as well as the following primary without much opposition.

In all of the ten states either party has a chance to win the governorship. Texas and Tennessee are newcomers to this two-party league, but there were Republican governors in both as the nomination process started. This even competition controls for the probability of success in winning the nomination in the initial resource distribution (Chertkoff 1966). V. O. Key also hypothesized that the potential electoral success of a party influenced the number of contestants in a primary. In this study I wanted to rule out the factional contests within the dominant Democratic party in the South as well as the uncontested and seemingly cohesive endorsement within the minority Republican party.

Observation and Interviews

In order to test the assumptions discussed previously, which are drawn from individual state studies and voting statistics, I turned to observation and interviews. I decided to put some flesh and blood on theory drawn from statistical analyses. What appears to be coalition durability, as measured by statistics, may be a succession of strong gubernatorial candidates with ad hoc followings. What appears to be a bifactional voting pattern may disguise one durable faction and a succession of different factions formed to challenge it. A multifactional voting pattern indicates very little about the activities of the men and women who contend for the gubernatorial nomination under the party label.

Observation and interviews are appropriate to examine the way candidates fashion coalitions. I focused on the candidates in twenty gubernatorial nominating contests in the ten two-party states in 1982. I designed an interview schedule that asked for information concerning goals, party factions, resources, strategies and results (see appendix). I interviewed all announced candidates unless, in the view of political observers close to the scene, the candidacy was hopeless (a predicted vote of less than 10 percent of a convention or primary). When it was impossible to see a candidate, I talked to the campaign manager (nineteen out of forty-three cases). The names of those interviewed are listed in the appendix.

States with Preprimary Endorsements

I observed the preprimary endorsing conventions for both parties in Minnesota, New York, and Connecticut. I attended the Republican convention in Colorado. (Since the Democratic governor of Colorado was not challenged for the nomination, I did not attend that convention.) Nominations in Illinois are not open, and I had to glean information about the nominating process from the candidates and party officials. During the conventions, I talked to delegates, observed the proceedings, collected party documents such as campaign literature and roll call votes on endorsements, and monitored press accounts. I tried to interview the candidates as close to the endorsement as possible, but that was not always feasible. In 1994, to measure the continuing importance of endorsements, I studied endorsements in ten state parties, based on surveys of delegates and, in several parties, firsthand observation.

States with Primary-Only Nominations

Because of the frantic activity involved in campaigning for the primary nomination, I arranged interviews with the candidates as soon as possible after the primary, while their recollections were still fresh. I asked the same questions of these candidates (with the exception of the convention-strategy section). I had to track down these candidates in different locations because there was not the rallying point of a convention to draw them together.

The forty-three taped interviews of approximately one hour each are an exceedingly valuable set of statements of the ambitions, strategies, resources, personal observations of party factionalism, and philosophies of the gubernatorial hopefuls in 1982.

The Governor's Legislative Coalition

Ten successful candidates entered the governor's mansion. They provide a test for the hypothesis that there is a correlation between coalitions formed to win the nomination and coalitions formed to pass the governor's program. The assumption is that the legislative party and the statewide electoral party are joined in the forming of a governing coalition. I predict that a strong party coalition includes members of the legislature who are part of the governor's coalition. In states where the party is weak or divided, the governor will face a legislature where party loyalty is low. The loyalty of the legislators may also be affected by divided government in which the governor must negotiate compromises with the majority opposition party and hence alienate some of his or her own party members.

The dependent variable in this part of the research is legislative voting on governor's program bills for ten state legislatures in 1983. The package of bills a governor presents to the legislature as his or her policy program is the most important and hence the most controversial considered. In all of the states, the governor presents a program message to the legislature in which he or she outlines the substance of the program desired for passage. This program is translated into administration bills, which are introduced in most states by the governor's party leaders in the house or senate. A legislator's party voting support can be determined by analyzing roll call votes, which are an essential part of reaching decisions on bills. In this way an average loyalty score for each legislator can be determined.

It is also possible that electoral conditions in the legislators' districts can explain deviations in legislative support for the governor's program. Parties are made up of legislators pulled by the needs of their constituencies as well as demands for party loyalty imposed by state leaders. Hence, for the fifteen hundred legislators, both voting behavior and district electoral data were collected. Multiple regression analysis was used to determine the degree to which electoral conditions in the legislators' districts can explain the support that the governor receives from his or her legislative members.

How the Study Tests Party Theory

Party organization matters. But how it matters has rarely been specified. It matters to candidates whether they receive party support for the nomination and election. It matters to the governors, as they beseech legislators to pass their programs, if they can count on their legislative leaders. It matters to the people of the state if they can count on their governors fulfilling their campaign promises.

I study how forty-three prospective gubernatorial candidates formed coalitions in order to win their party's nomination. Such coalition formation involved the people they asked to join their campaign for the nomination, the resources those people had, the strategies they used to win, and the results. I follow the ten successful candidates into the governor's mansion and measure their coalition-building efforts in the legislature. I hypothesize that if the governor was successful in building a coalition in the primary, he or she was successful in building a coalition within the legislature to pass legislation. Alternatively, in the states where the outside party is weak, the prediction calls for weak legislative party loyalty.

This research tests the theory of party government that maintains that there is a linkage between the electoral party and the governing party. If legislators support the governor's nomination and election because they see their own election chances bound up with that of the governor, the party has a governing coalition. For the governor, legislative cooperation is crucial to policy-making. Policies that please the electorate are crucial to the next election. The degree to which this model is operative in the ten test states will help us understand how far American parties fulfill a theory that many despair as impossible in our country.

The research also tests how ambition is related to electoral opportunity. The ambition theory of party organization states that the office drives of the men and women in the party determine its character. If the party makes endorsements before the primary takes place and if these endorsements are seldom overturned, candidates must get the approval of the leadership coalition. This leadership coalition can recruit and promote candidates for governor, and the coalition of the party and the candidate are joined in the electoral effort. On the other hand, parties rent by two or more factions cannot agree on a candidate in advance and do not have any legal or informal machinery for doing so. In these parties, the candidate has to build his or her own coalition. Because I have selected states that endorse as well as states that do not, this theory can be tested.

The coalition model is based on four conditions that are present in the nominating and governing process and therefore make it an appropriate model to use: (1) individuals (actors) agree to pursue a common goal, (2) they pool their relevant resources in pursuit of this goal, (3) they engage in communication concerning the goal and the means of obtaining it, and (4) they agree on the distribution of benefits received when obtaining the goal (Kelley 1968). I describe the coalition-building efforts of gubernatorial candidates in terms of actors, resources, strategies, and results. I hypothesize that different types of coalitions form depending upon the character of the actors and their resources. Their strategies are based on the electoral rules, and the results differ according to structure, stability, and candidate success.

Outline of the Book

The order of chapters in the book follows the time sequence of coalition building. Chapter 2 describes the way candidates assess their opportunities for winning office based on competitiveness, primary rules, the potential for party endorsement, incumbency status, and party strength. Chapter 3 is concerned with the rules that structure the ambitions of the candidates for governor. The direct-primary form of nomination as well as the preprimary endorsement process will be discussed in general as well as the particular experience of each of our ten states. Campaign finance laws also have an impact on the ambition of the candidates, and they will also be presented in general as well as in the particular application to each state.

Chapters 4 and 5 discuss the actors, resources, strategies, organization, and outcomes for the direct-primary states and the endorsing states. The endorsing conventions in four states and the Illinois experience with central committee endorsements will be described. The candidates themselves are largely responsible for the material in chapters 4 and 5. They tell about their choice of coalition partners, their observations about their political party and its usefulness to them, their struggles to raise money for their campaign, their own strategies, and their view of those of their opponents. Included are the predictions of success on the part of those interviewed as well as the analysis of the actual outcomes. These outcomes are compared to recent developments in each state that confirm or change the events of the 1980s.

Chapter 6 is a statistical comparison of our ten states with all those (thirty-six) that nominated and elected governors in 1982. In particular, the impact of money on the nominating process is considered. Any finding of coalition cohesion and hence success would be suspect unless it could be shown that it was not the result of superior spending. Multiple regression analysis was used to estimate the relative influence of money and party effort on the primary or convention outcomes.

Chapter 7 focuses on legislative support for the programs of the successful gubernatorial candidates in the ten states. This legislative party voting analysis tests my previous research, which found a high correlation between the strength of electoral party coalitions and legislative party loyalty on the governor's program. The test involves roll call voting on governors' program bills for ten state legislatures in 1983. The test also considers whether the correlation may be affected by factors in the legislators' districts such as primary and general election voting strength.

Chapter 8 will conclude with a review of the findings and an analysis of the conditions that give rise to party government in some of the states in our nation. The forty-three candidates and the ten governors drawn from them will have given human form to party theory. Their efforts will tell us about factions and coalitions, money versus party effort, and the condition of political parties in ten states of our union. This chapter will include a comparison of the party endorsement process in 1982 and 1994 and an analysis of the types of party coalitions formed in the two time periods.

CHAPTER 2

Coalition Building for Electing and Governing

We have defined a political party as a coalition of men and women who seek office by gaining election. We have also stated that election is their main purpose and that they plan their campaigns by paying attention to the preferences of the voters and attempting to appeal to these preferences. They assess their opportunities for office based on their chances for nomination and election.

Opportunities and Ambitions

There are several factors that influence the calculations of candidates as they assess their chances of winning:

1. The competitiveness of the state: What chance do they have of winning office?
2. Primaries: Is this the only point of decision for the nomination? Is there a runoff primary? Do candidates have a preferential place on the primary ballot because they have an endorsement?
3. Endorsements: Does their party endorse a candidate before the primary? Does this endorsement bring party money and support?
4. Incumbency: Are they incumbent, or are they running against incumbents?

What we have just set out is a theory of the political party that is driven by ambition for office. The relationship between ambition and party organization will develop as we examine each of the factors. Political candidates adjust their political ambitions according to their chances for winning as well as the rules of the game. The coalitions that the prospective gubernatorial candidates form in order to win the nomination of their party are indicators of the organization of the party itself.

Electoral Competition

Increasingly, the people of the states vote as Democrats and Republicans in nearly equal proportions. Almost all of the states could be classified as having two-party systems, in the sense that both Democrats and Republicans seriously compete for the office of governor and each party has held the governorship at least once since the beginning of the 1960s. The greatest trends toward two-party competition in state politics have come in the South, beginning in some states in the 1960s and in others much more recently.

In 1976 there were five southern states that had not elected a Republican governor in modern times and in which the Republican gubernatorial candidate rarely ran a competitive race: Texas, Louisiana, Alabama, Mississippi, and Georgia. Since that time, the Republicans have won three gubernatorial races in Texas, beginning in 1978; two in Louisiana, in 1979 and 1995; three in Alabama, beginning in 1986; and two in Mississippi, in 1991 and 1995. The Republicans have failed to elect a governor in Georgia, but they came very close in 1990 and 1994. Since the mid-1970s most gubernatorial elections have been closely competitive in nearly all the states, both North and South. As voters have grown more independent at the polls, they have increasingly elected Republican governors in traditionally Democratic states and Democratic governors in traditionally Republican states.

The office-seeking theory of party, or the American-style party model, assumes competition between two relatively evenly matched contenders. Competition, according to this theory, is the best guarantee that the parties will be internally cohesive and, as a result, better able to perform the job of electing and governing.

It was V. O. Key's hypothesis that internal party structure is determined by electoral competition (1950, 1956). Key's studies of the eleven southern states support his contention that lack of competition results in weak, multiple-faction parties that cannot control nominations or enact programs. Key asserted that no external pressure from a minority party existed to drive the majority party toward internal unity and discipline. The corollary of this hypothesis is that parties will be cohesive in states where there is close competition between them. Each must be united to fight the common enemy and hence will be able to control the type of men and women who are nominated for public office. Because winning is the primary goal, candidates who represent majority opinion will be selected by party leaders. Factions within the party will be appeased by the promise of policy, patronage, prestige, and the like. A slight modification of this basic theme was offered by W. Duane Lockard (1959) and John Fenton

(1966), who claimed that parties will most likely be cohesive in states that are polarized by parties along rural-urban lines. Thus, it takes a particular kind of economic and political competition to produce cohesive parties.

However persuasive the hypothesis, competition has only a moderate impact on party cohesion. V. O. Key discovered that the two-party states were not producing consistently the disciplined parties he had predicted. I found that the correlation between two-party competition and party strength was not high (.40). In a group of twenty-two states where competition was strong, only nine showed unity in the nominating process for both parties during the period studied (1956–78). It is only in the five southern states mentioned earlier that the hypothesis appears to be proved. Here the main competition for the governorship during this period took place within the Democratic primary where opposing factions represented a conflict of personalities or amorphous issues.

Primary Election Laws

When V. O. Key found that the northern states were not unified in their internal organization, he hypothesized that it was due to the influence of the direct-primary form of nomination. The uniquely American direct primary exists in all states, although it takes on different forms. Ushered into the state political systems in the period 1896 to 1915, the primary replaced the delegate convention as a means of selecting candidates to run for governor and other statewide offices. Convention nominations had been indirect, with delegates chosen by mass meetings, caucuses, and conventions in counties or other local areas. The adoption of the direct primary, under the guise of making the internal control of the party more democratic, struck down the intermediate links between the party rank and file and would-be candidates, allowing the voters to express their preferences for the nomination.

The primary system first came into use in the southern states—those most stubbornly attached to a single party. It permitted a measure of popular government within the dominant Democratic party. Since nomination was tantamount to election, the voters were given a choice within the confines of the party. Outside of the South, statewide direct primaries first took hold in the Progressive western states and then spread to the eastern seaboard. The fact that there was a semblance of an opposition party in these states may explain why they embraced the primary procedures later on. Before the primary form of nomination, leadership factions operating within their respective party conventions bargained and fought over the nominees their party would present to the voters in the general election.

The lottery of the direct-primary form of nomination was a serious setback for the party leadership, which was the intention of the reformers. It made it very difficult for the leaders to recruit candidates for public office by using the assurance that they would win in the primary. Too often, last-minute challengers entered the scene, declared their candidacy for the nomination, and then swept the primary. It is debatable whether they were more qualified than the party-sponsored candidate carefully chosen by the leadership.

Primary turnout is about 60 percent of each party's vote in the general election, although in a few southern states the Democratic primary turnout is still higher than that party's turnout in November (Jewell and Olson 1988, 111). If primary voters reflected the preferences of the party's rank and file, there would be no problems with this unusual turnout pattern. But those people who vote in primaries are not representative of the whole: they are better educated, wealthier, and older, with much more interest in politics. In most states, about 30 percent of the potential electorate determines which candidates will contest the general election. This fact has undoubtedly affected the overall health of the political party in the United States. Candidates appealing to small groups of voters can make it difficult for politicians to present popular slates. These blocs of voters may be rooted in an ethnic, religious, or professional group, or any group that is strongly committed to certain issues (such as a pro life or pro choice position on the abortion issue) and is well organized during the primary.

In addition to requiring the primary as a nominating device, some southern states have imposed additional rules that also affect electoral ambition and hence party organization. In particular, runoff primaries offer greater incentives to candidates to compete than do single primaries. In most states, the primary candidate with the plurality of votes is the nominee. However, in a number of southern and border states, laws require a runoff primary between the top two candidates if the leading vote getter does not win over 50 percent (or in a few states 40 percent) of the vote. The possibility of a runoff primary may offer incentives to additional candidates to enter the first, as the odds of surviving are increased.

In a recent study Berry and Canon test for the effects of both competition and primary electoral laws on the factional structure of the political party. They find that when competition is weak, runoff primaries can produce greater contesting among the factions within the majority party. The possibility for primary candidates to bargain for rewards with the candidates competing in a runoff makes the expected reward from entering a double primary greater than the reward from participating in a single primary. As the minority party becomes stronger, the difference between double and single primary systems in the expected rewards they create for potential candidates diminishes, and both kinds of primaries are marked by equal amounts of factionalism (Berry and Canon 1993; M. Black and E. Black 1982).

In most of the northern states, competition is close and either party can expect to win, and the single ballot is used; yet factionalism exists within many, but not all, parties. The requirements for voting in primaries may affect factionalism. The basic distinction is between closed primaries, which are limited to members registered with a party, and open primaries, which are open to anyone qualified to vote in the general election. In open primaries it is considerably easier for voters to shift from one party primary to the other (Jewell and Olson 1988, 89–94). Tobin, Keynes, and Danziger found that closed primary systems encourage the control of a single leadership coalition in the nominating process, whereas open primary systems frequently provide nonpartisan groups such as chambers of commerce with the opportunity to influence nominations by endorsing and sponsoring candidates (Tobin and Keynes 1975; Keynes, Tobin, and Danziger 1979).

To summarize, it appears that the number and strength of factions within a party organization are related to both competition between the parties and the primary electoral laws. But neither of these conditions can explain the wide variation in types of factionalism found in most party systems. Factions are, after all, led by men and women. The economic, social, or geographic bases of factions lie dormant until they are activated by human effort. We need to explain why parties in some states have a tradition of unified leadership and in others are marked by intense intraparty factionalism. Practically speaking, gubernatorial candidates in some states seek the support of a leadership coalition; in others they must build their own out of the existing factions or any others they can mobilize.

Preprimary Endorsements

In about a third of our states, party leaders and officeholders are able to exert an influence over nominations. They make preprimary endorsements as a way to increase party control over the nomination or to guide the primary voters toward choosing a party-endorsed candidate. States with strong parties are most likely to have preprimary endorsing procedures (McNitt 1980; Morehouse 1980; Mayhew 1986).

Recall that the direct-primary movement was an effort to undermine the power of the leadership of political parties, particularly in states dominated by a single party. Groups and interests that lacked political power could mobilize voters in primary elections to win the nomination. Party leaders in states where the parties were competitive opposed the primary because it encouraged factions within the party to mobilize a block of primary voters, unrepresentative of the party's supporters, to nominate a candidate who might well lose in the general election.

Malcolm Jewell observes that the institution of the direct primary was a weapon used by the reformers against the party leaders, and the preprimary endorsement process was a weapon used by the party leadership to maintain power (Jewell 1984, 40). Eight states passed legal provisions for party conventions or committees to make endorsements for the primary. In five of these, the endorsement system was part of the initial primary legislation and was undoubtedly proposed by strong parties to give the leaders a method of controlling the nomination outcome. These states are Colorado, Rhode Island, Connecticut, New York, and Delaware. Delaware has recently repealed its law requiring endorsements.

Party leaders in several states felt their influence over nominations was weakened, with disastrous results. In three of these, North Dakota, Utah, and New Mexico, experimentation with endorsements resulted in legal party endorsement systems. In North Dakota, the practice of informal endorsements has existed since the early years of the direct primary. When the state legalized the practice in 1967, it gave the endorsees the right to get on the ballot without petitions. In Utah, the primary system was adopted relatively late (in 1937), and by 1948, the endorsing convention was given legal status. The duty of the endorsing convention is to select two candidates to compete in a primary, unless one gets 70 percent of the vote and becomes the single endorsee. In New Mexico, endorsing conventions have been thrice legalized and then repealed. Following the last period of disuse (1982–93),they were reinstituted in 1994. Many New Mexico politicians believe that conventions offer the best way to achieve slates balanced between Hispanic and Anglo candidates (Jewell 1984, 48–49).

In another ten states, endorsements by one or both parties are by party rule, and again the endorsing is done in party conventions or committees (Jewell 1984). Illinois is an example of a state that adopted the primary method early, and experience with it prompted the leaders of both parties to make informal endorsements. In Minnesota the new Democratic-Farmer-Labor party's leadership believed preprimary endorsements were essential to maintain party control over candidate selection, which was particularly important for a new party that was in a minority. In addition, Minnesota's open primary system permitted Republicans or independents to enter the DFL primary, so a strong party-backed candidate was key. In 1979 the Wisconsin Republican party amended its constitution to make endorsements optional rather than mandatory; a majority of the delegates must vote to have endorsement for a race. The change occurred because the gubernatorial endorsee lost the primary in 1978 and the party believed that endorsement no longer carried the weight it had in earlier elections (Jewell 1984, 44). Most of these states that use informal endorsements are found in the urban-industrial states of the Northeast and Midwest. In addition to the three just mentioned, parties in Delaware, Massachusetts, Michigan, Pennsylvania, Ohio, and Virginia make endorsements (evidence for Michigan and Ohio is sparse). California joined this group in 1988 after a federal court overturned state law, which forbid the practice.

If party leaders in one-third of our states see the advantages of endorsements and regularly practice the endorsement process, why don't leaders in the remaining two-thirds? We would not expect to find endorsing in states where the majority party is an umbrella over factions and groups that contend for the nomination. In those border and southern states, no set of party leaders can gain control over the process, and until recently there has been no real threat from the Republican party to make party unity necessary. Outside these states, there are about twenty in which endorsements are not used, and it is hard to speculate why party leaders have not embraced the process, either informally or legally. Parties are competitive, and unity should be important to winning. Perhaps this book can shed light on the meaning of party in a few of these.

Advantages of Endorsements

While there are many advantages that endorsement, either legal or informal, brings to a candidate, the legal endorsement process offers primary-ballot access. This access may be given to the winner of the endorsement or to all candidates who reach a minimum percentage at the convention or meeting. In several states, the candidate who wins the largest number of convention votes gets the top position on the ballot. Those who fail to reach this percentage may be denied access to the ballot or may have to clear an additional hurdle by getting petitions signed. In Connecticut, for instance, it is necessary to get 15 percent (on at least one ballot) in order to enter the primary. In states where endorsements are informal, without any legal sanction, endorsed candidates have no advantage in getting on the primary ballot and must gain access by petition.

A party endorsement made under law or custom confers potential political advantages. One such advantage is that nonendorsed candidates may be discouraged from running in the primary. In the elections from 1960 through 1994, endorsees had no primary opposition 56 percent of the time in states with legal endorsements and 24 percent of the time when parties make informal endorsements. Contrast these endorsement figures with that for all other primary elections in northern states during the same time period, in which only 20 percent of the primaries were uncontested.

Party endorsement may bring to the party's choice tangible campaign resources, such as workers and funding, or intangible advantages,
such as momentum. Voters in the primary may also be inclined to support the endorsed candidate. One indication of the impact of endorsements might be the margin by which the nominee wins. I found that, in
the elections from 1956 through 1978, gubernatorial nominees who
received preprimary endorsements won by bigger margins in the primaries than did nominees in primary-only states (Morehouse 1980).
About 44 percent of gubernatorial candidates in parties with endorsements won at least 80 percent of the primary vote, with those in legal systems doing better than those in informal ones. Only about 22 percent of
nominees in nonsouthern states without endorsing systems won by such
a high percentage.

Another measure of the impact of endorsements is the proportion of
endorsees who win those primaries that are contested. In the 1960 through
1980 elections, endorsees were very successful; they won 82 percent of contested primaries, with almost no difference between legal and informal
endorsements. In elections from 1982 through 1994, that rate of success
dropped to 46 percent. If we take into account both the frequency and the
outcome of primary contests, we find that the proportion of endorsees
being nominated has dropped from about 90 percent to 70 percent.

In order to better understand the conditions that affect the success of
endorsees in the nominating process and to determine whether those conditions have been changing during the 1980s and 1990s, I have analyzed
the endorsing process in ten state parties in 1994, including most of those
studied in 1982. The results of that analysis are described in some detail in
chapter 7.

In view of the success record of endorsees, a candidate with the ambition to become the party's candidate must join forces with the party leadership coalition in the attempt to obtain the endorsement in a convention.
The delegates who are elected to endorsing conventions are persons who
have worked actively in their state and local parties. Each candidate needs
to go about the state and convince these potential delegates that she or he
should be the party endorsee. Occasionally there are close contests for delegate positions among persons who are committed to candidates seeking
the endorsement. In this case, the election of delegates may determine who
is going to win the endorsement.

In 1982, Malcolm Jewell conducted surveys among delegates to the
Democratic and Republican endorsing conventions in five states (Jewell
1984, 125–41). Most of the delegates believe that the endorsement process
is good for their party. They say that delegates are the backbone of cam-

paign committees that the candidate needs to win the primary and the election. They have the best knowledge of a candidate's background and are likely to pick a winner.

Based on these responses and observations, there are several reasons why a potential candidate for governor wants the endorsement. The most important is money and services the party provides, such as organizational assistance and personnel. In Minnesota the state party organizations provide the endorsee with fund-raising assistance, computer facilities, phone banks, access to lists of voters, and campaign workers. Local parties in New York and Connecticut provide the endorsed candidates with support services. In most states, a candidate who wins the endorsement is likely to attract campaign workers and contributions.

If all these resources are bestowed upon an endorsee, it is likely that she or he will eliminate other primary candidates. Rivals may be eliminated because they do not receive the required convention vote. Or, they may drop out because they believe a challenge would be futile in the face of the endorsee's resources. They may want other support from the party's leadership at a future time, and party loyalty to the endorsee is a way of obtaining it.

Voters may not pay attention to endorsements per se, but they are probably aware of the attention the winner of an endorsement contest receives in the media. Endorsements are able to structure the primary election by providing the voters with cues about the party favorite that provide him or her with the momentum needed to win a challenged primary.

The party leaders recognize that convention endorsements provide the party with incentives for party activists, which helps maintain the party organization. V. O. Key (1956) suggested that the growth of the direct primary and the elimination of party conventions and caucuses resulted in the atrophy of party organizations. In states that maintain endorsing conventions, we would expect to find strong party organizations. Closely linked to the strong party organization is the candidate's own coalition, which is nourished by the linkage.

The incentive for a gubernatorial candidate to gain a party endorsement is high. Capturing the support of the necessary number of delegates is a manageable task and less draining and expensive than in states where the only route to the nomination is the direct primary. After the endorsement, the candidate benefits from party support, which may fend off all challengers. If challenged, the party often provides money and campaign support that follow the candidate into the general election. We would predict that governors who emerge from such a process would have a party in the legislature ready to vote favorably for the governor's program.

Incumbency

Incumbent governors are almost guaranteed renomination and have a good chance of reelection. During the period 1977 to 1993, 76 percent of those eligible ran again (Beyle 1994, 37). For four years they have built their strength with the rewards and punishments that come from office. They have been the leaders of their parties and have dealt with local party leaders all over the state. If they want to be renominated, they can count on the party to help them. The stronger the party organization, the less likely there will be a challenge to a governor who wants to run again. Since the abandonment of an incumbent by a party will likely cause a divisive primary and a potential loss in the general election, it is natural that the party organization and the incumbent are unified.

In the elections from 1960 through 1994, about two-thirds of governors in primary-only states and just over one-fourth in endorsing states faced contested primaries, and only about one-tenth of those facing contests in either type of party failed to win renomination. Governors face a higher risk in the general election, where they confront the candidate from the opposite party under competitive conditions. Even so, they win on average 72 percent of the time (Beyle 1994, 37). Governors have the opportunity to build a favorable image through the use of the media. A skillful governor can use speeches, press conferences, and television to create a positive impression in the voters' minds.

To summarize this discussion of electoral ambition and the conditions that shape it, candidates must assess their chances of success based on four factors: electoral competition, primary rules, the potential for party endorsement, and incumbency. An incumbent has already won party support and is likely to keep it. Hence, challenging an incumbent is risky. In a competitive electoral situation with an open race, a candidate with a party united behind him or her has an advantage over the opposition candidate who does not.

The Structure of Party Coalitions

To repeat what we have already said about political parties: they are a collective effort directed toward capturing public office and governing once that office is attained. But this effort takes many forms. In some states, the party organization is so weak that a political candidate receives the party label after a hard-fought primary and goes forth into the campaign with his or her own coalition that does not contain any party elements. In other states, the party leadership and the party coalition are so strong that the candidate is supported from the start, given organizational help for the nomination, election, and governing. We have already referred to the elements of a party organization or coalition as factions and groups, but we have not defined them. It is appropriate to set out the concepts and definitions we will use in our study of party coalitions.

Factions

The basic elements of party coalitions are also called factions. State parties are characterized by the number, strength, and durability of the factions within them. V. O. Key defined a *faction* as "any combination, clique or grouping of voters and political leaders who unite at a particular time in support of a candidate. Thus, a political race with eight candidates will involve eight factions of varying size. Some factions have impressive continuity while others come into existence for only one campaign and then dissolve" (1950, 16). Thus, for Key, a faction was a subset of a political party that might or might not contest nominations over a series of primaries. Key also included the voters in his definition of faction, probably because he measured factional strength by primary voting strength. I do not include voters in my definition of a party faction, although votes are a resource that groups and individuals bring to the faction. As I have said before, voters are choosers among factions and coalitions, not an organizational part.

Generally, three types of factional organization within parties are observed. The first is the unifactional party, which features a leadership coalition that is continuous and can control nominations. The second is the bifactional party, which has two reasonably continuous groups, each claiming considerable electoral strength and the ability to compete for the nomination. Under this arrangement, the party leaders remain neutral or back their factional candidate. The third type is the multifactional party, in which nominations are often contested by three or more candidates. Party leaders are weak and remain neutral unless they are the instruments of the incumbent. Since we are studying contests for governor, we will focus on factions and coalitions contesting for this office, although an elected office at any level would be subject to contesting factions.

Jewell and Olson have described factional patterns within the parties of northern states. By *faction,* they refer to "any sign of disagreement within a political party, to any divergence of opinion, to any effort to contest nominations, platforms, or party offices" (1982, 52). They agree that factions may be transient or durable. Describing their bases as regional, ethnic, religious, ideological, personal, economic, generational, and candidate oriented, they claim that the main task of the party leaders is to manage the ever present potential for factionalism and to channel the aspirations and energies of rival groups into a semblance of party unity. By my definition, this unity would be called a party coalition.

While Jewell and Olson generally classify parties according to the same typology used by Key, there are some differences. They do not depend upon primary percentages to measure the strength of factions, relying on observation and expert testimony as well.

Calling the unifactional party a cohesive party, Jewell and Olson describe it as one that has a single source of leadership. That leadership may be a powerful individual, such as the late Senator Harry Byrd of Virginia, a state chair, such as Ray Bliss of Ohio, or a governor, such as Mario Cuomo of New York. The leadership might be collegial, such as a state committee, or an informal council of regional or county leaders, as among the Republicans of Pennsylvania. Cohesion may be engineered by a state convention, as in the Minnesota Democratic-Farmer-Labor party. States that endorse are placed in the cohesive category if their endorsements are usually ratified in the primary by a sizable share of the vote.

The cohesive party is able to compromise factional differences internally and present a united front in both the primary and general elections. Jewell and Olson guess that the major factions within this type of party are ethnic and geographic rather than economic or ideological ones that are harder to compromise. This supposition introduces a distinction between factions that may be compromised and those that are more durable and less prone to compromise. I predict that factions based on ethnic or geographic or personal-ambition candidacies would be prime ones for negotiation and compromise.

Jewell and Olson describe the types of factions within the multifactional party, none of which is large or cohesive enough to dominate. They are not willing to compromise with others generally, except in a runoff primary when they have no hope of winning alone.

The components of all factions include groups and individuals, such as the candidate, party leaders, or delegates to party meetings, who take a traditional part in electoral activities. In addition to them, the newspaper publisher, the interest-group leader, and the financial donor contribute to the faction. Usually a faction will be composed of like-minded groups and individuals. For instance, middle-class liberals and labor have frequently joined the same faction. These groups and individuals bring such resources to the faction as money, information, votes, legislative support, legitimacy, and a variety of other things.

Factions and Change

The development of factions within parties has been studied by Baer and Bositis (1988). They find that factions structure conflict and consensus within the political party. Factions are organized informally because they compete with other factions within the party, while they retain "the opportunity to negotiate, transact and compromise." Baer and Bositis claim that social movements, represented within the parties as factions, bring about a change in party factionalism and in many cases the substitution of new elites for the old, which means that American parties are permeable to outside groups that are moving into positions of leadership. The party has integrated the values and norms of the different groups, accounting for the increased cohesion noted by many scholars.

Coalitions as Alliances between Factions

Coalitions are alliances between factions. By definition a unifactional party is a grand coalition. It is also possible that geographic, ethnic, and candidate factions will compromise to form a party coalition. I do not expect that factions in bifactional and multifactional parties will form a single party coalition. In the bifactional and multifactional parties, where the primary is the major decision point for determining the nomination, there is little to gain by joining a coalition if the faction can win a primary alone with as little as 30 percent of the vote.

In the interviews with forty-three candidates for the gubernatorial nomination, I asked about their coalition-building efforts. I made the assumption that in order to win the nomination, they would have to fashion a winning coalition. In the case of the unifactional or cohesive party, the party coalition and the candidate coalition are joined in the nominating process. In the bifactional or multifactional party, there is no party coalition, and the candidates build or inherit their own factions. Occasionally two candidate factions join after a primary is over, but there is no certainty that this will occur. In these situations, the party label is the most a party can offer a candidate.

Party Coalitions and Party Bureaucracies

The concept of party as an electoral and governing organization includes the party coalitions as well as the formal party apparatus. State party bureaucracies have become stronger in recent years. The Party Transformation Study that was the work of four political scientists (Cotter, Gibson, Bibby, and Huckshorn [1984]) documented the growth in strength of state and local organizations over a twenty-year period (1960–80). They found that state budgets had grown and that over 90 percent of the parties had either full-time state chairs or executive directors. The revivified state party bureaucracies ran campaigning seminars for party candidates, and a majority of them had mobilization programs through which to identify and turn out their party's likely voters. Many parties were increasingly active in providing campaign services to candidates. These findings were confirmed by the Advisory Commission on Intergovernmental Relations survey of state party chairs in 1983–84 (ACIR 1986, 111–18).

The relationship between increased bureaucratic strength and winning elections, which I believe is the major motive of political parties, has not been proved. The authors of the Party Transformation Study documented the fact that Republican state party bureaucracies were considerably stronger than their Democratic counterparts. In several southern states where the Republicans have not yet achieved electoral strength, they have built up the party apparatus in anticipation of attracting votes. Therefore, we would not expect an immediate correlation between bureaucratic organization and electoral strength. Leaving out the southern states, for that reason, the authors test for party organizational strength (POS, as they call it) and party electoral success in contests for governor. Their findings show that the relative strength of Democratic state party organization (over the Republican party organization) correlates .46 with Democratic electoral success (Cotter et al. 1984, 93–104). This is a modest correlation, but in the right direction.

The coalitions that gubernatorial candidates build to receive the party nomination may be related to the party's bureaucratic strength. We do not know how this increased organizational capability matters to candidates for the gubernatorial nomination. My hypothesis predicts that most state parties, even those with ample budgets, hold back on campaign contributions and fund-raising assistance until a candidate emerges from the primary process. My hypothesis also predicts that strong party leadership can commit effort and resources to its favored candidate for the endorsement and the following primary.

Parties as Governing Coalitions

Is it true that party organization affects the quality and distribution of services to the people? Based on the party coalition model, we would expect that in states where the governor's electoral coalition is strong, the governor would be able to obtain loyalty from the legislators in the party. In states where the party is weak or divided, the governor will face a legislature in which sit remnants of the factions that opposed him or her in the primary contest. My previous research has found moderate to high correlations between the strength of electoral party coalitions and legislative party loyalty on the governor's program. This is, to my knowledge, the only research that tests legislative voting loyalty on governors' program bills (Morehouse 1966; 1973; 1981a, 246–52; 1992; 1993).

Until the research of Erikson, Wright, and McIver, there was no proved connection between the preferences of the people and the policies that state legislatures made for them (1993). This research convinces us that there is a correlation between public opinion and state policy. Individual states differ in the ideological direction of their electorates, but the policies reflect that, with liberal states producing liberal policies and conservative states producing conservative policies.

What is fundamental for those studying party organization is their finding that party organizations matter. Within each party, there is a compromise between the electoral elites, those who run and get elected to office, and the activist elites, those whose values and ideologies define what the parties stand for. In this process, state parties position themselves at the public opinion midpoint from fear of electoral sanctions. And the parties' legislators reflect this midpoint in the policies they produce. This research sets the stage for compelling investigation of the coalition-building efforts of party elites and factions in the struggle to nominate, elect, and govern.

The Activity of Coalition Building

There are few comparative studies about how gubernatorial candidates go about coalition building for nomination, election, and governing. The next step is to discover how they do it and the rules, ambitions, resources, and political structures that contribute to this effort. The coalition-building model is suited to the task of examining this process. It is based on political activity that involves individuals or groups who work with initial resources and the rules of a game to bring about an outcome that will reward all of them. I will describe how coalition research can be applied to the gubernatorial nominating and governing process. Bear in mind that the coalitions built during the electoral process follow the governor into the government and affect his or her relationships with the legislative party.

Coalition behavior involves four major components: actors, resources, rules of the game, and results. We will examine how the prospective gubernatorial candidates form coalitions in order to win the nomination of their party. In this study, the *actors* are the candidates for the gubernatorial nomination, the party leaders, the legislative leaders, and the leaders of various factions and groups. The factions may be based on geographic divisions within the party, such as counties, or they may represent ethnic, ideological, or economic bases. The actors bring resources into the coalition that they offer in exchange for future payoffs such as political positions, legislation, and jobs. Thus, winning the nomination is the goal, but the actors have a variety of incentives for joining the coalition. We want to discover how much the political party offers the gubernatorial candidates in their coalition-building efforts.

The *resources* are party leadership support, group support, votes in the convention, votes in the primary, money, information, media attention, popularity in the polls, issues, and so forth. A major resource is incumbency. It is important to discover how each candidate evaluates the initially strongest player (front-runner) and the probability of success of the different candidates.

Rules of the game involve state laws, party rules, and informal practices. As we have seen, parties in one-third of the states make preprimary endorsements by law or by party rules. Consider the different strategies that the various gubernatorial candidates would use in each different situation. If by winning a convention vote by 81 percent all rivals would be eliminated and nomination would be won, the candidate and the party leaders would strive for such a result. On the other hand, factions might join in order to keep this result from occurring—hence forcing a primary in which the unpredictable electorate would help select the winner. It is important to know how the candidates and party leaders view the rules and how they try to gain advantage based on them.

In most states, gubernatorial nominations are made solely by primary elections. Here a plurality is sufficient for the nomination. In these direct-primary systems where there is no endorsement process, we do not know how party leaders and candidates build coalitions. Factions with economic, personal, or ideological bases challenge each other or combine to defeat the front-runner. Bargaining takes place among factions without the forum of a convention to aid in the information process. Little is known about how this bargaining occurs.

To summarize, there is at least one point and frequently two where the candidate must have coalition support before the election: (1) the convention, (2) the primary, and (3) the runoff (in southern states). Andrew McNitt (1980) demonstrated that a candidate needs more than a minimal winning coalition in the endorsing convention to be sure of winning in the following primary. In some direct-primary states a runoff is required if no candidate receives over 50 percent. How large a coalition needs to form at point one in order to be an effective coalition at point two? While the election is not part of this project, nominating strategies must be based on forming a future coalition large enough to win an election against the other party.

Results for the gubernatorial nominating process would include the type of coalition built by each candidate. This component would include the vote the coalition received in the convention or primary. Results would also include the decision of a prospective candidate to drop out of the race before the convention or primary and the disposition of her or his supporters. I am interested in the winner's choice of partners—predicting that in a situation where a strong party coalition exists, the winner will adopt this coalition. I hypothesize that the coalition will be composed of most of the county leaders. The coalition will have been responsible for recruiting the candidate and working for her or his endorsement. In a party with a multifactional structure, candidates are on their own to form coalitions with as many groups as are necessary to win. The initially strongest candidate may not win because of a coalition that forms against her or him. The vote on primary day is the test of the strength of the coalition—and brings victory or defeat.

To summarize what I have said in this chapter, ambition for office must be tempered by the existing political opportunities and the rules. If the chances of winning are very close, candidates need organization support and money. If the first does not exist, candidates must raise a huge war chest to contest the nomination. The character of the primary plays an important part as well. Open primaries widen the campaign to the whole electorate and hence much more uncertainty. If parties are strong in the state and have the resources to back candidates for the nomination, the game is a very different one indeed. The candidate can count on party help and the leadership and minions that the party can provide. Based on the rules, candidates plot their strategies. They represent a faction that can be merged with the party coalition, or they go it alone without the party help. Chapter 3 discusses the rules in all the states and details those in the ten states that form the base of this study.

CHAPTER 3

The Rules and the Game

Rules are important because they determine how the game is played. Our forty-three candidates for governor will use very different strategies depending upon which rules they must follow. This chapter sets out the rules that govern nominations in all states and describes with more detail the process that candidates follow in our ten states.

Chapter 2 traced the development of the direct-primary form of nomination in the early years of this century. The primary transferred to the voters the power to choose the party's nominee, which was traditionally done by the party leaders, officeholders, and activists. In about one-third of our states, the party elite fought back and established preprimary endorsements to protect their power over nominations. These states were the strong party states at the time, and most of them remain strong today.

A great threat to the internal cohesion of a political party is offered by the open opportunity for any faction or candidate to enter and contest the primary. The party is liable to be infiltrated by self-proclaimed ideologues. Advocates of any cause, far right or far left, can enter the party and attempt to convert it to their particular cause. In 1986, a coalition of right-to-life activists and religious fundamentalists imposed a loyalty oath on Washington state Republican candidates. The Republican party officials realized that the loyal candidates would receive energy and funds from the fundamentalists but wondered how they could retain the support of either their party or the electorate (Bone 1986, 4–5).

Factions can be based on almost any shared bias or belief. Religious groups as in the previous example, candidate aspirations, ethnic divisions, or regulars versus reformers all offer the substance for party fracturing. In addition, states are often divided by regionalism, illustrated by northern and southern California. Party leaders must be strong to hold a party together under such circumstances, and most cannot. They merely preside over the struggle for nomination and "ratify" the winner. It appears that few prospective governors can count on the support of a party organization to help them in their attempts to capture the governorship. In a sense, they must "capture" the party label in order to make a bid for the nomination and election.

Lucky is the gubernatorial candidate who has the backing of a party leadership with money to bestow and activists to mobilize. In the states that make use of a preprimary endorsing system, it is hypothesized that the parties are cohesive in the nominating process. The following conditions would apply. The party leaders in counties and towns are unified under a state chair. They can control the nomination for a gubernatorial candidate by sending local delegations to the convention who will back him or her. The candidate may not be challenged, but if a challenge takes place, these party leaders build a coalition for the candidate that will ensure a primary win. The gubernatorial candidate wins by a large percentage (80 to 100 percent). The coalition carries over into the election campaign and works to elect (or reelect) the candidate.

Party Nominations and Party Strength

A Measure of Party Strength

Table 3.1 sets out the relationships just discussed. The measure of party strength is the one developed by V. O. Key about half a century ago (1950, 16–18) and is based on the primary vote for governor. Key believed that the primary would ignite as well as reflect the factionalism within a party, and hence the primary vote indicates the degree to which the party is unified or divided. The states are listed by party system strength over a twenty-year period. This table measures the average percent of the primary received by governors of either party who served during this time. While the measure can be applied to a single party over time, this measure tells us to what extent the state's governors have come from parties that are unified or divided.

In table 3.1 party coalitional strength can be estimated from the magnitude of the governor's vote in the primary. If the average primary vote for each state's governors over the time period is 80 to 100 percent, I predict that coalition building for the nomination is not episodic—that there is a steady corps of party leaders within both parties who outlast individual gubernatorial candidates and can recruit and help each prospective candidate. If the average primary vote is between 60 and 79 percent, both parties may be making modest efforts to aid their candidates, or perhaps one party has made some effort and strong candidates have captured the apparatus only to be succeeded by weak candidates of either party, thus producing a moderate average. The weakest category, 35 to 59 percent, indicates that there is no steady corps of party leaders in either party (although in many of the states in the lower right cell of the table, the majority Democratic party is organizationally weak). Factions within the

TABLE 3.1. Gubernatorial Nominations and Party System Strength, 1994

	Party Nominations for Governor		
Party System Strength (1974–94)[a]	*Strong:* Preprimary Endorsements By Law	*Moderate:* Preprimary Endorsements By Party Rule or Practice	*Weak:* Primary-Only No Major Competitive Party Endorsements
Strong (14)	*Colorado* North Dakota Rhode Island *Connecticut*	Delware (R) Virginia[b] Iowa (post)[d] Michigan (D) *Illinois* Ohio	Vermont Indiana (pre-76)[c] Idaho (66–71)[c] *Tennessee*
Moderate (22)	*New York* Utah	*California*[c] (D) (90, 94) Massachusetts Wisconsin (R) *Minnesota* Pennsylvania	*Oregon* South Carolina North Carolina Maine Nevada New Hampshire Wyoming Montana South Dakota Missouri Arizona Arkansas *Texas* West Virginia Washington
Weak (14)			Maryland Florida Hawaii Georgia Oklahoma Alabama New Jersey *Kansas* Alaska New Mexico[c] (64, 66, 78, 82, 94) Nebraska Louisiana Kentucky Mississippi

[a]Party system strength is measured by averaging the governors' percent of the primary vote in gubernatorial primaries 1974–94 (inclusive). In states with strong party systems, the average primary vote received by governors-to-be was 80 to 100 percent. In moderately strong party systems, it was 60 to 79 percent. In weak party systems, it was 35 to 59 percent. The five most recent elections were used, with the following exceptions: AK (4), CT (4), ME (4), each of which elected an independent, and ten elections apiece for the states with two-year terms: NH, VT, RI. AR (8) changed to a four-year term in 1986, RI in 1995. States studied in detail in this book are italicized.

[b]State party officials may by law choose either the primary or the convention.

[c]Dates in parentheses indicate dates preprimary endorsements were used.

[d]Postprimary nominating convention if no candidate receives at least 35 percent.

party battle it out in the primary, and there is no effort on the part of the party leaders to influence the nomination contest.

Preprimary Endorsements

The matching of party system strength with strength of preprimary endorsement provides striking proof that it is only in states that have strong or moderately strong party systems that preprimary endorsements occur. Nine of the fourteen states with the strongest parties have preprimary endorsing conventions, and one additional, Iowa, has a postprimary convention to endorse a candidate if no candidate receives a majority in the primary. Seven of the twenty-two states with moderate party strength practice preprimary endorsements. In these sixteen states, the party leaders have devised ways to control the nominations. They may bargain among potential contenders. Bargaining might consist of agreements for appointments within the administration if the leading contender is elected. It might consist of a promise of support in a future endorsement contest.

Endorsements by Law

The preprimary endorsements differ according to whether they are mandated by state law or are permissive, allowing the parties to set their own rules. For the purposes of comparison, I call a strong nominating system one in which preprimary endorsements are made by law and apply to both parties. A moderately strong system is defined as one in which preprimary endorsements are permissive and are used by political parties. In this category also is Iowa, which has the postprimary option if no candidate receives a majority of the votes in the primary. A weak nominating system is defined as no provision by law or party regulations for preprimary endorsements for major or competitive parties. During the twenty-year period shown in table 3.1, some southern Republican parties nominated by convention rather than primary under state laws permitting such a choice when the party's vote in the previous election was low.

Preprimary endorsements also differ according to the advantage given the endorsed candidate. One advantage of a legal endorsement process is that the endorsed candidate can be given a preference over others in access to the ballot. In two of these states, Connecticut and Utah, the only challenge can come from the convention, and the challenger must have received a certain proportion of the vote in order to challenge (Connecticut, 15 percent). In Utah, the endorsing convention designates two candidates to run in the primary election. However, if one receives 70 percent, no primary is held. In North Dakota and Rhode Island another system exists. Others can challenge the convention-endorsed candidate who qualifies for the ballot and is listed first. Recently in both states others are exercising this option. In Colorado and New York, candidates qualify for the ballot by getting a certain percentage of the convention vote (Colorado, 30 percent; New York, 25 percent) as well as the right to petition. In most of these states, the endorsee has a distinct advantage. Hence, a front-runner seeks to get an impressive convention vote to discourage potential rivals from attempting to challenge. This continues to be the best strategy.

Informal Endorsements

In ten states, party endorsement of candidates is not authorized by law, but one or both of the political parties follow this practice. Table 3.1 indicates after some states the single party that endorses. (Iowa is not included in this discussion, but the fact that it has postprimary endorsements if no candidate receives at least 35 percent indicates that parties make the attempt to unify behind a candidate in the general election.) In a few states, the previous law was repealed and parties were permitted to endorse if they chose. Such is the case in Massachusetts and Delaware. After legal endorsements were abolished in 1973 in Massachusetts, the Republican party continued to make informal endorsements and in 1982 the Democratic party resumed the practice: both require a certain percent of the convention vote to qualify for the ballot (Democrats, 15 percent; Republicans, 10 percent). Delaware shifted from formal to informal endorsements in 1976 and only the Republicans now endorse.

In some state parties operating under both formal and informal rules, the endorsements are made by conventions meeting in public and attended by relatively large numbers of delegates. Such is the case for the endorsements made in Massachusetts, Connecticut, Colorado, Minnesota, Wisconsin, and California. Wisconsin Republicans, who endorsed regularly for thirty years up to 1978, changed their party rules to make endorsements "permissive," and it appears that they have not endorsed recently.

In other states, endorsements are generally made by groups such as state party committees, which meet without the fanfare of a convention. This process is typical of the Democratic party in Illinois. The Republican party there sometimes makes endorsements through its central committee or its county chair's association. Other states also follow this practice, but there is little knowledge about the details. Pennsylvania and Ohio are states where the party leadership has often played some role in recruiting and endorsing statewide candidates.

The traditional power of Ohio parties at the county and state level rests on their ability to build slates and to endorse in order to minimize primary conflicts and craft the strongest possible ticket. In early 1990, the state Republican chair convinced Robert Taft II to abandon his effort to oppose George Voinovich for the gubernatorial nomination and run for secretary of state instead. Promising Taft $500,000, chair Bennett told him that the party needed him in that office. Because of this accomplishment, neither Republican statewide candidate faced primary opposition that year and both were able to save their war chests for the general election. In November, both Voinovich and Taft won state office (Sturrock et al. 1994, 341–44).

Michigan Democrats, after a long losing streak, approved preprimary endorsements for state offices in May 1980. Perhaps this change can account for their winning three gubernatorial terms after that, although incumbents usually are renominated without much difficulty.

In Virginia, state party officials may choose either the primary or the convention procedure for nominating. The Republican party has consistently used conventions, which may help explain why the Virginia Republicans are among the must successful in the South. This success spurred the Virginia Democrats, a party rent by factions, to shift to a convention system. Both parties win the governorship at regular intervals.

Candidates who win the endorsement of informal party conventions gain no legal advantage of ballot access or position, but they gain the same political advantages as those who are endorsed in legal systems. They are just as likely to discourage other candidates from challenging in a primary. They are just as likely to gain organizational money and workers. And with the publicity gained from the endorsement process, they are also more likely than the challenger to gain voter support. While voters may not be aware of party endorsements, they may receive cues during the preprimary endorsement process that lead them to vote for the party's choice.

Exceptions to the Rule

Several states are interesting because they defy the hypothesis that preprimary endorsements are found in strong party systems. In the upper right cell of the table are four states with strong party systems that do not use preprimary endorsements. Idaho and Indiana did have legal endorsements at one time, however. In fact, Indiana's nominations were made in party conventions before 1976, when the mandatory primary law took effect. Since that time the Indiana state parties have not held nominating conventions for governor (they nominate by convention for other state offices), but I understand that the county, city, and district parties endorse a favored gubernatorial candidate. Since this favored candidate is a product of common negotiations among the subunits, the result may be the same. Idaho also had preprimary endorsements by law from 1966 to 1971. Since that time the Democratic party appears united and has won six gubernatorial elections. (Its success has been confined to the governorship because it has not controlled the legislature for more than twenty-five years.) Vermont needs to be accounted for because it has never engaged in preprimary endorsements, yet the parties in the Green Mountain State nominate for governor in an orderly and cohesive manner with infrequent primary battles. Furthermore, control of the governorship rotates between the parties. Apparently ruralism is an inhospitable environment for political conflict. The Vermont Republicans were marked in the first half of the century by a benevolent unifactionalism (Bryan 1981, 173). After the Democratic breakthrough, that party was able to siphon off a goodly amount of socioeconomic diversity, and both parties appear to limit conflict in order to win.

Strange though it may seem, Tennessee governors have shown such primary strength in recent years that the state appears in the strong party column. Since 1966, when the Republicans did not even run a gubernatorial candidate, until 1994, when they won office for the fourth time, both parties have attempted to consolidate their factions. Part of this attempt can be explained by the passage of the two-term allowance and the ability of the incumbents to prevent challengers. The energetic Lamar Alexander, the first governor to run for a second term, was able to consolidate the Republicans in 1978 and in 1982 when he ran again. His successor, Democratic Speaker Ned McWherter, had no primary challenger for his second term. In 1994, Tennessee Republicans nominated their prospective governor Don Sundquist by 83 percent of the primary vote. However, the "out party" in each election revealed factional stress, so Tennessee may be hovering insecurely in the strong party column. Time will tell.

While New Mexico appears in the weak party–no endorsement column, the state in 1994 revived for the fourth time its traditional system of preprimary endorsements by attempting to instill order into chaos by legal means. New Mexico now occupies the lonely position of a weak party state that periodically adopts a strong endorsement system. The parties in this state experimented with the preprimary endorsing conventions twice in the 1950s, twice in the 1960s, and again for 1978, 1982, and 1994. Under this endorsement system, candidates qualify for the ballot by getting 20 percent on a single convention vote. Others qualify by petition if they fall short of 20 percent or choose not to seek endorsement. Many candidates seek the nomination in this state. The conventions are seen as a way of cutting down on the number of contestants, rather than a way of declaring an endorsee. The failure to get 20 percent of the convention indicates that a candidate is in serious organizational trouble. Parties are not strong in

New Mexico and cannot keep conflict from breaking out. For the party leaders, a legal endorsement system appears to be the only way to provide some order in the nominating process.

History and Tradition: The Primary-Only States

The states selected to represent those that nominate by primary only are a diverse lot, and they are italicized in table 3.1. Two (Texas and Tennessee) are from the South, two (Oregon and California) are western, and one (Kansas) is in the middle of the plains. (California Democrats began to endorse in 1990, hence its placement in the moderate column.) Table 3.2 presents the 1982 primaries, showing dates and candidates. A major requirement for a state to make it into the study was that it be competitive between the parties. Eyebrows might be raised over the inclusion of Texas, but the state had a Republican governor as the 1982 election year began, and Republicans have won regularly since.

Texas: Conservatives versus Liberals

Republican governor Clements of Texas was the first of his party to claim the office in more than a hundred years. Furthermore, Republicans traditionally held only a small bloc of seats in the legislature. Texas provided the classic case of a dominant Democratic party torn from within by a major conservative faction challenged by a liberal coalition of minorities and labor. V. O. Key observed this split back in 1949 and concluded that Texas had "developed the most bitter intra-Democratic fight along New Deal and anti–New Deal lines in the South" (1950, 259). This factionalism continued as conservative Democratic governors were able to rally conservatives to their side in the open primaries and beat the liberal coalition candidates. Then in the general election, the Democratic voters remained in the fold and the GOP lost each match. The Democrats fought another bitter primary fight in 1978 and moderate-liberal candidate, state attorney general John Hill, won over the incumbent governor, Dolph Briscoe, and provided the opportunity for a Republican win. Afraid that the liberal Hill would take over the Democratic party if he won, the conservative voters supported the Republican Clements. For conservatives of either party, the biggest threat are the liberal Democrats, and hence party lines are not as important as economic class lines in the Lone Star State. Class lines are aided by an open primary system with a runoff if no candidate receives over 50 percent.

A study of Republican primaries in southern states characterizes the

Texas Republican primaries as combining elite competition with low rates of turnout (M. Black and E. Black 1982, 130–40). The Republican primary turnout has not exceeded 55 percent of the Democratic turnout in Texas. The Republican party remains a party of the right and far right.

Tennessee: Crump vs. Clement

Tennessee has joined the ranks of a competitive state in contests for governor. Since the mid-1970s either party could count on winning the highest

TABLE 3.2.   Party Primaries, Dates and Candidates, 1982

State	Party	Primary Date	Type	Filing Date	Candidate	Current Office or Occupation
Texas	R	May 1	open	Feb. 1	William Clements	Governor
	D	(June 5 runoff)			Mark White	Attorney General
					Buddy Temple	RR Commissioner
					Bob Armstrong	Land Commissioner
Tenn.	R	Aug. 5	open	June 3	Lamar Alexander	Governor
	D				Randy Tyree	Mayor, Knoxville
					Anna Belle Clement O'Brien	State Senator
Kans.	D	Aug. 3	closed	June 21	John Carlin	Governor
					Jimmy Montgomery	Disc Jockey
	R				Sam Hardage	Businessperson
					Dave Owen	Former Lieutenant Governor
					Wendall Lady	House Speaker
Oreg.	R	May 18	closed	March 9	Victor Atiyeh	Governor
	D				Ted Kulongowski	State Senator
					Don Clark	Multnomah County Executive
Calif.	D	June 8	closed	March 12	Tom Bradley	Mayor, Los Angeles
					John Garamendi	State Senator
	R				George Deukmejian	Attorney General
					Mike Curb	Lieutenant Governor

Note: A closed primary is defined as one for which the voters declare their party affiliation prior to election day. California has an open blanket primary as of 1996.

office in the system, and lively contests within the primaries of both parties take place. Still, as is true of many southern states, the Republicans have not held majorities in the state legislature. The mountains of eastern Tennessee are the stronghold of the Republicans, dating from the Civil War conflict and the Unionist sentiment of the mountaineers. Middle and western Tennessee were secessionist and became Democratic strongholds.

Sectionalism and factionalism intertwined have dominated politics in this state and still appear with regularity in the Democratic primary contests for governor. It has traditionally been a bifactional rivalry marked by durable factions, notably those of Frank Clement and E. H. Crump, each of whom held the governorship for eighteen consecutive years (E. Black and M. Black 1982, 106–8). Crump's Memphis–Shelby County machine held sway until the mid-1950s. By enlisting support from the minority Democrats in eastern Tennessee, Crump gave them patronage in state government denied them in their Republican stronghold. Middle Tennessee was the center of the Clement operation, which fought the Crump machine in statewide primaries and eventually took over. Up until 1970 statewide elections went to the Democrats by default after the factions within the party fought for the nomination. Each governor faced a legislature that included a hostile faction within his own party as well as the cohesive Republican contingent from eastern Tennessee.

While middle Tennessee has remained strongly Democratic, shifts in eastern Tennessee toward the Democrats and in western Tennessee toward the Republicans have made the state the most competitive in the South. Traditionally driven into the Republican party by the race issue in the 1960s, some Democratic sections of western Tennessee have continued to support the GOP, although the race issue has subsided. In eastern Tennessee, Democratic economic policies have appealed to the poorer whites. Primaries within the Democratic party rarely provide the nominee with as much as 50 percent of the vote, as many factions battle and heirs of one of the two traditional contenders, the Clement dynasty, emerge to fight some more. After a multifactional fight in 1974, a former member of Congress from western Tennessee, Ray Blanton, won the Democratic gubernatorial nomination with 25 percent of the vote. Blanton went on to win the governorship. The Clement faction emerged to fight Jake Butcher and Mayor Randy Tyree from Knoxville in the 1978 and 1982 primaries, respectively, providing another intraparty type of contest.

In both of those elections, however, Republican Lamar Alexander from Nashville won. Initially he had benefited from the scandal-ridden administration of Democrat Ray Blanton, who was convicted of extortion, conspiracy, and mail fraud (Lamis 1984, 173–74). The second time, he won because of his popularity and skillful campaigning, thus proving that Tennessee is a competitive state. Black and Black note the shifting mass base of the Republican primary electorate from small-town and rural counties to the large cities, which furnished 59 percent of the vote in 1978 (M. Black and E. Black 1982, 135). Thus, the party sought to appeal to those outside its original locus in rural eastern Tennessee. By 1978, party unity prevailed as Alexander received scanty primary opposition in that year and was unopposed in 1982. Party unity was short-lived, however, as the gubernatorial primary contender won with a slight 52 percent in 1990.

Kansas: Party Leaders Run for Cover

Kansas, formerly as Republican as Tennessee was Democratic, is considered competitive now, although Democrats must struggle to take control of the legislature. Neither party shows much internal cohesion, although the Democrats have consolidated behind their incumbents since 1956, when George Docking began the party's frequent success in gubernatorial politics. The Republicans rarely nominate a candidate for governor with over 55 percent of the vote, and in 1994, neither the Republican nor the Democratic nominee received that much. During the first hundred years of the state's history, Republicans won consistently at all levels of government by comfortable margins. During the 1950s, however, election outcomes were less predictable. Candidates came to depend less upon the party organizational support, and financial resources became more important in primary elections (Harder 1986, 170).

Sam Hardage, the winner of the Republican primary in 1982, did not believe a party organization should become involved in an open primary contest. Hardage, as might be expected, believed that the party should remain neutral, but he had just successfully beaten David Owen, a party organization leader who had spent a year and a half seeking the nomination.

David Owen, loser of the Republican primary by three percentage points, said that he was favored by the party leaders because he was the only candidate who had done any work for the party. But the party leaders do not support candidates in the primary in Kansas, as Owen points out: "Frankly, I think that's one of the problems with the system that we use. All the party leaders all want to run for cover until after the fact. Their lack of input or lack of work in the primary process really throws the thing up for grabs and it allows people who really don't have the experience or background to win the nomination" (1982, 5).

Oregon: Independents All

Oregon's political parties are weak, although they are competitive, which flies in the face of hypotheses that state that competitive politics force cohesion on both parties to fight the common enemy. Neither party has a social-group profile from election to election. Therefore, each candidate has to establish an independent power base. The parties do not stand for clear-cut issues: each candidate has to exploit issues of the moment. The primaries are competitive, but no identifiable factions continue from election to election. Republicans are not exclusively probusiness. In 1986, Neil Goldschmidt, the Democratic candidate for governor, ran on a probusiness, economic development program statewide, while relying on support from his traditional Democratic home base in Portland. Goldschmidt's politics were described as a contrast both to national Republican conservatism and the labor liberalism of the Democrats.

Some of this independence from the national party profiles can be explained by the fact that Oregon does not have the economic makeup that provides the bases of traditional parties. Timber and agriculture are the major industries. The New Deal split the Democratic party between the progressives, the backers of Roosevelt, and the conservatives, who wanted to continue in power. The Republicans had their roots in populism and Progressivism and were the more liberal party. While the parties of today are not quite as incongruent as they were for twenty years after the New Deal, they still contain both conservative and progressive factions. If the Republicans move in the direction of the national party, they lose general elections. If the Democrats become more liberal and less moderate, they also lose. The conservative areas of Oregon are those where conservative candidates from either party could win, and Republicans win in liberal areas.

The parties in Oregon are impotent when it comes to recruiting and nominating candidates, hence party loyalty is not a strong factor, and candidates run independent campaigns in the direct primaries. The candidates in 1982 agreed that parties should play no role in primary campaigns, even when an incumbent is running. And so the system continues with the support of the candidates as well as the citizens of Oregon.

California: Amateur Parties and Elite Consultants

The interaction of the rules with the political culture of a people accounts for the type of party system. California's weak parties are not an accident. An elite group of Progressives emasculated the parties during the early part of the twentieth century. Not content with imposing primary laws as they did in most states at that time, the California Progressives inflicted another injury on the body politic. Cross-filing was passed in 1913 to introduce a strong measure of nonpartisanship into the state's primary system. This reform allowed a candidate to run in both parties' primaries.

Republican Earl Warren used cross-filing to win both party nominations in the primary and proceeded to win a unanimous victory in the 1946 gubernatorial election because he was the only candidate appearing on the ballot. The cross-filing system had a devastating effect on the political party organizations because it prevented them from having any influence over nominations. Candidates who were elected to office as a result of winning both primaries seldom had any sense of loyalty or obligation to their party, if indeed they could be identified as having a party. The ultimate in successful cross-filing was reached in 1944, with 80 percent of the districts in the assembly and 90 percent in the state senate (Rowe 1961, 23). The cross-filing system was one reason for the great weakness of party discipline in the legislature, making it almost a nonpartisan body.

It was the Republicans who first tried to establish some control over nominations. After the FDR landslide and the loss of congressional and state legislative seats, a group of Republicans established the California Republican Assembly (CRA) outside the structure of the official state party. The major purpose of the group was to revitalize the party, but the CRA moved cautiously toward the practice of making endorsements. In 1942, for the first time, the CRA endorsed a slate of candidates for statewide office, including Earl Warren for governor. The slate was successful in the primary, and the practice of Republican Assembly endorsements was well established. The CRA-endorsed candidates were virtually assured of the Republican nomination. The great number of uncontested nominations suggested that the assembly's success may have been in forestalling contests rather than winning them (Rowe 1961, 37).

It was the Democrats' turn to worry, because the endorsed slate of Republicans were often able to win both primaries, which Governor Warren accomplished in 1946. Democratic leaders decided to follow the Republican example and establish an organization, the California Democratic Council (CDC), to make endorsements at a statewide convention (Rowe 1961, 46). The CDC made its first endorsements in 1954, and in most cases it succeeded in persuading nonendorsed candidates to stay out of the primary; partly as a consequence, the endorsed candidates were able to win the Democratic primary against cross-filing Republicans. Preprimary endorsements and the CDC were important elements contributing to Democratic unity in the 1958 campaign and the sweeping victory that year. The Democrats won most statewide races, including the governorship, and won legislative control. One of the first orders of business in 1959 was the abolition of cross-filing in the primary system (Rowe 1961, 53).

One might think that the California parties, thus encouraged, would try to get control of their organizations and begin to make endorsements themselves, instead of "farming out" this operation to their respective club movements, but that was not to be. Considerable concern was voiced by the press, by some members of the legislature, and by certain party officials that in the absence of cross-filing, the direct primary would become subverted and meaningless since the party could make preprimary endorsements, which would deny the voters a genuine choice among persons seeking party nominations. The actual selection of candidates would be by party conventions or, even worse, by party hierarchies, "machines," or "bosses." This attitude prevailed, and in 1963 the California legislature adopted a law that provided, in part, that the party "state convention, the state central committee, and the county central committee in each county shall not endorse, support, or oppose, any candidate for nomination by that party for partisan office in the direct primary election" (Jewell 1985, 16). Beaten down again and deprived of their major function, the parties could only hope that their club affiliates would present them with good candidates.

Twenty years later the CDC and the CRA had ceased to be the major prolocutors for their parties. Neither was adequately representative of the distribution of its party's registration or voting strength throughout the state (Rowe 1961, 79). The CDC was tailored to a California electorate that was young, issue-oriented, and homogeneously middle class. Low-income groups and unskilled workers were not attracted to the movement. The club types were social liberals who were not representative of Democratic registrants and voters. By 1982 Tom Bradley, the Democratic front-runner, decided not to seek the CDC endorsement, and it lost its influence over the nominating process in California.

The CRA declined because it could not contain all the interests within the Republican party. A number of other Republican groups representing different ideological positions sprang up and made their own endorsements. The California Republican League represents the moderate wing of the party, while the United Republicans of California represents the right wing. The gubernatorial candidates endorsed by the CRA in 1974 and 1978 both lost the primary. In 1982 the CRA was unable to reach the two-thirds majority needed for a gubernatorial endorsement: Lieutenant Governor Mike Curb got 198 of the 200 required votes in the convention but lost the primary.

The history of California nominating politics ends with another chance for the parties to assume some control over the choice of their standard-bearer. In February 1989 the U.S. Supreme Court issued its ruling in the case of *Eu, Secretary of State of California, et al. v. San Francisco County Democratic Central Committee et al.* By a vote of 8–0, the Court declared that several provisions of the California Elections Code were invalid, because they "burden the First Amendment rights of political parties and their members without serving a compelling state interest." In particular, the Court ruled that a ban on preprimary endorsements was invalid because it violated the rights of parties and their members to free political speech and freedom of association. Since early 1989, therefore, the California parties have been free to organize and endorse candidates in partisan primaries.

The Democratic party has begun to endorse candidates in legislative and statewide races. As table 3.1 indicates, California Democrats now endorse by party rule, the gubernatorial primary of 1990 being the first effort. The State Central Committee of approximately three thousand members endorses for governor. To be endorsed, a Democratic incumbent has to receive 50 percent of the votes, while a nonincumbent needs 60 percent. Convention participants also have the right to vote for no endorsement. In 1990, John Van deKamp was the Democratic party's endorsee for governor, but Dianne Feinstein beat him in the Democratic primary. If party endorsees lose regularly in the primary, the endorsement becomes meaningless, if not counterproductive. The bylaws encourage nonendorsed candidates to withdraw from the race to encourage a unified effort on behalf of the endorsed candidate, but it was hard to envision Dianne Feinstein withdrawing. In 1994, the party leaders convinced the gubernatorial candidates not to seek endorsement "in the interests of party unity."

The California Republicans have opted not to endorse, fearing that it could be divisive and lead to rigged meetings. Moreover, if party endorsing were to be adopted, there could be conflict between Republican legislative leaders (who have at times given endorsements) and local GOP leaders over which Republican candidate should be supported in a primary (Price 1992a, 203). There may be more incentive for the Republicans to endorse now since the voters approved a blanket primary in March 1996. Now voters from any party as well as independents can vote for party candidates on the primary ballot. Both party chairs opposed the initiative, and the motivation to endorse to exert some control over the nominating process should be obvious to both parties.

Because of the traditionally weak parties in the state, candidates do their own fund-raising, hire their own campaign manager, and only occasionally join a coalition with other members of the ticket. The 1990 California gubernatorial race featured presidential-like expensive media-centered campaigning. A number of high-priced, high-profile political consultants spoke in a postelection symposium at the Institute for Governmental Studies at Berkeley in January 1991. A reading of the report of the conference reveals that California politics is professional business. The consultants for the John Van deKamp, Pete Wilson, and Dianne Feinstein campaigns are members of a small elite corps of consultants who regularly emerge in the California election contests. Some of them, such as Richie Ross, Clint Reilly, and Michael Berman, are based in California. Others, such as Dick Dresner and Bill Carrick, are national consultants who have been brought in to help particular candidates. They are all formally independent of the Democratic and Republican state committees, but they work exclusively for candidates of one party or the other (Cain 1991, 202). In the absence of party organization, candidates make their own. It was probably never the case in California politics that a candidate turned to a party organization rather than a special interest. In fact, in the early years of California politics, organizations were the captives of special interests.

Thus ends the brief background of the five states that nominate exclusively by primary. It is obvious that their primaries reflect the factionalism that exists within each party. To what extent the primaries are responsible for igniting the factionalism and to what extent they expose it may be a chicken-and-egg question. The strong progressive sentiment maintains that the people should determine their candidates. But are the majority of the people in the Democratic party in Texas really represented in the open primary process when conservatives of both parties can ensure a Democratic candidate in their own image? Are the people of Oregon served when a candidate can muster a plurality of interests within a party and capture the party banner? These interests may be the same as those represented by their rival in the opposite party. The parties stand for very little other than a familiar label for the election. Each candidate is independent and owes nothing to the party. California alone in this group may be a case study in a growing awareness of the advantage of party organization. It has abolished its ban on endorsements, and its Democrats are struggling to foster them. The Golden State may join the ranks of endorsing states.

States with Preprimary Endorsements

In table 3.1 the five states chosen to study the effects of preprimary endorsements are italicized (Colorado, Connecticut, Illinois, New York, and Minnesota). This section will give a bit of the history of the endorsement process in each of the five states and indicate what the candidates think about the process. Table 3.3 gives the dates and locations of the endorsing conventions and the candidates for 1982. Table 3.4 sets out the 1982 rules for the endorsement process for each state, which the candidates for endorsement must follow. The order gives the states that have legal endorsements first, and among them, those with the most restrictive rules.

Connecticut: Always a Strong Party State

Strong disciplined parties are a fact of life in Connecticut. They are accepted by the political culture and protected by strict state laws. True, some of the toughest restrictions have been loosened recently, such as the requirement that primary challengers to the party-endorsed candidate now

TABLE 3.3. Party Conventions, Dates and Candidates, 1982

State	Party	Convention Date	Convention Place	Candidate	Current Office or Occupation
Conn.	D	July 16–17	Hartford	William O'Neill	Governor
				Ernest Abate	House Speaker
	R	July 23–24	Hartford	Lewis Rome	Former Senate Majority Leader
				Richard Bozzuto	Former Senate Minority Leader
				Gerald Labriola	Senator
				Russell Post	Senator
N.Y.	D	June 21–22	Syracuse	Mario Cuomo	Lieutenant Governor
				Ed Koch	Mayor, New York City
	R	June 15–16	New York City	Lewis Lehrman	Businessperson
				Paul Curran	U.S. Attorney
				James Emery	Assembly Minority Leader
				Richard Rosenbaum	Former Party Chair
Colo.	D.	June 18–19	Denver	Richard Lamm	Governor
	R	June 26	Denver	John Fuhr	Former House Speaker
				Phil Winn	Former Party Chair
				Steve Schuck	Businessperson
Minn.	D	June 4–6	Duluth	Rudy Perpich	Former Governor
				Warren Spannaus	Attorney General
	R	June 17–19	St. Paul	Wheelock Whitney	Businessperson
				Louis Wangberg	Lieutenant Governor
				Glen Sherwood	House Minority Leader
				Paul Overgaard	Former State Legislator
Ill.	R	—	—	Jim Thompson	Governor
	D	Nov. 1981	Chicago	Adlai Stevenson	Former U.S. Senator

TABLE 3.4. Gubernatorial Preprimary Endorsement Procedures, 1982

State	Party	Name, Size	How Selected	Percent for Endorsement	Qualifications Primary Ballot	Primary Date	Primary Type
Conn.	D	Convention, 1,300	Caucus	51	20%[a]	Sept. 7	closed
	R	Convention, 933	Caucus	51	20%[a]	Sept. 7	closed
N.Y.	D	Central Committee, 357	Assembly District Primary	51 (weighted voting by ballots cast last gub. election)	25% or petition	Sept. 23	closed
	R	Central Committee, 402	Assembly District Primary	51 (weighted voting by ballots cast last gub. election)	25% or petition	Sept. 23	closed
Colo.	D	Assembly, 510	Caucus (precinct to county)	20[b] or more, one ballot	20%[b] or petition: listed in vote order on ballot	Sept. 14	closed
	R	Assembly, 3,576	Caucus (precinct to county)	20[b] or more, one ballot	20%[b] or petition: listed in vote order on ballot	Sept. 14	closed
Minn.	D	Convention, 1,220	Caucus	60	petition	Sept. 14	open
	R	Convention, 2,025	Caucus	60	petition	Sept. 14	open
Ill.	D	Central Committee, 24[c]	Congressional District Primary every 4 years	51 (weighted voting by ballots cast last primary)	petition	March 16	open

TABLE 3.4.—*Continued*

State	Party	Name, Size	How Selected	Percent for Endorsement	Qualifications Primary Ballot	Primary Date	Type
Ill. (cont.)	R	Central Committee, 24[c] Informal consensus	Congressional District Primary every 4 years	51 (weighted voting by ballots cast last primary)	petition	March 16	open

[a]Changed to 15% in 1993
[b]Changed to 30%
[c]Now 20 members

must get at least 15 (instead of 20) percent of the endorsing convention. And the Republicans for a time courted nonaffiliated voters in their primaries, but that was a short-lived courtship, and the party has ruled them out and returned to party registrants. Neither reform can be seen as the end of strong parties in the Nutmeg State. The strength of Connecticut's parties, according to an astute observer, is a result of three factors: electoral competition, control over nominations, and internal agreement (Lockard 1959, 244).

Connecticut has generally been a closely competitive state since 1930. Republican party strength is drawn mainly from the small towns and suburban communities and the upper-income urbanites. The greatest support for the Democratic party comes from cities and particularly from labor and ethnic populations. The major dependence of the party is on the larger urban centers of Hartford, New Haven, Bridgeport, and Waterbury. Thus, a delicate balance of forces has preserved the competitiveness of Connecticut parties. After 1954, the Democrats began to build a registration advantage and controlled the statehouse for thirty-six years with only one interruption (1971 to 1975, when Thomas Meskill was governor). Connecticut elected an Independent governor, Lowell Weicker (previously a Republican Senator), in 1990 and a Republican, John Rowland, in 1994. Both races featured three major party candidates, indicating a time of flux for the state.

The two party machines that have received the most notice have been on the state level, perhaps because Connecticut does not have a "major city" from which a machine could gain control over the state party. Middle-size cities vying for control may have necessitated a state "boss." The Republican boss was J. Henry Roraback, who held sway from 1912 until 1937. Roraback combined rural organizational strength, businessmen's money, conservative government policy, and a disciplined organization. His main control over the party lay in his ability to determine who would run for office. He controlled the state conventions of the party and hence the slate of statewide officeholders. No successor to Roraback has held the power he had, but subsequent party chairs have been able to exert power over nominations and party strategy in campaigns (Lockard 1959, 245–51).

The Democratic counterpart, John Bailey, held power from 1946 until his death in 1975. Gone were the days when a state chair could exert dictatorial power. Bailey had to consolidate and persuade. He had to work around a challenge primary law that took effect in 1955 and provided that convention nominees could be subject to primary challenges. The structure of the Democratic party forced him into alliances with various city bosses, the labor unions, and ethnic minorities. At the height of his power, Bailey was able to control nominations as well as legislative policy, but it was by patronage and consensus (Lieberman 1966, 1981). Liberal white-collar professionals have emerged within the party ranks, making a balancing act even more urgent (Rose 1992, 12). Since Bailey's time, party chairs have generally kept the party unified for nominations and campaign strategy.

The Connecticut party conventions best fit the model of delegate selection controlled by the party organization (Jewell 1984, 72–80). The first step in the process is the endorsement of a slate of delegates by a local party committee, or a caucus, depending on local party rules. These selections can be challenged in a primary, by another delegate slate, but that is rare. In 1982 only 4 percent of the Democratic delegates and 11 percent of the Republican ones were involved in a primary election. More than two-thirds of the Democratic delegates and half of the Republicans reported that their local delegations made some effort to reach consensus on one or both of the major statewide races (Jewell 1984, 73). Connecticut convention delegates are experienced in party activity. Over 60 percent of the Democrats and half of the Republicans held a party office at the state or local level and attended the previous convention (Jewell 1984, 79). The convention delegates were asked what advantages the endorsee gains from endorsement if there is a primary challenge. Delegates from both parties mentioned money (in good times), expertise, personnel hours, telephone banks, and support from town committees (Jewell 1984, 137–39).

The convention system remains strong, and it is rare for a candidate for statewide office to be unseated in a primary election after winning the endorsement of a majority of the convention delegates. State law provides that the winner of the party endorsement may be challenged in a primary only by someone who receives 15 percent of the vote in the convention (changed from 20 percent in 1993). Convention rules traditionally made it difficult for a challenger to get 20 percent, because they allowed vote changing at the end of a ballot, and there are pressures to shift votes to the winner. The party norms against running in the primary are strong. Traditionally candidates at the convention make a commitment to abide by the endorsement if they should fail to receive it. Only six gubernatorial primaries have been held since 1955, and only in the Republican challenge of 1986 and the Democratic challenge of 1994 did the convention endorsee lose.

New York: Designation by State Committee

New York is another competitive strong party state, but the parties reflect a different type of cleavage. The New York City area, accounting for about half of the state's population, is dominated by the Democratic party. Long Island and most of upstate New York are safely Republican, but the larger upstate cities of Buffalo, Syracuse, and Albany are Democratic strongholds. Statewide elections are usually quite competitive, with a small edge going to the Democrats. Of the ten gubernatorial elections from 1994 back, five were won by Democrats and five by Republicans. In the New York Legislature, the assembly is solidly in Democratic hands and the senate protects a Republican majority due to a creative gerrymandering of senate districts.

There is an enduring upstate-downstate division in the political culture of New York that ignites the party conflict. New York City is home to the vast majority of the state's African-Americans, Hispanics, and Jews, reinforcing ethnic differences between upstaters and city dwellers. Yet the need for a Republican senate and a Democratic assembly to do business leads to titanic truces. Well-organized political clout is mutually admired, and both political parties have plenty of it. There is a common expectation that parties are legitimate actors in the political life of the state and that they should nominate, elect, and govern.

Both parties in New York have traditionally exercised control over nominations. From 1921 until 1967, New York remained one of the few states to nominate statewide candidates by convention. Nominations from the twelve hundred to fifteen hundred delegates at the conventions were the product of bargaining among blocs of uncommitted delegates or, more realistically, among the county leaders who typically engineered the results. In response to attacks by good-government groups and the *New York Times,* Governor Rockefeller reluctantly signed into law in 1967 the bill that abolished the convention system of nomination (Scarrow 1983, 43). Designation (endorsement) for statewide office is now made by a party's state committee, whose members are elected in state assembly districts. A candidate can force a primary by either of two routes. In the first, a challenger can get on the primary ballot by receiving at least 25 percent of the weighted votes at the designation session of the state committee in any vote taken. The second, the petition method, allows individuals to challenge the party's designee in the primary by gathering petitions (fifteen thousand signatures properly distributed throughout the state). Furthermore, party organizational expenditure on behalf of the designee's primary contest is prohibited. These last two provisions make New York's rules less strict than Connecticut's.

The hope of the bill writers to keep parties in control of the nominating process after the introduction of the challenge primary has not worked as envisioned. At first the Democrats had to deal with the stigma of "bossism." At the first designating committee meeting in 1970 their choice, Arthur Goldberg, announced that he wished to renounce the designation so he would not be a "creature of the bosses" and would prove the fact by collecting the necessary signatures to get on the primary ballot (Scarrow 1983, 45). In 1974, the committee designee, Howard Samuels, lost in the primary. In 1982, the issue of bossism seemed to have subsided, because both major contenders for governor sought the party's designation. However, the designee, Mayor Ed Koch, lost in the primary to Lieutenant Governor Mario Cuomo. As incumbent, Cuomo was endorsed regularly without significant challenge.

The Republicans do not suffer from cries of bossism, but they have fallen prey to another provision of the challenge primary law, namely, the prohibition against funding the candidate of their choice if challenged. In 1982 the designee, Lewis Lehrman, had never been active in the party and had never run for public office. But as a successful businessperson, he had millions to spend to win both the nomination and the general election and successfully forced himself on the party. "Clearly money and television had replaced party organization as kingmaker" (Scarrow 1983, 46). Since 1982, however, the party has had only one challenge to its endorsees.

It would be premature to say that the New York parties are folding up their tents. In the first place, party organizations in the state have always been decentralized. County party leaders have been more powerful than state party leaders, and bargaining among them to select a nominee has been traditional. In answer to a questionnaire of member-delegates of the 1982 Democratic and Republican designating committees, more than two-thirds of the Democrats and half of the Republicans reported that efforts were made by the party organizations at the local level to reach consensus on major candidates. When asked why these efforts were made, delegates emphasized the following points: the local organization would gain political clout or leverage, improve its chances of getting state patronage, increase its influence on the candidate selection process, and avoid the dangers arising from a split in the local ranks (Jewell 1984, 73–75). Committee members were also asked what advantages the endorsed candidate might receive. Tangible campaign resources topped the list for those asked: 40 percent of the Democrats and 31 percent of the Republicans mentioned them. Since the party cannot fund its nominee in the primary, the delegates must have had county and local participation in mind (Jewell 1984, 137–41). For example, the chair of Suffolk County, Dominic Baranello, initiated a "Suffolk Democrats for Koch" committee and raised funds independent of the party (Piscatelli and LoCicero 1982, 28).

Colorado: Caucus-Convention by Law

Colorado comes next in terms of the rules that encourage party strength. The state has mandatory endorsing conventions, and those who receive over 30 percent get on the ballot automatically, with the valued "top line" designation going to the one who receives the most votes. Those who fail to receive 30 percent of the convention vote have the option of petitioning their way to the statewide primary ballot. The primary is closed, but unaffiliated voters can register with the party of their choice on primary day and remain registered.

In 1910, the Colorado legislature passed an election bill that introduced a novel nominating system to the American scene. This system has remained essentially unchanged. The law provides for preprimary party designation of candidates, who are placed on the primary ballot in the order of the number of votes they received at the designating assemblies, with the name of the top designee appearing first. Provision for candidates' names to appear on the primary ballot by petition was included in this law. What makes the law weaker than the ones in Connecticut and New York is that the primary is not a challenge primary, with the right to challenge given those who receive a certain percentage of the convention vote. All candidates who receive 30 percent are automatically placed on the primary ballot with the party's blessing. In practice they may wish to withdraw, and most do, leaving the highest vote getter on the top line. Originally set at 10 percent for primary designation, later changes increased party control over the nomination of candidates by increasing the convention vote requirement to 20 and then 30 percent.

The foundation of the Colorado preprimary designation system is the precinct caucus, where delegates are chosen by registered party members to attend county assemblies and conventions. At the county level, delegates are chosen to attend district and state assemblies and conventions.

(In strict legal parlance, conventions nominate or elect, while assemblies designate candidates to run in primaries, but common parlance refers to both as conventions.) The precinct consists of approximately a thousand registered voters who live in the same neighborhood. On the first Monday in April of each election year, precinct caucuses are held in every precinct to start the nominating process (Cronin and Loevy 1993, 132). In many precincts the same people are elected delegates to the county convention. Candidates for governor get lists of these party "regulars" and contact them in an effort to get their votes at the county and state party conventions. "Working the party regulars tends to be a more fruitful endeavor than attempting the considerably more difficult task of turning out supporters at the precinct caucuses" (Cronin and Loevy 1993, 135). At the county convention, candidates for governor may be competing for delegates to the state convention. County party leaders attempt to resolve disputes by balancing the recommended list of state convention delegates among competing candidates, but if that fails, delegates may have to choose between competing lists of state convention delegates, with each list committed to a different candidate.

As V. O. Key said, clearly a nominating system, by itself, cannot produce party unity. Political parties are creatures of their environments and must respond to and serve the needs and expectations of those from which they draw support. Inspection of the Colorado nomination contests since 1962 reveals that incumbents are assured of their party's designation without competition. But when there is an open seat for governor, both parties have lively contests, and the top-line designee almost invariably wins.

Because of the geographic clustering of the population along the corridor immediately east of the Front Range, politicians cultivating a statewide constituency play to this urban audience, while many state legislators are creatures of the mountain and plains communities. A study of the partisan preferences of Coloradans drawn from CBS–*New York Times* polls reveal that the two political parties evenly split Colorado voters willing to identify as partisans. Approximately 30 percent of the voters identified themselves as Republicans and 30 percent as Democrats. The liberal-conservative makeup of the Republicans, Democrats, and independents indicate that Colorado is one of the seven most ideologically polarized states (Erikson, Wright, and McIver 1993, 40–41). The balance of power in Colorado remains with the independent voters who display no leanings toward either philosophic extreme.

It is therefore in the interest of both parties to offer moderates to the voters, and it would appear that this is what they have done, although candidates from the ideological wings of both parties have tried to get the assembly designation. A comparison of the ideological self-classification of state convention delegates surveyed in 1980 revealed that 66 percent of the Democratic activists regarded themselves as somewhat to very liberal. Ninety percent of Republican delegates classified themselves as somewhat to very conservative (Simmons 1984, 75). The Republicans were split between the conservatives and moderates in the gubernatorial nominating campaign of 1978 (Klein 1982, 31).

The Colorado preprimary assembly system provides parties with control over nominations (Eyre and Martin 1967). It enables them to limit the number of candidates who enter primaries as well as choose the nominee by giving him or her the top-line designation on the primary ballot. The nature of the assembly makes it resistant to dictation from a single source, although unity can be forged by an incumbent, by an extremely popular candidate, or by an unusually strong coalition of interests.

The Republican gubernatorial candidates in Colorado supported the preprimary designations as the best way to unify the party. A few had changes to offer. Republican candidates John Fuhr and Steve Schuck thought the state chair should become involved in the designation process. As Walt Klein, Steve Schuck's campaign manager, put it, the state chair should try to "force events to happen" (Klein 1982, 23). Apparently the state chair does get a promise from all candidates to support the party's nominee. According to Phil Winn's campaign manager, a neutral chair can better unite the party after the nomination (Diepenbroch 1982, 22). Governor Richard Lamm's campaign manager also believed that a neutral chair was preferable until after the primary.

We can conclude that while the preprimary system of endorsement as it functions in Colorado has tended to strengthen the parties, the party leadership is limited in the degree of control it can exercise over the actions of the assemblies because they are composed of delegates who reflect the strong spirit of independence and localism.

Minnesota: Caucus-Convention by Party Custom

The direct primary came to Minnesota in 1912. The Republicans were the first to experiment with preprimary endorsements by holding an "eliminating convention" in 1920. Being the majority party, they did not see fit to endorse with any regularity until the 1950s (Kunkel 1987, 8). In 1959 the party amended its constitution to permit endorsements, and they have been made frequently since that time.

Because of the weakness of the Democrats in the first half of the century, that party's main problem was to find candidates, not eliminate them. As the fortunes of the national Democratic party improved, factions began to fight to control the small Minnesota party, and after its merger with the Farmer-Laborites in 1944 it began to endorse regularly. The Farmer-Labor party had a strong rural base and the Democratic party had an urban Catholic base. A new generation of liberal Democrats under Hubert Humphrey's leadership forged the alliance. The leaders of the new Democratic-Farmer-Labor party believed that preprimary endorsements were essential to maintain party unity and elect candidates who would be committed to DFL principles. That was particularly necessary because the party was in the minority and Minnesota has an open primary system that would permit "raiding" by Republicans or independents.

The endorsements have seldom prevented primaries, particularly in the DFL, but the endorsees have usually won these primaries by comfortable margins, often against token opposition. Although the party endorsement does not actually appear on the primary ballot, endorsement still may help a candidate defeat his or her opponent. Until 1982, there had only been one example of an endorsee losing; that occurred in 1966 when the DFL endorsed a challenger to the incumbent governor (Lebedoff 1969). The most common pattern in the DFL has been for a candidate to be endorsed without opposition in the convention and to face minor opposition in the primary, although the competition has become more intense since 1982. In the DFL party some splits have occurred between liberals and moderates, and regional differences between the Twin Cities (Minneapolis–St. Paul) and the Iron Range also exist in the party.

The Republican party has had more close and prolonged contests in its convention, but its gubernatorial primaries (until 1982) have been infrequent and lopsided. The normal pattern has been for those candidates who are beaten in the convention to support the endorsed candidate. In all of the six contested primaries in the Republican party from 1960 to 1994, the opposition came from candidates who did not seek endorsement. There is no limit on the number of ballots for endorsement, and occasionally many are taken before a winner receives the required 60 percent. The Republican party (called the Independent Republican party) has a split between traditional Republicans and Christian fundamentalists, which has been dividing the party since the gubernatorial convention of 1982. In 1994, the Christian Right denied the endorsement to the incumbent Republican governor, Arne Carlson, because he did not espouse their principles.

Minnesota's caucus-convention system begins with a precinct caucus, held separately by both parties in each of the state's nearly four thousand precincts. Since Minnesota's precincts are relatively small in size, the precinct caucus is essentially a neighborhood meeting. By state law and party practice, the precinct caucuses are open to any party supporter who feels inclined to attend. State law specifies the time and place for the caucuses and even regulates their order of business. At these quasi-public, quasi-private caucuses, attendees vote on delegates to attend the district and state conventions. These caucuses serve not only as the basis for the party organization, but also as a debate forum for the party faithful. At the precinct caucuses, participants may propose, discuss, and pass or reject policy resolutions. Later at district or state conventions, these resolutions may be written into the platform. It is most common for local party leaders to be elected as convention delegates, apparently with little opposition. Things were different in 1982, as we will see.

In 1982 the Republican precinct caucuses were invaded by large numbers of persons with strong ideological commitments to pro life, pro-family, and morality issues. Many were evangelical Christians mobilized by local church groups. A large proportion of them were supporting the candidacy of Glen Sherwood, whose platform was based on these issues. When delegates elected at the precinct meetings gathered at district and county caucuses to elect state convention delegates, party leaders attempted to reduce their numbers to include more party regulars. A delegate survey showed that 58 percent had attended the previous convention, which is high, but 54 percent said that they had been opposed in the caucus. Almost 50 percent said they were interested in issues (Jewell 1984, 76–77).

The delegate selection process used by the Minnesota DFL is unique. It is not dominated by the party organization, although two-thirds of the delegates had attended the previous convention. Issues played a larger role in party conventions and in the delegate selection process than any other parties being studied. When asked about their major interest in becoming delegates, 80 percent mentioned issues. Most listed the question of abortion (a slight majority were pro choice), but large numbers mentioned the Equal Rights Amendment, the nuclear freeze, and a variety of economic issues (Jewell 1984, 77).

Issues are incorporated into the DFL delegate selection process in an unusual fashion. When delegates chosen in precinct caucuses meet at the district or county level to elect state delegates, they usually organize into subcaucuses. Anyone at the caucus can try to organize a subcaucus by attracting enough persons to elect one state delegate. Elections are strictly proportional; if the county is entitled to ten state delegates, and a hundred persons attend the caucus, any subcaucus of ten persons can elect one delegate. Of the DFL delegates who answered Jewell's survey, 82 percent were elected by a subcaucus. Subcaucuses are wrapped around issues primarily, or a combination of issues and candidates (Environmentalists against Abortion, for example). It is surprising that a party with such a commitment to issues sends convention delegates who are party officeholders! Sixty-seven percent of the Democrats and 58 percent of the Republicans hold party office (Jewell 1984, 79).

On balance, the endorsing system in Minnesota seems to have achieved its purpose by uniting the parties in the nominating process. The candidates for the nomination supported the endorsing system. Even though both Republican Wheelock Whitney and Democrat Rudy Perpich chose not to try to receive the endorsement in the convention, they supported the system and said that the party chair should support the endorsee by using the party's resources. Minnesota's popular culture, described as issue oriented, reformist, purposive, and moralistic, has been supportive of strong parties.

Illinois: Slate-making

Unlike the first four states with preprimary endorsements that we examined, where hundreds of delegates gather amid bands and balloons to endorse candidates for the primary, Illinois parties choose to make their endorsements in "smoke-filled rooms." No attempt has been made to incorporate endorsements in the law, the endorsed candidate is not designated on the ballot, and the primaries are open. The parties go about the process of endorsing—or slate-making, as it is called in Illinois—with efficiency and minimal fanfare. Because the Republicans have such a closed process, little is known about it. One source says the Republican party has made endorsements intermittently (Jewell 1984, 43). Another claims that in Illinois, GOP politics is personality rather than organization oriented. Hence. Republican slate-making is left in the hands of a few prominent leaders who use their clout and money to influence the nomination (P. Green 1986a, 8).

Governor Jim Thompson's campaign managers claimed that the Republican party state central committee did not have a slate-making process. As far as the governor was concerned, the only issue was whether or not he wanted to run again; there was never any question that he would be renominated. But the county, ward, and township organizations do endorse, and they played a major role in 1976 when the governor ran for the first time. Bob Kjellander assumed that Governor Thompson tried to get the county and local endorsements when he first ran. He was opposed in the primary by Dick Cooper, founder of Weight Watchers, who spent a lot of his own money (Kjellander 1982, 32).

From 1955 to 1976, the powerful Chicago mayor Richard J. Daley was unquestionably the leader of the Democratic party in Illinois, even though he held no state office. His candidates were usually nominated in Democratic primaries, and he usually delivered the Chicago vote for statewide candidates. The reason he was so successful is due to the weight given Chicago in the slate-making process. The state central committee of each party, created by statute, is composed of member(s) elected in the primary from each congressional district (now twenty); the law also provides for weighted voting, based on the primary turnout in the district. In 1986 the city of Chicago cast 54 percent of the total Democratic primary vote, and the percentage was undoubtedly much higher in the past. Hence, those members on the Democratic State Central Committee from Chicago could control the slate and the nomination itself.

Usually both the state and Cook County (where Chicago is located) central committees held sessions at which those seeking endorsement presented their cases. However, those sessions were a facade because Daley decided whom to slate; other party leaders went along after they received "the word." There is some disagreement about when Daley made his decisions known. It was commonly supposed that "the Boss" passed the word in advance of the slate-making meetings, which were a procedural sham. Not according to Adlai Stevenson, however. He said that Daley would not indicate his choice until the last minute so that the losers could not get organized and take the organization down in the primary. In return for organization support, potential candidates were required to pledge to support all endorsed candidates. Stevenson also presents a more benign portrait of the great boss, saying that he would listen to the opinions of others before he made up his mind: that he got his power by being an accommodator (Stevenson 1982, 24). After the slate-making process, Democratic workers delivered the votes in the primary for slated candidates (Gove and Masotti 1982, 213).

Since Daley's death, some of the non-Chicago members on the state central committee have tried to ensure that suburban and downstate members have more clout in the slate-making process. The Chicago Democratic "machine" was split by a civil war along racial lines between black Chicago mayor Harold Washington and white Cook County Democratic chair Edward Vrdolyak. Mayor Richard M. Daley, a son of the former mayor who was elected in 1989 after Washington's death, has sought racial reconciliation in a city that is now about 40 percent black. While the golden era of Chicago's machine politics is over, the machine is not dead. But the advent of new demographics, technology, antipatronage court decisions, and age (in some neighborhoods, the leading occupation is "widow"), have wounded its strength (P. Green 1986b, 13).

An account of the 1985 Democratic gubernatorial slate-making describes the "College of Cardinals" that met on November 25 at Chicago's Bismark Hotel. "Most committee members truly view themselves as 'Princes of the Party' as they glory in the hierarchical structure and political ritual associated with slatemaking" (P. Green 1986a, 7). The Democratic state central committee slate-making session was the first held under the party's new rules, which mandate that each congressional district be represented by one male and one female who cast equally weighted votes based on the formula established by law. The state central committee met on the hotel's third floor to endorse the Democratic ticket for statewide offices, while the Cook County central committee gathered in the basement to select its slate. Illinois Democrats came up with the strongest slate possible: endorsing four incumbents, a famous name—Adlai Stevenson III, son of the late governor—for a rerun for governor, and a woman for secretary of state.

The parties in Illinois go about the process of slate-making in a businesslike manner, aware that this process is crucial to their electoral success. The Republicans draw most of their strength from the five suburban counties around Chicago and the 96 counties in downstate Illinois, which can deliver 57 percent of the primary turnout. Hence, contests occur between metropolitan and rural candidates within the party and erupt occasionally into the primary. Governor Jim Thompson, who held office from 1976 to 1990, hailed from Chicago; his successor, Jim Edgar, was raised downstate. According to Mildred Schwartz, the Illinois Republicans display a robustness and vigor that permit them to survive the extremes of internal dissent or electoral rejection (1990). For the Democrats, internal cohesion is difficult to forge since the party has many ethnic groups within it, particularly in Chicago. The traditional strength of the Chicago organization has prevented the state party from playing a stronger and more positive role. This situation may be changing as the state committee is playing a dominant role in slating for state offices.

A review of how governors emerge in the ten states we are studying reveals vividly that, in the primary-only states, we must look to the factions that make up the parties if we are to locate potential leadership. In the Texas Democratic party, the liberals and the conservatives battle for the soul of the party. In Tennessee, vestiges of the Clement machine versus challenges from Knoxville or Memphis hold the power to nominate in the Democratic name. Kansas Republicans are divided geographically, and in Oregon it is difficult to locate any concentration of power. In California the sheer size and diversity of the state is making organizational cohesion a necessary condition for governing, and the Democrats are beginning to feel this need for endorsing in order to compete. The direct primary ignores the existence of political organizations and leadership by conferring ultimate power over nominations directly upon the individual voter.

In the preprimary endorsement states, a process, not a faction, brings forth leadership. The convention system fixes formal responsibility for nominating candidates upon party officeholders, leaders, and activists. It comprises a hierarchy of conventions and assemblies held at various levels of government to convey the will of the rank and file of the party through delegates to a central point where the candidates are nominated. This process permits accommodation of intraparty differences before, rather than after, the campaign and allows a consultation process in the selection of candidates.

Money

At a time when people say that money is dominating politics and hence parties, we must investigate its power to control nominating contests for governor. Our task is to compare the relative power of money and party strength in the race for the gubernatorial nomination. My hypothesis predicts that the importance of money varies with party effort. To test it, I need to make a comparison between party effort and money in states where the primary determines the outcome of the nominating process and in states where the parties make gubernatorial endorsements. Any finding of primary voting strength would be suspect unless it could be shown that it was not the result of superior spending.

The relationship between spending and winning votes is complex. For instance, in 1982, Rudy Perpich, former governor and Democratic primary challenger in Minnesota, spent $139,000 and beat the endorsed candidate in the primary, Warren Spannaus, who spent $990,000. In California, meanwhile, George Deukmejian spent over $4 million for the Republican primary to beat the lieutenant governor, Mike Curb, who spent nearly as much. Hence, we cannot say that money buys votes.

Money spent on a nominating campaign may be the best surrogate measure of many of the other resources possessed by a candidate. Common to all contestants is the need for exposure. The candidate who starts the campaign without any previous officeholding or political experience needs the most funding in order to gain visibility and develop a public image, which is usually purchased at great expense. In some states party leaders can help this effort; in others they are powerless. When the candidate is an incumbent, he or she benefits from a reservoir of public recognition and has less need for large-scale funding. Ironically, those candidates who are most experienced and have the least need for funds are also most able to raise funds because they are perceived as having the best chance to be elected. All of these observations point to the need to understand the relationships between campaign money and the characteristics of candidates.

Paying for Exposure

The mass media are a means by which candidates bypass the party to communicate directly with the voters. A party with a precinct organization at campaign time makes personal contact with the voters. In the terminology of political campaigns, this operation is called *ground war*. Mass media, however, are aimed at the general public through impersonal means and stress candidate images. This type of operation is called *air war*. Ground wars stress party leaders and precinct workers and are labor intensive. Air wars, by contrast, need only money.

A primary election campaign spends more time, effort, and money on the media than any other single activity. By 1980, the average gubernatorial candidate spent up to 30 percent of the total campaign budget on television alone (Sabato 1980, 150), and most campaign finance analysts think the percentage is rising. Lew Lehrman, winner of the 1982 New York Republican gubernatorial primary, provides a poignant example of the advantages of big money and the advertising it can buy. Lehrman, a multimillionaire businessperson, was totally unknown to the average voter when he launched his television campaign early in 1982. By mid-July, he had already spent $3 million on advertising and had an overwhelming lead over his three opponents for the nomination (Jewell and Olson 1988, 128–29). After the convention, which endorsed him for obvious reasons, all but one of his opponents dropped out, and he defeated the remaining one in the primary by spending another $4 million in a media blitz. We will hear about the campaign in his own words later.

Gubernatorial candidates need specialized help in today's world. When the only way to reach people was by speeches in public places, torchlight parades, whistle-stop tours from the back of the train, newspaper ads, and other publicity events, campaigns were manageable by the candidate helped by the party's minions. But now candidates need specialized help. Specialized commercial firms with politics as their business charge huge fees. The modern gubernatorial campaign needs a political consultant, and political consultants are expensive.

Some professional campaign consultants specialize in public-opinion polling. Gubernatorial candidates need to know many things about their voters. An initial benchmark survey discovers their own strengths or weaknesses as perceived by the electorate. Follow-up telephone polling; panel surveys, which measure shifts in attitudes; small focus-group interviews of typical voters; and tracking surveys, which measure the impact of advertising and other campaign events on different groups of voters, are all offered by the polling consultants (ACIR 1986, 252).

In addition to TV ad production and public-opinion polling, commercial firms handle many other activities. Direct mail can now be used to raise funds as well as persuade. Instead of office tables occupied by loyal party workers (traditionally women) addressing envelopes, computers can spin out thousands in short order. Contributors are identified and hit again. Phone banks identify voters and try to persuade them. Bumper stickers, campaign buttons, and other traditional items are also designed and produced by campaign firms.

In the foregoing litany of the need for campaign consultants, it becomes obvious that these services are provided to single candidates, rather than to parties or groups of candidates, which tends toward an atomized politics, with little joint activity between candidates running on the party's slate. It also means that the voters respond to individual candidates rather than a joint ticket. All of this fulfills the prophecy that parties are becoming weaker and voters less loyal to them.

The parties have been learning to adjust to these new circumstances by assuming the role of a management firm that delegates much of its fund-raising responsibilities. The services of professional consultants and specialized firms are increasingly contracted by political party committees (Jewell and Olson 1988, 154). The consultants, necessarily, are becoming partisan and work within the party of their choice, whether on the state or national level. Parties direct candidates to consultants often as a condition for obtaining party support.

In several states, political action committees (PACs) have become partners with parties (R. Jones 1984, 197). Party leaders can match their candidates with the appropriate PACs, outline the needs of the campaign, and determine the magnitude of the support required to win. A team concept emerges, with the PAC as the financial backer, the party as the initiator and strategist, and the candidate as the focus.

Financing the Campaign

Where does the money come from to finance such expensive campaigns? Are those who are independently wealthy more likely to win because there is no limit to the amount of their own money they can spend? Are those who must obtain their money from groups likely to be beholden to these backers? As we shall see, some states try to limit the power of groups and individuals by prohibiting or limiting contributions. But first, where does this money come from?

Figure 3.1 diagrams the sources and flow of money in state elections. While this study is primarily concerned with the people and groups who give to our candidates, the diagram indicates the potential recipients from each source. The major sources of campaign funds in state politics are individuals and political action committees. In some states, corporations and labor unions may contribute directly to candidates and parties. In some states, public funding is given to candidates for primaries or general election campaigns or directly to the political parties. Candidates are not limited in their own contributions to their campaigns and may incur personal debts through bank loans to finance their candidacies.

Individuals provide the majority of the funds for gubernatorial campaigns. Most gubernatorial nominating campaigns depend upon individual donations for well over 50 percent of their total receipts. However, these individuals are not giving $25 contributions. Most of them give much more than that, as we shall see. In the gubernatorial primary race in Tennessee, for instance, fewer than 10 percent of Randy Tyree's individual donations came in under the $100 figure. Compare that to opponent Anna Belle Clement O'Brien's supporters, 50 percent of whom gave less than $100. I have arbitrarily defined a *large donor* as one who gives more than $5,000 to a campaign. In Texas, California, and New York, several candidates received over 35 percent of their total contributions in large-donor amounts. Since there are no limits on how much individuals may give in Texas, one fellow gave over a million dollars to the candidates he supported. Each state has its own definition of large or small donations, and some states, such as Connecticut and Kansas, place limits on the amount individuals (and PACs) can give.

Individuals, meaning the candidates and their families, give personal money to their own campaigns, sometimes in huge amounts. One suspects that personal money may play more of a role in primary campaigns than in general elections. A recent study reports that most gubernatorial candidates contributed only very limited amounts to their campaigns and that Lewis Lehrman's profuse self-funded campaign was an exception (R. Jones 1984, 185). Among our other candidates, several contributed over 40 percent of their total receipts to fund their own nominating campaign. Among those were Buddy Temple (D) in Texas, Sam Hardage (R) in Kansas, Richard Bozzuto (R) in Connecticut, Steve Schuck (R) in Colorado (a whopping 96 percent!), and Wheelock Whitney (R) in Minnesota. All these generous self-funders, with the exception of Lehrman and Whitney, were seeking to be challengers to the incumbent governor. Four—Lehrman, Hardage, Whitney, and Schuck—were exceedingly successful business executives who did not hold public office and needed to spend huge amounts to become known. The first three of these candidates

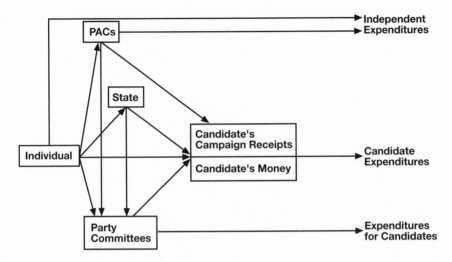

Fig. 3.1.   Sources and flows of money in state election campaigns

"bought" their nominations but could not buy the election. Schuck's money could not buy either.

While corporations and labor unions are legally prohibited from making direct contributions in federal elections, many states allow it. In California, Colorado, Illinois, and New York, among our ten states, neither corporations nor labor unions are prohibited from giving directly to state campaigns. In fact, half the states do not prohibit such direct donations—and in about ten of these, the size of the contribution is unlimited as well. Since the amount of union giving is so much smaller than corporate giving, the ability of labor to give is limited by funds, not legislation. Three of the largest states, California, Illinois, and Pennsylvania, have no limitations on corporate or union giving. In both New York and California, where corporations are not prohibited from direct giving, their identity is obvious and they give generously to gubernatorial primaries. Corporations may also give indirectly through their corporation executives. They may also give indirectly through attorneys and public relations firms who have been provided with large fees for that purpose.

Half the states now prohibit direct corporate giving. Businesses may, however, directly pay the overhead cost (personnel solicitation, administration) of the political action committees that they must form to distribute campaign money. In these states, their identity is often hidden behind a legal pseudonym—such as BWH-PAC, standing for Beer Wholesalers—and their contributions are more difficult to categorize.

While the major sources of nominating campaign money are from individuals (including the candidate's personal bank account) and PACs, some political parties give money to primary campaigns, but these are insignificant amounts—less than 4 percent of the total. In some states, parties are legally forbidden to contribute to primary campaigns. The major contributions parties make to nominating campaigns are endorsements. Endorsements are more powerful than money in determining the outcome. Malcolm Jewell suggests that parties should be legally able to contribute funds to candidates in a primary or use state funds provided for that purpose (1984, 293). One of the strongest challenges to party endorsees comes from candidates who have large amounts of money to spend on media advertising.

A recent development which should be mentioned in any discussion of political party giving is the role of "soft money." The flow of soft money from national parties to state parties for party-building activities has evolved since 1980. This money is called "soft" because it does not have to conform to "hard" federal guidelines for raising and spending for congressional and presidential campaigns. Funds from corporate treasuries, union dues, and large individual donors are legal in many states, and the national parties attract and collect them for distribution to their state affiliates. While most of this money is expended in presidential election years and is intended to directly or indirectly benefit presidential candidates, state parties have become stronger because of it. Voters registered during national election years vote in state elections as well. Party recording studios help the majority of gubernatorial candidates two years later. Audio and video equipment, computers, voter lists, fax machines, and high-tech phone systems stay in place for the state parties to use for their own campaigns. The 1992 elections were the first in which political parties had to report how they spent soft money. In an unofficial report, the Democratic National Committee specified sending 38 percent of its unregulated funds, or $9.2 million, to state parties for telephone banks and door-to-door voter drives (Donovan 1993, 1198).

Another source of money, as figure 3.1 indicates, is state public funding. While none of our candidates in the 1982 primaries benefited from public funds, several states now donate public funds to primaries as well as general elections. Currently twenty-four states provide some public funding, but their systems differ immensely. The motives behind these systems are to try to level the playing field between wealthy and modest-income candidates. In addition, the great advantages of incumbency can be eroded if the challenger has more money. Also, in return for receiving public funds, candidates may have to agree to spending limits. Twenty states raise money through their income tax systems. Some states like California give the money so raised to the political parties, some give only to candidates, and some give to both. Some fund both primaries and general elections. New Jersey allocated up to $1.6 million each for qualified gubernatorial candidates in the 1993 primary election and another $3.9 million for gubernatorial candidates in the general (Alexander and Schwartz 1993, 9). It would appear that public funding stimulates a large field of primary candidates in that state. In some states, candidates receive such small amounts that they can not justify the attached limits on spending.

It is difficult to measure how much the availability of public funds has increased candidate participation. Rudy Perpich, former governor and Democratic primary challenger in Minnesota, counted on the infusion of public funds for his general election campaign in 1982. However, Wheelock Whitney, the Republican nominee, did not participate in the funding program, did not sign the agreement, did not adhere to expenditure limitations, and lost the election!

Parties, however, appear to benefit from public funding. None of the fourteen states that give funds to parties mandates that the funds be spent on candidates or campaigns. When states permit the spending of public funds directly on campaigns, there may be a prohibition against supporting any candidate in a primary. Nonetheless, parties are given a cushion from which to operate. In Rhode Island, public funds are used exclusively for organizational headquarters and staff maintenance (R. Jones 1984, 198).

Finally, the flow of money in the model reaches the spending stage. Both individuals and PACs may spend as much money as they desire to urge the election or defeat of a candidate. They may use TV or newspaper ads or direct-mail messages. Political parties may be subject to some restrictions if they receive public funding. Some general patterns were observable as parties began to report their campaign spending activities in the 1980s. First, they were more extensively involved in state legislative campaigns than any others. Second, they concentrated more on in-kind services than direct financial support. Candidates are constitutionally permitted to spend as much money as they desire, which is limited only if they accept public funding. Generally candidates spend all they collect.

Campaign Regulations: Prohibitions and Contribution Limits

Every campaign needs a fund-raiser, a treasurer, and a legal expert. The regulations are demanding. Campaign treasurers must file with the appropriate state official both before and after elections and itemize all contributions and expenditures (some states require only those over a certain minimum: $50 to $100). The timing of these campaign finance reports is a sensitive issue. Wendall Lady, candidate for the Republican nomination in Kansas, suspected that the oil industry was pumping money into Dave Owen's campaign and that Sam Hardage was spending his own money and telling the press he was not, but there was no way to prove it because the report was not due until one week before the primary (Henley 1982, 13).

In some states, as table 3.5 reveals, direct contributions are prohibited from corporations and labor unions. PACs must be formed to contribute money. In addition, states limit contributions from individuals, PACs, and parties. Table 3.5 lists the regulations for the ten states in our study. They are typical of the types of regulations found throughout the fifty.

Table 3.5 is accurate for 1996 and indicates which states have changed their contribution limits since 1982, the year of the study. It is interesting that in the states where changes were made, they were more restrictive. Six of our ten states limit contributions; in the others, individuals and PACs may give as much to a candidate as they wish, and some of them give very large amounts indeed. In states where corporations are prohibited from giving directly, they form PACs for the purpose and are not greatly restricted. In Texas, for instance, bank loans are not considered corporate contributions. A wealthy business owner like Governor Clements could ask the bank for a million dollars worth of loans. Buddy Temple, a Democratic candidate in Texas, loaned his campaign a million dollars and his father paid it off (the elder Temple owned Temple-Eastex, which in 1982 owned more than 10 percent of Time, Inc.) (Daniels 1982, 35).

Minnesota, Oregon, and Tennessee limit the political party contributions to a candidate. Governor Thompson received $29,000 from the Illinois Republicans before the primary in which he had token opposition. Incumbents usually receive party funds, but the amounts are usually much more modest than that and are less than 3 percent of their war chest.

To summarize the discussion about nominating campaign money, the major source is individual donations. Most gubernatorial campaigns depend on individuals for well over half of their campaign funds. To be sure, there are exceptions when unknown business executives bankroll their own campaigns. It takes money to become known to the voters, and primary campaigns provide the voters with few voting cues, so money must buy exposure.

In states where the party endorses, the voters are provided with useful information about the party's choice, information that helps that candidate win. To the extent that parties are prepared to put their stamp of approval on a candidate, that candidate has a much better chance. The endorsee may receive tangible campaign help, such as funding, personnel,

TABLE 3.5. Campaign Finances for Governor, 1996: Prohibitions and Contribution Limits per Candidate, Primaries and Elections (in dollars)

State	Individual (other than candidate)	Corporate PACS, Corporations	Labor PACs, Unions	Party Committees	Other PACs
Calif.	No limits	No limits	No limits	No limits	No limits
Colo.	No limits	No limits	No limits	No limits	No limits
Conn.	2,500	5,000; corporations prohibited	2,500; unions prohibited	No limits	No limits
Ill.	No limits	No limits	No limits	No limits	No limits
Kans.[a]	2,000	2,000	2,000	No limits	2,000
Minn.[b]	2,000	Prohibited	2,000	20,000	2,000
N.Y.[c]	.05 × party voters	.05 × party voters	.05 × party voters	No limits; primary prohibited	.05 × party voters
Oreg.[d]	500	500; corporations prohibited	500; unions prohibited	25,000	500
Tenn.[e]	2,500	7,500; corporations prohibited	2,500	250,000	7,500
Tex.	No limits	No limits; corporations prohibited	No limits; unions prohibited	No limits	No limits

Source: Adapted from COGEL 1984–85, 7–8; and COGEL 1993, Table 13 and Table 14, 72–86. Also adapted from Council of State Governments, 1996, Table 5.11 and Table 5.12, 177–94.

[a]In Kansas, the limit on contributions in 1982 was $3,000. In a contested primary, the party is restricted to same limits as PACs.

[b]In Minnesota, the limit on contributions in 1982 was $60,000; party committees could contribute $300,000.

[c]In New York, for all statewide offices, the formula used is the number of enrolled voters in candidate's party × .05 for the primary but not less than $4,500 or more than $13,400 for the primary and more than $28,000 for the general election. Spouses are unlimited but other family members are limited. Overall limitations for individuals are $150,000. Corporations are limited to $5,000 per calendar year.

[d]Oregon had no limits in 1982. The $500 limit is waived if the opponent and family raise over $25,000.

[e]Tennessee had no limits in 1982. The candidate is limited to $250,000 for statewide office and may not receive more than 50 percent of total contributions from PACs.

and technical assistance from the state and local party organizations. The endorsement may provide publicity and momentum for the endorsee's campaign, which helps attract campaign resources.

Hypotheses: Gubernatorial Nominations as Coalition Building

The following hypotheses are based on the discussion of the rules and the game as they are played in our ten states. They predict that the success of gubernatorial candidates in obtaining the nomination will differ according to party leadership strength, the rules governing the nominating process, and the resources available.

> Hypothesis 1: In states where the party leaders are not unified, they cannot control the nomination. Preprimary endorsements do not exist.
>
> A. The incumbent governor's personal coalition will ensure that he or she wins the primary. Because the party leaders are not important to his or her success, they may or may not be included in the coalition.
>
> B. A candidate (nonincumbent) for the nomination will try to build a front-runner coalition by:
>   1. Spending on media coverage, and
>   2. Support from unifactional or factional party leaders.
>
> C. Party leader support for the candidate does not ensure the nomination.
>
> D. Money is a controlling resource in these primary-only contests.
>
> Hypothesis 2: In states where the party leaders are unified, they can secure the gubernatorial nomination for their favored candidate by preprimary endorsing conventions (or other legal or informal endorsements).
>
> A. The incumbent governor will work closely with the party leadership coalition and will be its choice for the nomination. This governor-leadership coalition will ensure that the governor wins the preprimary endorsement as well as the following primary by a large percentage.
>
> B. A candidate (nonincumbent) will strive to include the party leadership coalition in his or her coalition in order to secure the preprimary endorsement.
>   1. The candidate backed by the party leaders will win the preprimary endorsing convention by a large percentage.
>   2. The endorsed candidate will strive to enlarge the coalition

after the party endorsement by including defeated coalitions in order to discourage opposition.
3. If challenged, the endorsed candidate will win the primary by a large percentage.
C. Money is not a controlling resource in these contests.

The next two chapters will test these hypotheses by examining the statements made by the forty-three candidates for nomination in the ten states in the study (see appendix). They explained their coalition-building efforts by detailing those party leaders and factional leaders they asked to back their campaign. They described their resources in terms of initial advantage and money and their strategies in terms of their campaign organization, information, and media support, If the contest was over, they analyzed the results in terms of their initial goals and predictions. We expect to find that candidates for the nomination in primary-only states (states where the primary is the only point of decision for the nomination) build organizations backed by factions and do not strive for or include party leadership, although they are generally aware of who is receiving leadership approval, however weak or clandestine it may be. Much money is needed in these contests in order to reach the voters. I predict that candidates for nomination in preprimary endorsement states follow a different strategy, which must include negotiations with party organizational leaders from local to state level. Money and media may be a strategy to influence the leaders, but it does not necessarily buy convention votes. We turn now to a description of coalition building in the direct-primary states.

CHAPTER 4

Resources, Factions, and Strategies: Direct-Primary States

Our nineteen candidates for nomination in the five direct-primary states have exceedingly good credentials, but they must fashion their own campaigns. True, there are formal party organizations, but they do not help them win the nomination. The party leaders have preferences, but they do not help. The party does not provide money or effort for the nomination. The candidates are on their own. The plan for this chapter is to see how our nineteen candidates organize to capture the party label, which is what they covet. We would expect that the four governors would win renomination, because governors almost always do. As for the candidates, we observe a scramble in which the lead changes, constant polling is necessary to discover the mood of the electorate, and money determines the results.

The Actors

Table 4.1 lists our candidates and their prior office careers. All of them except for Jimmy Montgomery, the Kansas disc jockey who challenged the governor, have public-office experience, which would indicate that they are trained leaders. (Sam Hardage of Kansas had been a candidate for the U.S. Senate, which qualifies him for running, if not governing.) We might expect that outsiders would be more likely to defeat insiders in nonendorsing states. Systematic evidence is not readily available on the careers of winning and losing gubernatorial candidates in primaries in recent years, but one study examined the candidates in seventy-seven nonincumbent primary races during the 1984–92 period (Jewell 1994). During this period, insider candidates defeated other insiders in 68 percent of the primary elections. In another 15 percent, insiders defeated outsiders. In 9 percent, both candidates were outsiders. In only 8 percent were inside candidates defeated by outsiders, usually businesspeople. Our candidates in 1982 were even more likely to be insiders than in Jewell's study. In only one case, Kansas, did a businessperson defeat an insider in the primary.

Several studies have examined the public experience of elected gover-

TABLE 4.1. Primary-Only States: Office Experience of Candidates, 1982

State and Party	Name	Age	Governor	State Office	State Senate	State House	Other
TX-R	Clements	65	1978–82				U.S. Deputy Secretary of Defense 1973–77
TX-D	White	42		Secretary of State, 1973–78, Attorney General 1978–82			
TX-D	Temple	39		Railroad Commissioner 1980–82	1972–80		
TX-D	Armstrong	49		Land Commissioner 1970–82	1962–70		Comanager of McGovern, Carte campaigns
TN-R	Alexander	42	1978–82				Gubernatorial candidate 1974
TN-D	Tyree	42					Mayor of Knoxville 1975–82
TN-D	O'Brien	59			1976–82	1974–76	
KA-D	Carlin	41	1978–82			Speaker 1970–78	
KA-D	Montgomery	33					Disc jockey
KA-R	Hardage	43					U.S. Senate candidate 1978
KA-R	Owen	43		Lieutenant Govenor 1972–74	1968–72		Manager, Kassebaum 1978, Dole, 1974, 1980
KA-R	Lady	51				Speaker 1968–82	
OR-R	Atiyeh	59	1978–82		1964–68	1958–64	Gubernatorial candidate 1974
OR-D	Clark	48					County executive 1979–
OR-D	Kulongowski	41			1976–82	1974–76	
CA-R	Deukmejian	54		Attorney General 1978–82	1966–78	1962–66	
CA-R	Curb	36		Lieutenant Governor 1978–82			National Committee Reagan 1976
CA-D	Bradley	65					Mayor of Los Angeles 1973–82
CA-D	Garamendi	36			Majority leader 1976–82	1974–76	

nors. Our candidates hold their own against these career patterns. According to Thad Beyle's "frequency trees" for 194 elected governors serving between 1970 and 1989, 22 percent of governors had served in the state legislature immediately before their election as governor (Beyle 1990, 203–8). Thirty-two percent of our candidates held legislative office just prior to running for governor. Our candidates had the same amount of legislative experience (53 percent) as Beyle's sample and were more likely to have held statewide office just prior to running for governor (32 percent compared to Beyle's 25 percent). Overall, our candidates were much more likely to have held either state legislative or statewide office prior to running for governor than the sample of elected governors in Beyle's study. Sixty-three percent of our candidates and four of our five elected governors advanced from elective state offices (compared to 50 percent for Beyle's group). I discovered the same southern Republican career pattern as did Beyle, in that the Republican governors of Tennessee and Texas had not had previous state office experience, indicating that the pool of available, electable Republicans was not large.

What these statistics show is that candidates for governor in nonendorsing states are just as likely to be insiders with office experience as governors everywhere, which means that, when elected, they will not be lacking the experience to govern. However, this study makes the claim that the circumstances under which they will govern will be more difficult than those faced by their counterparts in endorsing states. The resources and strategies they must use to become governor take their toll on their future as state leaders.

Resources: Risks and Front-runners

The resources that attach to each candidate are material, organizational, personal. Money is a most important resource in direct-primary states, and most observers believe it is the most important ingredient for success in a primary contest fought without the party label. The chances of winning are another resource. Table 4.2 presents, in extremely abbreviated form, the initial resources of our candidates in terms of primary risk, front-runner status, party leader support, factional support, and money raised. Following the discussion of these resources, we will turn our attention to money, the most important resource except incumbency.

The Risks of Running

For most of our candidates, the primary is risky business. Rarely does a nominee in these direct-primary states receive 70 percent of the vote, indicating that competitors are a continuing threat and that the outcome is not secure. Incumbents are usually renominated in spite of a challenge, and table 4.2 shows that the average primary results for their respective parties are higher. Why? One might expect that both parties in a state would contain similar degrees of cohesion.

TABLE 4.2. Primary-Only States: Candidate Resources, 1982

State and Party	Name	Previous Primary Average[a] (in %)	Front runner	Party Leaders	Factional Support	Money Raised (in $000s)
TX-R	Clements (I)	67.7	Y	Y	Conservatives, business	4,402
TX-D	White	55.6	Y	Neutral	Conservatives, Brisco faction, some labor, ethnics	2,322
TX-D	Temple	55.6	N	Neutral	Southeast Texas, populists	2,548
TX-D	Armstrong	55.6	N	Neutral	Liberal coalition: blacks, Mexican-Americans, some labor	802
TN-R	Alexander (I)	65.1	Y	Y	East Tennessee	1,658
TN-D	Tyree	41.4	N	N	Knoxville, Butcher faction	976
TN-D	O'Brien	41.4	Y	Y	Old guard, Clement faction	298
KA-D	Carlin (I)	91.0	Y	Y	"New guard"	469
KA-D	Montgomery	91.0	N	N	Discontented	2
KA-R	Hardage	51.3	N	N	Wichita, Reagan conservatives	595
KA-R	Owen	51.3	Y	Y	Party organization, Ford supporters	642
KA-R	Lady	51.3	N	N	Northeast, urban, liberals	124
OR-R	Atiyeh (I)	71.1	Y	Y	Moderate conservatives	335
OR-D	Clark	57.9	Y	Y	Social liberals	104
OR-D	Kulongowski	57.9	N	N	Liberals, labor	119
CA-R	Deukmejian	66.6	N	N	Endorsed by party moderates (CRL)	4,088
CA-R	Curb	66.6	Y	Y	Endorsed by party conservatives (UROC)	3,700
CA-D	Bradley	62.7	Y	Y	Hispanic leaders, blacks, labor	3,190
CA-D	Garamendi	62.7	N	N	New Left	1,068

[a]Average primary vote for gubernatorial nominee in last five elections

In Texas, Tennessee, and Kansas, the traditional minority party has the governorship. Traditional minority parties have customarily put up sacrificial candidates to contest the certain winner from the majority. Hence, the average primary results for the Republicans in Texas and Tennessee and the Democrats in Kansas reflect this sacrificial quality of primaries past. In Oregon, both parties have moderate strength, but it appears that the Republicans are slightly more unified. California, where there was an open contest in 1982, revealed slightly more unified parties. However, even Richard Nixon and Ronald Reagan did not receive over 65 percent as nonincumbent candidates in the Republican gubernatorial primaries, nor did Jess Unruh and Jerry Brown as nonincumbents in the Democratic primary contests. California parties cannot guarantee that their nominees will win decisive victories. Thus, running for the nomination in direct-primary states means taking risks. There is no party organization to help provide workers and money. You are on your own.

Front-runner Status

The four governors were front-runners, of course. None was seriously challenged. Governor Alexander of Tennessee had no opponents, and Governor Clements's primary challenger received 8 percent of the vote. Governor Atiyeh of Oregon had four opponents in the primary, no one of whom received over 8 percent. Even Governor Carlin did not find it unsettling to have a Wichita disc jockey take 21 percent of the primary vote away from him. He said that there "was no primary campaign; it was a general election from the very beginning. We never acknowledged that we had an opponent. We knew that there was going to be a protest vote of some size . . ." (Carlin 1982, 4).

For those who contested in the four nonincumbent primaries, as well as those who fought in both open primary contests in California, front-runner status was sought, but it was not a guarantee of success. In fact, those who wore the front-runner crown in the beginning had reason to keep a sharp watch over their shoulders for those who were trying to stop them. In only two of the six open contests did the front-runners win the primary. In other words, the lead can change in direct-primary races.

Texas Triad

The race for the Democratic nomination in Texas was an unstable affair. In the first place, the front-runner, Senator Peyton McKnight, who had been campaigning since the summer of 1981, dropped out of the race on

February 2, 1982, citing lack of money. The senator came from eastern Texas and was an independent oil operator and a conservative. His withdrawal opened up the "slot" for another eastern Texan, and Buddy Temple, railroad commissioner and heir to a multimillion-dollar timber and publishing fortune, entered, reportedly with McKnight's backing. Thus the three-way race became a different contest, changing from two conservatives and a liberal—McNight, White, and Armstrong, respectively—to one conservative and two liberals—White, Armstrong, and Temple, respectively—jockeying for first place.

Mark White took the lead, although many thought the Temple fortune was necessary to beat Governor Bill Clements. As attorney general, White was the most widely known of the triad, partly because of his well-publicized challenges to Governor Clements during their common term in office. White brought suit on behalf of the state against Sedco, Clements's oil-drilling corporation, charging water pollution violations. Bob Armstrong, land commissioner, tagged a liberal because of his support for Democratic presidential candidates (!) struggled for five months to overcome that label and his image as an underfinanced long shot to unseat the governor.

Tennessee: Miss Anna Belle the Front-runner

When state senator Anna Belle Clement O'Brien, the sister of former governor Frank Clement and heir to the Clement machine, entered the Democratic gubernatorial primary race in May 1982, she was considered the front-runner. Her fellow Democrats in the senate voted her the only candidate with enough name recognition to tackle popular governor Lamar Alexander. She was backed by Nashville lawyer and business executive John Jay Hooker, a former gubernatorial contender, who was looking for a consensus candidate who could win in the general election. Knoxville mayor Randy Tyree, who started building a campaign network the year before, did not convince many important Democrats that he could compete with Governor Alexander. Because Tyree was mayor of a large city, he had championed many issues that O'Brien as senator had voted against. She was in favor of a death penalty and opposed to an equal rights amendment, the opposite of the positions of Mayor Tyree. The mayor hoped to benefit from his association with the 1982 World's Fair in Knoxville, which was a success and boosted the local economy. He had many powerful connections and a slick advertising campaign, which eventually upset the old-fashioned courthouse campaign of "Miss Anna Belle."

Kansas Triad

Another triad locked in deadly battle occurred in Kansas. As in Texas, there appeared to be a clear front-runner and a clear third place, but in this race, as we shall see, the front-runner lost in the primary. Dave Owen, the former state senator and lieutenant governor, campaigned for eighteen months, built a solid organization, and was the clear front-runner most of that time. He claimed that his strong grass roots organization would win the race. Sam Hardage, the Wichita businessperson who tried unsuccessfully for the GOP nomination for the U.S. Senate four years before, entered the race and put his money into a media campaign to gain voter recognition. Professional pollster V. Lance Tarrance of Houston, who conducted tracking polls on behalf of Hardage, said the campaign was a "cliff-hanger" two days before the primary, but Hardage pulled an upset.

Wendell Lady, state house speaker, ran third throughout and succeeded in taking votes from Owen. He did offer a position on taxation different from his two rivals. Agreeing with the Democratic governor that a severance tax was needed to solve the state's financial crisis, he could not count on the vote from Wichita, the center of the oil and gas industry. Saying "Big Oil" would pay the tax, Lady hoped to get enough support from Johnson County suburbs of Kansas City plus the more populous northeastern counties to offset the Wichita and western vote. But both Owen and Lady came from Johnson County, the state's most Republican county, and necessary to offset Hardage's Wichita base. Lady was unable to match either Owen or Hardage in funding or organization.

Oregon: A Democratic Duel

Before State Senator Ted Kulongowski entered the race for the Democratic nomination in February, Multnomah County executive Donald E. Clark of Portland had been considered the front-runner. The sudden entry of Kulongowski dislocated Clark's campaign, which Clark said had been planned for an extended run concentrating on kaffeeklatches and similar grass roots organizing. Clark's twenty-year political career was all in the Portland area, and he had not made a statewide campaign. Clark was described as a liberal progressive Democrat with a reputation for innovative administration. He led in fund-raising until a month before the primary, when Kulongowski started to overtake him.

Kulongowski was the Democratic nominee for the United States Senate in 1980 and was defeated by Republican Bob Packwood. His base was in the Eugene area, the second most populous county in the state. As a legislator, Kulongowski continued to practice law, and most of his major clients were labor organizations. Also a liberal Democrat, Kulongowski's main assets were a residual organization from his past campaign two years before, strong labor support, and more money for media than Clark had. With these assets he overtook Clark's lead, bringing him front-runner status that he maintained. This race between two liberal Democrats shows that in unstable direct-primary races, the lead can change.

California Republicans: Curb, the Uneasy Front-runner

George Deukmejian, the state attorney general, was far behind the younger and more colorful lieutenant governor, Mike Curb, as the nominating contest got under way in February 1981. According to Deukmejian's campaign manager, Curb had the establishment, he had the money, he had much better name recognition. The bold, explosive lieutenant governor, a former recording executive, had ties to some of the wealthy business executives who served in Ronald Reagan's "kitchen cabinet." While both candidates came from Los Angeles, each had statewide experience and support outside of his home base. According to the polls, Curb enjoyed big leads in the vote-heavy Republican areas of San Diego, Los Angeles, and Orange counties. Curb was the more conservative candidate, supporting the Proposition 13 tax-cut measure in 1978, which Deukmejian opposed. Deukmejian, even though a moderate, sought to appeal to the conservatives by reminding them that he wrote the state's death penalty statute and California's mandatory sentencing law for criminals who use handguns.

The two candidates disagreed over a ballot question on the Perpheral Canal—a waterway that would divert water from the northern San Joaquin–Sacramento River delta toward the aqueduct system that serves the parched Los Angeles area. Deukmejian favored the project as a necessary link in the water distribution system for southern California. Curb, who once favored the plan, now opposed it as a project plagued by cost overruns. In this way Curb tried to gain support in the north. Two weeks before the primary, Curb was seen in the lead, but his lead evaporated in the highly volatile contest.

California Democrats: The Front-runner Keeps the Lead

According to the California Poll of February 1982, Los Angeles mayor Tom Bradley was the front-runner for the Democratic party nomination for governor. The mayor never lost this overwhelming lead in this typical California race with thirteen candidates. Only one of his competitors established any credibility as a force in the primary. State senate majority leader John Garamendi, former football hero at UCLA, Harvard Business School graduate, and former Peace Corps volunteer, had everything but name recognition going for him, and name recognition is what gets primary votes. Garamendi was also frustrated at every other turn in efforts to raise money and receive key Democratic party backing.

The son of poor sharecroppers in Calvert, Texas, Bradley came to California at the age of seven. He won a scholarship to UCLA, where he was, among other things, a track star. Later he joined the Los Angeles Police Department while studying law at night. After twenty-one years on the force, he left and soon was elected to the Los Angeles City Council during the racial tumult of the 1960s. After challenging Mayor Sam Yorty in 1969 and losing, Bradley was successful in winning the mayoral race in 1973.

This 1982 Democratic race in California was clearly the only one among the nonincumbent races where the front-runner lead never changed. It showed that publicity, money, and group support all flowed to the leader. It was, in that respect, unlike any of the others, where the candidates had to campaign continuously for that uncertain primary decision, and then the bruised winner had to pick up his troops and gear up for another campaign.

Resources: Support of the Party Leaders

The Governors

It is customary for the governor to choose the party chair, so it is no surprise to find that each governor in our study had his chair's support. In Texas Governor Clements ran against the Republican party chair, Ray Hutchison, in 1978 and beat him by a margin of three to one. Needless to say, Hutchison was replaced with an oil baron from Mineral Wells. The governor's aide said that Texas Republicans want a "businessman" for governor over a "politician compromiser" like a party chair. They want someone who can say: "I've got the money. I can give us a chance in the fall" (Daniels 1982, 6).

Governor Alexander's spokesperson said that the governor can "anoint" the Tennessee party chair. He explained that the chair's power came from the governor, not the other way around (Campbell 1982, 13). According to Governor Carlin, the Kansas party chair is "my person although I brought him out of the older faction simply to provide some unity" (Carlin 1982, 19). Governor Atiyeh of Oregon had an uncomfortable time with a "born-again" party chair, Huss, who was one of those who ran against him in the primary (receiving 7.2 percent). Atiyeh had been instrumental in replacing Huss with a party chair who was right wing, a Reagan supporter (Atiyeh 1982, 12). One senses that the party in Oregon was not strong enough to make much difference to the governor one way or the other.

The Other Candidates

Texas Democrats: Weak Party, Weak Leaders

Since there had been a Democratic governor in Texas for the past hundred years, the party chair had traditionally been "the governor's anointed." But 1982 was different because the chair had been elected in a convention where there was nobody to name, bless, and anoint. According to Clark Jobe, campaign treasurer for Buddy Temple, the chair who was elected, Bob Slagle, represented the old guard (Briscoe faction). However, the chair is exceedingly weak and prevented from consolidating the party by the other factions within it who do not want to give over the reins of control to one faction. The Texas Democratic party does not keep a list of voters because that might give information to a rival faction.

Tennessee Democrats: Party Leaders Favor Clement

Anna Belle Clement O'Brien represented the Clement faction of the party. While her brother Frank Clement was governor, she had been in his cabinet as patronage director. He retired in 1966, and after a few years she returned to state politics, serving a term in the house and then winning a senate seat in 1976. Her nephew, Bob Clement, ran in the Democratic gubernatorial primary in 1978 and was defeated by Jake Butcher of Knoxville. Perhaps this defeat is what drove "Miss Anna Belle" to make another try at beating the Butcher Bank's candidate Randy Tyree in 1982. She was supported by leaders in the Democratic party who believed the Clement faction was still alive and could prevail. The end of May, a poll indicated that O'Brien was the favorite among county Democratic leaders (Pigott 1982a, D-10).

Randy Tyree, meanwhile, had the backing of the Butcher banking family in Knoxville, who were angry that O'Brien had not given their candidate more than token support in 1978. The Butchers wanted to keep control of the party in case Jake Butcher might want to run again. More of the Democratic leaders supported O'Brien, but the party was divided and there was no unity in the primary process.

Kansas Republicans: Weak Party, Leaders Favor Owen

According to David Owen, one of the three Republican candidates in Kansas, he was favored by the party leaders although they didn't come forward. He believes that their failure to work in the primary "throws the thing up for grabs and it allows people who really don't have the experience or background to win the nomination" (Owen 1982, 5). Owen said it becomes very difficult when the party is not involved in the nominating process to integrate it into the campaign after the general election campaign begins.

Both of Owen's rivals discounted the party as an organization. Wendell Lady was the antiparty candidate, and hence there was no support from the party leaders. Sam Hardage, the business executive from Wichita, acknowledged that he was not the favored candidate. Dave Owen, Hardage claimed, was "out there" a year and five months before Hardage was ever a candidate. Owen "took an awful lot of the traditional party leadership" (Hardage 1982, 7). He had an organization in every county, which made it difficult for Hardage to recruit people.

In Kansas, as the Republican candidates tell us, the parties are weak. So accustomed are they to this fact that they do not believe the parties should support a candidate in a primary. In other words, the recruiting role of the party is not considered a party function.

Oregon Democrats: Moderately Weak and
Little Structure

At least that is how Ted Kulongowski described his party. And Don Clark, who started out as the de facto nominee and went to the decided underdog when Kulongowski entered, said that, "Nobody really runs the party, if there is such a thing" (Clark 1982, 9). Clark went on to explain why he thought Oregon was not receptive to party organization: Oregon is a fiercely independent state. It has taken great delight in having mavericks such as Wayne Morse. People in Oregon like their government to be above partisanship.

When he announced, Clark was favored by the party leaders. He appeared surprised at my request for party hierarchy and said that "they don't call big meetings" in Oregon (Clark 1982, 7). "It's much more informal; it's much more ad hoc-ish. They're encouraging you" (Clark 1982, 7). The incumbent chair had to keep a neutral kind of profile and she did.

Kulongowski reaffirmed that the party's ability to recruit and back candidates is minimal in Oregon. Part of the reason the party is so weak is that it has no funds. Under Democratic governor Bob Stroub, a dollar checkoff plan was passed to allow citizens to contribute a dollar of their state income tax to the party of their choice. The coffers of the state Democratic party went from $40,000 to over $200,000. But when the Republicans got back in to office in 1978, they repealed the plan and the Democrats were again impoverished.

California Republicans: Where's the Leadership?

As Rex Hime, campaign coordinator for Mike Curb, patiently explained, "basically what you do with the party is say, 'I'm running.' The party chair is someone who is elected by the delegates to the convention. It's a very nebulous power. Party chairs are not able to go out and say (at least in the Republican party), 'You will run for this and you won't run for that,' whereas in some states they are able to do that kind of stuff" (Hime 1982, 6). At that time, party endorsements were prohibited in California by state law, but Republican bylaws went still further. If an elected state party officer endorsed in the primary, he or she was immediately removed from office. According to Hime, those bylaws were adopted in 1976 after the state chair endorsed Gerald Ford over Ronald Reagan.

Each candidate must engineer his or her own coalition. Mike Curb, lieutenant governor at age thirty-six, had already cultivated many prominent Republicans who were much more powerful than the California party. Through his connections with Ronald Reagan, Curb became associated with an elite Republican organization called the Statesmen and met the power brokers in the Republican party. Their financial backing was crucial to his campaign for the nomination. Curb also had the endorsement of a majority of the Republican legislators, a group that has not often been mentioned by other candidates in other states. In California, the legislative leaders had developed strong party organizations with considerable funds, so that backing was significant.

Because the party was banned from endorsing, several unofficial groups representing ideological factions within the party endorsed, although their strength was waning in 1982. Curb received the endorsement of the very conservative United Republican Organization of California, although its numbers were exceedingly small. He was disappointed that the conservative California Republican Assembly, the traditional unofficial party group, failed to endorse him by two votes of the needed two-thirds majority (198 out of 200).

"Duke," as Attorney General Deukmejian was called, entered the gubernatorial race long after Lieutenant Governor Curb, the heir apparent, had made his intentions clear. In fact, Deukmejian was being pressured by the power brokers backing Curb to run again for attorney general.

The California Republican League, the moderate unofficial Republican group, backed Deukmejian, although it is agreed that none of the Republican extraparty groups play a decisive or even modest role in GOP nominating politics anymore. Thus the identifiable party leadership is composed of kingmakers and legislative party leaders. The state party was too weak to perform any role in one of its major functions, namely, recruiting and nominating its candidates for office.

California Democrats: Where's the Leadership?

Mayor Tom Bradley's prolocutor said that the Democratic party in California "is not really a mobilization type of an organization" (Sullivan 1982, 10). In each race you have to get your own workers, get your own people to help. Officially, the party is neutral until after the primary is over, but Mayor Bradley had been the front-runner for the nomination among the party leaders, the contributors, and registered voters for nearly six months before he announced, and he never lost that advantage. The party leaders gave their support as individuals, but not as party members.

Because of his obvious strength, Bradley decided not to seek the California Democratic Council endorsement, and as a result, the CDC decided not to make any endorsement. It seems unlikely that the CDC will regain any significant influence over the nominating process in California. Now that the parties can endorse in the primaries, and the Democrats have incorporated the procedure into their bylaws, the CDC will lose its strength.

Because Bradley was the favorite among the Democratic party leaders, John Garamendi could not count on any help, even though informal, from party sources. And so, Garamendi tried to pull together key Democratic activists in various regions of the state and to build a grass roots campaign around issues.

Weak Parties Don't Support Candidates

Except for the incumbent governors who had picked their own party chairs and hence could count on their support, weak parties do not support candidates. Mayor Bradley was the only exception to this rule, and he did not have overt support from the Democrats because California parties were prohibited from endorsing at that time. As we will see, direct-primary races are unstable, and those favored by the leaders do not win. To repeat the familiar theme about parties in direct-primary states, they are denied their most important function, that of grooming and presenting leaders for election. This function is performed by an electorate that may or may not contain loyal partisans and is necessarily informed by the media under the direction of wealthy candidates.

Factions and Money

The following section will describe the factions that supported the candidates in the direct-primary states as well as the candidates' sources of money. We would expect a high association here. The discussion of factions will come directly from candidate interviews. The information on sources of contributions was obtained from official sources, generally from a state board of elections. Most states require primary candidates to file financial statements before a primary and again twenty to thirty days after. The postprimary summary report was used to calculate primary contributions.

Texas Republicans

The Republican party primary supporters are located in Dallas–Fort Worth and Houston. They are well-to-do, and most of them were Reagan-Bush conservatives. Governor Bill Clements's representative said that in those two cities, you have the campaign financing for Republican candidates nationwide. Party supporters are young professionals, young businesspeople, older businesspeople (Daniels 1982, 10). Republican gubernatorial primary turnout grew from 265,851 in 1982 to 557,340 in 1994. Again, most of this support is from the Dallas–Fort Worth and Houston areas.

Texas candidates spend millions for the gubernatorial race. Governor Clements borrowed money for his first race in 1978 but knew that there was enough money in contributions to back up his borrowing. (In all, for both the primary and general election in 1978, Clements spent $7.4 million, including $4.5 million of his own money.) Clements's opposition in the 1982 primary was insignificant, and so he could concentrate on building funds for the general election. It is common strategy on the part of incumbents. However, if they did not prove that they were amassing a huge war chest, they might be challenged by stronger candidates. They do not want to take that chance, so they begin to build a campaign chest early to discourage opposition.

Table 4.3 confirms this strategy of early accumulation. Governor Clements had collected $4.5 million by primary time, and most of it he held for the general election. Recall that there are no limits on contributions in Texas. The Governor received 25 percent of his campaign chest from large donors: those hundred individuals each giving $5,000 or more. Most of the rest of his total was from other individuals (sixteen thousand of them).

Texas Democrats

Front-runner Mark White referred to himself as a "moderate conservative," although he was clearly the most conservative of the three Democratic candidates and an heir to the Dolph Briscoe faction of the party. He said party factionalism was ideological, based on ethnicity, urban-rural, and geographical divisions. East Texas and West Texas fight over water. "South Texas is viewed as a separate political entity almost, because it's dramatically Mexican-American in population and Anglo" (White 1982, 11). White believes the conservative-liberal split is the strongest. He said, however, that he had the support of a portion of every group. Organized labor did not endorse in the primary, largely due to the lobbying efforts of Mark White and Bob Armstrong, who tried to ensure that a pro-Temple endorsement drive could not succeed.

TABLE 4.3. Sources of Contributions for Gubernatorial Primaries in Texas (in percentages)

	Democrats			Republican
	White	Temple	Armstrong	Clements
Candidate and candidate loans	4.4	42.0	21.4	0.2
Other loans	20.7	42.9	0.0	0.0
Transfers	0.0	0.0	0.5	0.0
Party	0.0	0.0	0.0	0.3
Interest groups				
Business	0.9	1.2	0.2	1.5
Professional	1.6	0.3	2.3	0.3
Labor	0.1	0.1	0.0	0.0
Agriculture	1.0	0.1	0.0	0.3
General/Policy	0.7	0.5	0.2	1.1
Other	0.0	0.6	0.0	2.1
Large donors	15.9	2.4	54.8	25.2
Other individuals	54.7	9.9	20.6	69.0
Total percentage	100.0	100.0	100.0	100.0
Total dollars	$2,321,732	$2,548,064	$801,743	$4,401,765

This was Mark White's first race for governor, and he needed money to hold the place of front-runner, especially after the young millionaire Temple entered. He loaned his own campaign $100,500 and borrowed nearly $500,000 from banks and individuals. The largest chunk of interest-group money came from law firms, reflecting the fact that White was attorney general and they were a natural source. As the numbers in table 4.3 indicate, White received about 16 percent of his contributions from big donors. White's most generous benefactor was southern Texas oil baron Lucien Flournoy, who gave him $94,000.

Buddy Temple did not have to worry about money. While he said that he expected to have to use some of his family money, most of his campaign funds would be raised from contributions. A quick glance at table 4.3 shows that 85 percent of the money contributed was in the form of loans from Temple himself or Temple-Eastex, the family company, which owned by far the largest amount of timberland in the state.

A description of Temple-Eastex and the company town follows: "On any given day, a procession of log trucks loaded with Temple timber rumbles through Diboll on Temple Drive, headed for one of the Temple mills, passing by the new $7 million Temple headquarters, the Temple Memorial Library and the Temple day-care center" (Blow 1982, 18A). Buddy's father gave his blessing for his son's last-minute entry into the race.

Buddy Temple came from southeastern Texas, an important base of the Democratic primary voting strength. Before Peyton McNight dropped out of the Democratic race, Temple could not hope to win in the primary because McNight came from northeastern Texas, and the eastern Texas vote would be split between the two. It had been a long time since eastern Texas had produced a governor, and Temple believed it was time; he counted on the geography to produce a primary win.

Temple also had support among minority voters, although he found that the Mexican-Americans were split along class lines, between the conservative upper class and the blue-collar workers. Nearly 40 percent of the total Texas population is African-American or Hispanic. Temple's campaign director, Clark Jobe, described the situation faced by the Temple campaign in wooing the black vote in Dallas and Houston. Groups exist in both cities that screen and endorse candidates: the Progressive Voters' League of Dallas and the Harris County Council of Organizations in Houston. It is necessary to pay for their slate card, if you are the fortunate endorsee.

Temple was considered a moderate-to-liberal candidate who had more support from liberal and "progressive" interests than did White. Temple received the backing of many labor organizations but not the largest labor union, the AFL-CIO, which did not endorse for governor. (Kinch 1982).

The third-place candidate, Bob Armstrong, was the underfinanced liberal. Armstrong said he received endorsements from African-American organizations, Mexican-American organizations, gays, the Women's Political Caucus, and the Consumer Association. In addition, newspaper accounts reveal that he received endorsements from the Sierra Club and the Texas League of Conservation voters, who have between them more than twenty-five thousand members in Texas. The largest chunk of money Armstrong received was from one person, Clinton Manges, a rancher, banker, and oil company executive. A combination of Manges's direct gifts and the PAC he controlled, Texans for Good Government, accounted for over $363,000, almost half of Armstrong's total contributions.

While much was said about consolidating the Democratic party for the match against the first Republican governor in a hundred years, the primary race was a bitter struggle. The three contenders tried to establish distinct factional bases in order to win. White, the conservative and the front-runner, was backed by business and conservatives, but he realized that moderates and liberals could consolidate against him and thus tried to woo the moderates as well. Buddy Temple, the pine-woods populist, was also backed by business but gained the support of minorities and labor. Armstrong, the liberal, got the support of the traditional liberal coalition. White had money because he had been working on his campaign for his four years as attorney general. Temple had money from his father's fortune. Armstrong tried to run a "poor boy" campaign but accepted a huge gift from a wealthy and controversial donor at the last minute. Each tried to expand beyond his original coalition to win enough primary votes for the runoff.

Tennessee Republicans

Governor Alexander was not opposed in the primary and spent his time consolidating his campaign for the general election. His press secretary said the Republicans were unified this time. He admitted that there were factions in the party that might surface in the election in 1986, when the governor would be ineligible to run again. The traditional Republican base is eastern Tennessee, which dates back to the Civil War conflict and Unionist sentiment. Eastern Tennessee tends to be a lot more conservative, a lot more "grass roots," and would certainly back a candidate for governor next time. In western Tennessee, a new group of Republicans has emerged as a result of the growing suburban population of Memphis. This faction would be likely to back a candidate as well. Bracey Campbell said that Republicans in both ends of the state were vying for the governor's "anointment."

Although unopposed in the primary, Governor Alexander built a campaign war chest larger than the combined contributions of his top two challengers. Table 4.4 shows that he raised about $1.6 million, nearly 80 percent of it through contributions from nonlarge individual donors (who numbered more than twenty thousand).

Tennessee Democrats

"Miss Anna Belle," as Anna Belle Clement O'Brien was called, hailed from middle Tennessee, home of the Frank Clement faction of the Democratic party, and geography was her main factional support. The county sheriff from middle Tennessee, Fate Thomas, said that vestiges of the Clement machine helped her. "There are still some dyed-in-the-wool Clement people out there—if they are still alive," Thomas said (Fletcher and Locker 1982).

TABLE 4.4. Sources of Contributions for Gubernatorial Primaries in Tennessee (in percentages)

| | Democrats | | Republican |
	Tyree	O'Brien	Alexander
Candidate and candidate loans	0.0	0.0	0.0
Other loans	44.0	21.8	0.0
Transfers	0.0	0.0	0.0
Party	0.0	0.0	0.4
Interest Groups			
Business	0.1	2.0	3.1
Professional	0.0	0.6	0.1
Labor	0.0	5.5	0.3
Agriculture	0.0	0.0	0.1
General/Policy	0.0	0.2	0.2
Other	0.0	1.1	1.0
Large donors	39.3	0.0	15.0
Other individuals	16.6	68.8	79.8
Total percentage	100.0	100.0	100.0
Total dollars	$976,284	$298,461	$1,657,820

O'Brien was supported by leaders of key constituencies, such as labor, teachers, state employees, and blacks. Her experience as chair of the state senate education committee brought her the endorsement of the Tennessee Education Association. She promised the association that, if elected, she would give it veto power over her choice for state commissioner of education. Some labor groups supported her, but not all. The state labor council did not endorse, although she had expected to receive the endorsement. The United Auto Workers and the Memphis-based Association of State, Federal and Municipal Employees backed her. O'Brien pledged to appoint a card-carrying member of organized labor as commissioner of labor.

When her primary campaign began, O'Brien announced that she planned to raise $500,000. This effort was to center around low-priced breakfast gatherings and bean dinners at $10 to $25 per person. Table 4.4 shows that with $298,461 collected, she realized only about three-fifths of her goal, and $65,000 of that (21.8 percent) consisted of loans from two banks. Her largest donation was from the PAC of the Tennessee Education Association. Most of her money (68.8 percent) was raised from small contributions.

Randy Tyree, the mayor of Knoxville backed by the Jake Butcher faction, was strong in large urban areas, including Memphis. He counted on the media to win the primary for him in the major media markets in the state, where voters were concentrated. His campaign coordinator, Jan Smith, said that Tyree had received almost all of the labor endorsement, hence both Democratic candidates claimed labor was supporting them.

Smith asserted that the Democratic party has strong factions and that Tyree represented the new guard within the party while Anna Belle Clement O'Brien represented the old guard. Without question, the major factor in Tyree's ability to mount a campaign against a well-known candidate like Senator Anna Belle Clement O'Brien was his financial backing by one group of supporters from Knoxville. As table 4.4 indicates, 44 percent of the money financing Tyree's campaign was loaned to him—by Butcher's United American Bank of Knoxville ($430,000). The monetary largesse from the Butchers was unprecedented in Tennessee politics. Jake Butcher and his immediate family gave $24,200. Counting his brother C. H. Butcher and brother-in-law Lionel Wilde and their families, the Butcher clan's total was $54,200.

In Tennessee we see that the Democrats are divided into strong and continuing factions that regularly present candidates to the voters. The Clement faction chose yet another of their name to carry the banner against a faction from Knoxville. In this case, the old guard was matched against a small group with tremendous resources that did not depend upon traditional loyalties and that may have upset for all time the geographical divisions of the party.

Kansas Democrats

Governor John Carlin described the major factions within the Democratic party as Docking and post-Docking. Before George Docking was governor in the late 1950s, the Democratic party was virtually nonexistent. The Dockings, George and his son Robert who was elected ten years later, built up the party and controlled it as a personal organization. The Docking faction tried to discourage Carlin from running for governor and backed the attorney general. The governor had tried to unify the party since his term began. He brought in a state chair "out of the older faction." In 1982 he was running with Thomas Docking, grandson and son of the former governors.

Governor Carlin said he had the support of business, agriculture, unions, and teachers. The unions have the money, but the teachers have the workers. Table 4.5 shows that Carlin received approximately as much from business as from labor: about 7 percent of his total from each (about $30,000). By far the largest chunk of money for the governor's campaign

TABLE 4.5. Sources of Contributions for Gubernatorial Primaries in Kansas (in percentages)

	Democrat	Republicans		
	Carlin	Hardage	Owen	Lady
Candidate and candidate loans	0.0	66.4	9.2	0.0
Other loans	3.6	0.0	4.2	0.0
Transfers	0.0	0.0	0.0	0.5
Party	2.6	0.0	0.0	0.0
Interest Groups				
Business	7.6	9.6	12.9	17.0
Professional	2.4	1.2	0.1	0.6
Labor	7.3	0.0	0.0	0.0
Agriculture	0.4	0.2	0.4	0.1
General/Policy	0.3	0.0	0.0	0.2
Other	1.6	0.1	0.3	1.7
Large donors	0.0	0.0	0.0	0.0
Other individuals	74.2	22.5	72.9	79.9
Total percentage	100.0	100.0	100.0	100.0
Total dollars	$469,357	$595,078	$641,733	$124,212

chest, 74.2 percent, came from individuals, proving once more that most campaigns for governor are funded by individual donors.

Kansas Republicans

David Owen believed that the Kansas Republicans were divided between the Reagan and Ford factions and that this division played a role in the governor's race. Owen had been chair of the Ford effort in 1976. "There is no way the Reagan people were going to be for Wendell Lady because he's a Democrat in disguise. So they would not have opposed me had not Sam Hardage got in the race and given them . . . a standard bearer for the Reagan troops" (Owen 1982, 12). Owen believes that the Reagan people encouraged Hardage to run. The Reagan-Ford division probably represents a continuing conservative-moderate split within the party that was there before that conflict personified it.

Compounding the ideological split between the Reagan and Ford factions is a geographical split. Western Kansas has a poor image of eastern Kansas. Owen believed that the people in the west preferred someone from Wichita as opposed to Kansas City for that reason.

Table 4.5 shows that Owen was the top fund-raiser in the gubernatorial race. He had been working on the effort for two years, carefully building his war chest. That took care, because Kansas did not allow any contributions in excess of $3,000 (now it is $2,000). Because a severance tax on gas and oil was a big issue in the campaign and Owen opposed it, he received $16,850 from oil and gas companies, as well as many contributions from drillers. Most of his campaign fund (about 73 percent), however, was built from individual donors in sums below the legal maximum of $3,000.

Sam Hardage, the oil millionaire and eventual winner of the Republican nomination, came from Wichita, the state's largest city, which had not produced a governor in thirty-one years, and the Wichitans wanted a governor. Most of the Prairie State lies to the west of Wichita, but a candidate from there is nearer to their interests than someone from the slick urban centers of Kansas City and Overland Park in the northeast. Hardage's conservative stand on cutting spending and his opposition to the severance tax made him popular in the western and southeastern portions of the state.

Hardage said repeatedly during the campaign that he would not contribute significant amounts of his own money to his campaign. But after the first campaign finance reports were due in the secretary's office the end of July, it appeared that Hardage loaned his campaign 66.4 percent of the total collected, or $395,000. Hardage was able to enter the race as a relatively unknown candidate three months before the primary and bankroll his own campaign to winning status.

Wendell Lady, spoke for the liberal northeast faction within the Republican party. Lady spoke for the Johnson County suburbs of Kansas City, which he represented in the statehouse. Lady represented liberal Republicans in a basically Republican state, although Republicans refer to their liberals as "moderates." His campaign manager Henley explained that moderates tend to live in the suburbs and cities in this state, and the conservatives live in rural areas. Lady did not have much money. Of the $124,000 he raised, nearly 80 percent of it was contributed from individual donors.

Oregon Republicans

Oregon's parties are weak yet competitive. Each election brings a different alignment of factions within the parties. Each candidate has to establish his or her own coalition of interests. The parties cannot be defined as representing distinctly different constituencies. In this setting, party loyalty is not a strong factor, and parties are not counted on to promise and enact programs. It is the individual candidates who make the promises. While Democrats have a 45–36 percent advantage in voter registration, they lose statewide elections regularly.

Governor Victor Atiyeh said the amount of factionalism in the party had been high but was moderate at the time. He mentioned the "born-again" takeover of the party, which had been temporarily resolved. He said that very liberal Republicans constitute a narrow base. There is an urban-suburban split in the Willamette Valley region stretching from Eugene to Portland. Atiyeh placed himself as a moderate, although he claimed, "Some like to shove me to conservative, but I'm not a conservative" (Atiyeh 1982, 11).

Governor Atiyeh received the support of the AFL-CIO building trades unit at the time Oregon was suffering its most devastating economic problems since the 1930s. Therefore, it was unusual, although more in Oregon style, for a Republican governor to win not only the endorsement of a major segment of labor but also a $3,000 check. This support for Atiyeh also represents a potential split in the Oregon labor force, since Kulongowski, one of the Democratic primary candidates, was endorsed by the Oregon AFL-CIO and given a check for $2,500.

Table 4.6 reveals that the governor raised close to three times more than either of the major Democratic contenders. Just over 25 percent of his contributions came from interest groups, mainly business. Sixty-seven percent came from individual donors (who each gave under $5,000). Governors can raise money easily.

Oregon Democrats

Donald E. Clark, the Multnomah County (Portland) executive, came from the most urban and populous county, which is also liberal and Democratic. He admitted that his and Ted Kulongowski's politics came from the same end of the spectrum but that he was the "issue candidate." Clark believed that factionalism within the party was moderate. Labor is one faction. The superliberals are another faction. There are the public-power liberals, which is a different group from the superliberals, and then there are the old party-regular kind of people. Clark said that the factions drop out for a few years and then come back. But the party is of little consequence and really doesn't mean very much.

Clark could not recover from the threat posed by the late entry of the liberal Kulongowski, who was able to raise more money in two months than Clark raised in six. Clark depended upon small contributions from

TABLE 4.6. Sources of Contributions for Gubernatorial Primaries in Oregon (in percentages)

	Democrats		Republican
	Kulongoski	Clark	Atiyeh
Candidate and candidate loans	8.8	11.6	0.8
Other loans	0.0	0.0	0.0
Transfers	0.2	0.0	0.0
Party	0.0	0.0	0.4
Interest groups			
Business	7.5	2.9	19.2
Professional	0.9	0.0	0.6
Labor	33.2	0.4	0.6
Agriculture	0.0	0.0	0.6
General/Policy	0.4	1.1	2.7
Other	4.3	0.2	2.1
Large donors	0.0	4.8	6.0
Other individuals	44.7	79.0	67.0
Total percentage	100.0	100.0	100.0
Total dollars	$118,833	$104,144	$334,804

many people (individual donors made up 79 percent of his support), and his campaign finance statement shows that he achieved his goal. Clark and his family loaned the campaign $12,100.

Enter Kulongowski on March 4. He said that he walked into the process with a series of ready-made groups because of his professional background as a labor lawyer. His law firm is legal counsel for the Oregon Education Association (OEA) representing twenty-six to twenty-seven thousand teachers who put people out on the streets working on campaigns. They also provide technical expertise and have their own in-house printing system. Kulongowski was supported by the different environmental groups because of his opposition to nuclear power and herbicides. The National Farmers' Union endorsed him because he was a strong proponent of public power. He was also supported by the social workers because of his support for social programs. Women's groups supported him for the primary because he was pro choice. The Jewish community in Portland supported him.

Labor was split between Kulongowski and Governor Atiyeh. Kulongowski also had the endorsement of the national AFL-CIO's Committee on Political Education and $5,000 for the primary, with more to come for the general election.

Kulongowski believed that the amount of factionalism in the state was extremely high. He described the Portland group "where the bulk of the population lives, where the bulk of the income is, where high technology industries and service-oriented industries are located, as not compatible with other areas of the state, which with its forest products, tends to be more conservative, tends to have less diversity of its economy, have less cultural opportunities" (Kulongowski 1982, 33). Table 4.6 confirms the fact that Kulongowski was backed by labor: 33.2 percent of his funding was from labor unions. He received slightly under half of his funds (44.7 percent) from individuals.

Where parties are not strong as in Oregon, and groups shift from candidate to candidate, personal campaigns are the order of the day. Candidates can win primaries without general electoral appeal. The personal campaign structure disappears after the campaign is over and no organization remains behind.

California Republicans

Michael Curb, the front-runner, brought together the groups that had worked for him in the 1978 campaign for lieutenant governor. Curb's campaign coordinator, Rex Hime, said that the factions within the Republican party were ideological. The major faction was the conservative one, and the major litmus test of Republican candidacy was support for Reagan. Hime identified Curb's major rival Deukmejian as basically of the same conservative faction, but more on the liberal fringe of the faction. He said the liberal wing did not represent more than 10 percent of the party. This assertion was confirmed by a California Opinion Index of October 1985 (Bell and Price 1988, 66). Hime said that the conservative faction had been joined by two more recent groups: the Richardson Gun Owners and the Christians. Hence, both candidates within the party had to run as conservatives, and both had to establish a personal base to woo the conservative Republicans of California. Both had to raise lots of money to win the primary. It took over $8 million to pick a gubernatorial nominee to run for the Republican party in 1982. Curb loaned his campaign $100,000 and received another $125,000 from three companies. Table 4.7 reveals that he acquired about a third of his money from interest groups, primarily business.

George Deukmejian also needed to get conservative support, and he had to put together a different personal coalition to do so. The Armenian community was most supportive, as the campaign finance reports reveal. The Jewish community provided organizational help. The Attorneys' Committee was evident throughout the campaign as cochairs and "name value."

TABLE 4.7. Sources of Contributions for Gubernatorial Primaries in California (in percentages)

	Democrats		Republicans	
	Bradley	Garamendi	Dukmejian	Curb
Candidate and candidate loans	0.0	8.0	0.0	2.7
Other loans	0.0	12.6	0.0	9.9
Transfers	0.0	0.0	0.0	0.0
Party	0.2	0.0	0.0	0.0
Interest groups				
Business	19.0	7.9	20.9	26.8
Professional	1.7	2.3	1.5	1.6
Labor	9.7	1.5	0.1	0.0
Agriculture	0.3	1.4	1.3	1.4
General/Policy	0.9	0.2	0.5	0.6
Other	0.9	0.0	0.0	0.1
Large donors	12.8	34.0	7.0	16.8
Other individuals	54.5	32.1	68.7	40.1
Total percentage	100.0	100.0	100.0	100.0
Total dollars	$3,190,342	$1,068,000	$4,087,500	$3,699,681

Deukmejian's southern California finance chairs, Bill Erwin, Jerry Prewoznik, and Karl Samuelian, were new and generous, giving substantial amounts of money and bringing in new friends. The same operation occurred in Orange County, where a new group brought in new donors. Deputy campaign director Fred Karger said a lot of new people emerged—people who had made money in the last ten years who wanted to get involved. This operation proved successful, because Deukmejian raised much more from individuals than did any other candidate.

California Democrats

This race, unlike all the other nonincumbent races, had a clear front-runner from start to finish. Mayor Bradley built upon his record as mayor and his partnership between business and labor and the government to redevelop downtown Los Angeles, create jobs, and stabilize black neighborhoods. Labor was very important in identifying support and help. Bradley had the endorsement of the California Teachers' Association, a powerful and sought-after group. Bradley was former president of the California League of Cities as well as the National League of Cities, and people all over the state "would voluntarily ask to help out" (Sullivan 1982, 9). Mayor Bradley's base was Los Angeles county, where the Democrats had a twenty-six-point registration edge over the Republicans and a significant share of the state's Democratic electorate.

There are two significant minorities in the Los Angeles area, blacks and Hispanics. The press pointed out that while Bradley had considerable black support, he was reluctant to take controversial positions that would alienate the white Los Angeles citizenry, a majority of the electorate. Probusing advocates criticized him for failing to provide leadership on the issue. Bradley knew that a coalition of black voters would not be sufficient to elect him to any office in California.

Bradley's representative Tom Sullivan spoke of a Hispanic uprising that was manifested in one of the minor candidates for the nomination, Mario Obledo. It was basically a protest within the party for more recognition for the Hispanic community. Bradley had the support of most of the Hispanic leaders and beat Obledo by about a two-to-one margin among Hispanics in the primary.

Mayor Bradley had a very broad-based coalition within the party. According to the California Opinion Index, the Democratic voters were divided ideologically as follows: 29 percent in the conservative wing, 53 percent in the liberal wing, and 18 percent in the middle (Bell and Price 1988, 66). The mayor appealed to most of the groups within the party, except for the most liberal (16 percent).

Table 4.7 shows that the mayor received nearly a third of his campaign funding from business and labor, with business accounting for 19 percent of the total. According to Sullivan, Bradley had a "lock on most of the money in the campaign . . . we made a very concerted effort early on to contact those people and lock them in" (Sullivan 1982, 5). And the figures showed that he had a great deal of money from individual donors, both large (12.8 percent) and smaller (54.5 percent).

Most people believed that Bradley's major foe in the primary, John Garamendi, was in the race to establish a name for future contests, although the candidate protested and said he hoped to win. (He ran again in 1994.) His supporters were key Democratic activists all across the state who supported him on issues "people who share my ideals" (Garamendi 1982, 3). Garamendi said he had almost no labor organizations because Bradley had garnered their support long before he got into the race. Garamendi believed that there were stable factions in the party, such as north-south and urban-suburban-rural, but that the party was itself so weak, factionalism was not that important.

Fund-raising became a problem for Garamendi because "the mayor worked very diligently to turn off the tap . . . He shut down Los Angeles, shut down all the money on the Wilshire Corridor. From downtown L.A. to Santa Monica—that's where the money is in Democratic politics and he shut it off" (Garamendi 1982, 4). Table 4.7 shows this fact very clearly. Garamendi was able to raise a bare third as much as Mayor Bradley. He loaned his campaign 8 percent of his campaign's total funds ($85,000) and borrowed another 12.6 percent ($135,000), and 66.1 percent of the total came from individual donors, 34 percent of them large donors.

Strategies and Results

The candidates are on their own to build their personal nominating coalitions and try to maintain front-runner status or overtake the front-runner. The incumbents have the advantage, because they are the front-runners in their party and are not seriously challenged. However, they described how they built a large war chest to discourage meaningful opposition. For the six contests in which governors were not candidates, those who were front-runners had to look uneasily over their shoulders, for the lead was insecure, as we shall see.

The hypotheses predict that incumbent governors will win primaries. They are, by definition, front-runners. They have planned to run again since their first election. They have power that comes from the distribution of rewards and punishments. Money and loans come easily because those who have money know that governors will be reelected. Even if the party is weak, the governor has placed the party chair in position and expects cooperation. The governor's personal coalition that helped him or her before will reemerge the second time ready to win again.

The hypotheses also predict that candidates for nomination in the "out" party will construct their own coalitions, building on factional advantage and hoping to add enough groups to establish front-runner status. The races are unstable, the front-runner is likely to be overtaken, and the party does not help its favorite, if indeed it has one. Because exposure is the most important ingredient for success, money is a controlling resource, and the candidate with the most money wins the nomination.

The Governors

None of the four governors in these weak-party states was worried about his nomination. They all used the primary season as a springboard for the general election, raising money, challenging any opponents from the rival party, and perfecting their campaign organizations. Three of the four were not worried about the general election, counting on their records and contacts and name to ensure another win.

Clements of Texas

Governor Bill Clements did not consider the 1982 Republican primary a contest. His opponent, free from a mental hospital after a successful court battle against commitment, raised only $1,000. As governor, Clements managed to raise enough money to repay his loans left from the 1978 campaign and at the same time build up a substantial campaign fund for 1982. The governor had already spent $3 million by the end of April without a serious opponent in the primary. This was obviously a move into the general election.

Around the middle of April, the governor formally launched his reelection campaign. He cited polls that showed him leading any Democratic contender by a 60–40 margin. However, he said it would be a hard, tough race. He said he would have more than forty thousand volunteers working for him, compared to the twenty-six thousand he had in 1978 (Attlesey 1982). His organization gave the appearance of a presidential campaign, featuring pollster Lance Tarrance, political consultant Stuart Spencer, and media consultant Don Ringe. The governor announced a big fund-raising dinner, "Victory '82," featuring President Reagan, Gerald Ford, George Bush, and Jim Baker, where he planned to clear over $3 million.

Alexander of Tennessee

Governor Lamar Alexander had absolutely no opposition in the 1982 Republican primary, so he also concentrated on the general election. His campaign featured many who had helped him in his last two campaigns. The expense account shows that Bailey, Deardourff and Associates of Washington, D.C., helped with planning, consulting, and media to the tune of $250,000, a fairly hefty chunk of the campaign spending up to the primary.

The governor based his campaign in 1982 on the same human effort he had used in 1978, when he took six months to walk from Mountain City to the Mississippi, staying in homes of supporters and meeting their friends. This effort, of course, helped develop a grass roots organization in all ninety-five counties. In 1982, building on this grass roots organization, the Alexander campaign featured hands-on community self-help projects all over the state. A minor scuffle ensued when he tried to work on the Hill-topper center for the mentally retarded in Crossville, the home territory of Democrat "Miss Anna Belle," who was vying for her party's primary nomination. Anna Belle Clement O'Brien succeeded in thwarting the effort, saying that "politics has gotten in the way of community effort" (Pigott 1982b).

Carlin of Kansas

Kansans for Carlin, the governor's personal operation, never went out of business after John Carlin won in 1978. It was reactivated in the fall of 1981 when the governor began to run again. It had maintained a Carlin coordinator in each county who worked in conjunction with the Democratic chair but kept distinctly separate operations.

In 1982 there was no primary campaign. It was general election from the very beginning. Unlike in 1978, Kansans for Carlin had a sophisticated operation in 1982. Their single primary opponent, Jimmy Montgomery, a disc jockey from Wichita, represented mid-Kansas discontent with Carlin's stand on the severance tax and the death penalty, so that gave them some reason for addressing these issues on TV. Even though the governor was in no danger, he paid D. H. Sawyer $86,400 in radio and TV advertising for the two weeks before the August 8 primary. The major media markets were Kansas City, Wichita, Topeka, and Pittsburg, an area in the southeast corner of the state. The governor won the primary with 79 percent of the vote, a comfortable margin, against the barometer of negative feedback.

A disc jockey who received 21 percent against a sitting governor was worth an interview, however, and I finally found him at Democratic county headquarters in Wichita. Jimmy Montgomery, unemployed and without a permanent address, dropped by the office regularly to use the phone. Dressed in a maroon leisure suit and a black embroidered cowboy hat, Montgomery told me the governor was very liberal for Kansas and that he, Montgomery, represents the dislike Wichitans have for the severance tax and the governor's stand against the death penalty. He invited me to the club where he was a disc jockey, but I left him a tape and my questions and asked him to mail the answers plus a little music.

Atiyeh of Oregon

"My opponents were not very formidable opponents," recalled Oregon governor Victor Atiyeh (Atiyeh 1982, 1). He considered the Republican primary a general election campaign and built his organization accordingly. He stressed a volunteer program as important and the reason for his success in the primary, in which he received 82 percent over four weak opponents.

The Challengers

The Texas Triad

The Texas Democratic party has more conservative than liberal identifiers, and the Republican party is one of the five most conservative parties in the country (Erikson, Wright, and McIver 1993, 40). An open primary and a weak party system mean that a conservative Democrat like Mark White could hope to attract the conservatives from both parties to vote for his nomination. However, interesting Republican races for state senate and Congress in Dallas and Houston might induce Republicans to vote in their own primary, leaving the Democrats with a real contest among conservatives, liberals, and minorities. In 1980, for the first time in memory, the Republican primary in Dallas County outdrew the Democratic primary. In fact, almost twice as many people voted in the Republican primary (attributable to the Reagan-Bush presidential primary). That would not be good for a Democratic conservative, and Mark White and his two liberal opponents were calculating the odds.

In the general election, the majority Democratic party would traditionally win. Close to 35 percent of Texans claim they are independents who lean conservative. Clearly it is difficult for a liberal to be elected governor. But ideology may be overcome by short-term factors like candidate personalities, geography, or the economy.

Mark White, the front-runner, established himself as the most conservative of the three Democrats contending for the nomination after Peyton McKnight, a very strong conservative from eastern Texas, dropped out on the day of the filing deadline. White was the front-runner, even though many of McKnight's supporters went to Buddy Temple, out of geographical loyalty as well as a sense that they could not join the former enemy.

White's campaign organization, which he had used in the tough fight for attorney general in 1978 (he beat James Baker III, who became President Reagan's chief of staff), came back together. White had traditional organizational support in the conservative panhandle and rural counties where neither Republicans nor liberals had a base. However, 45 percent of Texas votes are in Dallas–Fort Worth and Houston, and all three candidates had to get votes there.

Part of White's strategy was to deny endorsements to his rivals. He succeeded in blocking the endorsement of the Texas Teachers' Association to McKnight while he was still in the race. In a second attempt to stop an endorsement that would not have gone to him, White, along with Bob Armstrong, lobbied the AFL-CIO convention to make sure a pro-Temple endorsement drive could not succeed. Therefore, none of the candidates for governor appeared on the top of nearly three hundred thousand slate cards. "White wanted labor neutrality so he can work union halls while courting his mostly conservative supporters" (Kinch 1982).

When Buddy Temple entered the race at the last minute, he had several big assets. He had just run for railroad commissioner two years before and had an organization in place. Obviously Temple was counting on a small Democratic primary vote in the big cities, one that would feature the moderates over the conservatives. Another plus for Temple was his family fortune, which meant he did not have to spend time on fund-raising. Temple's strategy was to finish second in the primary and get into the runoff and beat Mark White there. His advisers thought that was possible, even though he started late.

One of Temple's major strategies was not to antagonize the Armstrong people, because he would need to form a coalition with them in the runoff in order to beat Mark White. Clark Jobe, campaign treasurer, described how their strategy was to stop the Mexican-American Democrats from endorsing either Armstrong or White because Temple needed their votes in the runoff and did not want to have them commit early.

Temple had to go on the air to compete in the primary, and the campaign became an air wars operation. "We were going to have to go on the air with close to a million bucks worth of TV and just hammer away at it because we did not have the time to build an organization on the ground" (Jobe 1982, 17).

Bob Armstrong, the most liberal of the three, had entered the campaign in November 1981 when the field was not set. He had been encouraged by a variety of liberal and minority groups. His organization was basically one of people with whom he had worked in the past, including his former law partner. Many things did not work for Armstrong. His fundraising efforts in the three major cities and southern Texas did not produce the needed money. He had hoped to "take" central Texas (Austin) and to be more successful in the western Texas farm and ranch area. He said he was the only candidate who knew which end of a cow gets up first: "Mark White, to this day, can't remember nor does Buddy know" (Armstrong 1982, 16). Armstrong was forced to conclude that in Texas, a suitable record, hard work, and individual endorsements do not bring electoral success. You have to raise the money and buy television time to communicate with the voter.

On May 1, the Democratic primary was won by Mark White with 45 percent of the vote. Buddy Temple placed second with 31 percent, and Bob Armstrong received 19 percent. Armstrong and Temple ran strong enough in eastern Texas and central Texas to deny White a primary victory without a runoff. White ran first in rural western Texas, the Gulf Coast, and populous Harris (Houston) and Dallas counties. Temple won the border counties in eastern Texas and Armstrong won or ran close to White in central Texas (Austin). The heavily courted Mexican-American vote in southern Texas was favorable to White, with Temple generally running second and Armstrong a poor third. The Democratic turnout was low in Dallas and Houston, and Temple and Armstrong split the liberal vote.

On May 6, Buddy Temple withdrew from the runoff primary. This action surprised many of his supporters, because his entire strategy had been to make the runoff and overtake White in the five weeks between the primary and the runoff. But Temple strategists said that his showing was not good enough. He was 15 percentage points behind White, and he would have had to get almost all of Armstrong's votes. Several factors influenced Temple's decision: organized labor's failure to get behind him, Armstrong's intent not to endorse him in the runoff, and the general impression that he was too far down to catch up. Besides, a runoff would have cost him another million dollars, and most of it would have been borrowed from his family fortunes. Temple said that the runoff would have left both contestants mortally wounded and the party spent and divided.

The race for governor within the Democratic party was unstable. The announced front-runner candidate dropped out on filing day, and another candidate threw his hat into the fray. That left the race with a conservative front-runner and two other candidates to split the liberal vote between them. While the front-runner won, he did it under stress and uncertainty. White knew that Temple could outdistance him given more time and certain money. It was a campaign totally dependent on candidate personalities and geography, not issues.

This contest in the Democratic party was the first in more than a hundred years in which the real enemy was the Republican governor. And Mark White was the first Democratic gubernatorial candidate in Texas history to be placed on the general election ballot with less than a majority of the primary vote; it was assumed that Governor Clements would win. It was the most expensive gubernatorial campaign in Texas history as well. Clements spent $13.3 million and White spent $5 million. On election day, White scored an upset victory over the incumbent: 53 percent to 46 percent. One reason for White's victory was the tremendous voter turnout, probably influenced by general economic conditions and a high-stimulus campaign. More than 3 million Texans turned out, compared to only 2.4 million in 1978. Analysis credits traditional rural Democratic straight-ticket voters, a group that White courted actively during the election campaign. Others believe the increased turnout of minorities contributed to White's win (Wiggins, Hamm, and Balanoff 1985, 383).

Tennessee Democrats

Randy Tyree's campaign was built around the electronic media. His campaign fund-raiser, Douglas Morrison, was a former law partner. Matt Reese from Washington, D.C., was hired to do consulting, and polling was performed by Pat Caddell. Thus Randy Tyree had in place a network of the most distinguished campaign managers in the nation by the time his major rival entered the race.

June polls indicated that Tyree was behind Anna Belle Clement O'Brien by 18 percent, but 44 percent of the potential voters were undecided. Jan Smith, Tyree's campaign chair, said they had to get their candidate out before the public by media. Tyree shunned traditional courthouse campaigning, with its reliance upon established political machines (Fitzgerald et al. 1986, 307). At one point in the campaign, Tyree said that he didn't need the support of local political organizations for the nomination.

The Tyree "crunch month" was a media blitz that began on July 5 and poured $600,000 into radio and TV ads. A lot of money and TV media coverage were focused on western Tennessee because Tyree was not known there. Apparently this effort worked well. It was commonly agreed that Tyree's media blitz was well done, competent, and diverse and brought previously uncommitted voters into his column.

In spite of his announced dislike of local machines, the Tyree campaign accepted the help of U.S. Representative Harold Ford, Memphis's top black vote getter. On the Sunday before the primary election at Tyree's Memphis headquarters, Ford and Tyree workers sat side by side stuffing envelopes with "the Ford ticket," a facsimile of Thursday's ballot that showed Ford's choice for various posts and called for Tyree's election with a big green circle around Tyree's name on the ballot. The Ford ticket was mailed to a hundred thousand people in inner-city Memphis. Ford also accompanied Tyree to several black churches (Pigott and Fletcher 1982, A1, A8).

Tyree's carefully cultivated strength in western Tennessee and urban areas by effective use of the media changed his unlikely nomination into a certainty, proving once again that the type of campaign that succeeds in a state where the party has no claim on the voters' loyalties is a personal campaign that rises and falls on political advertising.

State senator Anna Belle Clement O'Brien entered the Democratic race on May 6, exactly three months before the primary. Her campaign manager was Bryant Millsaps, aide to state house speaker Ned McWherter. O'Brien is an old-time stump orator, populist, and unabashed true believer in patronage. She learned her style from her brother, former governor Frank Clement. Her style went over well in rural areas and places like Nashville where she is well known. And so her campaign wound its way through the hilly terrain of middle Tennessee, visiting courthouses, nursing homes, and political gatherings, shaking hands and encouraging small groups of people to ask ten of their friends to "vote for Miss Anna Belle." Yet, she ran into difficulty with this campaign style because of poor staff management and organization schedule mishaps.

Senator O'Brien and Mayor Tyree campaigned to a different beat. She was not able to raise the amount of money to match his TV campaign. When her TV campaign started the end of July, it was expected to offset the Tyree advantage. But her commercials, handled by Bill Hudson of Nashville, did not catch on. She appeared lost in the woods in one of them. In her own words, she said: "I realize that I ran an old-fashioned campaign. You don't win that way anymore. You win on television. You sell the package on TV" (O'Brien 1982, 2–3).

Tyree won the Democratic primary. His victory over O'Brien was 50 percent to her 40 percent. His victory was won largely in the urban areas and western Tennessee, where the Memphis political machine of Rep. Harold Ford delivered the black vote. O'Brien won in eastern Tennessee's

Second Congressional District, beating Tyree in his home base, Knoxville. She also won in the newly created and entirely rural Fourth Congressional District, which included her home county, Cumberland.

The odds are with the incumbent, and Governor Alexander won the general election handily with 60 percent of the vote. The election was a vote of confidence on the personality and style of the governor. Alexander continued his community day activities and successfully disassociated himself from Reaganomics and the sour national economy. Tyree never succeeded in unifying the Democratic party, many Democratic power brokers sat out the race, and the traditional Democratic vote never coalesced for him. Finally, in the closing weeks of the campaign, Alexander ran a series of Knoxville man-on-the-street interviews questioning Tyree's campaign financing. Alexander intimated that $1 million of Tyree's financing had come from Jake Butcher, a fact that was later proved in the finance reports. Tyree never recovered from this attack, and his campaign went on the defensive. In retrospect, Alexander's victory was for the person and not the party, and Tyree's defeat was clearly that of the person and not the party. When parties are not responsible, personalities and personal campaigns determine the election.

Kansas Republican Triad

David Owen's method of campaigning was very systematic and organization oriented. He planned it to shut out the opposition, and he believed it did dissuade former governor Robert Bennett as well as attorney general Robert Stephan from entering. He set up organizations in southeastern Kansas and in the First District, which is all of western Kansas, in a move to block efforts of potential rivals. After that he systematically put together an organization in every county in the state, 105 in all. But his efforts did not keep his two opponents from entering three months before the primary. Sam Hardage from Wichita calculated he could win the rural parts of the state over Owen, the "suburban" candidate from Johnson County. Wendell Lady should have been thwarted from entering the race because he shared the same heavily Republican Johnson County base as Owen. As Owen saw it, "If I had to single out one single cause, even with all the money spent on the other side, and even with all the other things that went on, had Wendell Lady not gotten into the race, I would have won the race handily. So Wendall Lady's entry caused me to lose home town support here" (Owen 1982, 8).

Owen said that no primary race in Kansas history had seen so much money spent in the last ninety days. He said Hardage had put half a million dollars into the media and had stolen the election away. Owen said he did not have funds for a last-minute media blitz. He said that he had spent his money over eighteen months building an organization.

Sam Hardage was sensitive to the fact that Kansans like homegrown campaigns, and his only exceptions were a pollster (Lance Tarrance) and two media consultants (Woodward and McDowell from San Francisco); fairly significant exceptions. Hardage said part of his advantage was based on geography, and here he agreed with Dave Owen that one candidate from Wichita—Kansas's biggest city, with ties to the rural western part of the state—could beat two from Johnson County. There was not much difference between Owen and Hardage on the issues.

The Wichitan complained that the press did not report that he had a people-oriented campaign in seventy counties that reached out by phone banks, at shopping centers, and on street corners. It is true that the press did stress the money Hardage poured into the media via the four major markets, Kansas City, Topeka, Wichita, and Pittsburg. During the last three weeks of the campaign, Hardage outspent Owen two-to-one and Wendell Lady three-to-one in media purchases (Ferguson 1982). Hardage said their goal was to gather the momentum to pull even two weeks before the primary and move ahead the last week. He peaked the Monday of primary week and watched the polls seesaw back and forth the last few days.

Wendell Lady, speaker of the Kansas House of Representatives, was the only Republican candidate to favor the severance tax, oppose reimposition of capital punishment, and advocate raising taxes to increase state revenues. He entered the race at the same time as Hardage, much to the discomfort of David Owen. A small support group in the legislature encouraged Lady to run and provided him with campaign personnel after he decided to make the effort. They targeted about seventeen counties and university towns and the eastern part of the state where the severance tax support was strongest and did well in those, but not as well as they planned. Lady's campaign staffer said with pride that they won every precinct and every city in Johnson County, receiving 55 percent countywide.

The outcome of the fiercely fought Republican primary race was a close win by Sam Hardage, who received 37 percent to Dave Owen's 34 percent. Wendell Lady, with only one-fifth of the funding of either his two rivals, received 26 percent of the vote, a rather remarkable result. Hardage's aggressive media campaign neutralized Owen's strength in rural counties and gave him a firm base in urban areas outside Wichita. Owen's loss came as much at the hands of Speaker Lady, however, who carried the more populous northeastern counties where the severance tax proposal enjoyed strong backing. His 33 percent of the vote in Kansas's metropolitan counties to Owen's 30 percent prevented Owen from making up the ground lost to Hardage in rural Kansas.

Again we see a nominating race where the front-runner loses to a media blitz coming in at the end of the campaign. David Owen's carefully planned organizational strategy fell before a slick media campaign waged by a candidate who could afford to spend $395,400 of his own money. If any party organ had existed to endorse, it would have indicated support for one of the candidates, and that support would have meant that party fratricide could have been avoided.

In the general election, the race between John Carlin and Sam Hardage was perceived as a referendum on the severance tax. Hardage, from the oil and gas industry's headquarters of Wichita, took a forceful stand against the tax. Governor Carlin's advocacy of the tax placed him on the side of majority opinion on the issue. Preelection polls indicated that about 58 percent of Kansas favored the adoption of the severance tax (Harder and Rampey 1982, 173). The governor's argument that the state's fiscal crisis left no alternative but to raise taxes with a severance tax or a property tax increase was convincing to many voters. While this stand cost the governor votes in the oil counties in the west of the state, this loss was made up by significant increases in votes received in Johnson County and counties in the eastern part. Apparently Wendell Lady correctly anticipated the Johnson County sentiment with respect to the severance tax. Democratic incumbent Carlin received 53 percent of the votes cast for governor. Republican candidate Hardage received 44.5 percent. In this Republican state, with weak parties, it appears that issues of the day and candidate orientation are more decisive influences on the vote than is party identification.

Oregon Democrats: The Lead Changes

Don Clark of Portland was the first Democratic candidate to announce (November 1981), and when he did, it looked like he would not have significant opposition. But as the Republican governor's ratings went down, the number of Democratic competitors went up. Clark put together a modest organization run by a steering committee with the speaker of the Oregon House of Representatives as chair of the campaign. He had chairs in all thirty-six counties, many of whom were county commissioners like himself. He said it was a very personal kind of effort.

Clark had several well-developed position papers for economic recovery, prison problems, and health care. The *Portland Oregonian* endorsed him for the nomination because of his vigorous stands on issues. But the people do not get their information from newspapers. "Most people get their information by perceptions . . . from television and I had no political advertising on television whatsoever. And I think that was the deciding factor" (Clark 1982, 5).

It was late in the primary season when state senator Ted Kulongowski announced on March 4, 1982. Although he had decided to run in December, he was prevented from making the announcement earlier because the special session of the legislature took so long. State law didn't allow fund-raising from lobbyists during a session, a fact that would have hurt his fund-raising effort and the momentum of his campaign. In December 1981, different interests in the Democratic party asked Kulongowski to run. This solicitation came after two prominent Democrats, U.S. Representative James Weaver and Mayor Neil Goldschmidt of Portland, had decided not to make the race, and these groups believed that Clark could not win the general election against the governor. Kulongowski's poll revealed that he had a good chance.

From his 1980 campaign for the U.S. Senate against Bob Packwood, Kulongowski recruited his fund-raiser and media consultants. His close friend Grattan Kerans, state house majority leader, came on board to run the primary.

Kulongowski developed his own philosophy of campaigning. He said that his greatest asset . . . is his ability to excite people "and get them believing in themselves" (Kulongowski 1982, 32). Kulongowski spent over $30,000 to go on television during the final weeks of the campaign, and this exposure brought him the victory.

Kulongowski prevailed in the Democratic primary by 60 percent to Clark's 19 percent. He scored a victory by taking a solid margin in the state's major population areas, including Multnomah County (Portland) and Clackamas and Washington counties, which both contain Portland suburbs. In Lane County (Eugene), the second most populous county, Kulongowski finished well ahead of the other two resident candidates. The *Portland Oregonian,* which had endorsed Clark, said campaign styles must be changing in Oregon. "A slick media campaign and a few well chosen slogans . . . carried more weight than detailed proposals with Oregon Democrats" ([Oregon] Editorial 1982).

During the general election period, Oregon's partisan identification was: 31.2 percent Republican, 30.2 percent Independent and 38.6 percent Democrat. Ideologically, the Independents were moderate—in fact, one of the most moderate independent groups in the nation (Erikson, Wright, McIver 1993, 15, 40). They held the balance of power between the two parties, with the Republicans moderately conservative and the Democrats moderately liberal. The gubernatorial race was perceived as a rift between the interests of organized labor, which heavily supported Kulongowski, and business, which was solidly behind the Republican governor Atiyeh. Kulongowski tried valiantly to blame the sick economy on the governor, but the governor was not held responsible for the national economy, and Oregon was not suffering enough to make a change. Parties played no role in the campaign as usual. Atiyeh as incumbent was able to raise over $1 million while Kulongowski raised only half as much and ran a disorganized campaign. Atiyeh won with 61.4 percent of the vote and carried every county by a margin of two-to-one. At the same time, the voters elected a Democratic majority in both houses of the state legislature. While the odds are always in favor of reelection, the lack of a strong party system forces both candidates to mount personal campaigns in which symbolism plays a vital role.

California Republicans: Too Close to Call

After his hero was elected to the White House in 1980, President Reagan's young California campaign manager, Mike Curb, decided to run for governor. Curb consulted key financial people, key business leaders, and political leaders throughout the state. This group included the assembly minority leader and most of the legislators who backed him.

The campaign organization was basically three-pronged. One part was the fund-raising arm; one was the volunteers; and the third was the media. The fund-raising arm was directed by the rich and famous such as the Tuttles of Tuttleson. Ken Rietz was campaign manager and media director (Hime 1982, 2). The organization divided California into twelve regions, according to population and ability to control, but focused on the top ten counties containing 65 percent of the vote. These were Riverside, San Bernadino, San Diego, Orange, Los Angeles, Sacramento, Santa Clara, Alameda, Contra Costa, and San Mateo (Hime 1982, 5).

Over the two years of active candidacy, Curb had several potential rivals for the nomination. George Deukmejian became an active candidate in March 1981. In a poll taken in August of that year, Curb and Deukmejian were tied among Republican state central committee members and county chairs. Deukmejian was much more popular among the 142 Republican contributors polled (48 percent to 23 percent), an interesting fact considering the powerful financial interests Curb had already attracted to his campaign. Curb held the edge among the registered Republicans (*Opinion Outlook* 1981, 7).

Curb's campaign used primarily an air wars media strategy, not ground wars. Curb announced his candidacy in a string of half-hour television commercials broadcast throughout the state. The campaign began

TV commercials in earnest during the first week in February 1982. By the last week of May, nearly $2 million had been fed to media markets in Los Angeles, San Diego, Sacramento, Fresno, and Bakersfield. San Francisco, home of liberal Democrats (a 40 percent registration edge), did not receive more than 6 percent of the total TV spending.

According to one analysis, Curb faced three great obstacles in his race for the nomination. First, he had a hard time conceptualizing political issues, offering platitudes instead of substance. Second, he faced the problem of integrity. In 1978, his campaign for lieutenant governor was one of the most unsavory campaigns in California history. The *Los Angeles Times* refused to endorse either candidate. Finally, Curb cracked under political pressure. In October 1981, he lashed out at a female reporter for the *Los Angeles Herald Examiner,* an incident that was reported nationally. To counteract his erosion in public opinion, Curb hired former Reagan White House aide Lyn Nofziger as a campaign consultant (Lerner 1982, 12–13).

When George Deukmejian decided to run for the Republican nomination, he was far behind. Curb had a million dollars plus a lot of key people—legislators and businesspeople—signed up already. The polls showed Deukmejian fifteen or sixteen points behind Curb in early 1981. He engaged the firm of Bill Roberts, which developed the campaign theme of MISE: maturity, integrity, stability and experience. This theme described their "product." Deukmejian had twenty years on Mike Curb and undisputed integrity; his maturity and stability were indicated by a twenty-five-year marriage and twenty years of experience in government. The press did snicker at MISE, but it caught on after awhile (Karger 1982, 3).

Over the summer, more strategy and more fund-raising occurred. Deukmejian's campaign met its goal of a million dollars by June 30, and another of $750,000 by year's end. By the end of December the campaign organizers had county chairs and cochairs in all fifty-eight counties of the state. In Los Angeles and the surrounding counties, they had regional organizations as well because "the San Fernando Valley has more Republicans in it than the entire Bay Area in San Francisco" (Karger 1982, 22).

A statewide "home phoner" campaign was the contribution of volunteers working from instruction kits. According to deputy campaign director Fred Karger, it was a tremendous success, and as he spoke, certificates were being sent to the volunteers acknowledging their efforts. Deukmejian won the primary by 150,000 votes, and Karger estimated that the 500,000 household calls made in the home phoner campaign made the difference.

In California, campaigns are won on TV, and this strategy was carefully planned for the last six weeks. Deukmejian sat by and watched while Curb went on TV early, but after April, when Deukmejian started on the tube, the polls showed the race getting even again. What was immensely interesting was that each candidate spent $2 million on TV, indicating a level playing field. It was an unstable game from then on, with polls showing first one candidate and then the other in the lead. Lance Tarrance conducted tracking polls for Deukmejian four nights a week.

The campaign was unstable from the start, a feature of open-primary states. There were four major periods in the campaign when the lead changed. In the beginning, Curb started with a huge lead in money and leader support. He was hurt badly by the antipress outburst in Palm Springs in November, and the campaign swung toward Deukmejian, who surged far ahead. Curb's campaign manager directed a comeback. First voters were reassured as to Curb's integrity and stability for leadership by GOP stalwarts on TV. Curb then took a stand against the Peripheral Canal, which was calculated to bring him the northern California vote. Then he sent mailings to every Republican household in the state questioning Deukmejian's loyalty to President Reagan. The polls soon showed Curb ahead by a substantial margin. In the last weeks of the campaign, Deukmejian countered with the fact that Curb did not register to vote until he was twenty-nine. Mailers, television commercials, and full-page ads hit Curb with charges that he had not voted for Ronald Reagan in either of his campaigns for the governorship. Pollsters report that the Deukmejian attack worked and that Curb lost his lead in the final week of the campaign (Salzman 1982, 238). The final results showed Deukmejian with 51 percent and Curb with 45 percent of the Republican primary vote.

California Democrats: The Front-runner Wins

Tom Bradley was the front-runner when he formed an exploratory committee to test the water. In August 1981, Bradley was the choice among Democratic politicians and contributors and led among registered voters (*Opinion Outlook* 1981, 7). Bradley believed he could win the nomination and announced his candidacy on January 27, 1982. The core of his campaign organization had been with him for a long time.

The African-American mayor's basic support was the city of Los Angeles, the five counties that make up the Los Angeles media market, primarily. Bradley was well known and had a high favorability rating in the polls. The fact that his city's population was only 19 percent black showed that his appeal cut across racial lines. The Bradley campaign looked at the media markets and organized campaign offices in five major ones: Los Angeles, San Diego, Sacramento, San Francisco (Bay area), and Fresno. That is where 46 percent of the Democratic electorate is located.

With public opinion polls showing him with a huge lead over John

Garamendi, the mayor could devote time and effort to his fall campaign. In April 1982 he set up a radio and media effort directed by the Garth group and spent well over a million dollars by the end of June. In keeping with front-runner status, Bradley's commercials were nonpartisan in nature and avoided any issues that might cost him votes. Television ads running in northern California did not mention him as either a Democratic candidate for governor or in connection with Los Angeles. Instead, they stressed Bradley's background as a police lieutenant, city council member, and mayor. The theme was Bradley "doesn't make a lot of noise, he just gets things done." In truth, Bradley did take stands on controversial issues: gun control, which he favored; the Equal Rights Amendment, which he supported; the death penalty law, which he would enforce; and construction of the Perpheral Canal, which he supported.

Garamendi was frustrated at every turn in efforts to get key Democratic party endorsements, raise money, and convince Bradley to debate. From the start, he had problems with organization, money, and media. The state senator believed he received good media coverage considering his standing in the polls. He kept hammering away on the issues, and the media gave him attention for that reason. He kept hoping that Bradley would be forced to debate the issues, but the mayor kept hiding. That hurt Garamendi because he could never get a conflict going between himself and Bradley. Garamendi spent a bare $85,000 on radio and television.

The Democratic race shows how a front-runner can capture the money and momentum and keep it throughout the campaign. Bradley won with 61 percent to Garamendi's 25 percent. Without money for media, you cannot hope to win a campaign in a state where each candidate must build his or her own organization.

The nominating campaigns in California show that money counts. There was no talk of party organization by any of the candidates. The Republican race was totally unpredictable since the lead changed from week to week. Eventually the front-runner lost. Curb was not the front-runner because he was backed by a party organization; he was the front-runner because he attracted some rich and famous names to his campaign in the early days. Deukmejian prevailed after personality became an issue. The Democratic race was a testing ground for potential candidates in the beginning, with hopefuls pawing the ground, sniffing the air, and wondering what their chances were. No party could mediate because the candidates were on their own.

In a general election campaign between those whom the *California Journal* (Carroll 1982, 229) termed Dull Tom and Cautious Duke, the odds were with Tom Bradley. He had been the front-runner in his party from the start, and this kind of unity should have carried him into office, where he would have been the first black governor in this century. In addition, the Republican primary fight had been bitter, leaving a bruised party. During much of the campaign, Bradley held a ten-to-twelve-point edge. In the last two weeks that lead narrowed and held steady at five to seven points for Bradley.

Deukmejian used his strong image as a crime fighter to develop support in blue-collar southern California, where he needed conservative Democratic votes. Bradley countered by stressing his twenty-one years with the Los Angeles police, adding that Deukmejian had never arrested or prosecuted anyone. He also worked to keep liberal Democrats in place with strong appeals to minorities, urban dwellers, and labor. The Democrats were concerned that the Hispanics might be reluctant to accept Bradley.

On November 2, Deukmejian received 49 percent and Bradley 48 percent of the 7.88 million votes cast, a margin of 1.19 percent. Why did Bradley lose his lead on election day? Because the election was so close, it is difficult to assign any single reason. Neither candidate made an issue of Bradley's race. However, in October, Bill Roberts, Deukmejian's campaign manager had volunteered that if his candidate were trailing only five points by election day, he would win. He speculated that there was a hidden 5 percent antiblack vote. Bradley expressed his dismay over the comment and Roberts resigned.

Another reason may lie with the presence of the handgun registration proposition on the ballot. The votes for and against this proposition totaled 7.64 million—only a quarter of a million fewer than the votes cast for governor. The handgun measure had strong opposition in many of the more rural counties, where the turnout was as high as 75 to 80 percent, far above the statewide turnout of 68 percent. In these counties, the vote for Deukmejian ran as high as 65 percent.

The absentee voters actually elected Deukmejian. In the election booths, Bradley received almost 20,000 more votes than his opponent. However, the Republicans provided two million GOP voters with stamped addressed cards to request absentee ballots. Of the 525,186 absentee ballots cast, Deukmejian won 61.5 percent to Bradley's 38.5 percent (Gable, Sektnan, and King 1985, 128).

Thus, Governor Deukmejian was elected to office without a clear electoral mandate. In addition, he had no other Republican constitutional officers to support him, and he faced a heavily Democratic legislature. He needed his party behind him, but the nominating process had left the party bloodied and divided.

Conclusions

In states where the party leaders are not unified, they cannot control the nomination for the party's most important state office of governor. Preprimary endorsements do not exist. There is no mechanism for encouraging some candidates and discouraging others. There is no organizational scheduling of ambition for office, no meetings with the candidates, no team loyalty or commitment. Candidates for governor in these nonendorsing states are just as likely to have office experience as candidates in strong party states, which means that when elected, they will not be lacking the experience to govern. However, the circumstances under which they govern will be more difficult than those facing their counterparts in endorsing states. The coalitions and strategies they must use to win the governorship take their toll on their ability to govern.

Front-runner status is an initial advantage, but it is hard to keep. The four governors were front-runners, of course. None was seriously challenged for the nomination. For those outparty nominating contestants as well as for those who fought in both primary contests in California, front-runner status was sought, but it was not a guarantee of success. In only two of the six races did the front-runners win the primary. The races were unstable and the lead changed in Tennessee, Kansas, Oregon, and (for the Republicans) California. In those races, the candidates had to campaign continuously for that uncertain primary decision, and the bruised winner had to pick up his troops and gear up for another campaign.

The party leaders are not unified in any of the weak party states. The governors have their support, because they put them in office and expect compliance, if not active help. For the other candidates, the leaders may support the front-runners, but they must maintain formal neutrality. Parties in direct-primary states are deprived of their most important function, that of grooming and presenting candidates for election. This function is performed by an electorate that may or may not contain loyal partisans and is necessarily informed by the media under the direction of wealthy candidates.

Candidates for the nomination in states where the primary is the only point of decision build coalitions from factions within the party that will assure them of more votes than their rivals. In each of the ten contests we studied, candidates described the factions within their parties in terms of ideology, geography, urban-rural, and personality bases. Within the Texas Democrats, the liberal-conservative split represented major economic and social differences among minorities and workers versus business. In Tennessee, the factions within the Republican party were based on geography and those within the Democratic party on personality machines. For the

Kansas and California Republicans, the Reagan-Ford conflict was still operative. It has probably become a more ideological split in present times. In Oregon, there is no regular factional conflict. Each primary election brings a different alignment of factions within the parties. Personal campaigns are the order of the day.

In terms of strategy, governors use the primary campaign where they have token opposition to build up the resources and organization for the general election. No party backs them and so they are on their own, and usually successful. Governor Clements of Texas was the only exception, and he was the state's only Republican governor in over a hundred years. In the other races, the strategy is to stop the front-runner. Doing that takes money, and if the challenger has money, the strategy is usually successful.

Nominating campaigns in weak party states allow the candidate with the most money to win. Organization does not prevail. Covert support of party leaders does not prevail. A platform does not prevail. In short, the campaigns are based on money. The citizens of those states must hope that money flows to the most experienced and virtuous. It will take much of both to govern where there is nothing after the election except the shreds of a personal campaign organization.

CHAPTER 5

Resources, Factions, and Strategies: Party Endorsement States

In our five party endorsement states, the political leaders established the practice of endorsing to protect their power over nominations. These states were the strong party states at the time endorsing procedures were initiated, and most of them remain strong today. In these states, the party leadership backs the candidate endorsed in the convention with money and party organization. I hypothesize that the party leaders in the counties and towns are unified under a state chair. They can control the nomination for a gubernatorial candidate by sending local delegations to the convention that will back him or her. The candidate may not be challenged, but if a challenge takes place, the party leaders build a coalition for the candidate that will ensure a primary win.

Preprimary endorsements differ according to whether they are mandated by state law or whether the parties set their own rules. In a strong nominating system such as those in Connecticut, New York, and Colorado, preprimary endorsements are made by law and apply to both parties, and the endorsed candidate has preferential access to the ballot. Candidates in states such as Minnesota and Illinois, where endorsements are made by party rules, gain no legal advantage of ballot access or party position, but they gain the same political advantages as those who are endorsed in legal systems. In this chapter, I will rank the five states in order of endorsing strength and follow that order in the report of the interviews with the twenty-five candidates for governor.

The Actors

As we would expect, and as table 5.1 demonstrates, most of our candidates are insiders. The exceptions are Lew Lehrman of New York, Steve Schuck of Colorado, and Wheelock Whitney of Minnesota, all wealthy business executives. (Whitney had previously run for the U.S. Senate.) Lehrman received the Republican endorsement (instant insider status) and beat Paul Curran, an insider. Whitney defeated Lou Wangberg, the lieutenant governor, in the primary. Steve Schuck did not receive enough support to continue the race and dropped out. Hence, two businesspeople with no statewide political experience won Republican nominations in New York and Minnesota. We would not expect outsiders to beat insiders in endorsing states where the party leadership rewards office experience and party loyalty. According to Malcolm Jewell, outsiders rarely beat insiders even in primary-only states (1994, 11). In only 8 percent of the primary contests in the most recent decade did that occur. But in the four contested primaries in our sample of endorsing states, two were won by outside businesspeople with no political governing experience, one of whom, admittedly, had received the endorsement of his party.

Table 5.1 gives the office experience of our twenty-five candidates for governor. Thirty-six percent of our candidates served in the state legislature just prior to running for governor, and overall 56 percent had legislative experience. Of those who received their party's nomination, 60 percent had served in the state legislature, and of those who were elected, three out of five had served. These statistics compare favorably with Thad Beyle's findings on the prior office careers of governors (Beyle 1990, 204–8). Legislative experience would presumably be helpful to a governor whose time is largely consumed with legislative compromise. Seven (28 percent) of our candidates came from statewide elected office, which includes the three incumbents. Thus, eight out of the ten nominees had experience sufficient to the need acquired from statewide office or state legislative office, and all five of those elected had been governor or lieutenant governor.

Resources: Risks, Front-runners, and Leader Support

The twenty-five candidates for the nomination in preprimary endorsement states follow a different strategy from their counterparts in states where the primary is the only decision point. This strategy must include negotiations with party leaders from local to state level. By convincing just over half of the two thousand delegates to a party convention that you are the favored candidate, you may be able to shut off most or all opposition to your nomination and achieve your goal without a primary. Winning the endorsement and the nomination in one effort is possible. While no set of rules can contain severe conflict, the party endorsement states provide a process whereby the endorsed candidate can count on party support, however subtle, in the nominating campaign. This fact can be used to persuade primary enemies to drop the race.

TABLE 5.1. Party Endorsement States: Office Experience of Candidates, 1982

State and Party	Name	Age	Governor	State Office	State Senate	State House	Other
CT-D	O'Neill[a,b]	51	1980–82	Lieutenant Governor 1978–80		1966–78 Majority leader	State Chair 1975–78
CT-D	Abate	38				1974–82 Speaker	
CT-R	Rome[a,b]	48			majority leader, minority leader 1970–78		Mayor 1964–70 Gubernatorial candidate 1978
CT-R	Bozzuto	52			minority leader 1978–80		U.S. Senate candidate 1980
CT-R	Labriola	50			1980–82		
CT-R	Post	44			1978–82	1972–76	
NY-D	Koch[a]	57					U.S. Rep. 1968–78 Mayor of New York City 1977–
NY-D	Cuomo[b]	49		Secretary of State 1974–78, Lieutenant Governor 1978–82			
NY-R	Lehrman[a,b]						Business executive, Rite-Aid
NY-R	Curran	49				1962–66	U.S. attorney 1973–75
NY-R	Rosenbaum	50		Superior Court 1970–84			State Chair 1973–77
NY-R	Emery	50				Minority leader 1964–82	
CO-D	Lamm[a,b]	47	1974–82			1966–74	
CO-R	Fuhr[a,b]	53				Speaker 66–74	
CO-R	Winn	56					State Chair 1978–80, Federal Commissioner 1981–82
CO-R	Schuck	46					Real estate magnate

(continued)

TABLE 5.1.— Continued

State and Party	Name	Age	Governor	State Office	State Senate	State House	Other
MN-D	Spannaus[a]	51		Attorney general 1970–82			State chair 1967–69
MN-D	Perpich[b]	54	1976–78	Lieutenant governor 1970–76	1962–70		Gubernatorial candidate 1978
MN-R	Wangberg[a]	41	Lieutenant governor 1978–82				
MN-R	Whitney[b]	56					Investment banker Mayor of Wayzata 1962–68 U.S. Senate candidate 1964
MN-R	Sherwood	48				Minority leader 1972–82	
MN-R	Overgaard	52			1970–72	1962–68	
IL-D	Stevenson[a,b]	52		Treasurer 1966–70		1964–66	U.S. Senator 1970–80
IL-D	Walker	59	1972–76				
IL-R	Thompson[a,b]	46	1976–82				U.S. attorney 1971–75

[a]Won endorsement
[b]Won primary

The Risks of Running

Table 5.2 presents the initial resources of our twenty-five candidates in terms of primary risk, front-runner status, leader support, factional support, and money. Endorsements make primaries less risky. Primary risk is measured by the average primary vote for the endorsed candidates in the last five elections in each state party. Obtaining the endorsement greatly improves the chances of winning the primary over the chances of the candidates in nonendorsement states. In all ten parties, endorsed candidates averaged comfortable margins in the primaries. In all but three parties, the average primary vote for endorsed candidates was over 75 percent. Compare this figure with the average primary vote in parties in nonendorsement states (table 4.2), only one of which was over 75 percent. Hence, as the nominating process started, candidates in each of our ten state parties could expect that if they were endorsed, they would win the primary. The 1982 races provided unusual upsets in the Democratic party in New York and both parties in Minnesota.

TABLE 5.2. Endorsement States: Candidate Resources, 1982

State and Party	Name	Previous Primary Average[a] (in %)	Front-runner	Party Leaders Support	Factional Support	Money Raised (in $000)
CT-D	O'Neill (I)[b,c]	93.5	Y	Y	Party regulars	204
CT-D	Abate	93.5	N	N	Antiestablishment progressives	294
CT-R	Rome[b,c]	76.4	Y	Y	Party regulars	374
CT-R	Bozzuto	76.4	N	N	Personal	399
CT-R	Labriola	76.4	N	N	Personal, medical association	206
CT-R	Post	76.4	N	N	Personal, environmental groups	187
NY-D	Koch[b]	60.6	Y	Y	Party regulars, public employee unions	3,677
NY-D	Cuomo[c]	60.6	N	N	Coalition of minorities, unions	1,940
NY-R	Lehrman[b,c]	100.0	Y	Y[d]	Conservatives, anti-party insurgents	10,178
NY-R	Curran	100.0	N	N[d]	Personal, "old guard"	395
NY-R	Rosenbaum	100.0	N	N	Rockefeller moderates	806
NY-R	Emery	100.0	N	N	Personal, upstate legislative	701
CO-D	Lamm (I)[b,c]	91.7	Y	Y	Broad-based coalition	270
CO-R	Fuhr[b,c]	75.9	Y	neutral	Personal, moderates	123
CO-R	Winn	75.9	N	neutral	Personal, conservatives	834
CO-R	Schuck	75.9	N	neutral	Personal	143
MN-D	Spannaus[b]	83.3	Y	Y	Party regulars	990
MN-D	Perpich[c]	83.3	N	N	Personal, Iron Range, pro life, Catholic	139
MN-R	Wangberg[b]	93.7	Y	Y	Party regulars, conservatives	225
MN-R	Whitney[c]	93.7	N	N	Personal, moderates	935
MN-R	Sherwood	93.7	N	N	Christian Right, pro life	82
MN-R	Overgaard	93.7	N	N	Personal, moderates	110
IL-D	Stevenson[b,c]	77.5	Y	Y	Party regulars from downstate and Cook County suburbs	35
IL-D	Walker	77.5	N	N	Personal	37
IL-R	Thompson (I)[b,c]	74.0	Y	Y	Party regulars, broad-based coalition	2,030

[a]Average primary vote for gubernatorial nominee last five elections
[b]Won endorsement
[c]Won primary
[d]Curran was put forward by three Republican leaders to stop Lehrman, but his primary campaign faltered and he lost their support. Lehrman received establishment support by July 1982.

As we will see, these three 1982 nominating contests in our endorsing states were more likely to predict the future than reflect the past because the endorsed candidates lost to their challengers. It was an exceptional year for conflict, and three cases make up an exceedingly small sample, but they indicate a trend toward more serious challenges during the 1980s, when endorsed candidates won contested primaries only 44 percent of the time (Jewell 1994, 5). While neither party in New York had a serious primary contest for governor after 1982, the change in the fortunes of endorsees has been particularly dramatic in Minnesota through 1994. In 1982, both endorsed candidates lost: Walter Spannaus, the attorney general, to former governor Rudy Perpich, and Wangberg to Whitney. Only once since the 1950s had either party lost an endorsed candidate in a primary. Since that time, both parties have seen close contests, and in 1994, governor Arne Carlson lost the Republican endorsement to a Christian Right candidate and had to win the nomination in the following primary.

Governors as Front-runners with Leader Support

The three governors—O'Neill of Connecticut, Lamm of Colorado, and Thompson of Illinois—were front-runners, and their campaign organizations were merged with those of their parties. They had chosen their party leaders, who supported them. Yet while Lamm was unopposed, both governors O'Neill and Thompson were challenged by weak candidates, which indicated that even governors must take front-runner status and party leadership seriously if they are to survive. Neither of Governor Thompson's challengers received even 10 percent in the primary. Governor O'Neill's challenger, the assembly speaker, generated significant support in the state convention, and the governor had to work to keep him off the primary ballot.

Governor O'Neill of Connecticut and the
Party Organization

Governor William O'Neill's description of his announcement strategy illustrates the strength of the party backing that incumbents possess. He inherited the governorship in January 1981 due to the illness and death of Governor Grasso. Hence, although O'Neill was the incumbent, he had never run for governor. "The organization was there, and I went definitely through the Democratic party organization . . . which is the Democratic State Central Committee. They were all invited. Then the Democratic chairman in each and every one of the towns and the vice-chairman—they were invited. The mayors and the selectmen of the Democratic Party and the Democratic legislators . . . So I had a built-in constituency within the Democratic Party, and that's really who I attempted to appeal to immediately for the nomination. That was successful" (O'Neill 1982, 2–3).

Governor Lamm of Colorado Announces on May Day

"What better could somebody do with their life than work on Colorado's problems," said Richard Lamm, a Democrat who sought a third four-year term as governor (Miller 1982a). First elected in 1974 in the Watergate protest, Lamm received the vote of the front-range Democratic counties of Denver, Adams (the northern suburbs of Denver), and Pueblo (a real-working class county). In 1978, he received over 60 percent of the vote and carried nine of the ten most populous counties. A Denver metropolitan area poll of May 20, 1982, found that 61.4 percent of those questioned rated Lamm's performance as "good" or "excellent," and it showed him to be the overwhelming choice against his Republican contenders (Westergaard 1982, 5B). Lamm, not surprisingly, faced no opposition in seeking his party's renomination.

Governor Thompson of Illinois: A Merged Coalition

It was a foregone conclusion that Jim Thompson would run for a third term as governor (he had served one two-year term, 1976–78, and nearly completed one four-year term, 1978–82). At the state fairgrounds in July 1981, the most prominent political figure was Governor Thompson, who had the least reason for being there since no one had announced a challenge to him for the 1982 governor's race. Thompson had a party united behind him. Phil O'Connor explained that an incumbent governor has a lot of power in terms of appointments and dealing with people in the party "and being able to pretty well stymie opposition—not that there really was any" (Kjellander and O'Connor 1982, 34).

Don Adams, the state Republican chair, kept in close touch with Thompson. He was a moderate person "interested in winning and an arbiter—a person who tries to keep any kind of factiousness or disputes to a reasonable level" (O'Connor 1982, 22). Adams tried to keep the party strong because there has to be some center of power. If parties were not strong, interest groups would take their place. Slate-making, as the endorsing process is called in Illinois, is left in the hands of a few prominent leaders who use their muscle and finances to influence the party-endorsed set of candidates.

Citizens for Thompson, an organization for the raising and spending of money and its reporting, was in continuous operation. "It never dies. It raises money all the time" (O'Connor 1982, 7). Even when there was no campaign, there was an ongoing need for dollars because the governor was not a wealthy person and needed political funds.

Front-runners in Endorsing Parties

We now turn to the seven nominating races in parties that did not have incumbent governors (with the exception of O'Neill's challenger in Connecticut) in 1982. In the preprimary endorsing states, front-runner status implies party leadership support. Presumably the state leaders encourage a candidate to emerge as the front-runner. Occasionally they wait until the contest stabilizes before they back their choice. That usually happens before the convention, and the delegates are aware of the favored candidate. In Colorado, an exception, the Republican leaders maintained neutrality until the convention chose John Fuhr over former party chair Phil Winn. And in New York, some Republican leaders tried to stop the front-runner, Lew Lehrman, until it was obvious nobody could keep him from winning. Thus, secure and gradual garnering of momentum builds delegate strength toward convention endorsement.

Connecticut Democrats: The Speaker Challenges the Governor

Ernest Abate, speaker of the Connecticut House of Representatives, thought the governor's support was "soft" and determined to challenge him. He was not the front-runner, nor was he backed by the party leaders, but he had some supporters in the legislature. Abate was impressed with the clout that the governor had. As chair of the Bond Commission (which consists of the governor's cabinet), the governor controls the multimillion-dollar programs, such as flood-erosion control projects or a new entrance or exit ramp. A close friend of Abate's, the mayor of Danbury, held out against the governor until he was told that he would not get his senior citizen's center unless he "came out" for the governor. Abate believes that chairing the Bond Commission is the single biggest factor in the governor's leverage. The governor and the party chair had a network of relationships with the mayors of the cities and towns because of their ability to sponsor projects. Since Abate's candidacy was designed to "throw that organization out," he did not consult the party chair (Abate 1982, 17).

*Connecticut Republicans: Rome the Front-runner with the
Blessing of Party Leaders*

Lewis Rome as the state senate minority leader in 1978 sought the party's
gubernatorial nomination, but he fell short in the convention to a U.S.
Representative who was backed by the party chair, Frederick Biebel.
Under pressure from Biebel and other party leaders, Rome reluctantly
agreed to abandon a primary fight and take second place on the ticket. The
Sarasin-Rome team was badly defeated. In September 1981, Rome was
pressured by party leaders to run for governor. He was the candidate qui-
etly favored by the state party leadership and was eventually backed
openly by the party chair a week before the convention.

The other major contender for the nomination, Richard Bozzuto, former state senate minority leader, had committed the unpardonable political maneuver of mounting an unsuccessful primary challenge to the U.S.
Senate endorsee in 1980. He was not favored by the party leaders, and in
fact it may have been his growing momentum for the nomination that
prompted them to pressure Lewis Rome to run. (Bozzuto 1982, 10).

Gerald Labriola, the friendly baby doctor, believed he could win the
primary, if not the convention, and originally counted on receiving 20 percent of the convention votes. The party leaders did not think a one-term
state senator had earned the right to run for governor, so they did not support him and he did not ask for their help. He realized that he was in third
place but reasoned that he was everyone's second choice.

State senator Rusty Post hired a Washington campaign-planning firm
to assess his chances for the governorship and to draw up a plan to achieve
it. Post had never heard of the town chairs in the Fairfield County towns
where he hoped to gain delegates, and they had never heard of him (Post
1982, 5). Post, an articulate legislator, had a patrician manner and a Yale
establishment mein that he counted on parlaying into support in Fairfield
County. He believed he could win in the primary, but the hardest hurdle
was the convention.

New York Democrats: Koch is Front-runner

The mayor of New York City, Ed Koch, did not confirm the hypotheses.
He was the clear front-runner, he was the choice of the party leaders, and
he received the party endorsement, but he lost the primary to Mario
Cuomo. The mayor had repeatedly pledged not to seek any other office
than mayor of New York City. In fact, he told a roomful of reporters in
early 1982 that living in Albany was "a fate worse than death" (Logan

1982a, 104). Following Governor Hugh Carey's surprise announcement on January 15 not to seek reelection, the mayor enjoyed the speculation and the ensuing political ruckus caused by his pondering the gubernatorial candidacy. Asked if he was considering running for governor and answering "maybe," he was reminded that he usually gave more direct answers to questions. He said: "You're looking at a new Ed Koch—modest and humble" (Logan 1982, 108).

At last the mayor announced for governor on February 22, claiming that it was an opportunity he could not miss. He announced with his customary modesty that he was in the lead—and he was correct. He quickly won the support of a group of the state's most powerful Democratic county leaders: four of the five New York City Democratic chairs—Meade Esposito of Brooklyn, Donald R. Manes of Queens, Stanley Friedman of the Bronx, and Nicholas LaPorte of Staten Island—and the Erie County leader, Joseph F. Crangle. Dominic J. Baranello, the Democratic state chair who was also the Suffolk County leader, eventually delivered Suffolk's nineteen votes to the mayor. These leaders, whose counties are among the largest Democratic strongholds in the state, controlled enough delegates to the state convention to assure Koch of the endorsement (called "designation" in New York). While Governor Carey remained officially neutral during the nominating contest, he endorsed the mayor in the final week of the primary campaign. Koch had the services of media consultant David Garth and quickly won endorsements from all the major New York City newspapers.

At the time of the mayor's announcement, there were six or so potential Democratic candidates for governor including the assembly speaker, the state attorney general, the New York City Council president, and the lieutenant governor. Opposition to the mayor quickly dissolved, and the lieutenant governor became the mayor's sole opponent. Mario Cuomo was an acknowledged though undeclared candidate even before Governor Carey decided not to seek a third term. He planned to run for statewide office either as Carey's running mate or by himself. Cuomo's political career began in 1974 when Governor Carey chose him to be secretary of state and then selected him to be his running mate four years later. In the meantime, the governor backed him for mayor of New York City. The mayoral race should have been won by Cuomo, but it was won by Koch after a crowded primary, a runoff ballot, and the general election. After Mayor Koch announced for governor, Cuomo said that his rematch would go beyond the state's Democratic convention into the primary and would end differently from last time.

Cuomo's gubernatorial campaign started with the open support of only one "big county" chair, Mayor Erastus Corning II of Albany, and the potential support of the Manhattan County chair, Herman D. Farrel. However, the day following the mayor's announcement, Cuomo was endorsed by the city's Central Labor Council, an endorsement that was an important indicator of his future coalition. According to Bill Haddad, his campaign chair, Cuomo was 35 percentage points behind Koch, and 95 percent of the political organization was against Cuomo (Haddad 1983, 8).

New York Republicans: Lew Who? The Front-Runner

New York Republican leaders played the game of "stop the front-runner," but they did not succeed, and finally they joined him. This was a most unusual performance for the New York Republican leadership, who for decades, under governors Thomas E. Dewey and Nelson Rockefeller, had been used to controlling the nomination. After spending $3 million on TV ads, Lew Lehrman, the multimillionaire who left the Rite Aid discount drugstore chain to run for governor, had become the best-known Republican candidate. In the words of Tim Carey, Lehrman's campaign manager, "When you have the ability that we had here to go directly to the people, to jump over the free media and go to the people, you don't have to worry about what the free media says. By direct mail, telephone, our own paid broadcast commercials, we could go directly to the people" (Carey 1982, 52).

By May 16, a month before the endorsing convention, Lew Lehrman was the choice of 52 percent of Republican voters (Omicinski 1982). He claimed to have the support of chairs of many small counties upstate and two downstate: Staten Island and Suffolk. On the last day, he obtained the support of the Brooklyn leader, which assured him 29.6 percent of the convention vote, more than enough to be on the primary ballot. However, Lehrman did not have the support of most of the party's major leaders, especially Joseph Margiotta, the Nassau County chair and the state's most powerful Republican leader, who led the "stop the front-runner" effort. For the first time in decades, the county leaders were divided and could not consolidate against the feared outsider. The leadership of state chair George Clark was weakened when he tried to stop Lehrman's gubernatorial aspirations by backing state comptroller Ed Regan. But Regan did not have sufficient backing of the other party leaders and decided to seek reelection.

Also in the race was Jim Emery, assembly minority leader. His legislative staff provided jobs for party leaders, twenty-one of whom controlled enough delegate votes to give him a place on the primary ballot. An upstate resident from Geneseo, he was everybody's second choice for governor. Emery had the support of only one large county leader, Anthony Calvita from Westchester. He was not well known and lacked resources.

Another candidate, Richard Rosenbaum of Rochester, was Governor Rockefeller's party chair in 1976. Rosenbaum, a lawyer, also lacked resources and recognition, but had the support of his Monroe County chair and the leader of Bronx County, John Callandra. He said that he had raised $800,000 and received many promises that failed to materialize (Rosenbaum 1982, 3). The party leaders tried to lure him into running for the U.S. Senate (against Moynihan) as a way to eliminate him from the race, but he did not agree. Hence, it appeared that the powerful county leaders who could have stopped Lew Lehrman were divided among several candidates.

As Lehrman's name recognition mounted, some party leaders tried to find a party loyalist who could beat him and turned to Paul Curran. A former state assembly member, and more recently a U.S. attorney, Curran had the support of Warren Anderson, majority leader of the state senate, and Malcolm Wilson, former governor. The Nassau County leader, Joseph M. Margiotta, promised to deliver all of his county, the Manhattan Republican organization supported Curran, and the Erie County Republicans were added soon after that. With this support, he could count on 25 percent of the convention, enough to get on the ballot. Thus, for a month, Curran was not the front-runner but had the support of some powerful members of the Republican establishment.

Colorado Republicans: Leaders Are Neutral

The lead changed during the course of the endorsement campaign between "the show horse and the workhorse" (a campaign slogan of the latter). The party leaders were neutral by party rule until the workhorse won the endorsement. It was another classic example of a grass roots campaign versus a slick media operation. The grass roots candidate won the delegates by a slow and steady accumulation of their support. John Fuhr, the workhorse, ran because he was the only candidate who had held an elected position, and he thought that the party should have a choice. He believed his eight years of state legislative experience, four of them as house speaker, were crucial to candidacy. Fuhr decided to run early in 1981 and announced in November, much earlier than the other major candidate, Phil Winn. Fuhr knew about Winn's potential candidacy when he announced. He also knew that he would have to match his potential rival's money and media with substance and shoe leather.

Phil Winn, former state party chair (1978–81), returned from Washington, D.C,. where he had been federal housing commissioner. His

"Draft Winn for Governor" effort in the summer of 1981 succeeded in placing him in the race. Winn discussed his potential race with state legislative leaders and with the state party officers, but his promise to raise a lot of money did not impress the Colorado Republican leaders as much as their colleagues in New York. Part of the "Draft Winn" campaign was the circulation of three thousand petitions asking Winn to leave his government post in Washington and come back to run. On February 4, Winn announced from the White House lawn that he was going to return to Colorado to run for governor.

Winn succeeded in obtaining the support of two former governors, John Love and John Vanderhoof, U.S. Representative Ken Kramer, but he did not succeed in getting the backing of the Republican leadership, who decided to remain neutral even though Winn's organization and money appeared to give him the only chance of beating incumbent Democrat Lamm.

Steve Schuck, a Colorado Springs developer, wanted to run for governor in August 1981. But just as Schuck was about to start, the "Draft Winn" effort was published in the newspapers, and Schuck pulled out and planned to support Winn. Schuck stayed out of the race until April, barely two months before the endorsing convention. At that point he believed that neither Fuhr nor Winn could beat Lamm and decided to throw his hat into the ring. On May 2, just as the first precinct caucuses were to take place to elect delegates to the county assemblies, Schuck urged Republicans to "keep all your options open." He announced for governor on May 19, promising that he would raise $150,000 before the convention by contributions and personal funds.

Minnesota: Front-Runners Endorsed in Convention
Lose Primary

For a second time, the hypotheses that predict that strong parties can endorse candidates who win the following primary don't hold. Curiously, Minnesota is still a strong party state in the 1990s in that it claims thousands of loyalists in each party who flock to the quadrennial statewide nominating conventions determined to endorse a winner. In 1982, two-thirds of the Democratic delegates had attended a previous convention (Jewell 1984, 77). The state party as a concept is still meaningful to Minnesotans despite the fact that endorsed candidates since 1982 have found opposition in the ensuing primary more formidable. In that year, both state party chairs said in interviews, speeches, and letters to the party faithful that the endorsement system was on trial. If outsiders (i.e., Perpich and Whitney) win, they said, the influence of political parties would diminish, candidates would no longer face the close scrutiny that a party gives, and wealthy candidates would forever have an advantage in political contests in Minnesota.

The advantage that a party gives its endorsee is significant. Party resources—including volunteers, voter name lists, financial support, advertising assistance, and get-out-the-vote support—provide an endorsed candidate significant advantages. In 1982, the Democratic-Farmer-Labor (DFL) party, which had discovered mail solicitation, had more resources than ever before. A Humphrey Day dinner concluded a successful fund drive and gave the party a million-dollar budget for the first time in its history. Meanwhile, the Independent Republican (IR) party was eyeing the DFL nervously from its $2.5 million vantage point. The two parties differ in fund-raising: in the IR, the local units do no fund-raising but rely on an appropriation from the state party for their operating costs; in the DFL, local units do their own fund-raising for operations. Both parties planned to give money to endorsed candidates. The IR party planned a telephone survey and a get-out-the-vote campaign based on its computer file of 1.3 million names. The DFL, not having such an extensive file, bought a list of Minnesota households and planned a survey and a voter mobilization campaign.

In the Minnesota Democratic party in 1982, Walter Spannaus, the state attorney general for three terms, was the front-runner after he announced in June 1981, backed by the party leaders and supported by former governor Wendell Anderson and U.S. Senator Walter Mondale. Spannaus said he was regarded as the candidate for a long time and, in his words, "I was considered the strongest candidate" (Spannaus 1982, 3). He said he had name recognition as attorney general and was well funded. Why then, did he lose the primary to Rudy Perpich?

Perpich, son of an immigrant miner from the Iron Range, prided himself on his populist image. Colorful lore about him abounds: it is said he kept his appointments in the brim of his hat. He was elevated from lieutenant governor to governor in 1976 when Wendell Anderson was appointed to the U.S. Senate. Endorsed by the party in 1978, he lost the election to Republican Al Quie. Perpich had enjoyed being governor for two years and determined to make another try. He returned from Europe, where he had been a trade representative for Control Data Corporation, barely in time to announce for governor in late April 1982. When he returned to "regain Paradise," Perpich read the Minnesota Poll, which showed that he had 93 percent recognition and that Spannaus had 87 percent. He also had a better approval rating than Spannaus and an impressively better rating than any of the Republican candidates (Perpich 1982, 5). He did not seek the endorsement because, in his own words, "I knew I could never be governor through the front door. There has never been someone from northern Minnesota, . . . there has never been a Catholic" (Perpich 1982, 2). Perpich said that the forces that controlled the party would not approve him for the endorsement, and he had to go directly to a primary. But both he and his campaign manager said they respected the endorsement process and were not calling for any changes in it.

The year 1982 was not a good one for the Minnesota Republican party, either. After a bruising convention contest, its gubernatorial endorsee lost to a wealthy investment banker who had never held state political office (Whitney had run for the U.S. Senate in 1964). Six weeks before the endorsing convention, the Minnesota Poll showed that the four early IR candidates to succeed governor Al Quie had failed to gain significant name recognition or favorable ratings. Lieutenant governor Lou Wangberg was better than the others but hardly a household word because 49 percent of the poll didn't know who he was (Minnesota Poll 1982, 1A).

Wangberg appeared poised for a guaranteed endorsement. On January 25, Governor Quie declared he would not run for a second term because of the state's severe economic crisis, which was widely perceived to be his fault. Wangberg was the first choice of top IR officeholders, the governor, U.S. Senator Durenberger, and Minnesota's five Republican U.S. Representatives. Wangberg was considered bright, intelligent, and attractive but lacking in issues and legislative experience. State IR party chair Bill Morris said the support cut two ways: a lot of people are impressed by leadership support, but the activists do not take too well to early endorsements (Dawson 1982). By April 7, Wangberg said he was leading in committed delegates. He did not maintain forward momentum, however, and four others sensing his weakness, threw their hats into the ring to stop the front-runner.

Glen Sherwood, state house minority leader, entered the race on February 16 with a list of specific proposals for "preserving family life and promoting decency" as well as improving the state's troubled economy. Sherwood was elected to the Minnesota House as a DFL member in 1972. It was his displeasure with DFL sponsorship of much of the "antifamily" legislation that prompted him to change parties in 1978. In 1981, he was elected minority leader but was not considered a strong one ([Minnesota] Editorial 1982). He became a lay Christian preacher and a leader of a "pro-life, pro-family" caucus in the legislature.

Of the three remaining additional contenders, Paul Overgaard was the strongest and nearly stole the endorsement away from the top two candidates. He was well qualified, having served six years in the state house and two in the senate. In 1982, he was head of Governor Quie's campaign, but he was suddenly without a candidate when Quie withdrew. Believing that Wangberg's campaign had not caught fire, Overgaard announced his candidacy on April 10, calling for an end to the "tax-and-spend policies" of the DFL, which had controlled the state legislature since 1973. Overgaard said that he anticipated the support of the party leaders because of the success of Senator Durenberger's campaign, which he ran (Overgaard 1982, 7). He claimed that he had the best finance organization, campaign organization, people, and floor organization and the strongest momentum. He believed his business background gave him an advantage, because people want that.

The other two candidates, state senate minority leader Robert Ashbach and state house minority leader David Jennings, also focused on the solution to the economy and jobs. They were fiscal conservatives and social moderates, which differentiated them from the two front-runners. Along with Overgaard, they claimed that Wangberg was linked to Governor Quie's budget problems. Jennings was the most conservative of all and advocated reducing the size of state government. These three candidates for the endorsement had similar appeals, but Overgaard was the strongest.

Wheelock Whitney, who announced on March 15, was the primary challenger hovering in the wings. Whitney said he believed in the endorsement system but knew he could not compete for delegates, because he did not have contacts in the party. Governor Quie's surprise decision not to seek a second term reawakened in Whitney a desire he thought he'd left behind: the desire to be governor. He said he had learned in the investment business that the best time to buy stock is when people say it can't get any lower. He believed that Minnesota was in that period. He said he was convinced that a primary contest would be good for the IR party. It provides the endorsed candidate with the opportunity to get media attention and name identification. Whitney believed he was the strongest candidate because of his financial advantage and the difficulty of fund-raising in such hard economic times. He prided himself in his investment business.

Illinois Democrats

While a half dozen Democratic hopefuls were viewing the Democratic nomination in the summer of 1981, Adlai Stevenson III decided to make the run and announced in September. Stevenson had one of the most illustrious names in modern Illinois politics. His father was governor and nominee for president in 1952 and 1956. Adlai III served in the Illinois General Assembly and as state treasurer before election to the U.S. Senate in 1970 to fill the last four years of Senator Everett Dirkson's term. He was reelected in 1974, but he always wanted to serve Illinois as governor, which is why he did not run for the U.S. Senate in 1980. He said that power was shifting from the federal government to the states. "The authority's in the executive branch—that's clear to anyone who has served in the legislative branch" (Stevenson 1982, 10).

Stevenson said after he decided to seek the nomination, he had many conversations with party leaders and traveled some of the state to develop support. At that time there were other candidates for the nomination who dropped out before the "slate-making." Dan Walker, former governor (1972–76), was the most formidable. Stevenson said he wanted to avoid a primary contest and win the support of the state central committee with as little acrimony as possible to get the party behind him and reserve the party's resources for the fight with the Republicans. It was a daunting task because Stevenson wanted to obtain the endorsement (be "slated") without the support of the Cook County "machine." This machine, formerly headed by the legendary Chicago mayor Richard J. Daley, could control the outcome of the slate-making process because it had the most votes on the State Central Committee (votes weighted according to the number of Democratic ballots cast in the last primary). The machine strategy was to wait until the last minute to pick the candidate for governor and hence control the process. According to Stevenson, it was a liability to be the machine-endorsed candidate in downstate Illinois. "I decided to try to organize the necessary support for the nomination without the support of the Cook County organization" (Stevenson 1982, 2).

Factions and Money

Our hypothesis predicts that candidate factions in strong party states are more personal and less durable than in weak party states. The strong party boasts one leadership coalition, which may consist of one or more factions with continuity and the power to control nominations. The main task of the party leaders in strong party states is to manage the ever present potential for factionalism and to channel the aspirations and energies of rival groups into a semblance of party unity (Jewell and Olson 1982, 52). Candidates are on their own to raise money for their endorsement effort, but I predict that money itself does not buy the endorsement. Once they have been endorsed, they can look forward to the status and organizational support that endorsement confers and hence the money will come more easily. If they are challenged in the primary, they can look forward to the party effort, both monetary and organizational, that attaches to the endorsee. In order to examine the flow of money from various sources, I compiled and summarized each candidate's contributions (tables 5.3–5.9). The information was obtained from official documents, generally from a state board of elections. Most states require primary candidates (whether challenged or not) to file financial statements before a primary and again twenty to thirty days after. For endorsements, the report filed closest to the convention was used. For primary spending, the postprimary summary report was used to calculate primary contributions.

Connecticut: The Leaders Prevail

Connecticut Democrats: The Governor and the Party Regulars

Governor William O'Neill stated that the party had conservatives, moderates, and liberals within it, but that they all melded together to support his candidacy since there was low factionalism within the party. The party chair, James Fitzgerald, was supportive from the start. O'Neill explained that most of the delegates to the convention are "political people rather than from an outside group whether it be labor or elderly or minorities" (O'Neill 1982, 20). Hence, the governor did not actively solicit the support of unions before the endorsement (he got the endorsement of the Teamsters and Building Trades Union), but counted on their support after he received it. Indeed, the members of the immediate "clutch group" that the governor identified as the hard core of his organization were all "political as well as personal friends." The campaign chair was former governor John Dempsey. O'Neill's preconvention money was raised in a series of receptions around the state. Table 5.3 shows that nearly 98 percent of it came in small donations (under $2,500; listed as "Other individuals" in the table).

O'Neill's opponent, Ernest Abate, speaker of the House of Representatives, agreed there was low factionalism within the Democratic party. Abate said most of the factions were personal and ephemeral and that the party was made up of regulars who were interested in power, not ideology. Abate said he represented the small progressive wing of the party organization, which included the progressive unions (e.g., machinists, United Automobile Workers, health care, Federation of Teachers) (Abate 1982, 18–27). As table 5.3 reveals, the unions did not contribute to his campaign fund, however, and over half of it was a bank loan. Abate believed that he could win a primary because, "In this state the progressive candidate is more likely to win a primary than one of the regulars" (Abate 1982, 20). His remarks predicted the gubernatorial primary race in 1994 when Bill Curry, state comptroller and progressive, beat John Larson, the endorsed senate president pro tem. In spite of all this, Abate said most progressives supported the regulars within the party organization because they were politically involved at the local level and did not want to buck the power structure.

Connecticut Republicans: Rome the Party Healer versus Opponents

Factions in the Republican party are based on personal followings that change from election to election. According to 1982 candidate Lewis Rome, not even the bitterness remains stable. Two strong personalities, Fred Biebel, former party chair, and Lowell Weicker, U.S. Senator, shared power in the party, but their personal alliances shifted for each election. Rome could support either alliance and survive: indeed, he considered himself the healer in the party. His campaign organization was broad based and included people on the state central committee, legislators, and town chairs. Rome admitted that his major opponent was busily collecting support from the same groups. Table 5.3 indicates that Rome's support was widespread in that about two-thirds of his campaign chest consisted of individual donations (under $2,500) and one-third his personal loans.

TABLE 5.3. Sources of Contributions for Gubernatorial Conventions in Connecticut (in percentages)

	Democrats		Republicans			
	O'Neill	Abate	Rome	Bozutto	Labriola	Post
Candidate and candidate loans	0.0	0.0	34.0	56.9	19.4	6.4
Other loans	0.0	52.1	0.0	0.0	0.0	0.0
Transfers	0.0	0.0	0.0	0.0	0.0	0.0
Party	0.0	0.0	0.0	0.3	0.0	0.0
Interest Groups						
Business	2.5	0.0	0.0	0.2	0.1	0.0
Professional	0.0	0.0	0.4	0.5	0.0	0.0
Labor	0.0	0.0	0.0	0.0	0.0	0.0
Agriculture	0.0	0.0	0.0	0.0	0.0	0.0
General/Policy	0.0	0.0	0.0	0.0	0.0	0.0
Other	0.0	0.0	0.0	0.0	0.0	0.0
Large donors	0.0	0.0	0.0	0.0	0.0	0.0
Other individuals	97.5	47.9	65.6	42.1	80.5	93.6
Total percentage	100.0	100.0	100.0	100.0	100.0	100.0
Total dollars	$203,961	$293,789	$374,255	$399,015	$206,039	$187,200

Dick Bozzuto agreed with Lew Rome that factionalism within the party was weak and that personal coalitions would shift over time. He said that he did not represent a faction within the party nor did he want that. He said that the endorsement process is party oriented and hence outside groups sit back and wait until a candidate is chosen before they commit. Bozzuto spent more than Rome in the attempt to capture the endorsement. As table 5.3 shows, nearly 57 percent of this money was given or loaned by the candidate himself; the rest came mostly from individuals.

Gerald Labriola did not announce until October 1981. He was a first-term senator, having been chosen Freshman Senator of the Year. He pulled remnants of his senatorial campaign together for fund-raising and publicity. He counted on delegate votes from Republican Fairfield County in southwestern Connecticut. He had few ties with the regular Republican organizations, however, and his support was meager and shallow. He agreed with the other candidates that the party had ephemeral factions based on personal followings and that he was in third place. As illustrated in table 5.3, he raised only half as much as each of his major rivals, most of it (80.5 percent) from one hundred individuals.

Rusty Post was an articulate state legislator best known for sponsoring the "bottle bill" (recycling) but stated sorrowfully, "A convention state rewards prior contact. So for me, all of the groups I had worked with . . . were of zero value in a convention where so much depends on who the town chairman happens to know of the different candidates, and decisions are based on prior knowledge and personal relationships, rather than on issues and coalitions" (Post 1982, 4). Senator Post discovered that there is a vast difference between building a legislative coalition and a nominating coalition. The first was public coalition building, the second was organizational, where prior political contact was key. Table 5.3 shows that Post raised less than the other candidates, and his contributions—nearly 94 percent from individual donors—had slowed to a trickle in the second quarter of the year. After eight months, he had garnered only 20 or so delegates out of 933 who were to attend the convention. Post withdrew on July 16, leaving the race to the three remaining contenders.

New York: Power Struggles within Each Party

New York Democrats: Endorsed Koch versus
Challenger Cuomo

While Mayor Ed Koch knew that he would receive the designation because he had enough votes on the State Committee, he realized that a primary fight was probable and he needed to put together a coalition of factions and voters. The municipal unions—engineers, police, firefighters, and teamsters—supported the mayor and worked for him. But the prize union, according to Koch's campaign managers, was the United Federation of Teachers, which supported Cuomo and helped him obtain the AFL-CIO endorsement on August 8. "If I had to point to anything in the campaign that was a major turning point, I would point to that," said Koch campaign manager Peter Piscatelli (Piscatelli 1982, 13).

Koch had just won the mayoralty the year before with 75 percent of the vote as the candidate of both the Republican and Democratic parties, and he counted on this support. He counted on the Jewish vote, which had always supported him and made up about 30 percent of the Democratic vote in a statewide primary. He could not count on the Italian vote or the votes of other minorities because Cuomo was appealing to them. Koch was habitually criticized for his rhetoric against African-Americans and Hispanics.

The state chair raised funds for Koch's campaign in Suffolk County, but he had to raise them independently of the party because party funds cannot be given to a primary campaign. Table 5.4 reveals Koch raised over $3.6 million, about half of it from interest groups (bankers, law firms, and real estate companies) and half from individual donors, both large and small. Koch was correct in insisting that he did nothing illegal in accepting this money.

Meanwhile, the Cuomo coalition was building toward an upset. It was, in the words of Cuomo's campaign manager, Bill Haddad, "a modern Roosevelt coalition." Cuomo took the union people and made them part of his campaign because he needed professionals. The coalition Cuomo put together encompassed unions, minorities, the disabled, the elderly, the liberals—"the Bobby Kennedy type coalition" (Haddad 1983, 4). He received labor endorsements from the United Auto Workers, the Communications Workers of America, and the United Federation of Teachers. The Civil Service Employees Association, claiming 225,000 members, was ready to put its members on the streets for the lieutenant governor. Fifty thousand Italian-Americans were identified by telephone as Cuomo focused on the primary from day one.

As Governor Hugh Carey's emissary on behalf of the governor's programs, Cuomo visited many New York regions that rarely saw top public officials. Albany mayor Erastus Corning said that those visits were remembered, and on primary day, Cuomo carried Albany County by a ratio of better than three-to-one.

A very important part of Cuomo's coalition was the Liberal party, which endorsed him for governor. This endorsement gave him a position on the ballot for the general election whether or not he won the Democratic nomination. It is difficult to assess the impact of the Liberal party. Cuomo believed he was advantaged by the endorsement and stated that in modern times, no statewide Democratic candidate had ever won without it (Cuomo 1984, 221–22).

Cuomo raised less than $2 million for the primary, nearly two-thirds of it (62.6 percent) from small donations (under $5,000). The disparity between his funding and Koch's was notable. Almost $1 million separated their spending up until the time of the convention, and almost $2 million overall. Part of this disparity was overcome by incorporating the unions into the Cuomo organization, providing the free bodies to walk the streets, make the phone calls, and shepherd voters to the polls.

One striking observation about this Democratic struggle for the nomination was the general agreement that the party as an entity was important. Both sides agreed that winning the governorship was paramount and that the groups and factions would get together for a general election victory. Haddad said the major rifts were over jobs and power. The minor rifts were ideological and had to do with the growing concern of the blue-collar workers over taxes and minorities. He said of the rival factions, "well, they were against us but they worked like hell for us in the general

TABLE 5.4. Sources of Contributions for Democratic Gubernatorial Nominations in New York (in percentages)

	Koch		Cuomo	
	Convention	Primary	Convention	Primary
Candidate and				
candidate loans	0.0	0.0	0.1	0.1
Other loans	0.0	0.0	0.0	0.0
Transfers	0.0	0.0	0.1	0.1
Party	0.0	0.2	0.1	0.1
Interest groups				
Business	36.4	36.6	9.1	12.6
Professional	3.9	4.5	2.0	1.8
Labor	2.8	3.3	11.0	13.5
Agriculture	0.1	0.6	0.3	0.2
General/Policy	0.7	1.2	0.8	2.1
Other	0.3	1.0	3.2	1.6
Large donors	24.0	23.5	10.1	5.3
Other individuals	31.8	29.1	63.2	62.6
Total percentage	100.0	100.0	100.0	100.0
Total dollars	$1,800,098	$3,676,695	$921,231	$1,940,070

election. The main part of that is due to the fact that they liked Mario"
(Haddad 1983, 15).

New York Republicans: Lehrman the Outsider versus the Insiders

Lew Lehrman billed himself as a supply-side economist, picking up the
torch that the Reagan administration dropped. He also promoted radical
reform that would reduce the scope and limit the nature of state government. In addition, he promised to reform the political process, which
explains why the party leaders tried to stop him. Lehrman's "coalition"
was amorphous: it was a TV coalition, backed up by some strategic
ground organization. He ran on his record as a business owner, worth
about $30 million. He built the Rite Aid discount drug store from a small
family business to a billion-dollar company and was its president from
1969 to 1977.

From the outset of the campaign, which began in December 1991,
Lehrman held a trump card. He was the choice of the Conservative party's
leadership and received that party's endorsement, which meant that he
would appear on the ballot whether or not he received the Republican
nomination. He was an obvious choice for the Conservative party. He
attacked Governor Carey's Democratic administration for high crime and
high taxes and promised to double the police force, sign a death penalty
law, and lower corporate taxes.

As table 5.5 reveals, Lew Lehrman provided most of the funds for his
record-setting campaign. He donated almost 60 percent of his contributions for the convention endorsement and about 75 percent of his primary
campaign funds. There is no limit on a candidate's own spending for his
campaign. The limit on campaign contributions by Republican donors
based on their party's enrollment was $12,984. The media advertising that
these funds made possible transformed the multimillionaire from a political unknown to the front-runner for the Republican nomination. Lehrman
outspent his primary competitor, Paul Curran, twenty-six times over.

Curran represented the "old guard" of the Republican party. Drafted
in mid-May by Joe Margiotta of Nassau County to run against Lehrman,
Curran was supposed to be the organization's alternative to the feared
"outsider." But we have noticed that the county leaders were not united in
this endeavor. Perhaps it was because Margiotta had been convicted of
federal mail fraud and extortion and was appealing the conviction at that
time. Hence, the strongest county leader was wounded, and the iron fist of
Rockefeller had disappeared. So, the foundling Republican party leaders
put up Curran in a hope for unity, which it did not achieve, and one by one

they left him dangling on the end of a limb. His contributions reveal his lack of support. He raised less for the nomination than any other candidate—and two of them dropped out after the endorsing convention.

These last two candidates, Jim Emery and Richard Rosenbaum, offered themselves as viable candidates. Emery's rationale for running was solid. He was the assembly minority leader and knew state government and the issues. He realized that he could not achieve what he wanted for the state as minority leader and began to think toward the governorship in 1979 when he hired George Humphreys to be on his staff. He counted on a network of fellow legislators and upstate county chairs, whom he helped with patronage. He represented the small-county upstate faction of the party. As did the others, Humphreys, Emery's campaign manager, said that the factionalism within the party was low and that it was mostly regional. Table 5.5 shows that he raised more than half a million dollars, 61 percent of it from individual donors (contributing less than $5,000 apiece). While this shows he had broad popular support, Emery was way behind Lehrman and even Rosenbaum in fund-raising.

Rosenbaum asked Lehrman during a debate why he kept knocking "professional politicians." Rosenbaum was proud to say he was a politician: politics is a way to help people. Rosenbaum represented the rem-

TABLE 5.5. Sources of Contributions for Republican Gubernatorial Nominations in New Y (in percentages)

	Rosenbaum Convention	Emery Convention	Lehrman Convention	Lehrman Primary	Curran Convention	Curran Prim:
Candidate and candidate loans	0.0	0.0	58.3	75.2	0.0	0.
Other loans	0.0	0.0	0.0	0.6	0.0	0.
Transfers	0.0	0.2	0.0	0.0	0.0	0.
Party	0.2	1.0	0.0	0.0	0.0	0.
Interest groups						
Business	25.9	26.5	3.0	2.6	21.7	15.
Professional	2.4	1.5	0.0	0.0	1.5	0.
Labor	0.0	1.5	0.0	0.0	0.4	0.
Agriculture	0.7	1.0	0.0	0.0	0.0	0.
General/Policy	0.0	1.2	0.0	0.2	0.0	0.
Other	0.0	0.0	0.0	0.1	0.0	0.
Large donors	38.7	6.1	9.8	6.0	28.6	30.:
Other individuals	32.1	61.0	28.9	15.3	47.8	53.:
Total percentage	100.0	100.0	100.0	100.0	100.0	100.(
Total dollars	$750,812	$578,998	$4,305,300	$10,177,955	$114,644	$394,992

nants of Nelson Rockefeller's once potent organization. The late governor made him state chair, and he was renowned for his anti-Reagan stance at the 1976 Republican convention. The New York Republicans have shifted to the right of their famous governor, and many of the party activists resented both Rockefeller and Rosenbaum for their former grip on party activities. Rosenbaum raised about $750,000, roughly one-third each from business, large donors, and other individuals. But his coalition did not work because it was too moderate and underfunded.

Colorado: Front-runner Coalitions Are Stronger

Governor Lamm's Broad-based Coalition

David Miller, Governor Richard Lamm's speech writer, believes factionalism is low in the Colorado Democratic party and tends to be based on personalities more than on ideologies. The governor had widespread support within the party. His original coalition included environmentalists, and he led the movement to prohibit the Olympics from coming to Colorado. During the 1974 campaign Lamm expanded his coalition to include the traditional Democratic groups: labor unions, many farm groups, African-American and Hispanic groups, and women's groups. In this process he had to keep his original base and move toward the business community—a considerable feat.

Governor Lamm had trouble holding on to his support from the Hispanic community, based on two issues: bilingual education and immigration. The governor incurred the wrath of the Hispanics by not vetoing a bill that abolished bilingual education. The second issue involved Lamm's position that immigration laws must be tightened or the economy would be in serious trouble. Lamm and the Democratic party knew that Hispanics were becoming a strong faction within the party and were rising to positions of leadership.

Table 5.6 shows that the governor received strong support from the private-sector business groups. His campaign finance statements showed that he received nearly 18 percent of his campaign chest from business. About 8 percent came from labor. Almost 60 percent was contributed by individuals, slightly under half of that amount (25.9 percent) from large donors (over $5,000).

Republicans: Fuhr the Moderate, Winn the Conservative

John Fuhr, the moderate, believed he appealed to all factions within the Republican party, although he believed factionalism was fairly high. He identified the Christian Right as one of the factions and said he took a moderate position on the issue of abortion and thus would receive some of its support. He estimated the strength of the Christian Right as 35 percent of the delegates to the assembly. He billed himself as a moderate with a broad coalition. As table 5.6 reveals, 66 percent of Fuhr's modest campaign funds came from small (less than $5,000) individual donors, and 31 percent he gave or loaned the campaign.

Phil Winn was the conservative, a Reagan person, who predicted that the party was going conservative like himself. His campaign researcher David Diepenbroch said, "If we could reestablish the conservative coalition we would have a very good shot at winning fifty percent of the delegate voters" (Diepenbroch 1982, 16). Although Winn was Jewish, he received support from some of the Christian Right who sent their children to Christian private schools and did not want state interference. Because Winn had been Republican party chair, he counted on support from the county party organizations. Diepenbroch believed that the factions were based on ideology but that they also were personal in that they grouped about the candidates themselves and lasted as long as the candidates strove for office and then floated into different coalitions.

TABLE 5.6.   Sources of Contributions for Gubernatorial Conventions in Colorado (in percentages)

| | Democrat | Republicans | | |
	Lamm	Fuhr	Winn	Schuck
Candidate and candidate loans	1.1	31.0	0.3	96.1
Other loans	0.0	0.0	1.1	0.0
Transfers	0.0	0.0	0.0	0.0
Party	0.0	0.0	0.0	0.0
Interest groups				
Business	17.8	0.8	52.9	0.0
Professional	0.4	0.0	0.2	0.0
Labor	7.6	0.0	0.0	0.0
Agriculture	0.9	0.0	1.9	0.0
General/Policy	0.7	0.0	0.0	0.0
Other	11.7	2.2	3.8	2.6
Large donors	25.9	0.0	15.2	0.0
Other individuals	33.9	66.0	24.6	1.3
Total percentage	100.0	100.0	100.0	100.0
Total dollars	$270,013	$122,734	$833,502	$142,621

Phil Winn was an energetic fund-raiser, as table 5.6 proves. The chair of the fund-raising committee, Larry Mizel, had strong banking, real estate, and oil connections. That gave the candidate entree into three of the major areas of fund-raising. More than half of Winn's money came from business interests, and a reading of his campaign finance reports shows that the building and construction industry gave a generous amount of that total. About 15 percent of his funds came from donors who each gave over $5,000. Thus, roughly 70 percent of Winn's money came from business and the wealthy. The money was raised for media.

The truth about the third candidate, Steve Schuck, was that he didn't have a coalition. According to Walt Klein, his campaign manager, Schuck had not been active in the party and "had none of that baggage with him on one side or the other" (Klein 1982, 21). But "that baggage" is what helps win endorsement votes. Klein said he believed factionalism was moderate and based primarily on ideology. Schuck got in the race too late to develop a coalition, and his campaign was financed almost totally by himself (96.1 percent, as shown in table 5.6).

Minnesota: Power Struggles within Each Party

Democratic-Farmer-Labor: Spannaus the Party Regular,
Perpich the Irregular

Walter Spannaus was a well-known and respected leader of the Democratic-Farmer-Labor (DFL) party. His moderately liberal stance seemed to be as close as possible to the mainstream of the party. DFL party chair Mike Hatch, Spannaus, and a group of three dozen party leaders calling themselves "the Centrists" organized to keep a lid on factionalism. They stressed jobs and the economy and tried to minimize peripheral issues such as abortion and gun control. Spannaus was vulnerable on both, however. The abortion issue remained a deep source of division in the DFL. Spannaus supported the party's platform, which approved "medically safe legal abortions," and opposed a constitutional amendment banning them. He said he was opposed by some pro lifers, but many were supporting him, and he estimated that they represented about 25 percent of the party. As state attorney general, he had gained the enmity of anti–gun control groups, including the powerful National Rifle Association, by pushing for tighter handgun controls. In spite of these two ideological issues, Spannaus believed that factionalism within the party was low. He was supported by most unions—including the Teamsters, UAW, Minnesota AFL-CIO, the Police, the Firefighters, United Transportation Union, Railway and Airline Clerks, and Locomotive Engineers—and the Sierra Club. As table 5.7 indicates, Spannaus raised more than $600,000 for the convention solely from individual donors, 84.2 percent of whom made modest contributions. His nearly $1 million for the primary included a few more varied sources, but still, more than 90 percent of his money came from individual contributions both large and small.

Rudy Perpich claimed that he belonged to the liberal wing of the DFL party but that he differed from Spannaus more in style and personality because factionalism in the party was low. His base was in the Iron Range in northeastern Minnesota, a depressed area for the iron ore miners. The area casts many votes in a Democratic primary, and they were likely to support one of their own. The range was proud of the miner's son who became governor, and they were prepared to support him for another term. Perpich favored qualified constitutional limits on abortion and ran advertisements in Catholic papers across the state emphasizing his pro life position. In the months before the primary, the National Rifle Association sent letters to its Minnesota members urging support for Perpich, even urging its members to cross over if necessary to vote against Spannaus in the Democratic primary. Perpich was not a good fund-raiser, raising about $140,000, almost all of it (90.4 percent) from small individual donations. The Perpich campaign cost only 48 cents for every vote he received

TABLE 5.7. Sources of Contributions for Democratic Gubernatorial Nominations in Minnesota (in percentages)

	Spannaus		Perpich
	Convention	Primary	Primary
Candidate and candidate loans	0.0	0.0	0.0
Other loans	0.0	0.0	0.0
Transfers	0.0	0.4	1.6
Party	0.0	3.1	0.0
Interest groups			
Business	0.0	1.2	1.4
Professional	0.0	0.1	0.7
Labor	0.0	0.0	0.8
Agriculture	0.0	0.0	0.0
General/Policy	0.0	0.3	1.1
Other	0.0	1.7	0.0
Large donors	15.8	10.2	4.0
Other individuals	84.2	83.0	90.4
Total percentage	100.0	100.0	100.0
Total dollars	$639,427	$990,344	$138,758

in the primary—less than was spent by any other gubernatorial winner in the country who had serious opposition (Jewell 1984, 258).

Independent Republicans: The Economic Conservatives,
the Moderates, and the Religious Right

Lou Wangberg's campaign manager said the factions in the Independent Republican (IR) party are based on temporary candidate followings—with the exception of one issue, abortion, dividing the party. Wangberg was an economic conservative who endorsed many of the tenets of the Christian activists, as had Governor Al Quie. He received the support of the retiring governor and the party regulars. As the campaign progressed and other candidates challenged him for the endorsement, he hoped to attract both Sherwood people and Overgaard people and win as a compromise. According to campaign reports shown in table 5.8, Wangberg, the front-runner, raised more than the other candidates for endorsement, and 100 percent of it was from donations under $5,000.

Glen Sherwood, the lay preacher from Pine River, had strong support from fundamentalist Christians. He had led a loose-knit "pro-decency"

TABLE 5.8. Sources of Contributions for Republican Gubernatorial Nominations in Minnesota (in percentages)

	Sherwood Convention	Overgaard Convention	Wangberg Convention	Wangberg Primary	Whitney Primary
Candidate and candidate loans	0.0	0.0	0.0	0.0	81.7
Other loans	19.0	0.9	0.0	0.0	0.0
Transfers	0.0	0.0	0.0	6.7	0.0
Party	1.4	0.0	0.0	1.8	0.0
Interest groups					
Business	0.0	0.5	0.0	0.2	0.0
Professional	0.0	0.0	0.0	0.5	0.0
Labor	0.0	0.0	0.0	0.0	0.0
Agriculture	0.0	0.0	0.0	0.0	0.0
General/Policy	0.0	0.0	0.0	1.3	0.0
Other	0.0	0.0	0.0	0.0	0.1
Large donors	12.2	29.0	0.0	0.0	1.6
Other individuals	67.3	69.6	100.0	89.5	16.6
Total percentage	100.0	100.0	100.0	100.0	100.0
Total dollars	$81,672	$110,203	$173,581	$224,849	$934,661

caucus in the state legislature that sought to ban abortions, cut down on the availability of pornography, reduce the accessibility of drug and alcohol paraphernalia for young people, and strengthen parental rights. Sherwood said that his coalition was a very broad coalition of people who had deep concerns about the family, that cut across all kinds of political lines and all kinds of denominational lines. He believed that he could tap this group in the same way that the Moral Majority brought conservative Christians to the polls for Ronald Reagan in 1980.

That belief notwithstanding, Sherwood felt that the amount of factionalism within the party was low to moderate and had economic and ideological bases. The new conservative Republicans, he felt, were a lot less elitist than the "old moderate Republicans with the diamond rings" (Sherwood 1982, 11). The new conservatives were lowbrows representing farmers, small-business people, resort owners. Sherwood called himself both an economic conservative and a social conservative.

The Christians Alert for Liberty and Morality (CALM), newly organized in 1980, made its debut in the 1982 precinct caucuses, sending training material to three hundred to four hundred Minnesota churches. Its directors conducted training sessions in churches around the state the month before the caucuses in February. It set up a caucus information hot line and distributed sample resolutions on such issues as abortion and school prayer. CALM published the voting record of IR candidates for governor, highlighting Sherwood's campaign for moral decency. The IR Prolife Caucus, a network of people already in the party, urged its precinct leaders to get abortion opponents to IR caucuses. Table 5.8 shows that Sherwood's campaign coffers did not fill as full as those of the other candidates, but he surely received more prayers.

Paul Overgaard began late after he perceived that Lou Wangberg's campaign was faltering. Because of his previous success as a campaign manager and his twenty-five years of party activity, including legislative service, he assumed the role as "healer" in the party. His appeal was based on experience as a party centrist: a moderate conservative. He believed that small-business people would be drawn to his campaign because their interests were denied by the Democratic-controlled state legislature. He counted on the support of forty Republican legislators in the house who would support him "on the first or second ballot." He thought factions in the party were moderate, and the main one was based on family issues. But he said that even the Christian Right could identify a second choice, "so I think they can be reasonable" (Overgaard 1982, 12). As a centrist, Overgaard was counting on support from more people who considered him their second choice than their first. In fund-raising, Overgaard was effective with business leaders like Apache Corporation's Ray Plank. He tapped some of the same sources as Wheelock Whitney, raising about a third of his money from large donors.

Wheelock Whitney said he took five weeks to decide to run for governor and ten seconds to decide not to seek the party endorsement. He believed that the delegates to the convention were outside the mainstream of the Republican party thinking. He said their main concern was the abortion issue and that he did not want to be judged on that one issue. "I am a stranger to them and they are a stranger to me" (Whitney 1982, 10). He perceived himself to be in the mainstream of the IR party, which he said believes that abortion is a private, personal decision and not a government decision (12). Other than that issue, he did not think the Republican party at large had continuing factions. It had a broad umbrella, and he said he represented a moderate position. He thought the most important issue in the state was the economy, and as a businessperson, he would be well suited to govern. As a multi-millionaire, he said he had money of his own to contribute, and the campaign finance records reflected in table 5.8 show that he raised nearly $935,000 for the primary, 81.7 percent of which was given by himself.

Illinois: Front-runner Coalitions Prevail

Illinois Republicans: Thompson in Control

Governor Jim Thompson represented a moderate metropolitan-area Republican. He was very much an arbiter of factions within the party, although his campaign aides did not think factionalism was strong. He courted labor and received endorsements and substantial contributions. Thompson attended the national and state AFL-CIO conventions to boost labor support for his reelection. The Teamsters, with a membership of 165,000, endorsed him. He did well with the individual trade unions, Operating Engineers, and Service Employees International, from which he gained financial, electoral, and campaign support.

Thompson's coalition included the professional groups, such as the Illinois Education Association. He raised nearly a fifth of his money from the business community. In 1982 he received strong support from the Illinois Chamber of Commerce, which had been cool before because of Thompson's closeness to labor.

Illinois politics has traditionally been a contest between Chicago and "downstate" for both parties. For the Republicans in 1982, which marked the first election with all single-member legislative districts, the contest became one of suburban versus downstate, with suburban being the stronger force. The party had to remain broad based. Party support in downstate counties depended upon old Civil War loyalties, and the Republican counties had been pro-Union. "The guy who serves on the local highway crew for the state may be a big Republican for the area," said Phil O'Connor, Thompson's campaign manager (O'Connor 1982, 17). So the party had to be broad enough to appeal to lunch-pail Republicans. Thompson always had the support of the ethnic white population of Chicago but never the black vote.

In Illinois, factionalism is a case of personal factions, a contest for control. "It is much more like the old style in South American coups where you never shot the guys you took over from because there might be a coup next week and you don't want to get anybody into bad habits," noted Phil O'Connor (O'Connor 1982, 26).

Table 5.9 shows that Thompson had raised a massive amount of money by late July 1991, the time when he launched his reelection campaign. Over $1 million of it was raised at a July fund-raiser attended by President Reagan and came from gifts under $5,000. Most of the rest was in the Citizens for Thompson account, the funds that never ceased. This money effectively stopped any significant opponent from challenging the governor in a primary and was put away for the general election.

TABLE 5.9.   Sources of Contributions for Gubernatorial Nominations in Illinois (in percentages)

| | Democrats | | Republican |
	Stevenson	Walker	Thompson
Candidate and candidate loans	0.0	2.7	0.0
Other loans	0.0	0.0	0.0
Transfers	0.0	30.6	0.0
Party	4.3	5.3	1.4
Interest groups			
Business	0.0	13.7	18.7
Professional	0.0	3.0	1.0
Labor	0.0	0.0	2.6
Agriculture	0.0	0.0	0.8
General/Policy	0.0	0.0	0.4
Other	0.0	0.0	1.4
Large donors	0.0	0.0	5.1
Other individuals	95.7	44.7	68.6
Total percentage	100.0	100.0	100.0
Total dollars	$35,050	$37,550	$2,030,189

Illinois Democrats: Stevenson Doesn't Fit the Pattern

Democratic gubernatorial candidate Adlai Stevenson III said "I don't put together coalitions: that's what my opponents do" (Stevenson 1982, 11). He said that appealing for funds from PACs makes a candidate so compromised as to be incapable of representing the general interest. With that attitude, he lost the support of most of organized labor because he didn't vote for labor while in the U.S. Senate. He received tepid backing from the United Automobile Workers (UAW) by winning a vote between himself and Governor Thompson with fourteen out of twenty-seven members of the union's governing board.

Education groups were cool to Stevenson because he suggested cutting back on what he deemed "garbage education" programs, such as drivers' education, physical education, health education, and the like (Stevenson 1982, 13). He also refused to support the demand of the Illinois Education Association for a state law that would mandate collective bargaining at the local level because he was in favor of local control. Thus, he lost the support of this group, which had always supported him in the past. He was supported by the Illinois Federation of Teachers, who usually supported Democratic candidates. Stevenson discussed the upstate-versus-downstate division within the party traditionally based on regulars versus the independents. Stevenson had traditionally won the support of both the independents and the regulars. This time, however, he won the nomination without the core of regulars from Cook County. The traditional division of upstate versus downstate is more fluid now that the Cook County base is weaker. The suburbs are becoming more independent as people move out of Chicago. The city of Chicago now contributes only about half of the total Democratic primary vote, thus lessening its influence. And in 1982, the Chicago organization was ridden with personal factions following the death of Mayor Richard J. Daley in 1976.

Stevenson prided himself that nearly all of his preconvention money—95.7 percent, as shown in table 5.9—came from "individuals, people interested in good government" (Stevenson 1982, 12). The paltry sum of $35,000 was all that was needed to convince a majority of the twenty-four-member State Central Committee that he should receive the endorsement.

Strategies and Results

The hypotheses predict that the party will be the vehicle through which the nominee is selected in the endorsing convention. The leaders will be instrumental in candidate selection by engineering, if not controlling, the outcome. If the party makes endorsements before the primary takes place and if these endorsements are seldom overturned, candidates must get the approval of the leadership coalition. There is a close relationship between the candidate and the party in the preprimary endorsement races, a relationship that is determined by the rules under which the party conventions are held and the process that permits the candidate to be well known by the time he or she sets foot in the convention hall. Since it is the party organization that confers the endorsement, not the electorate, money is not a controlling resource in these contests. If the endorsed candidate is challenged in the primary, the hypotheses predict that the party and party-affiliated groups provide services crucial to the primary campaign.

The Governors Win Hands Down

The governors and the party leaders had developed a symbiotic relationship for the four years in office, and the governors' renomination was assured. However, the governors amassed substantial campaign war chests to choke off and otherwise discourage challengers and to start spending for the general election.

Governor O'Neill of Connecticut

Governor William O'Neill said his first priority was his nomination and elimination of a primary threat. He called on the party network he had known for sixteen years, and it "came forward." Because of the network, he knew he could carry his own congressional district and the four big cities of Hartford, New Haven, Waterbury, and Bridgeport. Then he worked for 80 percent of the delegate vote in order to shut down Ernest Abate's primary challenge, which depended upon a 20 percent vote in the convention. In O'Neill's words, "I had to show that not only could I win the election, I could murder anybody trying to take the nomination away, which we did" (O'Neill 1982, 22).

The strategy succeeded. The Democratic convention gave Abate only 14 percent of the delegate's votes and later nominated O'Neill by acclamation. The party organization controlled the outcome. When it was clear that the governor had the votes to stop a challenge, Abate was allowed to second his own nomination as a means of addressing the assembled delegates prior to the first ballot. It was a well-received address, but it did not change the vote of any delegates. In accord with party unity, Abate pledged his support for O'Neill. After spending $294,000 on his challenge, Abate was prevented from going any farther. Abate lost the challenge due to one of the oldest unwritten laws of politics: It is nearly impossible to successfully challenge an incumbent governor who has made no major errors.

Governor Lamm of Colorado Builds Up the Party

The full-blown Lamm operation resembled a typical governor's organization. Press coverage was divided between Governor Richard Lamm's office for his official duties and his campaign headquarters for his campaign efforts. Media advertising was another activity handled by the campaign organization. Governors, of course, have the advantage that press coverage can advertise the candidate, and press coverage is constant.

Lamm wanted to show that he was not taking the Democratic party for granted and was not taking his nomination for granted. "So we probably worked just as hard as we would have if there was a primary," said David Miller, Lamm speech writer (Miller 1982, 10). Lamm announced his intention to seek a third term on the eve of the precinct caucuses on May 3, the first step in selecting convention delegates.

The 3,500 state assembly delegates made Lamm their gubernatorial candidate by acclamation. But as the other delegates gave Lamm an enthusiastic standing ovation, 75 of the assembly's 300 Hispanic delegates marched out of Currigan Convention Center to protest the governor's stance on immigration and bilingual education. Manny Rodriguez, chair of the Colorado Chicano Caucus, said that his group decided not to endorse Lamm but was not urging its members to vote Republican.

The governor had good relationships with the party and its candidates and offered them help. He was most eager to elect enough Democrats to ensure a "veto support" legislature, and he provided research and other assistance to the party's legislative candidates. Thus, the Colorado Democrats offered an example of a united party in which the merger of the governor's campaign organization with that of the party was accomplished.

Governor Thompson: An Assured Victory

Governor Jim Thompson did not consider the March primary a major event although he had two minor challengers. His media consultants were the firm of Bailey, Deardourff and Associates, and his pollster was Robert Teeter. He asked Bob Kjellander, his legislative liaison, to move to campaign headquarters and advise the campaign.

The governor's Citizens for Thompson continued to raise money for the general election. Thus the governor was able to take charge of his party, win the primary for himself and his lieutenant governor, and control the underticket. This was a merge of a personal coalition with the Republican party with the blessing of the party chair.

The Challengers

Connecticut Republicans: The Party Leaders Maneuver

Lew Rome had the support of the party leadership, and that meant votes of delegates loyal to the leaders. Bozzuto had a superior organization, which he had been cultivating for a year and a half. He claimed the existing organization reached "into virtually every town" (Bozzuto 1982, 6). Both Rome and Bozzuto hoped to come to the convention with 51 percent of the delegates (467 delegates), but neither was able to do so because it was so close, and because there was a third candidate. In one sense, Gerald Labriola, the friendly pediatrician, played the most crucial role of all. He held the balance of power and eventually threw the endorsement to Lew Rome. His plans were to obtain 20 percent of the votes in order to challenge in a primary. When he realized, shortly before the convention, that he would not receive that percentage, his strategy changed to that of deadlocking—hoping to be everyone's second choice after the first ballot commitments were off. But the party leaders could prevent that.

On the first roll call, the count was Rome 414 (44 percent), Bozzuto 392 (42 percent), and Labriola 122 (13 percent). Under the convention's rules, delegates can switch their votes before the closing of the ballot. Labriola's supporters began to switch to either Rome or Bozzuto. At that moment, Labriola entered the hall and released his delegates, saying, however, that he favored Rome. His delegates divided, with approximately 70 going to Rome and 50 to Bozzuto. Hence, the final vote was close: Rome garnered 52 percent and Bozzuto 48 percent. It was no surprise that Labriola accepted the candidacy for lieutenant governor. A Rome-Labriola alliance had been rumored for months before the convention.

The question that remained as the delegates packed up and went home was the possibility of a primary challenge by Bozzuto. Traditionally convention choices have not been challenged. Bozzuto had a hard choice to make since he came so close to winning. He had a sizable campaign debt ($113,000 out of pocket). Both Lowell Weicker, U.S. Senator, and Ralph Capecelatro, the party chair, urged him to shun a primary challenge. On August 5, Bozzuto announced that he would not primary, a customary choice in Connecticut where a party endorsement is taken seriously.

Connecticut: The Governor Is Reelected

Lew Rome and a united Republican party kicked off the gubernatorial campaign in Fairfield County, where one third of the party's enrolled voters are concentrated. Meanwhile, Governor O'Neill, who was ahead in the polls, initiated a low-key campaign with the hope that incumbency and traditional partisan advantage would carry him into office. (At that time the 1,644,498 registered voters were 40 percent Democratic, 27 percent Republican, and 33 percent unaffiliated; not too different from 1994, which was 38 percent Democratic, 26 percent Republican, and 36 percent unaffiliated). It turned out to be a successful game plan; Governor O'Neill campaigned as little as possible and maintained a low profile. Lew Rome could never convince the voters that there was need for a change in administration. While he charged the O'Neill administration with corruption and incompetence, the governor continued to cut ribbons and break ground. The polls taken in October showed the incumbent winning by a substantial margin (20 to 30 percent). This information had an effect on Rome's ability to raise funds. Because of it, he could not engage the "media blitz" over the New York City television stations to appeal to the Fairfield County voters. When the votes were counted, the governor beat the challenger by 7 percent. The results prove that an incumbent governor who has not made major errors can count on being reelected.

New York Democrats: Koch Is Designated, Cuomo Wins

This is not the way it is supposed to work, but New York Democrats are used to fighting and making up. The warriors admire each other's coalitions and tactics, and the primary factions come together for the general election. The convention provides a meeting ground for rival coalitions to watch each other and communicate. Nothing is more important than winning. Supporting the winner means the tangible things office can bring, such as leverage and patronage.

The Koch campaign, steered by David Garth, was confident that the mayor would receive the endorsement, because it had committed votes from 53 percent of the 357-member state committee by April 6. Most of the mayor's votes were delivered from the counties of New York City and Long Island, but Cuomo also received a fourth of these. They knew that Cuomo was trying to receive the 25 percent needed to get on the primary ballot and denied any attempt to keep him from obtaining it. Fund-raising was no problem for Koch campaign finance chair Ken Lipper because the people who supported the mayor for governor knew that if he lost, he would continue to be mayor of New York City.

Mario Cuomo faced a very difficult campaign. His campaign manager, David Garth, left him for his formidable rival, Ed Koch, the mayor of New York City; Cuomo had lost three times to Mayor Koch in the city elections in 1977 (in the primary, the runoff, and the general election); almost none of the county leaders, including the state chair, thought he could win and hence supported the mayor. Up until nine weeks before the state convention, Cuomo's campaign was a disaster, in the view of one of his staunchest supporters. But then Bill Haddad, a campaign veteran and former reporter for the *New York Post,* agreed to run the effort. Cuomo's son, Andrew, was in charge of operations. Patrick Caddell, President Carter's pollster, was also on board to identify Cuomo's strengths and weaknesses.

There was no possibility of Cuomo getting the majority of the convention vote. Haddad said that they planned on the 25 percent to get on the ballot without going the long course of petitions from every county in the state. Out of need and necessity, Haddad named union people as deputy campaign chairs. According to him, the unions "made a big thing of it" and said it was the first time that they'd been brought into a campaign as intimately as that (Haddad 1982, 6).

It was generally conceded that the convention in the Civic Center in Syracuse went according to Mayor Koch's plan. The mayor received 61 percent of the delegate vote, representing 61 percent of the weighted vote based on the last election for governor. According to his campaign strategists, he had "fifty-three hard" going into the convention. Most of his votes came from Long Island, New York City, and Buffalo. Cuomo received a surprising 39 percent of the votes, although he had predicted 33 percent. Half of these came from Manhattan (split with the mayor), Westchester, Monroe, and Albany. The upstate vote was split fairly evenly between the two candidates. To summarize, the convention endorsed the gubernatorial candidate who was ahead in the polls, in organization, in financing. It was their best informed choice.

Three months later, on September 23, Mario Cuomo defeated Ed Koch for the nomination, 53 to 47 percent, or by a margin of nearly seventy-five thousand votes. No voter poll ever gave Cuomo a lead. The Associated Press/NBC Poll gave Koch a 46-to-35-percent lead. A poll conducted for the *New York Post* by Century Opinion Polls and released the day before the primary said Koch was 18 percentage points ahead. One of the reasons for Cuomo's late surge was the street campaign put on by several major labor unions whose efforts were key to the Cuomo campaign. Campaign volunteers were provided by unions representing teachers, communications workers, state civil servants, and others. Cuomo voters, including the fifty-thousand Italian-Americans, were identified by telephone and then escorted to the polls on primary day by ten thousand volunteers. The turnout in the primary was overwhelming: 1,269,000 Democrats voted—almost 40 percent of those registered and twice as high a percentage as the one that had turned out in the last gubernatorial primary in 1978.

Cuomo's victory may be a triumph of traditional political organization over modern media. But is unlikely that any candidate can win without using television, and Cuomo used television cleverly, if not as much as his well-financed opponent (Cuomo spent $1 million for broadcast advertising and Koch spent more than $2 million).

To summarize, Mario Cuomo won by achieving the unusual coalition of upstate New York and liberal-labor-minorities in New York City. His solid upstate vote coupled with a close second in New York City brought him victory. Mayor Koch did his best in the New York City suburbs, where his hard line against crime brought him a receptive audience. After the primary, the Democratic party organization had lost its endorsed candidate. But in New York, winning forges cooperation, and the party organization embraced the primary winner. Bill Haddad claimed that a week after the primary, he had pulled all the Democratic factions together, had met with most of the leaders, and they all united for the general election.

New York Republicans: Lehrman Buys Both Contests

Unlike the Koch media campaign, which was overcome by Cuomo's massive grass roots effort, Lew Lehrman's "air war" strategy was instrumental to his success. Unknown in December 1991, Lehrman became the best-known candidate by mid-June through the efforts of Roger Ailes and Richard Worthlin. He had spent $3 million on TV ads to convince 69 percent (weighted vote) of the four hundred members of the Republican State Central Committee that he should receive the endorsement because he would win the primary anyway. Lehrman's air war campaign was backed up by an exceedingly sophisticated ground war operationalized by Tim Carey, vote director.

Several well-timed decisions were made by the campaign's board of directors early in the campaign. One was to stop the state chair, George Clark, from obtaining the support of the county chairs for comptroller Edward Regan as the party's choice for governor. Lehrman's board devoted a month to persuading county chairs not to support Regan and by February 6, the date of the proposed confirmation, they had succeeded in stopping him (Carey 1982, 6)

Getting on the Republican primary ballot was crucial to the plan of Lehrman's campaign managers because they were sure Lehrman could win the primary. Getting the required 25 percent of the weighted delegate vote at the convention was not certain. This was a political party constituency of 402 state committee people and 62 county chairs. They calculated that Lehrman was the second or third choice of a majority of the delegates, with only a minority of the "regulars" opposed to his candidacy. Media credibility was considered crucial to their campaign because it would convince a starving party that it had a wealthy, potential candidate. Not content with having secured two lines on the ballot, Republican and Conservative, they circulated petitions to get Lehrman a candidacy on the Independent party line as well.

Paul Curran, by contrast, had little to say about his campaign. Announcing late on May 18, he was the party establishment's alternative to Lew Lehrman. He said his goal was to get 25 percent of the convention, and that had been guaranteed as he announced. He had the support of the Republican organization in Nassau under the famed leader Joe Margiotta, Erie County (Buffalo), and Manhattan. These three organizations, plus a few more promised votes, gave Paul Curran his 25 percent of the convention. He counted on the party leaders to handle his campaign for him. But the party leaders were not united.

Jim Emery's campaign was run through the county chairs, who were also on his payroll. According to Emery's campaign manager, George Humphreys, Emery had the advantage, as a minority leader, of having in place an organization that was "very heavy on research and on logistical support and knowledge" (Humphreys 1982, 8). They could not raise money, a problem they had in common with Rosenbaum and Curran. Emery's strategist said that it was a "retail operation" making himself known, liked, and appreciated by organizational politicians upstate: state committee members, county leaders, and state leaders. He received the support of local government people: sheriffs, town officers. Humphreys said they did not recruit workers because they were not needed in a retail operation. The day of the convention, Emery had the support of twenty-two county leaders, giving him a bare 25 percent of the vote.

Emery knew that the price of a primary with Lehrman would be over $3 million, which his campaign could not raise. But it continued on the possibility that Lehrman might not get the 25 percent and would have to petition to get on the ballot—a process fraught with legal and technical difficulties. In that case, Emery would stay in the race, because he thought he could beat anybody else in a primary.

It is harder to understand why Richard Rosenbaum made the run for governor. He said he was approached as early as the spring of 1980 by party leaders and businesspeople. His strategy was to receive the party's designation, because he knew he could not raise enough money to battle Lew Lehrman in the primary without united party support. In the beginning, he had widespread and growing support, but it was thin, and when Curran came into the race, he took much of his support away from him in Manhattan and Erie counties. While Rosenbaum had entered early, events passed him by, and he was not taken seriously.

A lively contest was brewing in the Sheraton Centre's Georgian ballroom on June 15. Instead of an orderly convention traditionally controlled by the leaders and the front-runner, the Republicans had no one in charge of a party still in debt from the last gubernatorial campaign and bereft of state patronage.

At the end of the first ballot, Lehrman had 27.5 percent, Curran 26.6, Emery 25.8, and Rosenbaum 20. The first three had qualified for the primary and were in a virtual dead heat. After the second ballot, which brought little change, Emery and Rosenbaum dropped out of the race. This was no way to endorse, and the leaders hoped for a grafting of two hopefuls: Curran-Emery. The intended grafting, however, did not blossom the way the leaders intended. Emery's delegates joined forces with Lew Lehrman, and the combination of their votes plus those released by Rosenbaum produced a startling third ballot result: an endorsement of Lew Lehrman by 69 percent of the votes. Curran was left with the remainder, enough to enter the primary. The primary race would feature the endorsed multimillionaire versus the impoverished party alternative.

Yet another surprise was in store for the party leaders. It was nearly midnight when a county leader proposed suspending the rules and nominating Emery for lieutenant governor by acclamation, which was done rapidly and with enthusiasm. It was reported that this move had Lehrman's prior approval.

How to assess such unusual behavior for the Republicans? Was the party totally out of control? It is worth looking at the extent of bloc voting by county delegations. Most of the largest county delegations voted with complete or almost total unity for their favored candidate (Jewell 1984, 116). While the counties could deliver the vote, there had been no coalition candidate to unite them.

Lew Lehrman continued to pour money into the media campaign and continued to gain recognition. On July 24, George Clark endorsed Lew Lehrman for the Republican nomination, saying that Paul Curran was not waging a serious primary campaign. In the end, after spending $10 million on the effort, Lew Lehrman won the primary by 81 percent of the vote. One is tempted again to say that air war can overcome ground war, but that was not entirely true in this case. Lehrman had a well-ordered ground campaign as well, and an extremely weak opponent. He worked toward the general election while the Democrats engaged in a major primary battle.

New York: Cuomo Beats Lehrman

After September 23, Lew Lehrman knew his campaign opponent was Mario Cuomo, and the juggernaut rolled on to overcome a normal Republican deficit of one million registered voters. The conservative tenor of the time was favorable to the Republicans, and Lehrman had an excellent chance. He used all the techniques made possible by advanced technology and taught the nation the art of sophisticated campaigning. He mailed out three million letters during the last week of the campaign that almost made him governor, according to Haddad, Cuomo's campaign manager. But Lehrman's independently wealthy candidacy did not succeed. Cuomo won by a 4 percent margin (51 percent to 47 percent). This victory was testimony to the persistence of a class-based, economically sensitive politics. Cuomo successfully tagged Lehrman as a wealthy father of Reaganomics. New York City's New Deal party politics emerged in this ideological contest. Cuomo piled up the usual Democratic plurality in the five counties and beat Lehrman by 68 percent to 32 percent.

Colorado Republicans: The Workhorse Beats the Show Horse

John Fuhr's campaign was built on friendships within the party, and his strategy was built on shoe leather, which took him face-to-face with county delegates. He had the support of the leadership in the legislature: senate president and majority leader and house speaker and majority leader. The rest of his organization rested on county coordinators, present and former county chairs. The rural counties were loyal from the beginning because Fuhr is a rancher and veterinarian. Fuhr predicted that he would get endorsement votes in every one of the sixty-three counties.

John Fuhr slowly and steadily built up the delegate strength he needed to win first place on the ballot. He averaged about sixteen hundred miles of travel each week. Over oceans of coffee and mountains of cookies, Fuhr tried to convince the majority of the thirty-five hundred delegates to the June 26 endorsing assembly that his experience in the state legislature as member and speaker would make him the best candidate. His was a shoestring campaign, but it could overcome thirty-second spots put out by his closest competitor, Phil Winn. In fact, Fuhr's staff were opposed to spending money on advertising until after the endorsing assembly. Tests along the way came in the form of candidate forums, precinct caucuses, county assemblies, and straw votes at which Fuhr and Winn vied for votes. By May 5, after the precinct caucuses were over, both Fuhr and Winn were trailing "undecided" in the competition for delegates. After the county assemblies, particularly in the Denver area, Fuhr had more votes than either Winn or "uncommitted." Fuhr predicted the day before the endorsement that he would receive 44 percent of the delegates but said that he would not contest in the primary if he did not receive a solid top-line position on the ballot.

Phil Winn's campaign was a large and thoroughly professional one. By the time of the convention, there were sixteen salaried staffers. Winn's expenditures report shows that he had hired several consulting firms, several media firms, and a polling firm. Winn was billed as a "man of action" and ran prime-time television and large newspaper ads. His media consultants said that he was doing more than just trying to reach delegates: he was trying to establish the name and face of Phil Winn.

Winn came back to Colorado from the Federal Housing Commission in March and completed a thirty-day, sixty-three-county sweep through Colorado. He established campaign chairs in each county, although only a quarter of them were county party officers. Winn did not have a local image and was perceived as a metropolitan or statewide figure.

Steve Schuck announced his candidacy five weeks before the state convention, just before the county conventions were held to elect state convention delegates. His goal was to get enough Assembly votes (20 percent) to get directly on the primary ballot. Schuck was able to recruit county chairs in about six big counties (among them Jefferson, El Paso, and Arapahoe).

Armed with the names and addresses of all thirty-five hundred delegates chosen in the conventions, Schuck attempted to build a coalition out of those who were undecided. His biggest advantage was the lack of enthusiasm for the top two candidates. Schuck's biggest handicap was his late start. Since the essence of the convention endorsing process is building relationships of trust among the activists within the party, Schuck just didn't have the time.

On the eve of the convention, political columnist Carl Miller asserted that 40 percent of the 3,576 delegates were uncommitted (Miller 1982b). Each of the candidates claimed to have the 20 percent needed for the primary ballot, and both Winn and Fuhr claimed the coveted top-line designation.

The usual fanfare took place. Hospitality suites, hoedowns, delegate wooing parties, and arm-twisting campaign staffers were in full gear. Sophisticated floor operations were planned by Winn and Schuck. These two campaigns worked the floor of the assembly with walkie-talkies and sophisticated telephone hookups. Fuhr, on the other hand, did not plan on any out-of-state operatives and counted on his campaign chair, Tom Grimshaw, plus his county coordinators to keep delegates in line and pick up new commitments.

The results of the endorsing race were close, and the outcome was a surprise.

	Votes	%
Fuhr	1,522	42.5
Winn	1,104	38.8
Schuck	697	19.5
Grandbouche	236	6.6

At 5:30 P.M., Phil Winn rose to announce his withdrawal. With his wife Elle at his side, Winn told startled delegates that his campaign had made its decision early Saturday to withdraw if he didn't take the highest number of votes at the assembly. The former party chair said party unity was the most important thing: "We must beat Dick Lamm." Schuck also came to the podium to commit his support to Fuhr. (John Grandbouche, a Jefferson County tax protester just convicted of federal firearms smuggling charges, was not expected to place.)

The outcome was a triumph of substance and shoe leather over money and media. Winn had spent nearly seven times more than Fuhr in a campaign that relied on professional staffs and TV and newspaper advertising. In the assembly voting, Fuhr won in seven of the state's largest counties (Adams, Arapahoe, Boulder, Denver, Jefferson, Larimer, and Weld). Winn carried only Mesa and Pueblo counties. All told, Fuhr won or tied for the lead in thirty-nine of the sixty-three counties. He swept the small ones where there aren't many votes, but they all counted. His unopposed nomination would turn on a flood of contributions from party sources and political action committees. The Republicans deserved credit by nominating a candidate with the experience to govern if elected. They also deserved credit for dispelling the myth that public office can be bought and sold like soap by well-heeled candidates employing hired-gun professionals.

Colorado: The Governor Is Reelected

It does take money to win a general election, however, and Richard Lamm was a popular governor. A *Denver Post* poll of May 20, conducted by the Denver Consulting Group, showed that over 60 percent of both Republicans and Democrats polled thought Lamm's performance was "good" to "excellent." A Republican Party poll of six hundred people statewide by Market Opinion Research Corporation of Detroit showed that matched against either Fuhr or Winn, Lamm was the overwhelming choice (Westergaard 1982, 5B). The Lamm campaign was well organized. It drew in large numbers of volunteers and worked closely with the party organization both at the state and county levels. Financial support was generous and came from a wide array of groups. The AFL-CIO gave $10,000, and an oil billionaire gave $25,000 (Hero 1986, 55). Lamm received the support of the state's major newspapers, who said he had performed admirably and had studied state problems and set an agenda to deal with them.

A popular governor is hard to beat, and Fuhr did not have the money to publicize himself. His low-key campaign for the nomination had to change into a highly publicized general election effort. The Republican party, both state and national, provided funds, but they were insufficient. A series of debates was held around the state, and Fuhr took the offensive and criticized Lamm for lack of leadership and poor management. But the state had enjoyed relative prosperity, since the national recession had not affected it as hard as most other states. The setting was favorable to an incumbent governor running again. Lamm was elected to an unprecedented third consecutive term by a victory that was the largest ever in a Colorado gubernatorial election (67.5 percent). The day following the election, Lamm made the announcement that state treasurer Roy Romer had been appointed as his chief of staff. While Romer did not keep the post for more than a year, one political analyst suggested that the new arrangement put Romer in a stronger position to seek the governorship at some future point. As of 1995, Romer was a third-term governor of Colorado.

Minnesota Democratic-Farmer-Labor: The Endorsee Loses

Warren Spannaus sought the endorsement the old-fashioned way, and the party was effective in providing help. The seventy thousand DFLers who took part in the caucus-convention process in the spring of 1982 believed in the endorsement process as a way to make candidates commit to the party platform. Issues are incorporated into the DFL delegate selection process in an unusual way. Delegates are elected from issue-oriented subcaucuses, which may stress one (e.g., pro choice) or more issues (e.g., progressive-labor-nuclear freeze). A poll indicated that 82 percent of the delegates were elected by a subcaucus (Jewell 1984, 77). The twelve hundred convention delegates who emerged from this process were committed to the issues as well as to the unopposed candidate, Warren Spannaus. On a more personal level, they were glad to repay him for speaking to their Lions Clubs, helping with their legal problems, or remembering deaths in their families. He said he kept adding to "a kind of broad based committee that now totals 3,000 people" (Spannaus 1982, 8).

Spannaus was endorsed by 81 percent of the delegates at the DFL convention, well over the 60 percent required by party rules. Most of the other votes were cast for "no endorsement," by feminist, pro life, and Perpich supporters. Spannaus's overwhelming vote total showed that he had strong support from all factions, including feminists and abortion foes. Considering the fact that at least one-third of the delegates were pro life advocates, he obviously drew substantial support from that group. According to Spannaus campaign representative Bob Meek, the convention gave the candidate what he wished: approval by a steady, progressive, mainstream party that voters can trust (Sturdevant 1982b, 4A). As the endorsee, Spannaus could count on considerable help from state party headquarters. In the DFL this help includes a computer listing of registered voters that identifies Democrats, plus lists of local organizations, party officials, and campaign contributors. Spannaus received $30,000 from the state party for the primary.

Rudy Perpich did not challenge Spannaus for the endorsement and hence did not go to delegate selection meetings. His organization was a loose one: "I have gotten some people together . . . In about ten or fifteen days, you put it together" (Perpich 1982, 3). But his candidacy was supported informally by many delegates to the Eighth District convention in early May. The Eighth District in northeastern Minnesota was crucial to Perpich's success in the September 14 primary. Leaders squelched a straw ballot between the two, although both sides claimed they could win it. Spannaus's appearance was greeted by a polite standing ovation. Later at a DFL polka party nearby, Perpich received a hero's welcome. The crowd shouted "Rudy, Rudy," and the band played "Happy Days Are Here Again."

The primary campaign began immediately after that, with Perpich campaigning heavily in the Iron Range of northeastern Minnesota. He said that he had to take 85 percent of the vote in this Eighth Congressional District. Perpich did not have the funds to buy TV advertising. He limited his TV and radio advertising to ten-second get-out-the-vote messages. His campaign manager, Alvin Brustuen, said people "believe" in Perpich and they didn't need to promote name identification or sell people.

Spannaus, meanwhile, concentrated in the southern part of the state, the Twin Cities. He said that his experience in state government would give him the necessary edge. Mike Hatch, party chair, sent twenty-five thousand letters to party activists, warning them that the primary was a referendum on the endorsement process and asking for money to buy advertising for Spannaus. Phone banks, a million sample ballots bearing Spannaus's name, and two hundred thousand postcards with friendly messages deluged the voters. DFL luminaries went on radio and television to support him. DFL legislators distributed Spannaus campaign literature and went door-to-door with him. Observers did not think the issues of gun control and abortion were driving deep divisions within the electorate. They expected voters to divide on the basis of perceptions of candidates' personalities, styles, and records.

When the votes were counted, Perpich received about twenty thousand votes more than Spannaus out of five hundred thousand cast, for a victory with 50.4 percent. The results reflected the underlying regional split among Minnesota Democrats. Perpich received his victory in northern Minnesota as a child of the Iron Range. Spannaus won the liberal Twin Cities area—Minneapolis and St. Paul—by fifty thousand voters but trailed Perpich in the rest of the state by more than seventy thousand. Perpich's victory marked the first time in sixteen years that an endorsed candidate for governor lost a primary. At first DFL chair Hatch said that a Perpich victory would lead to the death of the DFL endorsement process, but shortly after Perpich's narrow victory became clear, he was on the phone to Perpich allies suggesting a meeting between Perpich and party leaders and offering to arrange a central committee meeting to endorse Perpich. Spannaus sent Perpich a telegram promising to rally to the support of the entire DFL ticket.

Minnesota Independent Republicans: A Bruising
Family Fight

Among the Minnesota Independent Republicans, it was a family fight and could be used to prove the old adage: "United we stand, divided we fall." Until 1982, the Minnesota Republicans had a history of successful endorsements. Those who failed to receive the endorsement at the convention accepted the convention's decision, and the endorsee, if challenged from the outside, always won. The 1982 convention's crosscutting conflict among economic conservatives, economic moderates, and the Christian Right was a prediction of the future direction of the IR party. The estimate was that antiabortion delegates controlled the convention by more than a two-to-one margin.

In the beginning, Lou Wangberg had a lock on the nomination. He moved into the campaign headquarters of MFQW (Minnesotans for Quie/Wangberg) and changed it to MFW, dropping Quie from the name. He had the support of the party's officeholders and the leaders, the best recognition, and the best finance. His campaign chair was Bill Frenzel, the senior member of Congress from Minnesota, and his first campaign manager was Marcie Leier, President Reagan's top organizer in 1980. But the campaign got overstaffed, and eventually it ran out of money. The campaign faltered until Bjarnie Anderson, former aide to Republican U.S. senator Rudy Boschwitz, took over just five weeks before the convention, and Wangberg's delegate count began to rise. The whole thrust of the operation after that was courting delegates. The delegate strategy included three personal letters to each delegate the week before the convention and a phone-bank operation. By the time of the convention, Wangberg had pulled nearly even with Glen Sherwood in delegate count.

Sherwood's campaign organization was put together "with what we had," a tremendous volunteer crew, a very small paid staff of about four, his wife, JoAnn, two sons, and two daughters-in-law. On the eve of his announcement for the endorsement on February 16, Sherwood urged all Christians to take part in precinct caucuses, which began the selection process for party convention delegates (Sherwood 1982, 2, 8).

Sherwood's people went to precinct caucuses to garner delegates, aided by effort from the Christian Right church communications network. Thousands of conservative Christians, concerned that decency and morality were under attack throughout society, turned to the IR caucuses as the way to fight back. Party leaders could not estimate how many evangelical Christians came to precinct caucuses for the first time on February 23. Wangberg's campaign manager estimated that if caucus participants had voted that night on IR gubernatorial candidates, Sherwood would have won more than 50 percent. Their influence was diluted in the legislative district and county conventions as party regulars won state convention delegate spots. At party headquarters, the chair's administrative assistant took phone calls for ten straight days from party regulars who moaned that they had been dumped by the "right wingers" (Sturdevant 1982a, 4A). IR chair Bill Morris estimated that about 39 percent of the 2,010 delegates to the state convention were newcomers representing those groups (Salisbury 1982a, 1B).

Paul Overgaard entered the campaign too late to work the precinct caucuses. According to IR party officials, 50 percent of the delegates reported that they were undecided on a gubernatorial nominee the eve of the convention (Spano and Leary 1982). Hence Overgaard and the other two latecomers, Robert Ashbach and David Jennings, had a chance if they could get publicity and hence momentum. Overgaard's commercials began before any of the others and ran just prior to the convention. They bought time during news broadcasts in every major TV market in the state. The ads used the theme "Fight Back Minnesota," which made Overgaard appear like an outsider and a strong fighter, ingredients that the campaign had been missing.

Overgaard's strategy for endorsement included one hundred floor leaders and two Apple computers. His strategy was that of a second-place candidate: obtaining second-ballot pledges from the supporters of minor candidates who would drop out first and then, after achieving momentum, obtaining the winning number of votes from Glen Sherwood's camp. He fashioned a contract button that said simply "O" and identified Sherwood's supporters and others who pledged second choice to him.

The great day dawned on June 18 at the St. Paul Convention Center, "pitting a candidate of the prayer book against four candidates of the ledger book." A computer scan of the delegates revealed that 24 percent said they were "very conservative," 51 percent said "conservative," 20 percent "moderate," and 4 percent "somewhat liberal" (Spano and Leary 1982, 4). Another questionnaire asked delegates about their primary interest in seeking election to the convention. Seventy percent of Sherwood delegates emphasized issues or issues and candidate. When the answers from all the other delegates were combined, only 38 percent said issues or issues and candidates and 47 percent said neither. Of those Sherwood delegates who expressed such an interest in issues, two-thirds mentioned abortion (pro life position), one-third mentioned "morality" issues, and one-sixth specified "family" issues (Jewell 1984, 93).

A test of these positions came when the delegates were asked to vote on various platform planks. Here are the ballot results on several of those planks:

Require the teaching of the scientific creation theory as well as the evolution theory in public schools: 1,167–586
Prohibit busing for racial integration: 1,527–289
Legalize lotteries: 591–1,198
Legalize pari-mutuel betting: 560–1,229
Prohibit abortion: 1,140–621
Allow freedom of choice in regard to abortion: 592–1,208

Before the balloting for endorsements, IR chair Bill Morris warned that the party's hands would be tied by the failure to endorse. As table 5.10 indicates, Sherwood led on the first three ballots, but he did not get the 40 percent he had predicted. If he had, he might have been able to block the endorsement of anyone else. Wangberg placed second on all three, ready to pick up second-place votes as the others faded. Staying power and second-place support would eventually bring victory to someone. Another strategy would bring about a win if two candidates combined, as Rome and Labriola did in Connecticut. It was rumored that Wangberg had proposed an alliance with Sherwood in which Sherwood would run for lieutenant governor, but he had refused.

After trailing on the first two ballots, state senate minority leader Robert Ashbach and house minority leader David Jennings dropped out of the race on the third ballot. Ashbach never had a chance because he was the only candidate in the field who supported legalized abortion. In withdrawing, both Ashbach and Jennings told their supporters to vote their conscience. But Jennings in private urged many of his supporters to switch their allegiance to Overgaard. On the fourth ballot, Overgaard picked up 141 of the votes that had gone to Jennings and Ashbach earlier, while Wangberg received 98 of those votes and Sherwood 26.

The fifth ballot was crucial. Wangberg and Overgaard gained strength at the expense of Sherwood. While his staff urged him to continue the race, Sherwood went to the podium and withdrew. He could not win the endorsement, but he could control who did. Wangberg was a conservative who supported the same "family" values. Overgaard wasn't conservative enough on social issues. Although he opposed abortion, many on the Sherwood team considered him a recent and questionable convert to their cause. Sherwood announced his withdrawal, saying, "I'm convinced we have made a change in the political spectrum of this state. The issues I feel strong about will never again be swept under the rug by any candidate. We still need a strong pro-life, pro-family candidate on the ballot" (Salisbury 1982b, 1A). Sherwood told reporters he preferred Wangberg and that most of his supporters knew his preferences.

The Overgaard strategy backfired. He had hoped to pick up most of the Ashbach and Jennings votes and force Wangberg out of the race, leav-

TABLE 5.10.   Votes for Gubernatorial Candidates in Minnesota Republican Convention (in percentages)

Candidate	Ballot						
	First	Second	Third	Fourth	Fifth	Sixth	Seventh
Wangberg	26.5	27.3	28.2	33.1	35.2	55.9	67.9
Overgaard	21.1	24.6	26.7	33.8	35.7	40.4	28.4
Sherwood	30.5	30.8	30.7	32.0	28.3		
Jennings	11.5	11.0	9.6				
Ashbach	9.6	6.0	4.3				
Others/Pass	0.8	0.3	0.5	1.1	0.8	3.7	3.7
Total	100.0	100.0	100.0	100.0	100.0	100.0	100.0

Source: Jewell 1984, 96.

ing the delegates with a choice between Overgaard and Sherwood. "We knocked off the wrong guy first," Overgaard campaign coordinator Al Johnson said (Salisbury and Dornfeld 1982). Many of the Wangberg delegates were party regulars who would have supported Overgaard over Sherwood. On the sixth ballot, Wangberg pulled ahead. The governor and U.S. Reps. Bill Frenzel and Vin Weber worked the floor on his behalf. The Wangberg floor operation, which numbered more than two hundred people, identified delegates whose votes could be switched as the contest grew tight. Most Sherwood supporters voted for him. On the seventh ballot, with some Overgaard delegates making a shift, Wangberg got two-thirds of the vote and the endorsement. The IR had an endorsed candidate at 1:30 in the morning.

Wheelock Whitney was correct in believing that he could not win endorsement at the convention because he supports legalized abortion. He reasoned that IR voters might view him differently. He spent $100,000 of his own money on TV ads before the convention and planned to resume immediately after. He opened up a campaign office in downtown Minneapolis and hired a campaign staff.

Whitney organized three support groups for his campaign. One was the business community of the Twin Cities, where he was well known. The second was the chemical dependency network of alcoholic treatment centers, halfway houses, and the like. His third group were the health promotion and wellness individuals: runners, nutrition people, stress management types. He was a community leader and taught a course at the University of Minnesota, both of which gave him sources of support. He believed that he would pick up support from people who thought Wangberg was too vulnerable or too conservative, and he was pleased that the former governor of Minnesota, Elmer Anderson, supported his candidacy.

The primary was an uneven match. The Wangberg campaign never recovered from its slow start in time to defeat the challenger Whitney; it lagged in money and staff. It was not until mid-July that the Wangberg campaign found a finance chair, who had never before headed fund-raising for a statewide campaign. A month before the primary, Wangberg had not obtained the $80,000 loan he sought to obtain two weeks of advertising, despite a cosignature from the IR party. The week before the primary, the campaign staff went unpaid and the campaign report listed over $61,000 in unpaid bills. Only a few radio ads went on the air. Wangberg had hoped a series of preprimary debates with Whitney would give him exposure, but Whitney, with good reason, agreed to debate Wangberg no more than twice.

Sherwood and Overgaard, loyal to the endorsement process, went on the radio vowing support for Wangberg. Sherwood's endorsement meant a lot to Wangberg, who was counting on the conservative Christians to get out the vote. But it takes money to fight, and Wangberg did not raise enough to give him the exposure he needed against his opponent's media-intensive campaign.

Meanwhile, the Whitney TV ads, acclaimed among political pros as among the most effective ever used by a statewide candidate, helped transform the name of Wheelock Whitney to a household word from one that respondents to an April survey had confused with the inventor of the cotton gin. But Whitney needed a high turnout to win, and he also carried out an extensive field operation to accomplish that. Whitney beat Wangberg decisively (59.9 percent to 33.8 percent). He won the Twin Cities by a margin of two-to-one. Wangberg carried only seven counties, most near his home base in the northwest corner of the state. IR chair Bill Morris recanted his previous position that a Whitney win would threaten the caucus convention system. He called the primary winner's operation "incredible" and hoped he would run the same kind of campaign against Perpich.

Did the results of both Minnesota's primaries put the state's endorsement system on trial? Both parties reached agreement in their conventions without leaving deep scars among the delegates. In the case of the Republicans, that was difficult because there were so many candidates running. Both parties performed many services for their endorsees in the primary campaign. Wangberg wrapped his party's endorsement around his campaign like a blanket and reminded listeners that he was the product of a quality political system respected around the world. Spannaus said the primary was a test of what the endorsement system was worth. After their defeats, both party chairs tried to soothe the party activists, and the defeated endorsees offered their support to the winners.

From that time, both parties in Minnesota have hosted lively convention contests, and until 1994, the endorsed candidates won over both inside and outside candidates. In 1994, as in 1982, the conventions were contentious. The Republicans endorsed a Christian Right candidate in place of their governor, Arne Carlson, and the governor beat him handily in the primary. The adage that a divisive primary hurts a candidate's election chances could not be tested in the elections after 1982 because endorsees from both parties have been strongly challenged.

Minnesota: Iron Range Perpich Wins Election

In the general elections of 1982, the two mavericks faced off, one the millionaire business executive from the Twin Cities, the other the populist from the Iron Range. Wheelock Whitney did not accept public financing, but Rudy Perpich did. The central focus of the general election was the financial condition of state government. Perpich liked to contrast the flush condition of the state treasury when he left office and its depleted condition four years later. He said he would consider an increase in the sales tax to balance the budget. Whitney said he would freeze state spending, including property tax relief. Voters were treated to six weeks of classic partisan debate over the role of government and how it should be financed. In the end, the populist former governor won over the well-financed media candidate. Perpich refuted for a time the political maxim that money wins elections. Returns showed a Perpich win of 59 percent to Whitney's 40 percent. In September 1995, Rudy Perpich, Minnesota's longest-serving governor, died of cancer. "He was an immigrant's kid who became a governor" was an epitaph he would have cheered (Klobuchar 1995, 1A, 7A).

Illinois Democrats: Stevenson Wins State
Central Endorsement

Adlai Stevenson III said he wanted to avoid a primary contest and win the support of the twenty-four-member State Central Committee with as little acrimony as possible. Because he did not want to be associated with the Cook County machine, he decided to organize support for the nomination without their help. The state chair, Jack Touhy, was friendly, but of little help since he was from Chicago and dared not cross the Chicago–Cook County machine. Stevenson had not run for office since his last U.S. Senate race in 1974, and when he decided not to run again, members of his staff who had been with him through his four campaigns and in the Senate disbanded and he had to "start from scratch." It was easy in the past, when he had high-powered staffs and was looked upon as the probable winner. This time he didn't have a staff and was not looked upon as the favorite. Larry Hansen, who had been on Stevenson's staff since he was state treasurer, came back for the slate-making campaign.

This slate-making effort was small, "mainly moving around the state and on the telephone with Larry Hansen and one or two others also on the phone and giving me advice as to who to call. I'd go to meetings that the party paid for and try to generate grassroots support. The county chairmen would get together and have meetings, and all the candidates would appear and make speeches. Then the press would typically measure the support by the applause levels" (Stevenson 1982, 7).

Stevenson had several undeclared opponents and one declared opponent, Dan Walker,a former governor. Due to the rather fluid personal politics in Chicago in 1982, Mayor Jane Byrne supported Walker because he was a traditional enemy of the Richard J. Daley machine, and son Richard

M. Daley was expected to challenge her in the mayor's race in 1983. On September 27, Stevenson said he might run against a "divisive" Democrat in the March primary even if the latter had the endorsement. This announcement made the mayor's decision more difficult because she would provoke anti–city hall sentiment by keeping Stevenson from the nomination.

By September 17, Stevenson announced that he had the backing of much of the State Central Committee, with the exception of a "handful of Chicago members." To strengthen his hand with the slate-makers, Stevenson released a list of 183 municipal, township, and county officials throughout the state who had endorsed his candidacy. On October 8, Stevenson reported the names of eight supporters on the twenty-four-member State Central Committee, all from the suburbs and downstate. Most of the city Democrats, who held a near majority of the votes on the state committee, waited for a signal from Mayor Byrne. Stevenson continued on with his quest and by October 23 had thirteen supportive committee members. But each represented votes equal to the number of Democratic primary ballots cast in the congressional district in 1978, and the thirteen did not have quite enough votes. By November 12, Stevenson had fifteen members and just over half of the weighted votes. Former governor Dan Walker had not received one endorsement and dropped out of the race.

Stevenson called Mayor Byrne to tell her that he had enough votes to assure his slate-making as the Democratic candidate for governor, and she agreed. She said her information was the same. The slate-making took place over several days in two locations, ending up at the Bismarck Hotel in Chicago on November 18. By the preceding Friday, however, it was settled that Stevenson was slated along with his choice for lieutenant governor, Grace Mary Stern. They did not face a challenge in the March primary. Dan Walker urged his supporters to support Stevenson. That is the way the game is played within the Democratic party in Illinois. It takes shoe leather and time to get the majority of the members of the State Central Committee, but not much money as Stevenson's campaign fund reveals.

Illinois: Governor Thompson Wins Third Term

The general election campaign between the governor and the senator centered on issues arising from economic recession. During the early months of 1982, there was general agreement in the media and among pollsters that Stevenson was the front-runner and that the weak economy was damaging Thompson's campaign. Thompson's image did not improve until early September, and then it improved dramatically after four debates that gave him the chance to recoup. Stevenson complained that he could not get the state focused on his strategy for its economic recovery. Stevenson was also dogged by the fact that his organization consisted of strangers, and, "We never really did get the whole organization chained down" (Stevenson 1982, 9).

Governor Thompson won the election by 5,000 votes out of nearly 3.7 million cast, and Stevenson's request for a recount was not rejected by the state Supreme Court until three days before the January 10 inauguration. The predictions the weekend before the election had Thompson leading Stevenson by a margin of 16 percentage points. Thompson's actual vote totals were 23 percent lower in Chicago than the polls had predicted. The vote resulted from registration drives in Chicago's black wards and an unprecedented turnout there. Stevenson emerged from the 1982 contest with 74 percent of the vote in Chicago. This extraordinary turnout has been laid to the resentment stirred by Reaganomics, and the awareness that Thompson as a Republican was the extension of the president. Another possible reason for the turnout was the use of the election by the black leaders as proof to Harold Washington that he should make another try at the mayor's race in the February primary (Keenan 1986, 150–54). Nevertheless, Governor Thompson had achieved an unprecedented consecutive third term, and he turned his attention to governing.

Conclusions

In the preprimary endorsing states, front-runner status implies party leadership support. Presumably the state leaders encourage a candidate to emerge as the front-runner. Occasionally they wait until the contest stabilizes before they back their choice. That usually happens before the convention, and the delegates are aware of the favored candidate. In Colorado, an exception, the Republican leaders maintained neutrality until the convention chose John Fuhr over former party chair Phil Winn. And in New York, Republican leaders tried to stop the front-runner, Lew Lehrman, until it was obvious nobody could keep him from winning. Thus, secure and gradual garnering of momentum builds delegate strength toward convention endorsement.

The three governors were front-runners, and their campaign organizations were merged with those of their parties. Both governors O'Neill of Connecticut and Thompson of Illinois were challenged by minor candidates, which indicated that even governors must take front-runner status and party leadership seriously if they are going to survive.

The candidates and the party leaders are in frequent communication. In Connecticut, Lew Rome was a Republican candidate for the gubernatorial nomination in 1978, and when he agreed to abandon a primary fight in the interests of party unity, it was implicit that he would run for governor in 1982. The party leaders backed him and did not support his rival. In Illinois, Adlai Stevenson garnered the needed votes within the State Central Committee, called the mayor of Chicago, and received the endorsement. Mayor Koch of New York was the clear front-runner and the choice of the state's most powerful county party leaders, who controlled enough delegates to the state convention to assure him of the endorsement. The New York Republican party had traditionally been united under governors Dewey and Rockefeller, who had controlled the nomination. When it was obvious that Lew Lehrman, the multimillionaire, could win the primary, the leaders backed him. Minnesota Democratic leaders supported three-term attorney general Walter Spannaus for the nomination. The Minnesota Republicans appeared united as the nominating season commenced, and although Lou Wangberg was the front-runner and favorite of the leaders and he faltered at the convention, he eventually received the endorsement. This review of front-runners and leaders shows that every leader-backed candidate won the endorsement. But occasionally, conventions are not representative of the party's voters, and such was the case three times in 1982.

Our hypothesis predicts that factions in strong party states are more personal and less durable than in weak party states. If the party boasts one leadership coalition, it may consist of one or more factions with continuity and the power to control nominations. The main task of the party leaders in strong party states is to manage the ever present potential for factionalism and to channel the aspirations and energies of rival groups into a semblance of party unity (Jewell and Olson 1982, 52). Candidates are on their own to raise money for their endorsement effort, but I predict that money itself does not buy the endorsement. Once they have been endorsed, they can look forward to the status and organizational support that endorsement confers, and hence the money will come more easily.

In eight out of ten endorsing contests, a single faction of *party regulars and leaders* controlled the outcome for their candidate. The major exception was the contest within the New York Republican party, since Lew Lehrman was definitely not an insider and had not paid his dues to the party. When it was obvious that he would win, they backed him. In Colorado, the party leaders waited until John Fuhr built up the delegate strength he needed to win first place on the ballot. His bare-bones campaign, costing a fraction of Phil Winn's, proved to be what the party regulars wanted, and Winn dropped out. The other type of faction in the endorsing states is the *personal* faction, which most candidates use to seek the endorsement. This faction is ephemeral and easily merges with the leadership faction or with the campaign organization of the nominee. The candidates were most likely to talk about low factionalism, which can merge to win in the general election.

Why did three endorsees lose? The New York Democrats were used to family fights. Hugh Carey, the incumbent governor, had challenged and beaten the endorsee, Howard Samuels. After 1982 the Democrats consolidated behind Governor Mario Cuomo. According to campaign operatives for Mayor Koch, rival factions can bury the hatchet and pull together for the general election. For the two parties in Minnesota, 1982 proved to be a forerunner of increasing conflict within both. Yet, the citizens of that state continue to want the rigors of face-to-face contact in unruly endorsing conventions as a preliminary to the loneliness of the primary election booth.

In the preprimary endorsement states, one senses an organizational presence. The party leaders, officeholders, and activists come together to confer endorsement in the party's name. The endorsee goes forth with the backing of a party and the status and support that represents. Intraparty differences are accommodated before rather than after the nominating campaign, which places the elected governor in a stronger position to govern.

CHAPTER 6

Money versus Party Effort: Nominating for Governor

Party organization matters. We recognize party organization when we compare the effort to receive coveted front-runner status in party endorsement states, versus the self-propelling and freewheeling campaigns for the nomination in direct-primary states. Strong parties can help candidates with campaign training seminars, computerized lists, sources of contributions, and recognition. But are strong parties more effective than money? Heretofore, money raising and spending has not been subjected to a rigorous comparative analysis, although casual inspection of the fund-raising reports in chapters 4 and 5 indicates that money plays a larger role in the direct-primary states.

Front-Runner Status

Students of the presidential nominating process note the drive to obtain front-runner status via early primary victories, which in turn capture national media attention (Aldrich 1980; Bartels 1988). Whether this front-runner status strategy transfers to gubernatorial nominations has not been widely researched. In chapters 4 and 5 we witnessed the candidates' need to outspend and outdistance rivals in order to ensure a primary or convention victory. Since the electorates differ in the primary versus the convention system, I hypothesized that the impact of front-runner status would differ. While front-runners achieve their status primarily by experience in office, courting party leaders, and media spending, the primary voters place a different value on success in these areas than do convention delegates.

Money

Money buys exposure, and exposure is the most important ingredient in determining the outcome of a primary contest fought without the party label. Larry Sabato has detailed the use of direct mail, telephone banks, personal organizations, opinion polling, and media advertising, which have become standard procedures for gubernatorial campaigns in most states (Sabato 1980; Jewell and Olson 1982, 175–85; Beyle 1983). Because state political parties are primarily labor-intensive organizations, they cannot provide the new technology, and candidates have to buy these services elsewhere. Accordingly, candidates in state primaries, as in national, need to build their own personal organizations and amass the money needed for exposure. Candidates who have the means to wage a mass advertising campaign on the electronic media are advantaged, but broadcast advertising has the most impact in elections where the candidates are not well known.

A spectacular example of this phenomenon is David Owen, who ran for the nomination in Kansas by wearing out three pairs of shoes walking up and down the streets and talking to people in every county. He was defeated in a last-minute media blitz by Sam Hardage, who spent as much money in the last ninety days as Owen had spent in eighteen months. Owen said ruefully that "the guy who can write the big check, or borrow the big bucks, is the guy who can win the race" (Owen 1982, 7).

Money and Electoral Success

The relationship between spending and winning votes is complex. For instance, in 1982, Rudy Perpich, former governor and Democratic primary challenger in Minnesota, spent $139,000 and beat the endorsed candidate in the primary, Walter Spannaus, who spent $990,000. In the California Republican primary, meanwhile, state attorney general George Deukmejian spent over $4 million to beat the lieutenant governor, Mike Curb, who spent nearly as much. Hence, we cannot say that money buys votes.

There are wild variations among the states in population size and density. In Minnesota, total spending on the Republican primary contest was just over $1 million: in California, the Republicans spent $8 million. Four million dollars spent in New York amounts to about 28 cents per voter; in California, it amounts to 20 cents. However, money spent per voting-age individual in one state is not a good reflection of the amount it takes to win in another. It takes less money per voting-age person where they are concentrated in major media markets than it does in Alaska and Hawaii. For example, Lew Lehrman in New York spent only 77 cents per eligible voter by laying out $10 million, whereas his Republican counterpart in Alaska spent $2.59 on each voter, a total of $572,000.

Primary elections combine minimal candidate visibility and lack of party cues, both conditions that enhance the value of electronic advertising. Incumbency is at a premium since it provides the only information the voters possess about a candidate, which was essentially the discovery of Gary Jacobson when he tested this hypothesis and found that both incumbency and broadcast spending had major impacts on the outcomes of primary elections for governor (1975, 789–91). Malcolm Jewell's study of gubernatorial nominations reaffirms this finding. Spending as well as officeholding explained 61 percent of the variance in the primary vote (1984, 259–61).

In preprimary endorsement systems, on the other hand, the strength of the party organization and its skills and resources can be brought to bear on the outcomes of the nominating contests. In these cases, the hypotheses predict that candidate spending will not be as important to the outcome because the party will expend effort and money of its own to aid its favored one.

A Preliminary Test: Ten States in 1982

Tables 6.1 and 6.2 compare the power of money and front-runner status on nominating success in the five direct-primary states and the five preprimary endorsement states. Recall that no leadership coalition can confer front-runner status in primary-only states. Party leaders may favor one candidate over another, but they cannot encourage one candidate over another, schedule ambition, or control the results. Candidates are on their own to raise campaign chests and try to become the front-runner. But this status is hard to keep, and the candidate with the most money can overtake the leader and win the primary.

Table 6.1 shows that money talks in the primary-only states. While we would expect governors Clements, Alexander, Carlin, and Atiyeh to amass war chests to discourage rivals and to win the primary without difficulty, the power of money in other contests proves conclusively that candidates who have more money win. In every case, the candidate who had more money to spend won the primary. It did not matter if the candidate was the front-runner and perhaps had the support of party leaders. It did not matter if a candidate had announced early and built up an organization in every county, as did Don Clark in Oregon or Anna Belle Clement O'Brien in Tennessee.

Money talked louder than organization. In races such as those for the Texas Democrats and California Republicans, where both candidates raised equally enormous sums, the character of the media contest became a highly charged personality-related campaign with intrigue and personal character on the line instead of issues. Media are the key to a successful race, and media take money. In Texas and Kansas, where the top two contenders had approximately the same amount of money, a third candidate was able to take votes away from one of them, permitting the other to win, again indicating the unstable character of races in these primary-only states. To summarize table 6.1: in primary-only states, if you raise more money, you will win; if you raise the same amount, your chances are 50 percent; if you raise less, you will lose. Front-runner status has very little to contribute to a win.

Table 6.2, which presents the power of money versus party effort in preprimary endorsement states, tells a different story. In these endorsement states, front-runner status implies leader support and party endorsement. In all ten cases, the front-runner won the party endorsement and money did not play a major role.

In Colorado, the leaders were initially neutral (Phil Winn outraised John Fuhr by an eight-to-one margin). Fuhr received the endorsement and Winn did not challenge.

TABLE 6.1.   Primary-Only States: Money Raised and Gubernatorial Nomination Results, 1982

	Front-runners			Nonfront-runners		
Primary Election Results	Raised More $s (%)	Raised Equal $s (%)	Raised Fewer $s (%)	Raised More $s (%)	Raised Equal $s (%)	Raised Fewer $s (%)
Winners	Clements R-TX (100) Alexander R-TN (100) Carlin D-KA (100) Atiyeh R-OR (100) Bradley D-CA (73)	White D-TX (41)		Tyree D-TN (77) Kulongowski D-OR (53)	Hardage R-KA (44) Deukmejian R-CA (51)	
Losers		Owen R-KA (47) Curb R-CA (49)	O'Brien D-TN (23) Clark D-OR (47)	Temple D-TX (45)	Armstrong D-TX (14) Montgomery D-KA (0) Lady R-KA (9) Garamendi R-CA (27)	

Note: Percentages in parentheses indicate proportion of total contributions for primary.

Candidates raised equal amounts if their totals were within four percentage points of their rivals': White/Temple (TX); Hardage/Owen (KA); Deukmejian/Curb (CA).

However, within the New York Democrats and both parties in Minnesota, the party endorsee was challenged in a primary and lost. In New York, Mario Cuomo did not receive the convention endorsement, but he won the primary over Ed Koch, the convention endorsee, by raising only 35 percent of the total. In the Minnesota Democratic contest, Rudy Perpich did not seek the convention endorsement but won the primary over Walter Spannaus, the convention endorsee, by raising only 12 percent of the total. In the Minnesota Republican contest, Wheelock Whitney did

TABLE 6.2. Preprimary Endorsements: Money Raised and Gubernatorial Nomination Results, 1982

	Front-runners			Nonfront-runners		
Nomination Results	Raised More $s (%)	Raised Equal $s (%)	Raised Fewer $s (%)	Raised More $s (%)	Raised Equal $s (%)	Raised Fewer $s (%)
Winners	*Assured*	*Assured*	*Assured*	*Risk Takers*		*Populists*
	Lehrman R-NY (86)	Rome R-CT (32)	O'Neill D-CT (41)	Whitney R-MN (69)		Cuomo D-NY (35)
	Lamm D-CO (100)	Stevenson D-IL (48)	Fuhr R-CO (11)			Perpich D-MN (12)
	Thompson R-IL (100)					
Losers	*Regulars*		*Neglected*	*Hopefuls*	*Hopefuls*	*Also Rans*
	Koch D-NY (65)		Wangberg R-MN (17)	Abate D-CT (59)	Bozzuto R-CT (34)	Labriola R-CT (18)
	Spannaus D-MN (88)			Winn R-CO (76)	Walker D-IL (52)	Post R-CT (16)
						Curran R-NY (3)
						Rosenbaum R-NY (6)
						Emery R-NY (5)
						Schuck R-CO (13)
						Sherwood R-MN (6)
						Overgaard R-MN (8)

Note: Front-runner implies party leader support plus endorsement. Percentages in parentheses indicate proportion of total contributions for the convention and/or primary. Candidates raised equal amounts if their totals were within four percentage points of their rivals': Rome/Bozzuto (CT); Stevenson/Walker (IL). Also-rans are third and fourth candidates at the Convention.

not seek the convention endorsement but outraised Lewis Wangberg and won the primary.

Money did not make the difference in these states. Four of the party-endorsed candidates won the nomination over those who raised the same as or more than they did. Hence, the power of the party organization is confirmed. Table 6.2 shows that the money odds for preprimary endorsement states are no better than chance: if you raise more, you have a 50 percent chance of winning; if you raise the same, you have a 50 percent chance of winning; if you raise less, you have a 50 percent chance of beating your closest opponent. In the preprimary endorsement states, party organization dominates money.

A More Extensive Test: Thirty-one States in 1982

We need more rigorous and extensive proof that money does not control elections. It is time to test statistically the relative power of money and party strength across many states. Research shows that state party organizations are increasing in strength concurrently with findings that money determines election outcomes—an apparent contradiction. The hypotheses we are testing predict that the importance of money varies with party effort. Where party organizations are strong, they can ensure that their favored candidate becomes the nominee; where parties are weak, the self-selected candidate with the most money will win the nomination.

In this chapter, the relative power of money and party effort are compared in three different nominating situations. In the first, the primary alone determines the outcome and offers the party leaders little control over the nomination. Here the prediction calls for the controlling influence of money because the candidate must spend to become known. In the second situation, the parties make preprimary endorsements in a convention or party gathering, which offers the maximum potential for party organizational control. Money is not as important because the candidate must court party leaders rather than media-feed the voters. The third situation is the postconvention primary. Party leaders can prevent a challenge to the endorsed candidate in many cases, but if the endorsee is challenged, the potential for party control is weakened. Both endorsee and challenger must spend to become known to the primary voters, and money may become important.

Nominating for Governor in 1982

This test uses political, financial, and electoral data for those who sought the gubernatorial nomination in 1982. It tests the aforementioned hypotheses in three different nominating models: contests where the primary is the only point of decision for the nomination (primary-only); preprimary endorsing conventions; and postconvention primaries.

In that year, thirty-six states elected governors. Before the general election contest began, seventy-two political parties selected a standard-bearer to do battle against the enemy. This research is concerned with sixty-one of those nominating battles. Contests in four southern states (Alabama, Arkansas, Georgia, and South Carolina) were eliminated on the basis of V. O. Key's hypothesis that the potential electoral success of a party influences the number of contestants in the primary. Hence, I ruled out the factional contests within the dominant Democratic party as well as the uncontested and seemingly cohesive endorsements within the minority Republican party in those states. Both Rhode Island candidates and the governor of South Dakota were also omitted because no primary finance reports were required, since the primaries were not contested.

In twenty-three states selected, the primary is the point of decision. Candidates raise a war chest, get themselves on the primary ballot, and proceed to campaign for the nomination. In some states, party leaders back their favored candidates, but they cannot deliver the money and support typically given the endorsee in the convention states. In these situations, the candidate has to develop a personal organization and try for early money in order to beat off other contenders. Incumbent governors are generally able to achieve renomination, although they may be challenged in the primary.

Parties in eight of the thirty-one states researched use some form of preprimary endorsement process, usually a state convention, to which delegates are chosen in party caucuses to endorse a nominee before the primary. In addition to the five states we have already studied, Massachusetts, New Mexico, Pennsylvania, and Rhode Island endorsed in 1982 (Rhode Island was omitted). Candidates must garner votes from party activists and state leaders if they are to receive the endorsement. The leaders, on the other hand, have the chance to influence, if not control, the nomination of a candidate who will be supportive of the party as well as electable. In these states, there is ordinarily a party favorite before the convention, as the hypotheses predict. After the convention, the endorsee has the backing of the party leaders and activists. Occasionally that means that opponents do not contest the primary, as was true in Connecticut, Colorado, Illinois, and Pennsylvania. Incumbents in these states will, generally, win the endorsement as well as the following primary without much opposition. (Governor Edward King of Massachusetts provided the exception.) Hence, the postconvention primary model offers few cases for analysis since six of the sixteen endorsees were unchallenged; two were not challenged seriously.

Multiple regression and correlation analysis will determine the individual and collective power of money and party activity in aiding candidates in obtaining the nomination or the endorsement. Experience as well as front-runner status will also be added to the equations.

Model Building for Nominations and Endorsements

Many variables were called but few were chosen for the final models. What follows is an account of the selection process by which predictors were chosen for the primary and endorsement equations. The dependent variables were straightforward: candidate percentage of the primary for the primary models and candidate percentage of the convention for the endorsement model. Several variables, such as leadership support and front-runner status, have never been quantified before, requiring an innovative approach to measurement. Money, however, has been measured since time began.

Money

The 1982 gubernatorial election year was the first in which state campaign finance data were widely available for comparative research (R. Jones 1984). All of the campaign finance information used was obtained from official sources. Most states require primary candidates to file financial statements before a primary and again twenty to thirty days after. This postprimary summary report was used to calculate primary spending. For the thirty-four candidates for endorsement, reports that preceded and immediately followed a convention were used.

Because there are such wild variations among the states in population size and density, total dollars spent conveyed very little information about the impact of money. To adjust for these complexities, candidate spending is measured as a percentage of the total or as the dollar amount of expenditures per voting-age person in the state.

Money raised as well as spent was gathered for each candidate because I anticipated that a war chest raised might create an invincible climate that would discourage both money and votes for the opponent. Apparently campaign money burns a hole in the candidate's pocket, because the correlations between measures of raising and spending are all over .90 and most over .95. I proceeded with the analysis using only the spending variables.

Primary Money

The candidate's percentage of total spending emerged as the most powerful money predictor. Figure 6.1 tells a potent story. Plotted there is a

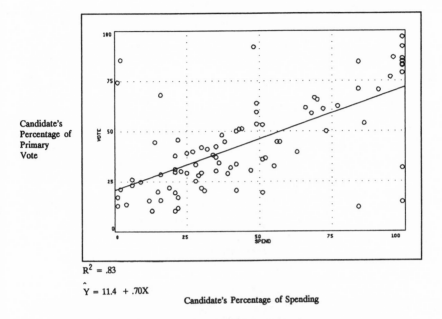

$R^2 = .83$

$\hat{Y} = 11.4 + .70X$

Candidate's Percentage of Spending

Fig. 6.1. Primary spending and primary success. Only contested primaries were included; five unchallenged candidates were eliminated from the analysis. (Reprinted from Morehouse 1990 by permission of the University of Wisconsin Press.)

strong relationship between the proportion of total expenditures a candidate can muster and his or her proportion of the primary votes ($R^2 = .83$). A 1 percent increase in the candidate's percentage of campaign spending brings a .70 percent increase in the percentage of the primary vote received. In the primary election, where the candidates are not known and the voters have no partisan cues, money talks.

Convention Money

Figure 6.2 tells another story entirely. In this plot, money does not predict the endorsement. In fact, in the bivariate correlations, spending accounts for less than half of the success of candidates who vie for the convention designation ($R^2 = .47$). The type of effort required for an endorsement is different. State party leaders provide essential organizational support. Delegates from towns and counties have to be persuaded to vote favorably at the convention. At times, local bosses can influence these potential supporters, so they must be convinced as well. Some media advertising helps,

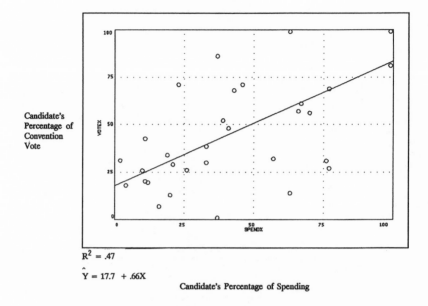

$R^2 = .47$

$\hat{Y} = 17.7 + .66X$

Candidate's Percentage of Spending

Fig. 6.2.   Convention spending and convention success. (Reprinted from Morehouse 1990 by permission of the University of Wisconsin Press.)

of course, but it is the convention votes that are crucial to the endorsement. Here a 1 percent increase in the percentage of campaign spending brings only a .66 percent increase in percentage of convention votes.

Postconvention Primary Money

Of the sixteen potential postconvention primaries, only ten were held, because six endorsees went unchallenged. Twenty-one candidates, including endorsed and challengers, faced the voters with varying amounts of money. Apparently spending could not explain success here any better than in the preceding convention, for the bivariate regression showed that only 43 percent of the postconvention primary vote could be explained by percentage of money spent. Here a 1 percent increase in percentage of postconvention primary spending brings only a .41 percent increase in the percentage of postconvention primary votes (see table 6.4). We have room to improve the predictions for both convention and postconvention support since we have not explained very much with spending. We turn to other variables.

Party Effort

Parties were defined in terms of factional organization and leadership. A single dominant faction within a state party is characterized by its own group of leaders who can prevail over the nominations for state office. Bifactional or multifactional parties cannot bring about a single leadership corps that can commit effort and money to the cause of a single candidate for the nomination. In order to quantify and measure such a concept as leadership support, I used the Delphi method of forecasting by consulting faculty experts in the states selected (see appendix). Party leadership support was scored on a six-point scale from "strongly supportive" to "strongly opposed" (see table 6.3). In the bivariate equations for primaries and endorsements, the leadership variable is strong. As a single predictor in the primary equation, it explains 50 percent of the variance in votes received. As a single predictor in the convention equation, it explains 46 percent. The postconvention primaries present the dilemma of too few cases to test leadership—a direct result of the success of the endorsement. Six of the endorsed candidates were unchallenged, leaving only ten primaries for analysis. Two endorsed candidates, Governor Jim Thompson of Illinois and Lew Lehrman of New York, won handily, but the other eight fought close battles, and four lost.

Experience

Gubernatorial incumbency plays a major role in the renomination process, as past research has assured us. To examine the potential of experience in other offices as well, I used Malcolm Jewell's measure of experience based on a scale of the relative visibility of previous officeholding (and hence campaigning) for several state and local offices (Jewell 1984, 259) (see table 6.3). Slightly over two-thirds of all candidates had officeholding experience.

When experience is the single predictor of primary voting, there is a tendency for votes to vary with this measure ($R^2 = .36$). This equation does not include four incumbent governors and one lieutenant governor who were not challenged in primary contests and hence eliminated from the analysis. In addition, there are several cases that weakened the strength of this relationship. Hawaii's Republicans, weak and demoralized, gave their sacrificial nonincumbent candidate 97 percent of the primary vote. Wisconsin's Republicans gave a good-size vote to Terry Kohler, a business executive, whose father and grandfather had been governors. In this case, Kohler himself did not have office experience but was drawing on the gubernatorial name. A few cases like this dampen a potential predictor.

The bivariate regression between experience and convention votes garnered by candidates for the endorsement is $R^2 = .18$. For the primary following the convention, experience could explain even less: $R^2 = .16$. Massachusetts Governor King's losses dampened the effects of experience from the start. Gubernatorial experience, however, continues a powerful predictor, since all remaining twenty governors in the research were renominated. The low predictive value of this multioffice measure may reflect the

TABLE 6.3.   Variables, Indicators, and Measures Used in Regression Analysis

Variables	Indicator: For Each Candidate in the Primaries and Convention	Measure
Independent:		
Party leaders	Strongly supported by leaders	3
support for	Supported by leaders	2
candidate	Supported by some; others neutral	1
	Leaders neutral or divided	0
	Opposed by leaders	–2
	Strongly opposed by leaders	–3
Experience of	Incumbent governor	4
candidate	Former governor	3
(Jewell 1984,	Elected state office holder, congressman,	
259)	house speaker, senate president, mayor of major city	2
	Former officeholder listed in measure (2),	
	current state legislator or mayor of small	
	city, former candidate for governor or for	
	U.S. Senator	1
	None of the above	0
Front runner	Yes	1
	No	0
Money spent by	Dollars spent by candidate divided by	
candidate	total dollars spent	%
	Dollars spent by candidate per	Actual
	voting-age person	
Dependent:		
Nominating strength	Primary only	% of vote
of candidate	Convention vote[a]	% of vote

Source: Morehouse 1990, Table 1, 715.

[a]A convention vote share was measured as the percentage a candidate received just prior to dropping out or losing. For instance, in the Republican convention in Connecticut, Labriola received 13% of the votes on a preliminary ballot. When he released his supporters, the remaining two candidates were the beneficiaries and their percentage was measured on the later ballot.

$N = 155$.

fact that other offices do not count for much in the nomination contest. After seven of the twenty-one governors were removed from the primary analyses because they were so successful (100 percent), experience so measured could not explain primary support.

Front-runner Status

This independent variable, a recent phenomenon of the presidential nominating contest, was used as a predictor in the three models. Front-runner status (yes or no) was assigned to each candidate by the panel of faculty experts. There appeared to be no hesitancy among those familiar with the campaign to confer this status on one candidate in each contest, although that was a hindsight judgment. The status is sought and perceived to be of importance in both the campaign for the nomination and the one for the endorsement.

Front-runner status is highly correlated with experience, leader support, and spending, although the correlations are not too high to eliminate any of these variables from the primary-only or endorsement equations. Front-runner status accounts for 53.8 percent of the variance in primary voting strength, which makes it a poor second to money as a predictor. In the primaries, front-runner status rests on voter perceptions, which are subject to change. People perceive a candidate as front-runner based on a poll, the candidate's money-raising ability, or even a gut feeling. One would predict that an incumbent governor, as front-runner, would receive a strong primary showing. However, of the fourteen challenged governors, half received considerably less than 80 percent of the primary vote. Other primary front-runners were not particularly advantaged. Of the twenty-six who were not gubernatorial incumbents, nine lost, and most of those who won did not receive impressive margins. Hence, one can conclude that in the primary-only states, front-runner status is unstable. It cannot be garnered steadily as a delegate count. Candidates substitute public-opinion polls, but those change daily. Money must be poured into media operations, and hence money is the most important resource in the primary nomination race.

Front-runner status is more secure in the endorsing states. The convention contest brings forth a different set of strategies because delegate votes determine the endorsement. Presumably the state leaders encourage a candidate to emerge as the front-runner. Occasionally they wait until the contest stabilizes before they back their choice. That usually happens well before the convention, and the delegates are aware of the favored candidate. Thus, secure and gradual garnering of momentum builds delegate strength toward the convention endorsement. A bivariate regression reveals that front-runner status has more explanatory power over the convention vote than the primary vote. A hefty 69.4 percent of the candidate's endorsing vote is explained by this variable. It appears that delegates respond to a front-runner, while a primary electorate is not as impressed.

The postconvention primaries have too few cases to measure the impact of front-runner status statistically. However, as we have seen, primaries make for instability in front-runner status, and the eight hardfought battles produced as many losing front-runners as winning ones.

Money versus Party Effort in Primaries and Endorsing Conventions

The explanatory power of money in primary-only contests was so strong that it is doubtful whether party effort could play much of a role. On the other hand, spending did not explain much of candidate success in endorsing states, leaving the hypothetically satisfying prediction that political party effort may emerge.

The Full Models

The hypothesis that predicts that money is a controlling resource in primary contests is confirmed. The overwhelming predictor is spending. Even front-runners must have money in order to keep their momentum, because, as table 6.4 reveals, front-runner status cannot explain much by itself. If a candidate aspires to be governor, where the primary is the only point of decision, he or she must outspend the opponent.

On the other hand, if a candidate aspires to the gubernatorial nomination in a convention state, he or she must consider the party leaders, who have influence over the endorsement. Endorsements are valuable: 70 percent of endorsees win the nomination. An endorsement takes a careful garnering of delegate votes in local caucuses and a building of support from party leaders. In this type of operation, money is not as important as party effort. Standardized regression coefficients may be compared, and this comparison reveals that spending comes in a poor third after front-runner status and leader support. Therefore, the hypothesis that money does not control the outcomes of convention contests is confirmed. Also confirmed is the hefty role of party leaders' support.

The fact that there were so few postconvention primaries indicates the success of the endorsing conventions but offers few cases to measure the impact of the variables we have discussed. I tried fitting several regression models, some using interaction terms involving the independent variables. None of these terms proved significant. Money can predict 43.3 percent of the vote for a postconvention primary candidate. Beyond that, idiosyncrasies of each contest prevailed, and no independent variables emerged to explain more.

By prediction, money will not play as large a role in these contests as in most primaries, since the party organization will commit the organization and services already in place. Party computers can provide voter lists, and party activists can hand out publicity. Thus, it appears that candidate spending is not as much a determinant of primary success in these endorsed-versus-challenger contests as it is in the standard struggles among self-anointed contenders.

TABLE 6.4. The Effects of Spending and Party Effort on Gubernatorial Primary and Convention Votes

Variables	Regression Coefficients		
	Unstandardized	Standardized	t-score
Primary-only candidates[a,b]			
Constant	12.14		6.76
Front-runner	8.40	.20	2.95**
Spending (%)	.60	.77	12.98**
Number of cases	89		
R^2	.84		
Adjusted R^2	.84		
Endorsing convention candidates:			
Constant	19.92		4.27
Front-runner	30.28	.51	3.86**
Leader support	5.59	.30	2.88**
Spending (%)	.22	.23	1.96*
Number of cases	34		
R^2	.78		
Adjusted R^2	.76		
Postconvention primary candidates:[a]			
Constant	26.41		4.38
Spending (%)	.41		3.81**
Number of cases	21		
R^2	.43		
Adjusted R^2	.40		

Source: Morehouse 1990, Table 2, 718.

Note: The dependent variable is the candidate's percentage of the convention vote or the candidate's percentage of the primary vote.

[a]Only contested primaries are used. There were five unchallenged candidates in the primary-only contests and six unchallenged endorsees in the postconvention primaries. These were eliminated from the analysis.

[b]Primary-only indicates that the primary was the only point of decision for the nomination.

*p < .05, one-tailed test   **p < .005, one-tailed test

Level of Spending

The impact of money has been examined, but not the *level* of spending in the three nominating situations. Table 6.5 compares winner and loser spending in the three types of contests. Again the hypothesis is confirmed.

Primary-only contests are much more expensive to win, and money distinguishes between who wins and who loses, as the significance indicates. Convention endorsements cost the candidate much less, and money does not make the difference between obtaining the endorsement or losing it. In postconvention primaries, candidate spending is still much less than in wide-open primary contests, partly because the campaigns are much shorter. In addition, money does not determine who wins or who loses. In fact, in this situation, losers averaged more than winners. Three endorsed losers spent considerably more than the winners (Lakian, [R] MA; Spannaus, [D] MN; Koch, [D] NY). Nevertheless, two winners were heavy

TABLE 6.5. Average Spending by Winners and Losers in Primaries and Conventions

	Analysis of Variance Test			
	Primary Only[a]	Endorsing Convention	Postconvention Primary[b]	F-score
Winner spending	.43 (.67)	.12 (.13)	.21 (.22)	2.46*
Number of cases	45	16	16	
Loser spending	.22 (.43)	.11 (.13)	.26 (.24)	.79
Number of cases	49	18	11	

	Two-Sample Test		
	Winners	Losers	t-score
Primary only[a]	.43 (.67)	.22 (.43)	1.82**
Number of cases	45	49	
Endorsing convention	.12 (.13)	.11 (.13)	.22
Number of cases	16	18	
Postconvention primary[b]	.21 (.22)	.26 (.24)	.56
Number of cases	16	11	

Source: Morehouse 1990, Table 3, 720.

Note: Spending is measured as dollars spent per voting-age person. The average is the mean. The standard deviation is in parentheses.

[a]Primary-only indicates that the primary was the only point of decision for a nomination.

[b]Postconvention primary spending included unchallenged or challenged endorsees. The endorsee was not the winner in four cases.

*$p < 10$ **$p < .05$

spenders. Winner Wheelock Whitney (R) of Minnesota outspent endorsed loser Lou Wangberg, 31–3, and winner Lew Lehrman (R) of New York (endorsed by his party) outspent Paul Curran 77–3. Presumably in most of these postconvention primaries, the party spends money for its endorsed candidate through media advertising, voter identification, and get-out-the-vote programs. In addition, both endorsed candidates and challengers are generally well known, having been convention losers or prominent political figures.

To summarize, less money is spent by the candidates, and the level of spending is not key to either convention endorsement or postconvention primary winning. Winners in primary-only contests spend much more money, and spending is significant in determining success.

The Impact of the Endorsement

In May 1986, a month before the Minnesota parties were to hold their endorsing conventions, the chair of the DFL party opined that the voting public wanted a full slate of candidates in the primary, "not just one person winnowed out and promoted by a comparative few caught up in the lockstep nominating process" ("Another Nail in Coffin" 1986). The voters apparently were not as exercised, because they later nominated both endorsed candidates (Kunkel 1987). However, in 1982, the year for this research, the Minnesota voters rejected both convention choices. The purpose of this story is to suggest that the endorsement is somewhat riskier than those who rant against the "smoke-filled room" would have us believe. In 1982, sixteen endorsed candidates emerged from their respective conventions. After the primaries were over, twelve of them were still in the running. Of the four who lost (Wangberg [R] and Spannaus [D] in Minnesota, Lakian [R] in Massachusetts, and Koch [D] in New York), three were beaten by challengers from the outside who had not gone the endorsement route. Thus, the odds for the endorsed candidate are good, but not spectacular. What predictions can be made about the impact of the endorsement?

One of the best ways to predict the primary success of a convention candidate is to examine his or her convention vote. The correlation between the two is $r = .66$. Endorsing conventions appear to be relatively representative institutions. A candidate's vote in the convention only slightly overestimates his or her following in the primary electorate (McNitt 1980). It appears that leaders are representative of the factions within the party. When there is a significant division within the party, the factions back their own candidates in the primary, as they did in the convention, and the primary results are in line with the convention vote. The "smoke-filled" coliseum, then, is not as unrepresentative of the primary voters as many claim. There is a relationship between the convention activists gathered in the convention and the primary electorate that they represent. If they bicker at the convention, this controversy is reflected in the primary. It is possible that this process of controversy and stability may characterize the inner workings of a party. In the case of the convention-primary syndrome, these factional divisions are acknowledged and represented in the convention and the ensuing primary.

The hypotheses that are most out of line with the realities of the nominating process in 1982 are those that predict the magnitude of postconvention primary voting outcomes. They predict that an endorsed candidate will obtain a large percentage of the postconvention primary vote. On the other hand, the prediction is that the winner of the primary-only contest will receive a bare majority because the party cannot control the nominating process. Such does not appear to be the case. The average primary win of the convention choice is only a few percentage points higher than that of front-runners from primary-only contests. Closer inspection reveals that front-runners in primary-only contests do better than those in postconvention primaries. In 70 percent of the cases, the front-runners in states where the primary is the only decision win by more than 20 percent over their opponents, while in convention-primary states, only half the endorsed candidates led by this margin. This finding challenges the hypothesis of V. O. Key, who predicted that the primary would ignite and reflect the factionalism within the party (Key 1964, 342). How can we explain the success of the winner in those primary-only states?

A plausible explanation may lie in the impact of the media in states where the only way to reach the electorate is through advertising on television and radio. The new technology takes the place of the political party as the intermediary between the voters and the candidate. The candidate with the most money to spend is ratified by the electronic media. Thus, media exposure confers winner status. This campaign is played far over the heads of party factions and party leaders. The primary results indicate commanding leads in most elections. It would appear that the electronic gatekeepers are more successful than the human ones.

In the convention states, a process exists that engages large numbers of party activists in face-to-face contact with a job to do—that of endorsing a party candidate for governor. If that candidate is not challenged, he or she becomes the nominee with a supportive party structure in place. That happened 50 percent of the time in 1982. Half the time, the endorsee was challenged and ran a hard-fought race. The primary electorate in these states had the opportunity of seeing its parties "handling the hot poker on the front porch" and ratified or rejected the endorsement. The primary provided the safety valve for the "smoke-filled room."

Summary and Conclusions

This research investigated the relative power of money and party effort in the race for the gubernatorial nomination. The hypothesis predicted that money would have more impact over outcomes of direct primaries than endorsing conventions. It also predicted that money would not have as much impact over primaries in which endorsed candidates faced challengers. The hypotheses were largely confirmed. Candidate spending was the overwhelming predictor of the outcome of the primary-only contests. Even experience in office was not as important as spending. In endorsing conventions, money was not nearly as important to the outcome as leader support or front-runner status. Likewise, in the primaries that followed conventions, money was not as important a predictor as it was in all other primaries. The reasons lie in the different character of the nominating contests themselves. In the direct primaries, where self-selected candidates battle for recognition, money is crucial because expensive electronic advertising is the only way to gain visibility, and hence the outcome usually rewards the one with the largest war chest. Conventions confer endorsements on candidates who have made themselves known to a thousand or so party delegates from the cities and counties of the state. It takes shoe leather and sweat to garner the convention votes. In the primaries that follow this face-to-face gathering, the endorsed candidate as well as the challenger are generally known to the voters. The party usually bestows time, effort, and cash on its endorsed nominee, and hence his or her spending does not play as large a role in the outcome.

A totally unexpected finding emerged from a scrutiny of the results from two different types of primary contests: those that are the sole decision and those that follow a convention. Since 1950, when V. O. Key wrote *Southern Politics in State and Nation,* primary voting was assumed to indicate the degree of party unity or diversity (16–18). However, contests within sole-decision primaries are producing winners who have commanding leads over their rivals. Do these results indicate that parties are backing them? More likely, it indicates the effect of electronic campaigning waged far above the factions and coalitions that make up the party organization. The media give the candidates a hefty lead, not the efforts of a leadership coalition.

On the other hand, primaries that are predicted to confer a rousing advantage to an endorsed candidate promote genuine contests. These primaries relate back to the endorsing convention and reflect the divisions within it. At times disruption may occur, as in Minnesota in 1982 when both endorsed candidates were defeated; at times unity may prevail, as in 1986 in the same state when the voters in both primaries ratified the endorsed candidates.

How can we explain why parties in sixteen states prefer to engage in the rigors of face-to-face contact in unruly endorsing conventions while their contemporaries disdain such a practice? This research was not charged to answer that question, although it should be answered. The task of a political party is to recruit leadership and to enable that leadership to govern. Nomination is parent to governing. Any process that connects with groups of people and their hopes and demands is preferable to one that is unconnected. A convention, however unruly the hand-to-hand combat, taps into reality more than does shadow boxing on a screen.

Tom Patterson comments that the media cannot possibly do things differently enough to organize the election in meaningful ways (1980). If that is true, then parties through endorsements are able to structure the primary election by providing the voters with cues—somewhat untidy and emotional, but reflecting a testing process rather than a single decisional event. Jewell's analysis of voters in primaries offers little evidence that they pay attention to endorsements per se (Jewell 1984, 143–47), but the process of preconvention garnering of votes, convention contests, and proclamation of the endorsement, followed by a second round of coalition building, may permeate the public's consciousness—providing a different opportunity for testing and weighing the candidates. In this case, the voters have been provided with an informed nomination process in which party effort dominates money.

CHAPTER 7

Governors and Governing

Ten of our candidates became governor. Among the endorsing states, Governors William O'Neill (Connecticut), Jim Thompson (Illinois), and Richard Lamm (Colorado) were reelected, and two nonendorsed nominees, Mario Cuomo (New York) and Rudy Perpich (Minnesota) were elected. Perpich had been governor four years before and was familiar with the legislators of his party. Cuomo, as former lieutenant governor, presided over the state senate by virtue of his office and hence had legislative experience. Both new governors had won exceedingly close primaries that had the potential for fracturing their parties, but as New York City mayor Ed Koch's gubernatorial campaign managers said, all the party factions pull together for the general election. (LoCicero and Piscatelli 1982, 23). This same sentiment was echoed in Minnesota by Democratic-Farmer-Labor party chair Mike Hatch following Perpich's primary win. Perhaps a family fight does not damage party support for its successful leader.

Three governors were also reelected in the direct-primary states: Governors Lamar Alexander (Tennessee), John Carlin (Kansas), and Victor Atiyeh (Oregon). The fourth, Governor Bill Clements (Texas), the state's first Republican governor in over a hundred years, lost to Mark White, the conservative Democrat (Clements won the rematch four years later). In California, an open race, Republican George Deukmejian won an exceedingly narrow one-percentage-point victory over Democratic mayor Tom Bradley of Los Angeles.

This chapter investigates factors that explain legislative support for the governor's program in ten states in 1983. It will test the hypothesis that there is a correlation between state party organizational strength and legislative party loyalty on the governor's program bills. This correlation may be influenced by divided government in which the governor must negotiate compromises with the majority opposition party and hence alienate some of his or her own party members. Support for the program will be stronger in the case of governors who have been endorsed and nominated by strong state parties.

The support of individual legislators for the governor's program may also be influenced by electoral factors in the members' districts, such as primary and general election voting strength of the governor or the legislator. Support may also be affected by socioeconomic characteristics of the districts.

Party Government Model

This chapter tests the party government model of a strong party system. In this model, the party coalition is composed of party leaders and activists who endorse candidates for governor, work for their nomination and election, and engineer support for their legislative program. This process occurs because many of those who attend the nominating conventions are state legislators as well as local party leaders who benefit from the governor's power and have a stake in the governor's success. Legislators are positively oriented toward their governor because they share the same policy affiliation.

The American model of party government does not require unified party government. Since in well over half of the states the governor's party does not control both houses of the legislature, unified party government would be an unrealistic condition to impose. In the ten states that form the backbone of this book, only three had one-party control of the governorship and both houses of the legislature. The model would predict that strong governors would gain strong legislative support, even if the party's legislators were in the minority. This support might be lessened because the governor has to negotiate compromises with the majority opposition party and alienate some of his or her own party members.

Coalition Building in the Legislature

Very little research has been done on the relationship between the political efforts of party leaders and gubernatorial candidates to capture the nomination and their success when in office in putting the party program into effect. Several works have dealt descriptively with the legislative leadership of governors (Sabato 1983; Jewell and Olson 1988, 244–49; Muchmore and Beyle 1980). In *Governors and Legislatures: Contending Powers,* Rosenthal (1990) describes executive-legislative jockeying as well as legislative independence from or dominance over the governor. He assumes institutional conflict, as the title suggests, and does not focus on legislative voting on gubernatorial initiatives.

The levels of partisan voting in state legislatures have been largely unexamined in the last two decades, although earlier research found that variations in the internal cohesion of parties affected the extent and direction of partisan voting behavior. Many years ago I found that governors who are successful in building primary and electoral coalitions outside the legislature are also successful in building coalitions within the legislature to pass their programs (Morehouse 1981a, 246–52).

Coalition Studies

The formation of coalitions by governors and legislative party leaders to win voting support can be examined by applying a model of legislative coalition behavior. However, early coalition theory was tested by experimental simulations or controlled conditions. William Riker, a leading theoretician, developed the size principle, which states that "participants create coalitions just as large as they believe will ensure winning and no larger" (1962, 32–33). Much empirical research has been devoted to investigating this theory in Congress and state legislatures, but efforts to prove Riker's minimum winning hypothesis have met with little success. Winning coalitions on the average are much larger than predicted.

Studies of coalition formation in state legislatures offer verification of the relevance of majority party size and cohesion. Wayne Francis (1970) studied the effects of party leadership strategy on coalition size in seven sessions of the Indiana legislature. A major part of the leadership strategy, Francis discovered, was related to the percentage of seats held by the majority party. The party leaders calculated the size of the coalition they wished to maintain, with an eye to the percentage of seats actually held by the party, and dispensed or withheld payoffs to party members accordingly.

David Meltz also studied the relationship between party competition and cohesion in the Indiana legislature (1973). He considered the majority party as three subsets: the leadership, the concerned, and the possible defectors. Neither the leadership nor the concerned constitute a winning coalition, so the leaders must bargain with the possible defectors and offer them sidepayments to obtain their vote. The number of potential defectors is a function of the majority party's size, and hence as the size goes down, the value of each unconcerned legislator goes up. Meltz found that cohesion is related to leadership and long-term competition.

These studies of coalition building confirm the fact that political party size and cohesion are the major determinants of the building of the winning coalitions. Members of the leadership of the parties are key actors in forming the coalitions. The leadership considers the votes necessary to win and does not waste resources on building oversize coalitions.

Legislative Coalition Building

Researchers have found that party alignments are likely to appear on the following issues: (1) the prestige and programs of the governor; finance, taxation, and administration; (2) social and economic issues that are associated with broad differences between the parties, such as labor; and (3) issues involving the special interests of state or legislative parties, such as apportionment, elections, and primaries (Francis 1967; Francis and Weber 1980).

The package of bills that a governor presents to the legislature as his or her policy program is the most important and, therefore, the most controversial legislation that is considered. A governor's program covers the three categories listed in the previous paragraph. It involves the major issues at stake on the legislative agenda. A majority of the major bills passed in an average session of a state legislature emanate from the governor's office. As a result, the governor must devote much time to the development of a legislative program and the strategy needed to secure its support. I found that governors are more likely to have support from their legislative party members if they are strong party leaders and if their formal powers are substantial (Morehouse 1981a, 246–52).

Coalition Actors

Coalition actors are the governor, the legislative party leaders, and the individual members of the state house or senate. A party coalition is defined as a joining together of the party's legislators in sufficient numbers to assume that it is not simply a chance combination. A party coalition may be said to occur when at least 80 percent of the party's legislators join together.

The Governor and the Legislative Leaders

The governor is assumed to be part of the legislative leadership. The governor may influence votes by rewarding or punishing legislators with resources such as appointments, public works projects, municipal loans, and the like. The leaders also have possession of resources such as patronage, power of recognition, flow of legislation, appointments, campaign money, and access to the governor. They can use these for payoffs to members who vote for the program.

The leadership supports the governor's program and sees that bills within it are guided through the legislature. When the governor has a majority in a chamber, this party leadership includes the speaker of the house, the presiding officer of the senate, majority leaders, and chairs of committees. This majority gives the governor a control over legislation that is absent when the governor has a minority.

Governors head the ticket on which legislators campaign for election, and legislators hope the governor's coattails will help them win, although Stonecash found that legislative electoral bases are much more stable than the governor's (1989). While most legislators have to run independent campaigns, there is a bond that comes from standing under the same umbrella. If governors have a strong interest in party coalition building, they will involve themselves in legislative elections (LeBlanc 1969, 49). While they will not usually get involved in a legislative primary, it is much more likely that governors will support legislators' general elections. Hence, the legislator in the governor's party has a personal stake in the governor's success.

There are several ways the state party leaders try to gain the support of the party's legislators. In states where parties are strong, like Connecticut and Minnesota, party leaders at the state or local level may recruit candidates for the nomination. In those two states as well as Ohio, Indiana, Pennsylvania, and Colorado, local parties endorse and work for candidates in legislative primaries. If the nominating system is open, as it is in most states, the party cannot control recruitment. Incumbents are less likely to have opposition in the primary, and only three percent of them lose. The picture emerges of legislative nominations going primarily to those who have already served and to self-starters who organize their own campaign, which does not leave too many vulnerable legislators willing to welcome party help.

However, a relatively recent development indicates that legislative leaders are taking an interest in legislative elections. It is in the marginal districts in closely competitive legislatures that legislative majorities are won or lost. Coupled with that, the cost of seriously contested legislative campaigns is escalating and candidates need help. Legislative leaders and legislative caucuses reason that raising funds to help both incumbents and challengers who face close races would make legislators more likely to cooperate with the party leaders and would help build or maintain a majority in the legislature. In addition, funding party members in open races would bring loyalty and gratitude on the part of the newly elected. In 1982 in Minnesota, endorsed candidates from both parties received advice, campaign money, fund-raising help, campaign schools, voter survey services, get-out-the-vote phoning, sample ballots, and, in the IR party, district-by-district polling (Sturdevant 1982c).

Governors and Divided Government

Governors in half of the states have minority parties in the legislature, and their strategies in these situations are different. In seven out of the ten states in our study, the governor's party was in the minority. Little attention has been paid to the consequences of divided government at the state level (Morehouse and Jewell 1992). In a divided government, the governor lacks many of the advantages that accrue to a governor who is backed by a majority. The house speaker, senate presiding officer, majority leaders, and usually all committee chairs are members of the opposition party and are in a position to control the legislative timetable and agenda.

The ability of the governor to get his or her program passed under conditions of divided government depends upon the strength of the statewide party as well as the cohesion of the legislative party. Charles O. Jones describes two types of coalition building that take place under conditions of divided government between the president and Congress: copartisanship and bipartisanship. These types assume the strong legislative party model. Copartisanship is the result of parallel development of proposals by the leaders of each party and the ability to commit their partisans to support the proposals. Bipartisanship, which is a rarer type of coalition building, involves leaders of both parties in a cooperative effort from the start and involves nearly unanimous support from partisans of both (C. Jones 1994, 20–22).

When there are strong statewide parties, there are likely to be strong parties in the legislature, but this situation is not universally true. When there has been a close balance between the two parties over a period of year and some alternation in majority control, divided governments are likely to have only modest majorities. A governor who is the effective leader of his or her party and commands broad party support is likely to follow a partisan strategy in the face of a narrow opposition majority. Such a governor may submit to the legislature an ambitious legislative program designed to carry out campaign promises and the priorities of his or her political party. Working within the legislature, he or she will mobilize support within the minority governing party and seek to expand this coalition by offering personal or constituency benefits to some members of the opposition. Where parties are strong, the potential for deadlock is great. But on the other hand, the leaders of cohesive legislative parties are better able to negotiate with the governor because the members are more likely to support any compromise that is negotiated. Opposition leaders will recognize more need to compromise if the governor is politically strong and has widespread public support. The most usual type of coalition building in this situation is copartisanship.

A governor whose statewide party is weak or divided will accommodate some of the priorities of the opposition party in a strong party legislature. The governor may be willing to negotiate with the leadership of the opposition and to make extensive compromises in order to get legislation passed. Members of the governor's party may object to these compromises and vote against the program. This is most likely a variation of copartisanship, but with the advantage lying with the opposition party.

When the governor's statewide party is weak, the legislative party is usually weak as well, and divided government may not have an impact. In weak party states, divided government often occurs when partisan control of the governorship has rotated, but the legislature traditionally remains in the hands of one party. Partisanship has some effect on voting on many issues, including the governor's program, but the effect is less strong and consistent than in the strong party legislatures. In the weak party system, the two legislative parties may have members with constituency interests that are less distinct. With less cohesive parties, the governor expects less success in winning unanimous support from members of his or her own party, but greater success in wooing some members of the opposition party.

Legislative leaders of less cohesive parties, of course, may be less able to commit their members to support of compromises negotiated with the governor. When a governor is elected from the traditional minority party, the hypotheses predict that she or he would be able to unite such a small legislative contingent but would have to obtain significant numbers of votes from the rival majority. For this situation, Jones suggests another type of coalition: the cross-partisan coalition, where one party (or a faction of one party) counts on support by a faction of the other party (C. Jones 1994, 22–23).

The third possibility is the southern party model. It is found in southern states where the governorship and the legislature have traditionally been under Democratic control. In the past this model has been virtually a nonpartisan one. The Republican minority was too insignificant to pose a threat or offer alternatives, and the majority party represented nearly all the constituent interests in the state and thus could not be very cohesive. There were only a few states, such as North Carolina, Tennessee, and Kentucky, where the Republicans had enough seats (ranging from one-fourth to one-third) to make possible a weak party model. More recently in most of the southern states, the Republicans have occasionally won the governorship but not a majority in more than one legislative chamber, thus creating divided government.

In most of these southern legislatures, the Democratic party's governor faces a divided party containing rival factions. Party voting is virtually

unknown, and governors must piece together factions based on geographical areas, ideology, personalities, and other components. Republican governors have an opportunity to win votes for their programs because many
Democratic legislators—perhaps a majority—share their conservative
viewpoints. Whether the Republican governor is able to use his or her own
partisans as the core of a winning coalition depends upon the size, cohesion, and organizational experience of the legislative party in that state. In
these states, the Republican governor may often face leaders of the opposition party who are very strong and whose power base extends to members of both parties.

Governors and Legislators

The majority of the legislators of either party are divided among the concerned and the possible defectors. For either party, the concerned are
those who are personally affected by the substance of the particular issue.
They include those whose constituencies are personally involved, those
whose future election chances may be changed by the fate of the bill in
question, and those who consider the issue a matter of personal conscience. The concerned in the minority party may be the core of support
for the governor's party when it is the minority. Since the number of concerned is proportional to the size of the party, the minority party contains
fewer than the majority party. In neither case, however, can those concerned together with the leaders form a winning coalition.

The possible defectors can be "bought" because they do not have an
intense commitment to, or are cross-pressured by, the bill in question. The
number of defectors is also proportional to the size of the party. If the governor's party has a large majority, there are many possible defectors. If the
governor has a minority, the number of defectors is small.

Legislative Districts

Parties are made up of legislators pulled by the needs of their constituencies as well as demands for party loyalty imposed by the state leaders.
Early studies of the links between a legislator and his or her district were
based on the relationship of district socioeconomic and electoral variables.
Studies of the relationships found between constituency characteristics,
electoral margins, and party loyalty were by no means comparable across
analyses. Researchers found that the impact of party and constituency varied between Democrats and Republicans and across issue areas, legislatures, and time (Collie 1984, 23–26).

The statewide party and the constituency party are interconnected in practice. The constituency influence research indicates that there is a link between constituency characteristics and legislative behavior but that this link may be partially explained by statewide party position, which would correspond to that of a majority of the constituencies and thus provide no conflict for the legislator. I suspect that political survival is at the base of a legislator's calculations and that much of the time survival is linked with the demands of the party.

Whether the political party can help the legislator electorally and professionally is related to the type of district he or she represents. At least 20 percent of the legislative districts (in a majority of states) are won by less than 55 percent of the vote (Tidmarch, Lonergan, and Sciortino 1986). It was originally assumed that legislators from competitive districts would tend to represent their districts first before the interests of their party, if the two were in conflict. However, it is precisely those competitive districts that are of interest to party leaders, particularly in legislatures where the party balance is close. These districts are the ones that can win or lose majorities. Caldeira and Patterson observe that partisan strength (measured as party registration) is the most important influence in voting for state legislators (1982). More of the votes in legislative races turn on the underlying partisan loyalties of the mass public. Campaign spending can confer an average advantage of 5 percent, but mobilizing partisan electorates is key to election success. In this endeavor, the money and electoral help provided by state legislative leaders bring victory as well as legislators' loyalty.

Tidmarch, Lonergan, and Sciortino (1986) report that a majority of districts are safe for one party or the other and that marginal seats are on the wane. Legislators from comfortably one-party districts do not need the support of a state party for election. If they want to advance within the legislative hierarchy, however, they must please their leaders, who control committee assignments and political positions. For about twenty years, a high percentage of incumbents have sought reelection. In 1986, ten out of fourteen states had at least one chamber in which 80 percent of its members ran again. On average, well over 90 percent of the incumbents win. What has changed, however, is the winning margin, which has increased dramatically (Jewell and Breaux 1988). Incumbents now win by about 75 percent on average (Garand 1991, 12). The high degree of incumbency and the increasing margins by which legislators win indicate that they may be independent of political parties as organizations. However, their advancement within the legislature depends on the party leadership.

Endorsements and funding are two ways the legislative party can help the legislators with elections in their districts. If the legislator needs the party's help to win, she or he will support its leaders and program. If the legislator's campaign was aided by a rival faction or interest group and not by the party, the legislator owes it little allegiance. On the other hand, a legislator from a noncompetitive district may face a primary and need the support of the party, and legislative caucus committees occasionally enter these races. From this discussion, it would appear that the more vulnerable the legislator electorally, the more she or he needs help and hence the more beholden becomes.

Not every vulnerable legislator turns to the leaders of the governor's party for help. A legislator is more likely to look to a governor who has strong support in the legislator's constituency. For example, Democratic legislators are more likely to support the governor's programs if the governor had high primary support in their districts. Those Democratic legislators coming from areas of high gubernatorial primary strength had a mean gubernatorial support score that was 25 points higher than those coming from low-strength areas. The causal connection between the gubernatorial primary vote and legislative support is provided by the governor's efforts to consolidate a winning coalition that includes the legislator (Morehouse 1973, 63–66).

It is highly probable that state legislators of both parties will also respond to the governor's general election vote in their districts. Congressional studies have shown that a member of Congress is more likely to support a president's legislative program if the president has won by a comfortable margin in the member's district and particularly if the margin has been larger than that of the member. The relationship between support for the president and his electoral margin was at least as strong for members of the opposition party as for those in his own party. Not surprisingly, this support was greater for those presidents who had won by a landslide (Harmon and Brauen 1979; Buck 1972; Edwards 1978). Members of Congress may interpret electoral support in their district for the president as evidence that constituents support the broad outlines of his policy, if not specific presidential programs. We can test whether this relationship also exists at the state level.

In order to build coalitions to pass the governor's program, leaders consider the electoral vulnerability or security of legislators and how they can affect their hopes for advancement by assisting them electorally or professionally. Jewell and Patterson have proposed that legislators from districts that reflect the basic economic orientation of the party are more likely to be loyal than those whose constituencies deviate from the mean (1986). These legislators, then, would be would be among the "concerned" on most issues. Legislators from districts that are not typical of the majority of those in the party would be cross-pressured between party demands and constituency needs and would make up the defectors. We do not know how legislators cross-pressured between the economic needs of their constituencies and the demands for party cohesion resolve these conflicts. Presumably they are constantly balancing the two, and adjustments are made on both sides.

To summarize, legislators have ambitions for advancement that are related to the political opportunities in their districts as well as the statewide party. If they see their chance for advancement bound up with the record of the party, they will support the party program if their party has the governorship. If legislators are from atypical districts and from a faction opposing the governor, they will support district or interest-group needs over those of the party.

Hypotheses

The following hypotheses are based on the discussion so far. They predict that governors in strong party states are able to command legislative party loyalty for their programs and that the strongest support comes from legislators from districts where the governor has a comfortable margin in the primary and general election.

I am measuring legislators' support for the governor's program and trying to explain variations in that support.

The specific dependent variables are:

(a) the average support scores of all Democrats and of all Republicans for the program;
(b) the individual legislator's support score for the program.

A. State party strength and legislative party support
   1. There will be larger differences between Democratic and Republican average support scores in strong party states using endorsements, with higher support coming from the governor's party and lower support from the opposition party.
   2. Average support scores in the governor's party will be higher in strong party states using endorsements than in other states.
      Endorsing states are generally states with relatively strong party organizations. The governor is more likely to win the primary by a big margin or unopposed. Thus, they are states where organizational partisanship can be expected to have a strong impact on legislative voting.
B. Unified or divided government and legislative support
   1. There will be larger differences between Democratic and Republican average scores in chambers where the governor's

party has control than in those controlled by the opposition party.

2. The average support score in the governor's party will be lower in chambers controlled by the opposition party.

In trying to build a winning coalition, the governor seeks votes primarily from his or her own party in a legislative chamber where that party holds a majority. If the opposition holds a majority in a chamber, the governor may have to negotiate compromises that will result in less partisan voting (smaller difference in Democratic and Republican support) in that chamber.

C. District electoral variable and support by individual legislators

1. A legislator in the governor's party will be more likely to support the governor's program if the governor's primary vote in the preceding or subsequent election in the legislative district was high.

2. A legislator in either party will be more likely to support the governor's program if the governor's general election vote in the preceding or subsequent election in the legislative district was high.

A legislator in the governor's party from a district where the governor has strong party organizational support will be part of the governor's coalition and will support the governor for mutual advantage. A legislator in either party interprets gubernatorial electoral support in his or her district as evidence that constituents support the broad outlines of the governor's policy.

3. A legislator in the governor's party will be more likely to support the governor's program if that legislator's primary vote in the preceding election in the legislative district is low.

4. A legislator in either party will be more likely to support the governor's program if that legislator's general election vote in the preceding election is low.

A legislator in the governor's party who is vulnerable in a primary may need help from the governor's organization. A legislator from either party who faces close competition will more likely support the governor because the district is so closely divided between the parties.

D. District socioeconomic variables and support by individual legislators

1. When districts represented by legislators from the two parties have distinctly different socioeconomic characteristics, a

legislator from the governor's party will be more likely to support the governor's program if the legislator's district reflects the basic orientation of the party.

2. When districts represented by legislators from the two parties have distinctly different socioeconomic characteristics, a legislator from the opposition party will be more likely to support the governor's program if the legislator's district does not reflect the basic orientation of the party.

Measuring Coalition Building

This book tests the ability of the governor to build an electoral coalition for the primary and general election that will be strong enough to carry over into the governing process and command legislative loyalty for the governor's program. The 1983 legislative sessions that followed the 1982 gubernatorial election test the coalition-building efforts of our ten governors. In the five endorsing states, the possibility of a strong coalition exists because gubernatorial candidates are endorsed in a convention or party gathering and party cohesion is traditionally strong (Colorado, Connecticut, Illinois, Minnesota, and New York). I hypothesize that a strong party coalition includes members of the legislature who come from areas where the governor has party organizational support. The assumption is that the legislative party and the statewide party are joined in the forming of an electoral coalition.

In the primary-only states, the parties have traditionally been weaker and do not use any endorsement process in primary elections (California, Kansas, Oregon, Tennessee, and Texas). The gubernatorial candidate must put together his or her own coalition because the party leaders have little influence and the primary determines the outcome of the nominating process. Incumbent governors are generally able to achieve renomination, but they may be challenged in the primary, as was true in Kansas and Oregon. In these states where the party is weak or divided, the governor will face a legislature in which sit remnants of the factions that opposed him or her in the primary contest.

In this study, the governor's party strength is measured by the primary vote of the party's gubernatorial candidates, averaged over the last five elections (1966–82). This is a summary measure of the strength of the coalition that the governor inherited to obtain the nomination, win the election, and control of the government.

Our hypotheses lead us to expect that legislators will support governors who show party strength in their districts. We also predict that if legislators need the governor's help in the next election, they will be more supportive of gubernatorial initiatives. To test these hypotheses, I collected the following data by legislative district. (See the appendix for the sources, computations, and problems with the data collection and processing.)

1. Legislator's primary vote for 1982
2. Legislator's general election vote for 1982
3. Governor's primary vote 1982 and 1986
4. Governor's general election vote for 1982 and 1986
5. Socioeconomic data for Illinois, Minnesota, California, and Texas

The dependent variable in this research is legislative voting on governor's program bills in the legislative session of 1983 for each of the ten states in the sample. In all fifty states, the governor presents a message to the legislature in which he or she outlines the substance of the program desired for passage. This message is translated into administration bills that are introduced in most states by the governor's party leaders in the house or senate.

In all but two of the states in this project, the governor needed to obtain 80 percent or more of his legislative party to build a winning coalition for passage. In the New York house, Governor Cuomo's party had 65 percent of the seats and needed only 77 percent of the party members to pass legislation. In Texas, Governor White needed only 66 percent of his party in the house and 62 percent in the senate to obtain the votes necessary to pass his program because he had such an overwhelming majority of the seats.

The first problem encountered in analyzing legislators' support for the governor's program is identifying exactly which bills embody that program. At the national level, *Congressional Quarterly* provides us with a list of all roll calls on bills, amendments, and other motions on which the president took a stand. At the state level, such information is lacking for governors, and therefore each governor's office must be asked for such a list.

The ten states varied in their ability to produce lists of the governors' program bills. In Tennessee and Minnesota the governor's office produced a tracking report of administration bills, describing each bill and stating what action had been taken on it in the two chambers and by the governor. In Connecticut, New York, Kansas, and Texas the governor's office provided a list of bills embodying the governor's program but no information on their fate. In Oregon bills could be identified in the legislative journals as being introduced "at the request" of the governor or (for budget bills) of the executive. In Illinois, Colorado, and California it was necessary to read the governor's state of the state speech and consult with administration officials about which bills were pertinent. Table 7.1 gives the number of bills contained within each governor's program for the 1983 session of the legislature. The numbers vary widely and do not appear to relate to size of the state. New York Governor Cuomo's program of 122 items (including seven on the budget) was rivaled by Governor Atiyeh of Oregon, one of our study's least populous states. Governor O'Neill of Connecticut and Governor Thompson of Illinois concentrated on taxes and appropriations for the 1983 sessions, which meant fewer program bills.

The second problem in identifying support for the governor's program is coding specific roll call votes on the bills that have been selected. State legislative roll call votes are found only in legislative journals, which must be obtained from a state library or law library. On each of the bills identified as being part of the governor's program, I recorded all roll call votes on amendments, motions, and final passage on which at least 10 per-

TABLE 7.1.   Contested Roll Call Votes on Governor's Program Bills, 1983 (by state and topic)

Topic	Number of Roll Calls										
	CT	MN	NY	IL	CO	CA	TN	KA	OR	TX	Total
Appropriations	27	19	20	25	6	8		18	106	27	256
Taxes	61	6	5	20	4	3	14	2	1		116
Administrative organization personnel		2	8		1				4	2	17
Courts, crime, prisons			3		1	1			2	2	9
Welfare, housing			2			9					11
Education	6	1		3		9		2	1		22
Health	7	5				11					23
Environment, water, agriculture	5	5		3		1		2	2	7	25
Transportation		5		1				2		2	10
Business regulation, economic development, energy		10	1			2	4		2	28	47
Labor		2	1	2							5
Civil rights, elections									2	4	6
Bond issues	4		2								6
Miscellaneous			2	1	2						5
Total roll calls	92	57	60	46	21	15	49	26	120	72	558
Total bills in program	7	39	122	14	25	57	85	26	125	36	

Note: Contested roll call votes are those on amendments, motions, or final passage on the governor's program bills on which at least 10 percent of those voting were in the minority. The numbers include votes in both chambers.

cent of those voting were in the minority—with a few exceptions. There were a few amendments on which the governor's position was unclear (such as one offered by an opposition legislator that might weaken the bill but make its passage more likely). Table 7.1 indicates that taxes and appropriations amounted to two-thirds of all contested roll calls in our ten states.

A yea vote did not always indicate a progovernor position. Occasionally a governor vetoed an item in a budget bill, and a nay vote on overriding the veto indicates support for the governor. Occasionally the opposition party (particularly when it was in the majority) succeeded in changing a "governor's bill" so drastically that the governor asked legislators to oppose it.

For each of the roll calls on bills in the governor's program, the vote of each legislator was recorded; a vote for the governor was scored as 1.0, an absence or abstention was 0.5, and a vote against the governor was scored as 0. A "gubernatorial support score" was calculated for each member, as the mean of his or her individual scores.

In each chamber for the 1983 session, the average gubernatorial support score was calculated for all Democrats and for all Republicans. The dependent variables used in this analysis, therefore, are the gubernatorial support score for each legislator, the average score for each party in each chamber, and the average score for each party in the legislature.

The Importance of Party in Voting for the Governor's Program

State Party Systems and Legislative Party Support

The hypotheses predict that governors in strong party states are able to command legislative party loyalty for their programs. Endorsing states are generally states with strong party organizations. In the five endorsing states in my sample, the governors' average percentage in the preceding five gubernatorial primaries (1966–82) was 80 percent. Thus, they are states where organizational partisanship can be expected to have a strong impact on legislative voting. In states where parties are weaker and nominations are made in primaries, governors cannot receive the backing of a party organization and must develop individual campaign organizations, which are very loosely connected with the party. In my primary-only states, the average vote for the governor's party candidate for the preceding five primaries (1966–82) was 70 percent.

Table 7.2 compares the five primary-only states and the five endorsing states with respect to legislators' support for the governor's program. This is a merged data program using all 1,550 legislators. The strongest finding is that the political party is highly correlated with the support for the governor's program in endorsing states (.754) and weakly correlated in primary-only states (.192). This contrast is caused by the exceedingly high correlation between party and support in Connecticut, Minnesota and the New York Assembly (.949).

In the endorsing states, members of the governor's party supported the governor's program 86 percent of the time, while opposition party support was only 38 percent, a difference of 48 percentage points. In the primary-only states, support from the governor's party was somewhat lower (71 percent), and support from the opposition party was much higher (65 percent), a difference of only 6 percentage points.

These data strongly confirm the hypotheses that there will be larger differences between the parties in level of support for the governor's program in endorsing states and that the support from the governor's party will be higher in endorsing than in primary-only states. This is the typical party government scenario. In primary-only states, there is much less partisan loyalty, parties are weak, and gubernatorial candidates must build their own electoral and governing organizations.

In all ten states except Texas (and the New York Assembly), the governor needs at least 80 percent or more of the governing party legislators to be sure that the program will pass or that he can bargain effectively with the opposition party. Legislators of the governor's party are much more

TABLE 7.2. **The Effect of Party on Legislators' Support for the Governor's Program (merged data)**

	Mean Support			
	Members of Governor's Party	Members of Opposition Party	Difference	Correlation (R) of Support and Party
Endorsing States (CT, MN, NY, IL, CO) ($N = 873$)	86.1 (15.0) ($N = 465$)	37.7 (26.4) ($N = 408$)	48.4	.754**
Primary-Only States (CA, TN, KS, OR, TX) ($N = 677$)	71.1 (15.6) ($N = 331$)	64.9 (16.4) ($N = 346$)	6.2	.192**

Source: Morehouse 1996, Table 1, 368.
Note: These data are for the 1983 legislative sessions. The Gubernatorial Support Score for each party is the mean of all scores for all Democrats and all Republicans. The vote of each legislator on each roll call was scored as follows: voted to support governor = 100, absent or not voting = 50, voted against governor = 0. The score of each legislator was the mean of individual scores.
Standard deviation in parentheses.
**$p < .001$.

supportive in endorsing states than in primary-only states. This finding we would expect, given the nature of the supportive party system found in the former and the loosely connected factional system in the latter.

As we would predict, support for the governor's program is higher in the governor's party than in the opposition party in both endorsing and primary-only states. It is particularly noteworthy that the opposition party's support for the governor's program is much higher in nonendorsing states. When the governor cannot obtain support from the governing party's legislators, he or she must turn to the opposition for votes. The opposition is able to provide these votes for a price—a price that may further alienate some of the governor's legislators.

Variations among the States

Strong Party and Weak Party States Compared

Although there is convincing evidence that partisanship is a much better predictor of votes for the governor's program in endorsing than in primary-only states, we need to examine variations within each group of states. Some parties may be stronger and some weaker within each category. Table 7.3 shows for each state the average support for the governor's program in each party and the correlation between support and party. It also shows the percentage of seats that the governor's party held in each chamber of the legislature.

The relationship between the party nominating strength and legislative support for the governor's program may be based on the long-standing level of cohesion in the party. In a party where the governor is traditionally nominated with broad party backing, there may be a tradition of strong support by his or her legislative party, which will survive an occasional narrow primary victory (more likely to occur for open seats). New York has a tradition of highly cohesive legislative parties, which has apparently not been eroded by the relatively competitive Democratic primary races in recent elections.

In three of the five strong party states that endorse for governor (Connecticut, Minnesota, and New York), the differences between Democratic and Republican support scores are much larger than in the five nonendorsing weaker party states (table 7.3). In the other two endorsing states (Illinois and Colorado), the differences are roughly comparable to those found in the moderate to weak party states. As we would expect, support for the governor's program is higher in the governor's party in every state legislature except Oregon, although there is not much difference between the parties in Texas.

In general it is true that the level of support in the governor's party is higher in the endorsing states than in the nonendorsing states. This difference is caused by the very high level of support in three of the endorsing states: Connecticut, Minnesota, and New York. In these state legislatures, the party coalitions are comfortably over the minimum needed for passage. The handful of legislators not needed in each coalition were undoubtedly loyal enough to continue their support at low cost to them-

TABLE 7.3. The Effect of Party on Gubernatorial Legislative Support, Controlling for Strength of Party (by state)

State	Gov. Party	% of Gov.'s Party House	% of Gov.'s Party Senate	Total	Mean Support Gov. Party	Mean Support Oppos. Party	Difference	Correlation Support and Party (R)
			Strong Party States: High Support Predicted					
Conn.	D	58	64	.566	.911	.068	.843	.971**
				(.428)	(.123)	(.063)		
Minn.	D	58	63	.652	.914	.270	.644	.953**
				(.333)	(.069)	(.134)		
N.Y.	D	65	43	.711	.901	.442	.459	.683**
				(.332)	(.152)	(.332)		
Ill.	R	41	44	.565	.674	.485	.189	.585**
				(.160)	(.135)	(.126)		
Colo.	D	38	40	.691	.785	.630	.155	.453**
				(.168)	(.117)	(.169)		
			Moderate/Weak Party States: Lower Support Predicted					
Calif.	R	40	38	.588	.705	.514	.191	.669**
				(.139)	(.115)	(.096)		
Tenn.	R	40	33	.685	.817	.607	.210	.601**
				(.170)	(.112)	(.149)		
Kans.	D	42	40	.734	.800	.688	.112	.350**
				(.158)	(.161)	(.140)		
Oreg.	R	40	30	.764	.665	.820	−.155	−.420**
				(.178)	(.190)	(.145)		
Tex.	D	76	84	.642	.643	.640	.003	.008
				(.126)	(.129)	(.113)		

Source: Morehouse 1996, Table 2, 370–71.
Note: These data are for the 1983 legislative sessions. The Gubernatorial Support Score for each party is the mean of all scores for all Democrats and all Republicans. The vote of each legislator on each roll call was scored as follows: voted to support governor = 100, absent or not voting = 50, voted against governor = 0. The score of each legislator was the mean of individual scores. The mean support score for all members is partially dependent upon the *number* of legislators in each party. In the last column, a positive correlation indicates higher support from the governor's party for his/her program.
Standard deviation in parentheses.
*p < .001   **p < .0001

selves and the leaders. Once again, Illinois and Colorado are not substantially different from the primary-only states in the support that the governor's party gives to the gubernatorial program. In these states, the opposition party controls both houses, and the governor's party leaders had to
recruit legislators from the opposing party to win votes for passage, probably at the risk of losing some of their own.

It is particularly noteworthy that the opposition party's support for
the governor's program is much higher in primary-only states; in fact, it is
higher in all five of these states than in any of the endorsing states except
Colorado. This finding gives credence to the idea that defectors come from
the opposition party under circumstances of weak or divided party government. The opposition party controlled the legislatures in four of the
primary-only states, all except Texas. A glance at the mean support for
each legislature indicates that all governors achieved the average support
necessary to pass most of their program, but most of them undoubtedly
had to make compromises with the opposition to do so, and, of course,
many lost on individual votes.

Another measure of the effect of party on support for the governor's
program is the correlation between the member's party and the member's
support of the governor's program (shown in the last column of table 7.3).
The correlation between party and support is higher in three of the endorsing states (Connecticut, Minnesota, and New York) than in any of the primary-only states (and it is surprisingly negative in the nonendorsing state
of Oregon).

Strong Party States and Strong Legislative Support

In Connecticut, party cohesion in the legislature is high, and legislators are
expected to support the program of the governor. The governor's support
is useful to them upon occasion and his or her opposition relegates them to
the back bench. Governor William O'Neill's budget was put to the test and
survived a challenge from the liberal wing of the party, which wanted an
income tax. This wing included the senate majority leader, Richard
Schneller, as well as the president pro tem, James J. Murphy Jr., who were
placed in the position of having to support their governor on the patch-
work tax extension program even though they opposed it. On the house
side, the speaker, Irving Stolberg, favored the income tax. In view of the
divisions within the Democratic party, it was not surprising that progress
on the budget was exceedingly slow.

As the session progressed toward a June 8 deadline, the governor made
it clear that he would not budge on the income tax question. But he tried a
new type of collegial decision making with the income tax liberals, who came

around to support his tax package. In the end the governor got what he asked for. Furthermore, he achieved his budget and tax program with well over 80 percent support from his party in both house and senate. Thus, party loyalty can be garnered in Connecticut. Occasionally it is reinforced by threatening to eliminate projects that will benefit legislators' districts, although this heavy-handed approach is used sparingly (Morehouse 1986, 84–86).

Governor Rudy Perpich of Minnesota took the oath of office in his hometown, Hibbing, in the Iron Range, rather than in the state capital with the rest of the elected officeholders. In spite of this deviation, the inaugural address, which emphasized the governor's commitment to quality public education, was well received. Legislators of both parties responded favorably to the state of the state address in which Perpich called for a partnership between business, labor, and government.

In Minnesota, legislators rely most heavily on the governor for information in deciding how to vote. More than three-quarters of the members rely on information from the governor regardless of party affiliation (Hanson 1989, 226–31). They support the governor's role as the principal policy leader in the state, including budget-making power and policy direction of state agencies. The governor's legislative leaders of their common party are understood to be the administration's "spokespersons" in the legislature.

The most important unwritten rule in the Minnesota House of Representatives is that the majority party runs the operation. Both party caucuses meet weekly during the session, and caucus discipline is required on organizational issues as well as substantive legislative issues. The speaker runs the caucus and is expected to exert strong centralized leadership. The power of the speaker and caucus leaders has been enhanced substantially by the campaign fund-raising effort. The ability to supply funds, information, and advice for campaigns is more important than ideology in producing loyalty and cohesion among caucus members.

The majority leader in the Minnesota Senate is the major figure, although she or he shares power over appointments, control of the agenda, and management of the process with members of the majority (DFL) leadership group. Under Roger Moe's leadership, beginning in 1981, more of the legislative agenda came under his control. The caucus meeting itself became a forum for informing the members of the position to be staked out by its leader, to test the water on a policy, to vent concerns or dissent and combat hardening of factional lines (Hanson 1989, 111). Thus, the Minnesota legislature is a highly partisan operation controlled by the majority leaders in each chamber. This leadership supports the governor when he or she is a fellow partisan, or dictates the conditions for cooperation with a governor of the minority party. In 1982, the governor was a fellow partisan and his program received overwhelming support.

Governor Perpich defended his budget as a step toward solving the fiscal crisis and helping needy citizens. The $9.3 billion biennial budget represented a 19 percent increase over the last one and contained a $250 million reserve fund to protect the state against faulty revenue projections. It introduced the notion of "shared risk," meaning that school and local government aids would be cut by as much as 4 percent if state revenues dropped below budgeted amounts. On the revenue side, it kept the income tax surcharge and sales tax and proposed a five-cent-per-gallon increase in the gasoline tax. Among the proposed expenditures was a $75 million jobs program, under which the state would subsidize the costs of hiring new workers (Gray and Hult 1985, 252). As table 7.1 indicates, 44 per cent of the contested votes on the governor's program were votes on the budget. While the Governor received over 90 percent support, on average, from his DFL party in the legislature, even his gas tax was passed by a loyal 80 percent support.

Governor Mario Cuomo's inaugural address asserted that New York government could be a "positive source for good." New Yorkers "should be able to find room at the table-shelter for the homeless, work for the idle, care for the elderly and infirm, and hope for the destitute" (Cuomo 1984, 458). In his state of the state message, the governor spoke of a partnership between labor, government, and business to foster economic growth. The governor also stressed the need for cooperative bipartisan action by New York's political leaders. Having served as lieutenant governor, the presiding officer of the state senate, the governor knew the legislative leaders well. The senate president pro tem and majority leader (same person) and the speaker of the assembly are exceedingly powerful and can control the passage, modification, or defeat of pending bills (Hevesi 1975, 6). The senate leader, Republican Warren Anderson, reacted positively to the message, saying, "I don't remember any governor reaching out this way before" (Benjamin 1985, 361).

The governor was faced with a $1.8 billion deficit that had to be paid back in his first budget year. On February 1, 1983, he offered a budget balanced by a $900 million tax increase and a reduction in state expenditures by the same amount. The unions, having been his strongest supporters, shared in the pain by the proposed elimination of 14,000 state jobs, 8,400 of them by layoffs. In offering his budget, the governor invited the legislature to improve on it. He also traveled through the state speaking in defense of his budget and defending the integrity of his decision making. The assembly speaker, Stanley Fink, said that the budget was honestly arrived at and nobody was trying to play games (Benjamin 1985, 368).

Strongly supported by his own party's legislators, the governor's budget was passed before the beginning of the fiscal year for the first time in four years. Because the governor's party held 65 percent of the seats in the New York Assembly, he did not need 80 percent loyalty to pass legislation. However, he received an average 94 percent support from his party's assembly members. Table 7.1 shows that over 40 percent of all contested roll calls were on appropriations and taxes. Tax increases totaled close to $1 billion. Programs were added but were balanced by the program cuts suggested by the governor. Education aid was increased without reallocation from wealthy districts, a concession to the Republican senate, and layoffs were reduced to about 3,400 due to pressure from the Democratic assembly. Governor Cuomo provided another example of a governor from a strong party state achieving partisan legislative success for his program. This accomplishment is more remarkable because of the party split during the nominating process. But, New York parties can fight and then coalesce to govern.

Strong Party States and Divided Government

In 1983, the opposition party controlled both houses in two of the endorsing states (Illinois and Colorado), and it controlled the senate in New York. In Illinois the usual pattern is for a Republican governor to face a Democratic legislature, but Democratic governors have also experienced divided government. In Colorado, a Democratic governor traditionally faces a Republican legislature. The legislature reflects the traditional pattern of Republican control, but the Democrats have had recent success in the governorship. In New York, competition between the state parties is common, but a Democratic governor traditionally faces a Democratic assembly and a Republican senate.

New York is the only state where partisan control of the legislature is split, with Democrats controlling the assembly and Republicans controlling the senate. In the New York Assembly, the patterns of partisan support and the correlation between party and support are comparable to those in states with unified governments. But in the New York Senate, party has less effect on support than in the other states with divided government. The reason for a lack of difference in support between senate parties was because opposition support was unusually high, not because support from the governor's party was low. The average Democratic support was .780 and the average Republican support was .793, and the correlation between party and support was −.040.

We would expect the governor of Illinois to be a strong legislative actor. Governor Jim Thompson, endorsed by his party and not significantly opposed in the primary, had just won an unprecedented third term. While control of the house had shifted to the Democrats, the governor had faced divided government before. Apparently the governor of Illinois does not approach the informal power or actual practice that accounts for the legislative dominance of the governor of New York (Rosenthal 1981, 251). The Republican leaders in the legislature generally exercised considerable independence during Governor Thompson's tenure (Van Der Slik and Redfield 1989, 87).

In 1983, Governor Thompson faced a complex legislative battle centered on tax increases, more controversial than any faced in his earlier administrations (Keenan 1986, 160–63). While the Democratic leadership of both houses favored a higher income tax and other revenue reforms, they refused to support the governor unless he sought support for new taxes among his fellow Republicans. Thompson could muster very little support among the Republicans in the General Assembly until he took a swing through southern Illinois at the end of April to influence his legislators through a public convinced that a higher income tax was necessary.

Two days before Memorial Day, Governor Thompson reduced his requested amount in an effort to gain votes in the senate. It had been difficult for the governor to obtain a senate sponsor for the tax increase, and he negotiated for some time before the senate Republican leader, James "Pate" Philip, accepted the dubious honor and duty of carrying the governor's bill (Parker 1984, 45–46). For a time it looked as if the leadership members could persuade enough of their colleagues to approve such a proposal. But on May 27, the last day before the recess, Governor Thompson and senate leaders came up one vote short in efforts to put the $1.5 billion comprehensive tax plan to a vote (Keenan 1986, 162).The governor could not persuade enough senate Republicans to vote for the measure because he had to negotiate with the Democrats and hence alienated his fellow partisans.

As the June 30 mandatory adjournment date approached, Illinois House Republican leader Lee Daniels offered the major alternative to the plan put forth by Governor Thompson; the final tax proposal was much closer to Daniels's proposal. Thompson agreed to support increasing taxes by only $1 billion, and the legislative leaders of both parties convinced enough of their flock to pass it. The governor's inability to obtain more of his partisans to support the tax may be laid to the distaste of most Republicans to increasing taxes plus the need to compromise with the Democratic leaders. This is a clear case of copartisanship, where each party has a plan and the strength to commit partisans to it.

In Colorado, where the legislature is considered very powerful, the opposition Republican party, in control of both chambers, was under very strong leadership. The speaker of the house is considered the power center and appoints the chairs and majority party members of the major house committees and assigns bills to committees. From 1981 to 1991 the speaker was Carl "Bev" Bledsoe, who served as speaker longer than anyone in Colorado history. Bledsoe, from the small town of Hugo on the eastern plains, used his powers as speaker to further conservative policies and programs by using the caucus as a mechanism to bind votes for bills he and the Republicans supported. The senate president is also powerful but shares appointment power with the Committee on Committees. He or she does have the power to assign bills to committees. Senator Ted Strickland from Westminster, a northern Denver suburb, was senate president in the 1980s and early 1990s. He was head of the Colorado Republican party and had run against Governor Richard Lamm in 1978. (He also lost the gubernatorial election in 1986 to Roy Romer.) Although a conservative, Strickland ran the senate in a more collegial manner, allowing minority Democrats to participate (Cronin and Loevy 1993, 177–90).

In Colorado, the budget process is centered in the Joint Budget Committee (JBC) in the legislature, which exercises enormous control over budgeting and spending decisions. Its six members, three from each chamber, contain two from the minority party. While the process starts with the executive budget prepared by the governor and the budget director, the JBC rarely feels constrained by the governor's budget plans (Cronin and Loevy 1993, 194–99).It writes the long appropriations bill referred to as the "long bill" for the following year. The Republicans then bind enough of their members via the caucus to support the budget.

Obviously, Governor Lamm had to engage in copartisanship to pass a budget. Confronting a critical budget crisis in 1983, he chose to negotiate with the Republican house speaker Bledsoe and senate president Strickland. For the past eight years the governor had engaged in partisan battles with the Republican legislators. In 1983, due to a $102 million deficit in the state government budget, he worked closely with the house and senate leaders. Lamm paid an impromptu visit to the Joint Budget Committee offices and conferred with the Republican chair and vice chair of the powerful committee. Lamm even considered appearing before the house Republican caucus to make the case against massive cuts in the state budget (Westergaard 1983).

The Republican caucus in both chambers provided a vehicle guaranteeing party unity on all provisions of the budget. The house speaker succeeded in forcing the governor to compromise on a number of issues, thus gaining the support of his Republican legislators for revised versions of the governor's program, which the Democrats also accepted. However, this Democratic support was hard to obtain, and the governor found leaders of his own party objecting to his conditional acceptance of a Republican idea to balance the state budget with a boost in the sales tax. In the house, average Democratic support was .780, average Republican support was .710, and the correlation between party and support was only .247. In the senate, however, there was less Republican support for these compromises, particularly the sales tax, and hence more party-line voting; average Democratic support was .794, average Republican support was .478, and the correlation between party and support was .854.

Moderate or Weak Party States and Divided Government

We turn our attention to states where we would expect lower support because the state party is not strong and governors do not have partisan backing. In the weaker party states, all but Texas, a southern party model, have divided government. In California and Oregon, divided government usually occurs under a Republican governor, as in 1983. In California, partisan control of the governorship has been balanced, but the legislature is almost always Democratic. In Oregon, the governor is usually Republican, and the legislature Democratic or split between house and senate. In Kansas, a Democratic governor traditionally faces a Republican legislature, which reflects the traditional Republicanism of the state. In Tennessee, a former southern party model, the Republicans have been increasingly successful in winning the governorship, but the legislature remains in Democratic hands, and so divided government occurs under their administrations.

We have no examples of how much support a governor can command if his or her party has only moderate strength and holds a legislative majority. We expect that the combination of moderate or weak parties and divided control contributes to lower support for the governor, because the governor's party leaders have to negotiate with the opposition and must make concessions in order to have their programs passed—concessions that will most likely result in loss of support from their own partisans.

Party appears to explain support better in California than in any of the other nonendorsing states, as previous research has indicated (Morehouse 1981a, 295). Statewide political parties are weak and divided in the Golden State. Filling the void in the 1970s and 1980s have been the Democratic majority and Republican minority legislative leaders in each chamber. The California Assembly has given birth to one of the most powerful speakerships in the nation. The person who was primarily responsible for making the speaker a powerful force in the state was Jesse Unruh, the assembly leader during most of the 1960s. Unruh united the Democratic party in the assembly and provided the legislature with the tools needed to make it an effective and independent branch of government (Squire 1992). He made the assembly speaker an important player in state legislative elections. Since Unruh, the speaker's office has been so important in shaping political outcomes that it is considered the most important position in the state next to the governor.

In 1980, Willie Brown was elected speaker of the California Assembly with the help of twenty-three Democrats and twenty-eight Republicans. Even though he had relied on the Republican party to gain control, Brown began consolidating his Democratic party soon after he was elected to the speaker's office. He gave his Democratic foes ten chair positions. Most important in establishing a party-based following was assuring party members that their primary goal of reelection would be among his major concerns. He became actively involved in the 1982 assembly elections and held two fund-raising dinners to help Democratic candidates. He provided relatively equal amounts of money to both his supporters and his former opponents within the party. His financial effort in the general election far eclipsed any previous total, as he directly contributed almost $2.2 million (Clucas 1995, 18). The result was that after the election, Brown was easily reelected speaker, but this time solidly supported by the Democratic caucus. Since that time until the mid-1990s, Brown used campaign support to maximize the party's control over the assembly to ensure that he would retain control of the speakership and that his followers would be able to attain the goals they sought. From 1982 to 1995 Republican governors had to deal with Willie Brown to ensure success of their programs. It is a clear example of copartisanship: Brown's cooperation is necessary for Republican bills to pass because he can engineer Democratic legislative support.

While Speaker Brown has provided a spectacular example of leadership power based on funding elections for Democrats, this phenomenon is paralleled in the California Senate, where the role of president pro tempore has evolved in a similar way, although the centralization is not so acute. Senator David Roberti was selected as president pro tem in 1981 with the understanding that he would raise campaign funds and help wage campaigns on behalf of Democratic senatorial candidates. The Republicans in both chambers also assume the responsibility for the election and reelection of the members from their respective caucuses (Capell 1988, 23–25). In both chambers, party caucuses and party-line voting are facts of legislative life.

In California, where we would not expect the governor to exert strong party leadership, we find that party and support are highly correlated (.67), which places the Golden State with the strongest party states. Governor George Deukmejian could not expect the traditional honeymoon with the legislature since members of his own party were at odds with each other. Assembly Republicans, who had supported Mike Curb in the primary, were more opposed to tax increases than their fellow partisans in the senate. Nevertheless, the governor received 70 percent support of his party, on average, and was opposed regularly by half of the opposition, but he was able to negotiate with the strong Democratic leadership who could guarantee a winning coalition, on their terms. Here copartisanship was present with the advantage on the side of the majority. Table 7.1 shows that almost all of the contested roll calls were on the budget, and since all money bills require a two-thirds majority in the legislature, it forced some form of partisan cooperation.

Governor Deukmejian faced a $1.5 billion deficit for the current fiscal year, and the immediate budget crisis preoccupied the legislature for the first month. On February 15, 1983, Controller Cory and Treasurer Unruh announced that the state would be "broke" by February 23. The assembly Republicans referred to as "Proposition 13 babies" (elected in 1978) were opposed to tax increases and were more obstructionist than the Democrats. Finally, on February 16, the legislature agreed to a budget-balancing plan that included cuts and a postponed deficit. The measure was supported by the assembly Democrats and only nine of the thirty-two Republicans.

The legislature was now able to turn its attention to the 1983–84 budget. The governor maintained his strong opposition to a tax increase, and the Democrats insisted that one was needed because of a projected deficit in the governor's proposed budget. An opportunity for compromise presented itself in early May when ten government efficiency teams, which Deukmejian had appointed, submitted their recommendations. Among them was a proposal to close tax loopholes. The Democrats praised the proposal and the Republicans denounced it, claiming that it was a permanent tax increase. Assembly speaker Willie Brown, acting like a diplomat, submitted the tax-loophole-closing package to the assembly as a committee of the whole, bypassing standing committees and giving opponents less time to negotiate changes or marshal votes. By the end of the day, seven Republicans joined the Democrats to provide the necessary two-thirds to pass the measure. Two of them were removed from their leadership posts by the Republican caucus for voting in favor of Governor Deukmejian's bill (Gable, Sektnan, and King 1985, 144). In view of the difficulty Deukmejian had with members of his party, it is surprising that party loyalty could explain an average coalition of 70 percent. The record of Deukmejian's first legislative year suggests that he did not achieve strong policy leadership, although he did achieve his budget goal. In dealing with a strong Democratic opposition, he had to negotiate with its leaders, who can determine the support he will receive.

In Tennessee, the parties represent distinctly different geographical sections, and partisanship was almost as important in determining support for the gubernatorial program as in California. Since the late 1960s, the cohesive Republican contingent from eastern Tennessee had hovered between 30 and 40 percent in each chamber (Morehouse 1981a, 295). Perhaps Republican legislators had a greater incentive to support Governor Lamar Alexander because Republican administrations had been so rare in that state, and they had an unusual opportunity to make their votes count.

Governor Alexander received a surprising 82 percent support from his state legislative party, even though Tennessee at that time was not a strong party state. As recently as 1966, the Republicans had not even run a candidate for governor. One would predict two weak parties and conservative cross-partisanship in such a situation. However, the Republican legislative minority based in eastern Tennessee had been cohesive over the years. The Tennessee governor shifted from "caretaker" to "program promoter" in his second term and promised to work diligently for passage and implementation of his budget and programs. Chief among these was his Better Schools Program designed to promote education as an instrument of economic development. Funding for this proposal was to be raised by a 2 percent increase in the state sales tax.

The governor won a significant level of cross-partisan support in the state legislature for the Better Schools Program as well as endorsements from major manufacturing, taxpayers, and teacher education groups. However, he faced a resistant and ambitious Democratic majority coupled with the enmity of the largest and most powerful state educational interest group, the Tennessee Education Association (TEA). The TEA objected to the merit pay part of the program. The combination of the TEA and the Democratic leadership was able to defeat the governor's plan in the Senate Education Committee (Fitzgerald et al. 1986, 314–17). The governor vowed to renew his fight for the program in the next legislative session and was successful. This episode shows how a governor's cohesive minority needs the support of the majority to build a winning coalition for its proposals. When the resistant majority is "loose, intermittent, and weak" (L. Green, Grubbs, and Hobday 1982, 103), it cannot commit its members to support the governor, and its disorganization blocks his program. Governor Alexander did accomplish many of his legislative proposals, which included adjustments to the sales tax and the severance tax and increased authority for the state Board of Regents. His legislators voted with a high degree of loyalty, and the opposition Democrats were divided.

Party may be less important as an explanation for support in Kansas and Oregon because these are less urbanized states in which the legislative parties do not represent such distinctly different socioeconomic interests and in which state party organizations are not traditionally strong. If the two parties do not represent very different interests, there may be smaller differences between them on the governor's program and thus greater possibilities for compromise. With less cohesive parties, the governor may have less success in winning unanimous support from members of his or her party but greater success in wooing some members of the opposition party. This is an example of cross-partisanship.

In the Kansas House of Representatives, there is no guaranteed majority that can be counted on to vote together all the time. Instead, different factions find themselves in the majority at different times, depending on the issue. Consequently, any majority in the house is a coalition of at least three factions. One of them contains several Republican factions and another a coalition of Democrats and liberal Republicans. This practice has continued over the years as a Republican rebel faction made a coalition with the Democrats in the 1989 house that rewrote the permanent rules and greatly diminished the Republican leadership's ability to dominate the legislative process (Loomis 1994, 56). In the Kansas Senate, two Republican blocs diverge along rural-urban lines but usually vote together against the Democrats, who vote with some cohesion (Harder and Rampey 1972, 131–46). In 1983, Governor John Carlin received support from both parties for the severance tax, a cornerstone of his legislative program, and this cross-partisan coalition enacted most of the appropriation bills he recommended.

In Oregon, legislators owe no party allegiance and tend to organize themselves along urban-rural or liberal-conservative lines. Splits within the Democratic party have led to bitter and lengthy contests for key leadership positions, as with the election of the 1983 senate president, Edward Fadeley. Republican governor Victor Atiyeh encountered difficulty with the legislature over his net receipts tax, which his party bucked, and a sales tax proposal, which split the majority Democrats. Otherwise, the numerous appropriation measures were passed with a cross-partisan coalition in which the governor received more support from the opposition Democrats.

To conclude this brief analysis of Kansas and Oregon, neither governor seemed moved to propose bold programs because they were faced with divisions within their own parties as well as an uncertain, but necessary, coalition with the opposition.

Texas represents the weak party model found in southern states where the governorship and the legislature have traditionally been under Democratic control. In 1983, party had little relevance in providing voting cues for the legislators. The overwhelming majority of seats were held by Democrats, and the corporal's guard of Republicans voted with the conservatives. Governor Mark White was a conservative, many of whose programs might be expected to generate as much support from Republicans as from Democrats.

That is not to say that a power structure did not exist. The traditional "speaker's team" in the house and lieutenant governor in the senate referred all bills, appointed all committee members, and controlled the flow of legislation to the floor. Governor Bill Clements, elected in 1978 as the first Republican governor in over a hundred years and defeated by White in 1982, opposed any form of Republican organization in the Texas legislature because it would consolidate Democrats and threaten the cozy relationship that existed between the Republican and Democratic conservatives. However, in the early 1980s, a house Democratic caucus was formed (Harmel and Hamm 1986). This caucus was initially opposed by the speaker and his "team," who saw it as a threat to the established speaker-centered power structure. It gained in membership in 1983 to include most of the party, but the speaker and his team were notable exceptions. While the caucus did include representation from all of the party's ideological persuasions, on most votes when the party divided, it was a liberal bloc within the caucus that provided the opposition to the governor and the party leaders.

Summary: Partisanship and Divided Government

As predicted, the differences between support levels in the two parties are much higher in two states with unified government (Connecticut and Minnesota) and the New York Assembly than in the six states where the opposition party controls both houses (table 7.3). In fact, in these three states, support from the governor's party is higher, and support from the opposition party is lower, than in any of the six states with divided government. (Texas, the only other state with united government, has such a weak party system that partisanship has virtually no impact on support for the gubernatorial program.)

The findings suggest that both the existence of a strong party system and gubernatorial control of legislative chambers contribute to a stronger relationship between party and support for a gubernatorial program. That relationship is particularly strong when state parties make endorsements and the governor's party controls the legislature, as in Minnesota and Connecticut and the New York Assembly.

The findings also suggest that governors in strong party states faced with divided government cannot count on the coalitional strength that exists in unified government. Their support is not significantly higher than that for governors who are not supported by strong state parties and who also face divided legislatures. These findings differ from my research of 1981, which found slightly higher support among the governor's legislators in divided government. I did not test for the difference between strong and weak governors (Morehouse 1981b, 18).

The level of legislative partisanship was suggested as a factor that could affect the ability of a governor to get his or her program passed. In the cases where the hypotheses based on state-level strength could not account for the level of support that the governor received, legislative partisanship is a possible explanation. In New York, Governor Cuomo bargained with the powerful leader of the Republican party in the senate who could obtain legislative support for his program. In Illinois, legislative leaders of both parties could tell Governor Thompson what the terms for the tax package would be and elicit sufficient legislative support for the compromise. In Colorado, Governor Lamm dealt with the powerful leaders of the opposition party in both houses who could bind their legislative party in a caucus. In these cases, where the opposition could provide the votes necessary to pass the program, voting loyalty in the governor's party is lowered because the governor must negotiate with the opposition party. Hence, divided government accompanied by strong legislative parties does not prohibit governors from receiving legislative support for their policies (Morehouse 1996, 372–74).

In cases where the hypotheses could not account for the high support the governor received from his own party or the level of partisanship between the parties, legislative party strength also provides a possible explanation. In California, where party support and level of partisanship were higher than expected, Republican governor Deukmejian dealt with the Democratic party leaders, who attempted to cooperate on a budget but who dictated the terms, since a two-thirds majority was required. The governor's party members were less than fully supportive because of that, and a number of "Proposition 13 babies" opposed the governor, but he still garnered an average coalition of over 70 percent from his Republican partisans and sufficient votes from the opposition to pass the measures.

The examples summarized in this section illustrate how governors must cooperate with strong opposition legislative parties, even at the expense of losing support from their own. This is the typical copartisanship pattern. The leaders of the opposition parties negotiate with the governor and can guarantee legislative support, but they set the terms for the compromises, which come at the price of lower support from the governor's own party.

This state-level analysis of the relationship between state party strength and support for the gubernatorial program sets the stage for analyzing this relationship at the level of the individual legislator, which may help to clarify the ambiguities found at the state level. It is possible that the legislator's support for a gubernatorial program is affected by the electoral voting strength of the governor and the legislator in the member's own district as well as by its socioeconomic character.

State Party versus Constituency Party Strength

By examining district-level variables, I expect to find that legislators in the governor's party give more support to the governor's program if the governor has demonstrated district electoral strength in the primary and general election. If a governor was nominated or elected by a comfortable margin, for example, the size of his or her margin in a district might have more effect than in the case of a governor who won narrowly. I expect to find a similar relationship for members of the opposition party, but only in general elections. For 1982, the governor's general election strength is examined for each of the states, and his primary vote is examined for the six states where he had opposition.

We also expect to find a correlation between support for the governor's program in the 1983 session and his district vote in 1986 (if he ran again). The reason for this hypothesis is that legislators who recognize that the governor is politically strong and expect him to carry their district in the next election are more likely to support his program. In previous research I found that the hypothesized relationship between legislative voting loyalty and gubernatorial primary strength appeared in districts where the governor did well (over 60 percent) and not in districts where the governor was weaker (Morehouse 1973, 65). For 1986 there were six states where the governor ran again but only two states where he had significant primary opposition.

We would expect to find that legislators of either party would be more likely to support the governor's program if they had been elected by relatively narrow margins. This might be particularly true of members of the governor's party who might need political assistance from the governor to get reelected.

We would not expect that electoral variables would be able to explain as much of the variance in support for the governor's program in the endorsing states where party affiliation already explains over 57 percent of the variance. In the primary states where party does not explain voting support at all (4 percent), there is room for other explanations (table 7.2).

State-by-state correlations of support with electoral variables are shown in table 7.4, which includes only those correlations significant at the .05 level. (An "x" in the column indicates there was no contested gubernatorial primary election; it is also used for gubernatorial primaries where no correlations were calculated for the opposition party.)

We would not anticipate that electoral variables would be able to explain much of the variance in support for the governor's program in Minnesota or Connecticut, where party already explains over 90 percent of the variance in support, or in the New York Assembly, where it explains

85 percent. In fact, in Connecticut and in the New York Assembly and Senate, district-level electoral variables fail to explain legislative support for the governor's program (table 7.4). So much voting can be explained by party cohesion that there was little left to be explained by district electoral variables. Governors can benefit from their party's cohesion overall, and their district electoral records do not affect legislators' support. (In Connecticut the governor's endorsement was not challenged in a primary in either 1982 or 1986.)

In Minnesota, however, members of the governor's party were more likely to support him in those districts where he ran strongly in the general election in 1982 and those where he ran strongly in 1986; a similar, though

TABLE 7.4. Bivariate Correlations between Individual Support for Governor's Program and District-Level Electoral Variables (by state)

State	Party	Governor General Election (1982)	Legislator General Election (1982)	Governor Primary Election (1982)	Legislator Primary Election (1982)	Governor General Election (1986)	Governor Primary Election (1986)
Conn.	Governor			x			x
	Opposition			x			x
Minn.	Governor	.345**				.329**	.218*
	Opposition			x	x	.246*	x
N.Y.	Governor						x
	Opposition			x	x		x
Ill.	Governor			x			x
	Opposition	−.274**	.268**	x	x	−.211*	x
Colo.	Governor		−.410**	x		x	x
	Opposition			x	x	x	x
Calif.	Governor	−.329*					x
	Opposition	.487**		x	x	.471**	x
Tenn.	Governor			x		x	x
	Opposition			x	x	x	x
Kans.	Governor					x	x
	Opposition			x	x	x	x
Oreg.	Governor		.398*			x	x
	Opposition			x	x	x	x
Tex.	Governor	−.204*		.199*			−.177*
	Opposition			x	x	x	x

Note: Only those correlations are included in the table that are significant at least at the .05 level. A positive correlation indicates that when the district electoral variable for governor or legislator is higher, support for the governor's program is higher.

An "x" indicates the correlations were not calculated. For the governor's party, this occurs in 1982 when the governor was unopposed in the primary and in 1986 when the governor was not running or was unopposed in the primary. No primary correlations were calculated for the opposition party.

* $p = .05$ ** $p = .01$

weaker, relationship is found for the 1986 Democratic primary. In a multivariate analysis, these relationships remain significant, and there is also a modest negative relationship, as predicted, between the legislator's general election vote and support. There is also a modest positive bivariate relationship in Minnesota between opposition legislators' support for the governor and the governor's district vote in the 1986 general election (one that remains in a multivariate analysis).

Illinois and Colorado are endorsing states where the correlation between party and support is extremely modest; that correlation is only .59 in Illinois and only .45 in Colorado. Consequently, we might expect to find that district electoral variables have more impact in these than in the other endorsing states.

In Illinois, district electoral variables have no significant effect on support levels within the governor's party (Republican). Members of the opposition Democratic party, strangely enough, are more likely to support the governor in those districts where he does poorly (in either 1982 or 1986) and more likely to support him where they themselves do well. Governor Thompson did unusually poorly in Chicago's predominantly black districts, where Democratic legislative margins are traditionally high. In the 1983 session there were factional divisions among Chicago Democrats—between the black mayor Harold Washington and the traditional white leadership—and Governor Thompson was forced to negotiate with individual legislators. It appears that he was more successful in gaining support from legislators representing black districts than from other Chicago legislators.

In Colorado, where the governor gets relatively high support from his legislative contingent, he does even better among those Democrats whose elections are less secure and who may need his support at a future time. Republicans support the governor at a slightly lower level, but this support is not significantly related to district electoral variables.

Among the five nonendorsing states, California stands out as having the strongest relationship between party and support (only Tennessee comes close). Governor Deukmejian had significantly more support from the opposition Democrats in those districts where he ran well in 1982 and also in 1986. In a multivariate analysis, in both 1982 and 1986, the governor's district vote remains significant and the variables explain about 20 percent of the variation.

Deukmejian, who won his election narrowly in 1982 and ran behind most Republican legislators, gained significantly more Republican support in districts where his voting percentage was smaller—contrary to our expectations. A number of very conservative Republican legislators took strong, uncompromising positions in opposition to some parts of the governor's program, particularly those dealing with taxes. Some of these members had opposed Deukmejian in the closely contested 1982 gubernatorial primary. It seems likely that these very conservative legislators represented some of the safest Republican districts where Deukmejian ran strongly.

In Oregon, where Governor Atiyeh's Republican party gave him less support than did the opposition party, the governor gained significantly more support from those members of his party who ran stronger in their districts, contrary to expectations. We would expect to find that the governor got more support in districts where his electoral vote was highest. More research on the peculiarities of legislative politics in Oregon is called for.

In the two primary-only states where the governor received the highest support from his own party (.800 in Kansas and .817 in Tennessee), district-level electoral variables fail to explain variations in his support within either party.

Texas is the only state where partisanship has absolutely no relationship to support for the governor's program. There is a difference of only .003 in the support between the governor's Democratic party members and the Republicans, and the correlation of party and support is only .008. In 1982 there was a modest negative relationship between the governor's general election vote in Democratic districts and support from Democratic members. This negative relationship may have occurred because some of the safe Democratic districts where Mark White, a conservative, ran well were ethnic minority districts where some of his legislative proposals were unpopular. He gathered more support from Democratic legislators in districts where he did well in the 1982 primary, but also from those where he did poorly in the 1986 primary, though neither relationship is strong.

In a majority of cases there is no significant relationship between the governor's electoral strength and success in gaining support from legislators—although in several of these legislative parties there is a weak positive relationship. Several explanations can be offered for the shortage of significant district-level relationships between electoral strength and support for the governor.

In Minnesota, Connecticut, and the New York Assembly, the correlation between party and support is so high (explaining 85 percent or more of the variance) that there is little room for district electoral variables to explain more. That makes the significant positive relationship between electoral variables and support (particularly in the governor's party) all the more impressive in Minnesota.

We would expect the governor's district vote in the primary to be more important than his or her vote in the general election in generating tering their votes. The issues were on such matters as gas tax, farm fore-closures, education commission, education appropriations, energy authority, transportation appropriations, and capital improvements. Minnesota Republicans from high-income districts had the tendency to oppose the Democratic governor, as we might expect (table 7.5). District income level is by far the most dominant variable in the regression analysis for Minnesota. Loyalty characterizes the Democrats so much that almost every vote in the governor's program is supported with near unity. Minnesota is a strong party state.

Illinois presents a difficult case for analysis. In the legislative session, there were seven votes that appeared to split the Republicans between high and low income groups. Four were veto overrides on appropriation bills, and the low-income-district Republicans voted to override the governor's veto on spending. Three votes were on the motor fuel tax, a highly charged issue, and the low-income districts generally were against the tax while Republicans from wealthier districts voted for it. The regression shows that income was the only explanation for the support the governor received from his own party, and this explanation did not offer much (.216 of the variance).

The California legislative parties showed more cohesion than most of those in weak party states. In spite of that, Governor Deukmejian was opposed by many of his fellow Republicans. There was a highly partisan battle over the 1983–84 state budget that accounted for the four bills chosen for special analysis here. Involved was a possible increase in the sales tax, plus education bills that would pump $700 to $850 million into the public schools. The regression, which attempts to explain the support given to the governor on bills that were of socioeconomic interest, does not prove too much. Apparently, some Republicans representing Hispanic and elderly districts voted in favor of the governor on such issues as the budget.

Last but not least is the Lone Star State, where parties do not count, but many other forces do. Here, the regression considers all members of the Texas House of Representatives without regard to party, on bills that were of socioeconomic interest. It shows that a combination of electoral and socioeconomic forces can provide close to half of the explanation for legislative voting behavior. There were fifteen bills, nine of which were appropriations. The regression analysis shows that Governor White opposed by legislators representing Hispanics and African-American well as districts where he did well in the general election. The governo a moderate conservative who had to do business with the very conse speaker. In this way, he could get a cross-partisan coalition of Rep and conservative Democrats representing wealthier districts bound to receive the enmity of the liberals, who often represent

support from legislators in the governor's party, but there is very little evidence of primary voting having such an effect. In 1982, however, three of the ten governors were unopposed in the primary and three others won by 79 percent or better—margins so large that district variations might be unimportant. In 1986 only two of the six governors who were running again had serious opposition in their primaries. They were Governor Perpich of Minnesota and Governor White of Texas, and their 1986 primaries are the only ones in which the district vote correlates with support from members of the governor's party.

The relationship between support and the district vote in a contested primary may be complicated. If the governor wins a landslide victory (like the three who won with 79 to 84 percent of the vote), it probably makes little difference to the legislator whether the governor got 80 or 90 percent of the vote in the district. Variations in district vote might be more important in the case of governors winning the primary by less than 80 percent of the vote.

The fact that only six of the ten governors sought reelection in 1986 reduces the number of opportunities for studying the relationships between subsequent electoral outcomes and support for the gubernatorial program.

There may be another, more complicated reason why we seldom find high positive correlations between the governor's voting strength in the district and the member's willingness to support the governor. In theory, a governor who demonstrates electoral strength in a district should have an impact on the legislator in that district; the member should believe that the governor, and perhaps the governor's major programs, are popular among the constituents. The literature on support for presidential programs suggests that this relationship is stronger in the case of presidents who win by a landslide (Harmon and Brauen 1979).

A governor who wins the general election narrowly (as did six of the ten governors in 1982) is in a much different position. A Democratic governor who wins by a narrow statewide margin, for example, is likely to lose most of the districts won by Republican legislators and to run behind most Democratic legislators. Such a governor's largest vote is likely to be in safe Democratic districts, where the Democratic legislator's share of the vote may be even larger. Under these conditions, a governor may seldom be able to win support for a legislative program by demonstrating political strength. But it is not necessarily true that legislators in the gubernatorial party would vote against the program simply because they had larger percentages of the district vote than the governor did.

The relationship between district electoral variables and support for a gubernatorial program is a complex one, and the results from one state party to another are inconsistent and sometimes counterintuitive. Because the results in many of the states seem to be idiosyncratic, evidence needs to be gathered for a larger number of cases before more reliable generalizations are possible.

The Impact of District Socioeconomic Variables on Support for the Governor's Program

The discussion so far has stressed the importance of the electoral vulnerability or security of legislators and how the party leaders can affect their hopes for advancement by assisting them electorally or professionally. Jewell and Patterson have proposed that legislators from districts that reflect the basic economic orientation of the party are more likely to be loyal than those whose constituencies deviate from the mean (1986). These legislators, then, would be would be among the "concerned" on most issues. Legislators from districts that are not typical of the majority of those in the party would be cross-pressured between party demands and constituency needs, and they would make up the defectors. We do not know how legislators cross-pressured between the economic needs of their constituencies and the demands for party cohesion resolve these conflicts. Presumably they are constantly balancing the two, and adjustments are made on both sides.

In order to assess the influence of district-level socioeconomic variables on support for the governor's program, I examined data from four states where 1982 data were available at the legislative level: California, Illinois, Minnesota, and Texas. The hypotheses predict that the economic and social characteristics of the district affect the support the legislator gives the governor. If the two parties are based on different relatively homogeneous districts, legislators from the most typical districts will be the most loyal to the demands of their party. Legislators in the governor's party from such districts will be more likely to support his program, while comparable legislators from the opposition party will more likely to oppose the program. This assumes that the governor's legislative party supports most of his program and the opposition party opposes much of it, as we have found to be the case in most states.

Income data were available from districts in all four states, age data from all except Texas, and education data from only California and Minnesota. Data on ethnic minorities were collected from all four states except for Minnesota, where they make up only a small proportion of the population. Table A.1 in the appendix, which shows the state averages for these variables, demonstrates that districts represented by Democrats and Republicans differed substantially on income levels (measured either by

average income or the percentage earning over $25,000), ethni istics, and education: there were only small differences in age (1993, 18–21).

Because district electoral and economic characteristics a nected, legislators from districts most typical of their party w be the most secure in the electoral sense. Regression analysis the relative strengths of these electoral and socioeconomic v legislative support for the governor.

Votes on Issues with Socioeconomic Impact

A governor's program consists of a variety of issues. Members ernor's party may support him or her on most of these issues, party loyalty and partly because of the governor's political their district. But the socioeconomic characteristics of the di make some members more likely and some less likely to supp ernor, may be pertinent to only some of the issues in the gov gram. A bill to provide more generous worker's compensation ticular socioeconomic interests more than a bill to promo safety, for example.

For these reasons, I decided to examine a subset of roll governor's program on which socioeconomic variables might effect. I used district income as the criterion for selecting roll c further analysis. The first step was to compare the pattern of v each party, in districts above and below median income. If on the parties was split along district-income lines, that roll call v sidered for inclusion. (In almost all of these cases that qualif not both of the parties had such a split.) I next looked at the r partisan split. If, for example, Republicans were divided and higher-income districts were more likely to support a Repub nor, or less likely to support a Democratic governor, then the included in the subset for further analysis.

The procedure used in selecting these roll calls in Texas except that legislators from the two parties were considered to roll calls were included if the vote of those from higher-inco was substantially different from those from lower-income distr because party did not explain voting behavior in the Texas legi suspected that I could improve the explanation if other forc idered.

The Republican party in Minnesota appeared to be divid ues, with the high-income-district Republicans voting to op Perpich's program bills and the low-income-district Repul

with many black and Hispanic constituents. The reason for the high negative correlation between the governor's district general election vote and support is that he was likely to do well as a Democrat in the very districts that would oppose him later.

Harmel and Hamm performed a cluster analysis on three Texas legislative sessions, including that of 1983, and found two well-defined clusters in that session. These two clusters—a liberal-moderate cluster and a conservative cluster—accounted for nearly 80 percent of the house membership. They discovered fifty-eight members in the liberal cluster and sixty-one in the conservative cluster, which is exceedingly close to my groupings by district income. Most Republicans voted with the conservative Democrats, as I also found (Harmel and Hamm 1986, 86–90).

Some attempt to organize along party lines has begun in the Texas

TABLE 7.5. The Effect of Legislator's District Variables on Support for Selected Roll Calls in Governor's Program in Four States: Multiple Regression Analysis

| State, Party and Variables | Regression Coefficients | | | | Adjusted |
	Unstandardized	Standardized	t-score*	R^2	R^2
Minn. Republicans (Dem. Governor) ($N = 82$)				.132	.075
Income	−1.896	−1.023	−2.940*		
Education	1.720	.526	2.149*		
Age	−2.971	−.459	−2.166*		
Ill. House Repubs. (Rep. Governor) ($N = 48$)				.232	.216
Income	.003	.482	3.731**		
Cal. Republicans (Rep. Governor) ($N = 46$)				.235	.117
Hispanic	1.724	.392	2.633*		
Age	2.365	.394	2.354*		
Texas House—Both Parties (Dem. Gov.) ($N = 147$)				.474	.455
Gov. Gen. Elec. 1982	−1.156	−.559	−5.866**		
Hispanic	−.454	−.342	−4.772**		
Black	−.323	−.165	−2.008*		

*$p < .05$ **$p < .005$

legislature, where party has never been a cue for voting loyalty. The beginnings of the house Democratic caucus in the early 1980s has been described. The group was immediately labeled "liberal," and its formation was opposed by the speaker and his "team," who saw it as a threat to their power. In 1983, Speaker Gib Lewis's name appeared on the roster as "ex officio" only (Harmel and Hamm 1986, 85). The intent of the caucus was to unite all Democrats, and indeed, by 1983 many conservatives had joined the liberal and moderate founders. Sixteen of the twenty-seven Democrats who voted in the conservative cluster were also members of the caucus (87–89). These twenty-seven conservatives could not win on roll calls without the Republicans, and the speaker was well aware of that and rewarded selected Republicans with important committee chair and vice chair positions. Whether the speaker system will continue to reward Republicans as their numbers increase remains to be seen. One would suspect that the Texas legislature may be on its way to organizing along party lines if the Republicans can maintain unity and control important decisions.

Conclusions

This chapter investigated conditions under which the governor and the legislative leaders build a winning party coalition to pass the governor's program. The hypotheses predicted that in the five states with strong state parties in which party leaders endorse for governor, the governor's legislators would support the program. In the five states with weak or divided parties where there is no method of endorsing candidates for the nomination, the governor faces a legislature in which sit remnants of the factions that opposed him or her in the primary contest, and party voting would be low.

These hypotheses were confirmed when the legislators in strong party states (873) were compared with the legislators from weaker party states (677). The strongest finding is that the political party is highly correlated with the support for the governor's program in endorsing states (.754) and weakly correlated in primary-only states (.192). These results prove that the strong party governor's legislators are highly loyal to his or her program and the opposition is opposed, while in primary-only states there is much less partisan loyalty, parties are weak, and gubernatorial candidates must build their own electoral and governing organizations.

When we examined the states individually, we saw that the governor's party legislators are more supportive in endorsing states than in primary-only states. This difference is caused by the very high level of support in three of the endorsing states: Minnesota, Connecticut, and New York. Illinois and Colorado are not substantially different from the nonendorsing states in the support that the governor's party gives to the gubernatorial program. These two states are the only endorsing states where the governor's party does not control either branch of the legislature.

Party appears to explain support better in California than in any of the other nonendorsing states because of the strength of both legislative parties there. In Tennessee, where party explains almost as much, the legislative Republicans have a history of cohesion. Party may be less important for support in Kansas and Oregon be because they are less urbanized states in which legislative parties do not represent such distinctly different socioeconomic interests.

Among the endorsing states, party voting is highest where the same party controls the governorship and the legislature: Minnesota, Connecticut, and New York. In states with divided government, party voting is lower, in part because a governor has to make compromises to win votes for his program from the opposition party. In all ten states, with the exception of Oregon and Texas, the governor gets significantly more support for his program from his own party than from the opposition.

Where party does not explain most of the variation in support for the governor's program, we have hypothesized that district electoral variables would have significant explanatory power.(We would also predict that legislators in strong party states would follow the expected district relationships but that party would still be the major explanation for voting support.) In a majority of cases, there is no significant relationship between support for the governor and his district electoral strength. The electoral strength of the individual legislator does not appear to have much impact on his or her party voting loyalty.

Four states were selected to test the additional effect of socioeconomic factors. Two (Minnesota and Illinois) are strong two-party states; two (California and Texas) have weaker parties. A subset of roll calls in the governor's program were selected to test the impact of socioeconomic variables in the four states. Here the hypothesis that predicts that socioeconomic and electoral variables would have an effect on legislative voting was confirmed. For the Minnesota parties, where party explained over 90 percent of the voting support, district variables explained a paltry .075 percent of the Republican loyalty. In California, where party explained about 44 percent of the voting loyalty, district variables contributed only .117 percent of the explanation to the Republican party support. In Illinois, where party does not explain more than 34 percent of the support, more of the house Republicans' loyalty can be explained by their district forces. It is in Texas that the socioeconomic and electoral variables can explain what party cannot. More than 45 percent of the variance in voting loyalty in the

Texas House of Representatives can be explained by district factors. Thus, we confirm the hypothesis that where party cannot explain voting loyalty, district demands can help provide the explanation.

The results show that the linkage between the external party and the legislative party is strong in states that have a preprimary endorsement process. In states where the primary decides the nomination and there is no way for parties to have an impact on the nominating process, the linkage between the external party and the legislative party is weak.

CHAPTER 8

The Governor and Party Government

The governor is at one time the head of the party and the head of the government. His or her success as a party leader is vital to success in electoral coalition building as well as legislative coalition building. The importance of this relationship between electing and governing has been virtually ignored at the state level. This book filled that gap. Governors were first presented as campaigners and then as policymakers.

In November 1994, thirty governors assembled at the annual conference of the Republican Governors Association and asserted their independence from Washington. Governor Pete Wilson of California said flatly, "We believe the states that we have been privileged to govern are just that. They are sovereign, proud states of the United States. They are not colonies of the Federal Government." Listening to his speech were governors of seven of the ten states detailed in this book, four of whom, like Wilson, were the immediate successors of the governors we studied.

How different are conditions today from those when our governors were elected? Not very much. The first half of the 1980s set the stage for the following decade and beyond. The candidates, rules, resources, and strategies of the 1990s followed a pattern that was in place by the time our study was made.

Probably the most spectacular continued growth in state party strength occurred within the Republican party in Texas. In 1982 at the time of our study, Governor Bill Clements, the first Republican governor in a hundred years, was beaten by Mark White in what appeared to be a return to Democratic domination. But in the following election, Clements won the rematch, and Republicans won again in 1994. Behind these electoral triumphs was the solid buildup of the party organization since the early 1960s. During the next two decades, the party grew, elected larger congressional and statehouse delegations, and produced two governors and the conversion of a Democratic icon, former governor John Connally, to the Republican party (Appleton and Ward 1994). Republican primary participation has increased from 20 percent of Democratic party votes in 1982 to 52 percent in 1992, and Republicans have reached parity with Democrats and Independents in terms of party identification (Stanley

1992). The hypotheses would predict that the party leaders would see the need for preprimary endorsements, either formal or informal, to unify the party.

This chapter will review what we learned about the governors as party leaders in two types of states: those that nominate by primary only and those that engage in the raucous and disorderly practice of preprimary endorsements. We will review the efforts of those who sought the gubernatorial nomination in the two groups of states in 1982 and the success of the winners in their first legislative session in 1983.

A new study of preprimary endorsing states undertaken in 1994 by Malcolm Jewell and Sarah Morehouse offers a current comparison of party effort in the nominating process. We observed a number of endorsing conventions and sent questionnaires to the delegates. This new study revisits the endorsing states in 1982 that were analyzed in this book. I will present our findings and discuss the changes since then.

Two trends and a recent phenomenon in the legislative process will be discussed for their future implications. We observed the impact of divided government in our study, and this trend has attracted considerable attention in the last decade. The use of legislative party campaign committees has also aroused scholarly interest. A new phenomenon, term limits, has begun to have an impact on legislative leadership and operations. I will also speculate on its potential for the governor's relationship with the legislature.

The Governor's Party Coalition

Gubernatorial candidates inherit state political party organizations, which they will embrace, ignore, or reject. A party is defined in terms of coalition building: collective activity directed toward capturing public office and governing once that office is attained. Men and women who pursue and win the most important post in each of our fifty states offer a measure of the political party as an electoral and governing coalition. A governing coalition exists if there is leadership that has the capacity to nominate a governor and command enough votes in the legislature to pass executive requests.

This book set about to accomplish the following:

1. To investigate the types of coalitions that are formed by gubernatorial candidates to obtain their party's nomination.
2. To test the effect of party rules and practices on these coalition-building efforts, especially the effect of preprimary endorsements.
3. To examine the relationship between the type of nominating

coalition and the governors' ability to obtain legislative support for their programs.

The Governor's Campaign Coalition

The book examined gubernatorial coalition building in ten states during the 1982 gubernatorial election year by observation and interviews with the candidates. In the first group of states, typical of most of those in our union, the gubernatorial candidate must put together his or her own coalition because the party leaders have little influence and the primary determines the outcome of the nominating process (California, Kansas, Oregon, Tennessee, and Texas).

In the second group of five, drawn from about one-third of the states, the possibility of a strong party coalition exists because gubernatorial candidates are endorsed in a convention or party gathering and party cohesion is traditionally strong (Colorado, Connecticut, Illinois, Minnesota, and New York). Laws or informal rules authorize the parties to make preprimary endorsements as a way to increase party control over the nomination and to guide primary voters toward choosing a party-endorsed candidate.

Front-runners, Factions, and Money: Direct-Primary States

Interviews with the nineteen candidates for nomination in the five direct-primary states reveal that these candidates must fashion their own campaigns. True, there are formal party organizations, but these do not help them win the nomination. The party leaders have preferences, but they do not help. The party does not provide money or effort for the nomination. The candidates are on their own. I predicted and found that the four governors won renomination because governors have access to resources.

For those who sought to challenge the successful governors as well as those who fought in the open primary contests in California, front-runner status was sought, but it was not a guarantee of success. In fact, those who wore the front-runner crown in the beginning had reason to keep a sharp watch over their shoulders for those who were trying to stop them. In only two of the six contests did the front-runners win the primary. In other words, primary races are unstable in states that nominate by direct primary only.

The four losing front-runners had good reason to feel aggrieved. Anna Belle Clement O'Brien, heir to the Clement faction in Tennessee; David Owen, former Kansas lieutenant governor and party leader; Don

Clark, Oregon county executive; and Mike Curb, lieutenant governor of California, all had excellent credentials to win, but the lead changed during the campaign, sometimes at the very end.

Factions provide the base for candidates in direct-primary states. The interviews confirmed the fact that the factions were strong, long lasting, and less likely to cooperate after the nominating process. These factions were based on *ideology*, as illustrated by the conservatives versus the liberals within the Democratic party in Texas and Kansas. In California, Republicans were divided into conservatives versus the right wing, and the Democrats had a moderate-versus-liberal split. Factions were based on *electoral machines*, as within the Texas Democrats, where the Briscoe faction's heir, Mark White, battled the John Hill legacy in the person of Buddy Temple. In Tennessee, the Democratic Clement faction was perpetuated in the candidacy of Anna Belle Clement O'Brien and battled the Butcher faction of Knoxville joined by the Memphis machine of state senator John Ford. In Kansas, the Democrats were split between Docking versus anti-Docking factions, and in Kansas and California, the Ford-Reagan split was continued in the factional battles of 1982. *Geography* also plays a role in factional divisions in primary-only states. In Texas there is an east-versus-west split over water and natural resources. Buddy Temple assumed the eastern Texas candidacy when Peyton McKnight dropped out of the race. For both parties in Tennessee, geography plays a part. The traditional Republican base is eastern Tennessee, which dates back to the Civil War conflict and Unionist sentiment. In western Tennessee, a new group of Memphis Republicans back rival candidates. In the Democratic party, the rural middle and upper eastern parts of Tennessee are pitted against the urban areas of Knoxville and Memphis. For Kansas Republicans, Wichita, center of the oil and gas industry, battles the slick urban areas of the northeast. And in California, both parties divide north versus south over water and power. Oregon parties are not strong. Each election brings a different alignment of factions. Each candidate has to establish a different combination of interests. The parties cannot be defined as establishing distinctly different constituencies. Unlike the other parties in the primary states that have strong and enduring factions, Oregon parties are weak and the factions are ephemeral.

Money talks in the primary-only states. While we would expect governors to amass war chests to discourage rivals and to win without difficulty, the power of money in other contests proves conclusively that candidates who have more money win. In all ten races in these states, the candidate who had more money to spend won the primary. It did not matter if the candidate was the front-runner and perhaps had the support of party leaders. It did not matter if a candidate had announced early and built up an organization in every county as did Owen in Kansas or Clark in Oregon or O'Brien in Tennessee. Money talked louder than organization. In races such as those within the Texas Democrats and California Republicans, where both candidates raised equally enormous sums, the character of the media contest became a highly charged personality-related campaign, with intrigue and personal character on the line instead of issues. In Texas and Kansas, where the top two contenders had approximately the same amount of money, a third candidate was able to take votes away from one of them, permitting the other to win, again indicating the unstable character of races in these primary-only states.

Front-runners, Factions, and Money: Preprimary Endorsement States

The twenty-five candidates for the nomination in preprimary endorsement states follow a different strategy from their counterparts in states where the primary is the only decision point. This strategy must include negotiations with party leaders from local to state level. Winning the endorsement and nomination in one effort is possible. While no set of rules can contain severe conflict, the party endorsement states provide a process whereby the endorsed candidate can count on party support in the nominating campaign. This fact can be used to persuade primary enemies to drop the race.

In the preprimary endorsing states, front-runner status implies party leadership support. Presumably the state leaders encourage a candidate to emerge as the front-runner. Occasionally they wait until the contest stabilizes before they back their choice. That usually happens before the convention, and the delegates are aware of the favored candidate. The three governors were front-runners, and their campaign organizations were merged with those of their parties. Both governors O'Neill of Connecticut and Thompson of Illinois were challenged by minor candidates, which indicated that even governors must take front-runner status and party leadership seriously if they are going to survive.

The candidates and the party leaders are in frequent communication. In Connecticut, Lew Rome was a Republican candidate for the gubernatorial nomination in 1978, and when he agreed to abandon a primary fight in the interests of party unity, it was implicit that he would run for governor in 1982. The party leaders thus backed him in 1982 and did not support his rival. In Illinois, Adlai Stevenson garnered the needed votes within the State Central Committee, called the mayor of Chicago, and received the endorsement. Mayor Koch of New York was the clear Democratic front-runner and the choice of the state's most powerful county party leaders, who controlled enough delegates to the state convention to assure him of the endorsement. The New York Republican leaders tried to stop the front-runner, Lew Lehrman, and finally joined him. The party had traditionally been united under Governors Dewey and Rockefeller, who had controlled the nomination. When it was obvious that the multi-millionaire could win the primary, the leaders backed him. Minnesota Democratic leaders supported three-term attorney general Walter Spannaus for the nomination. Spannaus was regarded as the candidate for a long time, and in his words, "I was considered the strongest candidate" (Spannaus 1982, 3). The Minnesota Republicans appeared united as the nominating season commenced, but the front-runner and favorite of the leaders, Lou Wangberg, faltered at the convention, although he eventually received the endorsement, and was beaten in the following primary. In this review of front-runners and leaders, we see that every leader-backed candidate won the endorsement. But occasionally, conventions are not representative of the party's voters, and such was the case three times in 1982.

Our hypothesis predicts that candidate factions in strong party states are more personal and less durable than in weak party states. If the party boasts one leadership coalition, it may assume the continuity and the power to control nominations. The main task of the party leaders in strong party states is to manage the ever present potential for factionalism and to channel the aspirations and energies of rival groups into a semblance of party unity (Jewell and Olson 1982, 52). Candidates are on their own to raise money for their endorsement effort, but I predict that money itself does not buy the endorsement. Once they have been endorsed, candidates can look forward to the status and organizational support that endorsement confers and hence the money will come more easily.

In eight out of ten endorsing contests, a single faction of *party regulars and leaders* controlled the outcome for their candidate. The major exception was the contest within the New York Republican party, since Lew Lehrman was definitely not an insider and had not paid his dues to the party. When it was obvious that he would win, however, the party backed him. In Colorado, the party leaders waited until John Fuhr built up the delegate strength he needed to win first place on the ballot. His bare-bones campaign, costing a fraction of opponent Phil Winn's, proved to be what the party regulars wanted, and Winn dropped out. The other type of faction in the endorsing states is the *personal* faction, which most candidates use to seek the endorsement. This faction is ephemeral and easily merges with the leadership coalition or with the campaign organization of the nominee. The candidates were most likely to talk about low factionalism, which can merge to win in the general election.

Why did three endorsees lose? The New York Democrats were used to family fights before 1982, but after that contest they consolidated behind

Mario Cuomo, the challenger and winner of the primary. According to campaign operatives for Mayor Koch, rival factions can bury the hatchet and pull together for the general election. Not so the two parties in Minnesota. That year proved to be a forerunner of increasing conflict within both. Yet, the citizens of that state appear to want the rigors of face-to-face contact in unruly endorsing conventions as a preliminary to the loneliness of the primary election booth.

The power of party effort versus money in preprimary endorsement states is evident. In these endorsement states, front-runner status implies leader support and party backing. In endorsing conventions, money was not nearly as important to the outcome as leader support or front-runner status. In all of the ten races, the front-runner won the party endorsement, and in seven out of ten contests, the endorsed candidate won the nomination. However, for the New York Democrats and both parties in Minnesota, the party endorsee was challenged in a primary and lost. Money did not make the difference in two of these primaries (New York [D] and Minnesota [D]). In all but these three cases, party-endorsed candidates won over those who raised the same as or more than they did, hence the power of the party organization is confirmed.

The Governor's Legislative Coalition

Ten of our candidates became governor. To what extent does it matter if they led strong parties or weak parties to victory? The hypotheses predict that the governor's coalition in strong party states will carry over into the governing process and command legislative loyalty for the governor's program. In these states the possibility of a strong coalition exists because gubernatorial candidates are endorsed in a convention or party gathering and party cohesion is traditionally strong. The assumption is that the legislative party and the statewide party are joined in the forming of an electoral coalition.

In the weak party states, no preprimary endorsements exist, and the gubernatorial candidate must put together his or her own coalition because the party leaders have little influence and the primary determines the outcome of the nominating process. In these states where the party is weak or divided, governors will face legislatures in which sit remnants of the factions that opposed them in the primary contest.

Using the individual legislator's voting for the governor's program bills to test legislative party loyalty, I compared legislators in the ten states. At first I used a merged data program using all 1,550 legislators (table 7.2) and found that the legislator's political party is highly correlated with support for the governor's program in endorsing states (.754) and weakly correlated in primary-only states (.192). This finding confirms the hypotheses that predict that the governor's party members are highly loyal to his or her program in endorsing states while the opposition is opposed, which is the typical party government scenario. In primary-only states, there is much less partisan loyalty, parties are weak, and gubernatorial candidates must build their own electoral and governing organizations.

In all ten states except Texas and New York (the assembly), the governor needs at least 80 percent or more of the governing party legislators to be sure that the program will pass or that he or she can bargain effectively with the opposition party. The governor's party legislators are much more supportive in endorsing states than in primary states. It is particularly noteworthy that the opposition party's support for the governor's program is much higher in nonendorsing states. When the governors cannot obtain support from their own legislators, they must turn to the opposition for votes. These votes the opposition is able to provide for a price—a price that may further alienate some of the governor's legislators.

Although there is strong evidence that partisanship is a much better predictor of votes for the governor's program in endorsing than in primary-only states, we need to examine variations within each group of states. When we compare the individual states, we see that party voting is strongest in Minnesota, Connecticut, and New York. The other two endorsing states, Illinois and Colorado, are not substantially different from the nonendorsing states in the level of partisanship on the gubernatorial program. They are states with divided government where the opposition party controls both houses. In those states, the governor's party leaders had to recruit legislators from the opposing party to win votes for passage, probably at the risk of losing some of their own.

Party appears to explain support better in California than in any of the other nonendorsing states, as previous research has indicated (Morehouse 1981a, 295). In Tennessee, party also explains an impressive amount of party support, which may be due to the traditional loyalty of the small contingent of eastern Republicans spurred on by a Republican governor. Party is less important as an explanation for support in Kansas and Oregon because state party organizations are not traditionally strong. Texas represents the weak-party model where the governorship and the legislature have traditionally been under Democratic control. In 1983, the overwhelming majority of seats were held by Democrats, and the corporal's guard of Republicans voted with the conservatives.

The hypotheses about differences between endorsing and nonendorsing states in level of legislative support are supported. The obvious exceptions, Illinois and Colorado, are the only endorsing states where the governor's party does not control either branch of the legislature.

The state-level analysis of the relationship between state party strength and support for the gubernatorial program prompted hypotheses about the relationship between the individual legislator and support. By examining district-level variables, I expected to find that legislators in the governor's party gave more support to the governor if the governor had demonstrated district electoral strength in the primary and general election and if the legislator was vulnerable. I expected to find that members of the opposition party would give more support to the governor if the governor was strong in the general election and if the legislator was electorally vulnerable.

In general, the governor's electoral record in legislative districts did not explain as much party voting in endorsing states as predicted. So much voting can be explained by party cohesion that there was little left to be explained by district electoral variables. Governors can benefit from their party's cohesion overall, and their district records do not affect legislators' support.

Contrary to the hypotheses, there were few significant relationships between the governor's district electoral strength and success in gaining support from legislators in weaker party states. Additionally, there were even fewer significant relationship between legislators' elections within their districts and their support of the governor's program within strong or weak states. The relationship between district electoral variables and support for a gubernatorial program is a complex one, and the results from one state party to another are inconsistent and sometimes counterintuitive. The conclusion is that party organizational strength on the state level is vastly more important in explaining legislative support than district electoral strength or weakness.

The discussion so far has stressed the importance of the electoral vulnerability or security of legislators and how the party leaders can affect their hopes for advancement by assisting them electorally or professionally. Jewell and Patterson have proposed that legislators from districts that reflect the basic economic orientation of the party are more likely to be loyal than those whose constituencies deviate from the mean (1986). I examined a subset of roll calls in the governor's program on which socioeconomic variables might have more effect. I examined the relationship between district-level socioeconomic conditions and support for the subset of economic issues in the governor's program in the four states where such data were available for 1982.

Texas is the only state where partisanship has absolutely no relationship to support for the governor's program, and here a combination of district socioeconomic and electoral variables could explain a hefty amount of the nonpartisan voting behavior ($R^2 = .474$). The regression considered all members of the Texas House of Representatives without regard to party on bills that were of socioeconomic interest. The analysis shows that Governor White was opposed by legislators representing Hispanic and black constituents as well as those in districts where he did well in the general election. The governor, a moderate conservative, could get a bipartisan coalition of Republicans and conservative Democrats representing wealthier districts. To summarize, the regression explained nearly half of the voting in the Texas house on bills that were most likely to cause division along socioeconomic lines.

Strong Parties in 1994: Endorsing States Revisited

We know that in strong parties that make preprimary endorsements, the gubernatorial nominee has the opportunity to build a strong coalition that includes the major elements of party leadership and is likely to win nomination by a comfortable margin, and sometimes without opposition in the primary. Under these conditions, the party is likely to nominate its strongest candidate, one who is in the mainstream of the party and stands the best chance of being elected in November. We know that when such candidates win the governorship, they have the chance to transform this campaign coalition into a governing coalition and to win a high level of support for their program from the members of their party in the legislature.

What is the relevance of these findings from the early 1980s for the 1990s? Do a substantial number of state parties still make endorsements? How successful are endorsees in winning nomination, with or without a contested primary? Where endorsements occur, do they still have the support of party candidates, leaders, and activists? Can we define the conditions under which endorsees are most likely to win nomination, and what causes some of them to fail?

To shed light on these questions, we will examine the record of gubernatorial endorsees in nominations from 1960 through 1994, and we will look in depth at party endorsements in a number of state parties in 1994.

Most of the state parties making endorsements in the early 1980s have continued that practice since that time. New Mexico abandoned legal endorsements after the 1982 election and restored them before the 1994 election. Delaware abandoned legal endorsements after the 1976 election, but the Republicans have continued the practice under party rules. The Wisconsin Republicans stopped making informal endorsements after 1978. The California Democrats began making endorsements in 1990, after the courts overruled a state law preventing party endorsements.

In order to measure trends in the effectiveness of endorsements, we examine the success of endorsees in nominating races from 1960 through 1994 in eleven states where one or both parties currently make endorsements in gubernatorial nominations (table 8.1). In the elections from 1960 through 1980, there were contested primaries in 44 percent of the cases for legal endorsements and 71 percent of the cases for informal endorsements. In the 1982 to 1994 elections, there were small increases: to 45 percent for legal and 80 percent for informal endorsements.

This finding suggests that, where the endorsement process has a legal basis, nonendorsed candidates are more likely to drop out of the race than is the case in states where the process is an informal one, based only on party rules. In several states having legal endorsements, it is either impossible to enter a primary unless you get a certain proportion of convention votes (Connecticut and Utah) or it is more difficult to qualify for the primary if you fall short of that threshold (New York, Colorado, and New

TABLE 8.1. **Primary Competition and Success of Party Endorsements**

Years	Party	No Primary Contest Total	Contested Primaries Total	Contested Primaries Endorsee Wins	Percent of Primaries Contested	Percent of Contested Primaries Won by Endorsee
Legal Endorsements						
1960–80	D	20	13	11	39	85
1960–80	R	17	16	13	48	81
1960–80	Total	37	29	24	44	83
1982–94	D	14	12	5	46	42
1982–94	R	14	11	5	44	45
1982–94	Total	28	23	10	45	43
Informal Endorsements						
1960–80	D	1	5	4	83	80
1960–80	R	3	5	4	63	80
1960–80	Total	4	10	8	71	80
1982–94	D	1	8	5	89	63
1982–94	R	3	8	3	73	38
1982–94	Total	4	16	8	80	50
All Endorsing Parties						
1960–80	Total	41	39	32	49	82
1982–94	Total	32	39	18	55	46

Source: Jewell 1994, 162.

Note: The states with legal endorsements are: Colorado, Connecticut, New York, North Dakota, Rhode Island, Utah, and New Mexico; those with informal endorsements are Massachusetts, Minnesota, California, and Delware.

Mexico). Massachusetts is the only state with informal endorsements where a threshold requirement exists, which suggests that parties operating under a legal endorsement process are stronger and better able to make the endorsement stick.

There has been a much greater change in the success enjoyed by gubernatorial endorsees in contested primaries. The proportion winning has dropped from 82 percent in the 1960–80 period to only 46 percent in the 1982–94 period (with only modest differences between legal and informal endorsements). Based on the data in table 8.1, we can calculate that the chances of an endorsee winning the nomination, either by being unopposed or by defeating an opponent in the primary, have dropped from 93 percent to 74 percent in states with legal endorsements and from 86 percent to 60 percent in state parties with informal endorsements.

The 1982 elections signaled the beginning of a decline in the success for endorsed candidates in contested races. Four endorsees lost primaries, including three in my five endorsing states. Since that time, only in the 1984 and 1986 elections have a majority of endorsees facing opposition won primaries.

One way to shed light on this trend, and particularly the factors contributing to—or undermining—the success of endorsees in primaries, is to examine a number of the gubernatorial endorsements made in 1994. In the summer of 1994, Malcolm Jewell and Sarah Morehouse revisited four of the endorsing states in the 1982 study plus Massachusetts, New Mexico, and the California Democrats, who had recently (in 1990) decided to endorse. We were interested in assessing the effectiveness of the endorsement process as a method of party building and as a way of guaranteeing a strong candidate who has the best chance of winning in the general election (Jewell and Morehouse 1995, 1996).

The hypotheses were the same as in 1982. We hypothesized that preprimary endorsements offer party leaders the opportunity to strengthen the party as well as secure the nomination for their favored candidate. Primaries are risky for the party because a plurality of voters who participate in the primary may not choose the candidate most likely to win in the general election. There are several ways the party leaders can use the endorsement process as a method of party building:

1. Recruit candidates who have the potential for winning. The endorsement process gives the party influence over nominations, and the recruited candidate should win the primary election.
2. Foster unity and minimize risk of bitter antagonisms that result from divisive primaries. Lead activists to rally around the

endorsee, and lead nonendorsed candidates to drop out of the primary.

3. Endorse a candidate whose views on issues and whose record of accomplishments are in the mainstream of the party. A mainstream candidate should be more electable than someone holding extreme positions on issues.

4. Build up party strength by rallying activists and local organizations to participate in preprimary endorsements.

The Study

The research was based on a study of ten party gubernatorial endorsing conventions held in 1994, in seven states, where there were significant primary contests. The gubernatorial candidates endorsed by state conventions won contested primaries in five of the parties in our study: New York Republican, Connecticut Republican, Massachusetts Democratic, Minnesota Democratic-Farmer-Labor (DFL), and New Mexico Democratic. The endorsed candidates were defeated in four parties: Connecticut Democratic, Minnesota Independent Republican, Colorado Republican, and New Mexico Republican. The California Democrats decided at the last minute to make no endorsement for governor.

Incumbent governors were endorsed overwhelmingly and won primaries without opposition in the New York Democratic, Massachusetts Republican, and Colorado Democratic parties. These three parties are not included in this study. Endorsed candidates lost in both Rhode Island parties, which were not in our study.

We evaluate the effectiveness of the 1994 convention endorsement process as a method of party building and candidate success in each state. We rely in part on questionnaires sent to a sample of convention delegates in the ten parties, almost fifteen hundred of which were returned and coded. These sources are supplemented by firsthand observation in six conventions, some interviews at the conventions, and media accounts of the conventions and subsequent primaries. Table 8.2 summarizes the information about the fate of gubernatorial nominees in the nine state parties where the endorsees were challenged.

The Endorsement Process as Party Building

The tradition of preprimary endorsements is much older in some state parties than in others, and convention delegates are much more strongly committed to the endorsement principle. This statement is best illustrated by looking briefly at the 1994 Connecticut Republican and California Democratic conventions.

The Connecticut Republicans

The Connecticut Republican convention pitted former member of Congress John Rowland against Connecticut secretary of state Pauline Kezer. Everyone knew that Rowland, a strong conservative, was going to be endorsed. The only question was whether Rowland, and the party leaders supporting him, could keep Kezer from getting the 15 percent of the vote

TABLE 8.2. Convention Endorsements and Primary Results, 1994

State and Party	Candidates	Endorsed?	% of Convention Vote	% of Primary Vote	Background
NY-R	George Pataki	Yes	72	75	st. senator
	R. Rosenbaum	—		25	ex st. party chair
CT-R	John Rowland	Yes	85	67	ex U.S. representative
	Pauline Kezer		15	33	secretary of state
MA-D	Mark Roosevelt	Yes	53	48	st. representative
	George Bachrach		24	27	ex st. senator
	Michael Barrett		23	25	st. senator
NM-D	Bruce King	Yes	60	39	governor
	Casey Luna		40	36	lt. governor
	Jim Bacca	—		25	ex U.S. official
MN-DFL	John Marty	Yes	41	38	st. senator
	Mike Hatch		5	36	st. official
	Tony Bouza		3	25	ex police chief
CT-D	Bill Curry		35	55	st. comptroller
	John Larson	Yes	65	45	st. senate leader
NM-R	Gary Johnson		22	35	businessperson
	Dick Cheney	Yes	49	33	former st. house leader
	John Dendahl		29	19	ex st. official
	David Cargo	—		13	ex governor
MN-R	Arne Carlson		31	67	governor
	Allen Quist	Yes	69	33	ex st. representative
CO-R	Bruce Benson	—		60	businessperson
	Mike Bird	Yes	50	23	st. senator
	Dick Sargent		42	17	businessperson

Source: Jewell and Morehouse 1996, Table 1, 344–45.

Note: In the Minnesota DFL party, the convention vote is for the first ballot; after the first ballot, Hatch and Bouza dropped out. On the sixth ballot, Marty led Mike Freeman by 56–44% (with 60% required for endorsement). Freeman then dropped out and did not enter the primary. Four candidates entered primaries but did not seek convention endorsement: Rosenbaum (NY-Republican), Bacca (NM-Democrat), Cargo (NM-Republican), and Benson (CO-Republican).

that she needed to challenge him in a primary. The roll call went on for hours, with some thirteen hundred delegates voting one by one. When it concluded, the totals were not announced, but Kezer had twenty-one more votes than she needed.

The chair announced that delegates had the right to change their votes and kept repeating the invitation as he kept the voting open for more than an hour. Many of the delegates were chanting: "Shift, shift, shift! No primary! No primary!" Finally, after a few conversions, the chair reluctantly announced the end of the roll call. Pauline Kezer had held 15 percent of the delegates, with three votes to spare. There would be a primary.

The California Democrats

The story of the California endorsing convention could not be more different. In 1990 the party endorsed for governor for the first time since the turn of the century, as a result of the U.S. Supreme Court decision in 1989 overturning state law that forbade the practice. John Van de Kamp was the party's endorsee for governor, but Dianne Feinstein beat him in the primary. The leaders knew that if a party endorsee loses regularly in the primary, the endorsement becomes meaningless, if not counterproductive. Before the convention met, state chair Bill Press, with the apparent support of leading Democrats, decided that, in order to preserve unity in the party, there would be no endorsement for governor, and there would be no debate among the gubernatorial candidates at the convention. Press said, "We do not want to emphasize our differences. We want to emphasize the one common goal, which is getting rid of Pete Wilson" (Decker and Wallace 1994). The delegates evidently agreed with Press. Two-thirds of them, in our survey, opposed any effort to endorse for governor.

Delegates' Support for Endorsement

For the endorsement system to continue to function effectively in a political party, it must continue to have the support of party activists. Delegates to the endorsing conventions are not only a good cross section of activists but also have firsthand familiarity, often over several elections, with the endorsement process. Delegates to conventions in nine state parties (all except the New York Republicans) were asked in a questionnaire if they thought the principle of preprimary convention endorsements was good for the party or, in some states, if the party should continue to make such endorsements. Seventy-three percent of those expressing a viewpoint responded positively to endorsements, 20 percent opposed, and 7 percent gave conditional support (table 8.3).

There are some important differences among the states in the level of support for endorsements. It is highest in the two Connecticut parties and the Minnesota DFL party (table 8.3). The Connecticut legal endorsement system is particularly strong: candidates must poll 15 percent of the convention vote to get on the primary ballot. The Minnesota DFL has a long-standing commitment to the principle of endorsement.

We might expect that support for the principle of endorsements would be strongest among those delegates who support the endorsee. In general such is the case; 85 percent of those backing the top endorsee and

TABLE 8.3.   Is Endorsement a Good Idea? (by state party and by supporters of endorsee and losers, in percentages)

	Yes	Conditional	No
ALL	73	7	20
Endorsee	85	5	10
Losers	64	10	26
CT-D	82	7	11
Endorsee	92	5	3
Losers	67	11	22
CT-R	82	4	14
Endorsee	87	4	9
Losers	58	4	38
MN-DFL	78	10	12
Endorsee	87	8	5
Losers	70	11	19
MN-IR	77	5	18
Endorsee	98	1	1
Losers	37	13	50
CO-R	77	7	16
Endorsee	79	8	13
Losers	76	8	16
NM-D	77	5	18
Endorsee	84	4	12
Losers	64	10	26
MA-D	67	7	26
Endorsee	69	9	22
Losers	65	7	28
NM-R	63	10	27
Endorsee	64	8	28
Losers	61	12	27
CA-D	56	6	38

Note: In states where more than one candidate is endorsed, all but the top endorsee are included as losers. Because in California no endorsement was made, there is no breakdown between supporters of winners and losers.

only 64 percent of those backing other candidates (losers) favor endorsements (table 8.3).

Delegates were asked whether the endorsement process should be strengthened, and about half of them in the states as a whole supported a stronger endorsement system. In Connecticut, there was more support among Republican delegates than Democrats for making it harder to challenge the endorsee in a primary, because many Republicans were critical of a candidate who barely got 15 percent of the convention vote required for such a challenge. In Minnesota, a majority of DFL delegates agreed that candidates who unsuccessfully sought endorsement should promise not to challenge the endorsee in a primary. But a majority of Republican delegates opposed this idea because the battle for the endorsement was so divisive.

Using an open-ended format, we asked delegates to explain their reasons for favoring or opposing preprimary endorsements for their party. The overwhelming majority of reasons given for supporting endorsements fall into three major categories. Thirty-six percent stress the important role of party activists in the endorsing process, 25 percent stress advantages to the party, and 12 percent say the endorsement process selects better candidates (Jewell and Morehouse 1995).

Those who support endorsements most frequently argue that the endorsement system is beneficial to party activists. It gives them a meaningful role to play in the party, specifically in the nominating process. Implicit and sometimes explicit in this argument is the belief that committed, participating activists are essential to the life of the political party. A Colorado Republican delegate says, "The present system helps to build the interest of party members. It also helps us to build a core of active party members." A leader of the California Democratic party sees the endorsement process as a learning experience for delegates: "It gives valuable experience to the activists, who learn to count votes, be whips, plan strategy, and build alliances—all of which is valuable in developing party leaders."

The next most frequent group of reasons given for favoring endorsements are somewhat varied but have one thing in common: the belief that the endorsement process is good for the party. It increases party unity, helps the party win, and strengthens the party. Selecting nominees should be the role of the party. Delegates often assert that the endorsement process makes candidates more responsive to the party and more likely to support the party's position on issues. A conservative Republican delegate from Connecticut emphasizes, "A party must have a philosophy and an ideology, and the voters must be presented with candidates who bear the party's philosophy and ideology."

One of the most common responses is that the endorsement process leads to the choice of better candidates. The idea of "better" candidates is often defined as those with the best chance of winning the general election.

In a similar vein, some of the delegates stress the importance of using endorsements to eliminate candidates so weak that they should not be on the primary ballot. A Colorado Republican says, "The system tends to weed out individuals of poor character or extreme political positions."

Only about 20 percent of the respondents oppose endorsements. The most direct attack on the principle of endorsements comes from the 6 percent who say the voters should decide. About 10 percent of all respondents believe that, in practice, the endorsement process is flawed because it gives too much influence to one particular group, which increases the chance that a candidate will be chosen who does not represent the views of rank-and-file party members and is less likely to be electable. Some identify a group that is perceived as having too much power in the convention: the governor, party bosses, activists, members of a single-issue or fringe group, or members of the Christian Right.

Factors Affecting Whether the Endorsee Is Nominated

In order to understand why it is becoming more difficult for endorsees to be nominated, we need to understand what aspects of the endorsing process strengthen or weaken the endorsee's position. We hypothesize that there are several factors that can explain the success of endorsees in winning the nomination.

1. The convention chooses the strongest candidate to endorse. This means that the endorsee has political skills and reflects the views of the mainstream of the party's voters. The party's incumbent governor is the strongest candidate when the party is in power.
2. The convention delegates represent the views of the primary electorate.
3. The endorsee is backed by a united party that encourages nonendorsed candidates to drop out of the primary.
4. The endorsee gains tangible advantages, such as campaign funds and workers, from individuals and organizations including state and local party groups.
5. The endorsee gains a significant amount of publicity and momentum from being endorsed.

Strongest Candidate

If the convention chooses a candidate who is politically strong, that endorsee is more like to discourage other candidates and beat any who enter the primary. The best example of a strong candidate is an incumbent governor. Party conventions endorsed seventy of the seventy-four incumbent governors who sought renomination from 1960 to 1994, and all but two of them were nominated, fifty-one without primary opposition; two of the four who were not endorsed still won the nomination.

Delegates generally recognize the importance of endorsing a strong candidate, one who can be nominated and elected. Almost 60 percent of the delegates we polled in 1994 mentioned electoral strength as a reason for supporting their candidate, and the proportion was about 66 percent for candidates who went on to win the nomination.

Several of the 1994 conventions illustrate the success or failure in finding strong candidates. In New York, the party leaders had to search for a candidate with enough potential strength to challenge Governor Cuomo. In the months leading up to the convention, Republican party leaders held a number of meetings in an effort to unite behind one candidate. Senator Alfonse D'Amato emerged as the leader of this group and succeeded in enlisting the support of most state and local leaders for George Pataki, a relatively obscure state senator. By the time the convention met, it had become clear that most of its members were prepared to support Pataki. Some of the delegates we polled emphasized that there was a good opportunity to defeat Cuomo, and a number perceived Pataki as a particularly strong candidate.

The most dramatic example of a convention's failure to endorse a strong candidate occurred in the Minnesota Republican party, where a convention packed by members of the Christian Right and other pro life delegates rejected Governor Arne Carlson and endorsed Allen Quist, an obscure, defeated legislator. Quist was an ardent advocate of "family values" and the pro life position, which had been important to a minority of the party since 1982. Quist supporters among the surveyed delegates were most likely (95 percent) to list agreement with Quist's views on issues as a reason for supporting him; only 15 percent mentioned his electability. Carlson beat Quist in the primary by a two-to-one margin and then won the general election comfortably. Quist clearly could not have been elected even if he had survived the primary.

Representative Convention

Delegates to endorsing conventions are usually party activists who are likely to share the views of the party loyalists in their district or county, who will vote in the primary. They are politically sophisticated and capable of evaluating which candidates have the best chance of being nominated. But some persons seek election as delegates primarily to help a particular candidate or to promote a particular cause or interest group. Such delegates may be unrepresentative of partisans who vote in the primary and less interested in endorsing a candidate who can be nominated and elected.

Obviously a large majority of delegates to the 1994 Republican convention in Minnesota did not reflect the views and priorities of Republican partisans as a whole. They were less interested in endorsing a candidate who could win than in promoting the cause of the Christian Right and the pro life movement. The candidate they endorsed by a two-thirds majority, Allen Quist, lost the nomination to Governor Arne Carlson, who was much closer to the mainstream of the Republican party.

United Party

One of the purposes of an endorsing convention is to unite as many of the active members of the party as possible behind one candidate and perhaps even discourage other candidates from running. Occasionally a convention not only fails to accomplish this objective, but also further divides a party. The 1994 Minnesota convention was deeply divided because delegates from the Christian Right had seized control from mainstream Republican activists. There are several examples that demonstrate how endorsing conventions can help unify a party behind the endorsee in order to facilitate winning the primary. The Republican party leaders in the 1994 New York convention not only managed Pataki's endorsement, but they engineered a deal to persuade his most serious challenger, Herbert London, to run for comptroller instead of running for governor in the Republican primary or in the general election as a Conservative party candidate.

John Marty won the 60 percent of the vote required for endorsement at the 1994 Minnesota DFL convention after a prolonged struggle that engendered considerable bitterness. For a number of ballots, the vote of liberal delegates was split between Marty and Mike Freeman, with more conservative candidates trailing far behind. But after Freeman dropped out of the endorsement contest, he also carried out a pledge not to run in the primary. A major reason for Marty's victory in the primary was that he did not have to fight with Freeman for the support of liberal voters, who make up the largest share of the DFL primary electorate. Similarly, in the 1982 Connecticut Republican party, Richard Bozzuto, the runner-up, agreed not to challenge Lew Rome, the endorsee, leaving Rome unopposed in the primary.

The 1994 Connecticut Democratic party convention, however, is a clear example of one that failed to unite behind its endorsee, John Larson. For hours after Larson defeated William Curry for the convention's endorsement, party leaders scurried around the convention center trying to strike a deal that would persuade Curry not to challenge Larson in a primary. The effort failed, and many delegates left the convention frustrated by the process or by the lack of results. Larson lost the primary to Curry.

Tangible Support

We asked delegates to the 1994 conventions (in an open-ended question) what advantages, if any, they believed that a candidate gained in a contested primary from being endorsed. Over three-fourths of the delegates (77 percent) said they believed that there were advantages to being endorsed, 16 percent said there were none, and 7 percent were unsure or unresponsive (table 8.4).

Almost one-third (31 percent) of the delegates as reported in table 8.4 described tangible support that the endorsee could expect to get from political activists or organizations as a result of convention action. Seventeen percent of these mentioned explicitly support from state or local party organizations for the endorsee. This percentage was higher in states with particularly strong party organizations. Another 14 percent of these mentioned other tangible support, including greater access to funding and help from party activists.

The five state parties where delegates are most likely to perceive endorsement as giving a candidate an advantage in the primary are all

TABLE 8.4. 1994 Convention Delegates' Perceptions of Advantages Enjoyed by Endorsees (in percentages)

Perceived Advantage	All Parties	NY Rep	MN DFL	MN IR	CT Dem	CT Rep	CA Dem	MA Dem	NM Dem	NM Rep	CO Rep
Tangible party support	17	34	29	21	25	20	27	3	4	3	1
Other tangible support	14	7	19	14	25	20	15	14	12	7	2
Publicity and momentum	29	15	30	40	24	37	23	45	30	28	16
Voters will support endorsee	7	6	9	7	9	11	8	9	2	3	3
Ballot position helps	6	0	0	0	4	0	0	0	13	18	23
Miscellaneous	4	28	0	4	1	0	4	0	9	7	3
Total advantages	77	90	87	86	88	88	77	71	70	66	48
No advantages	16	4	6	9	7	6	16	22	20	21	46
Uncertain or unresponsive	7	6	7	5	5	6	7	7	10	13	6

Source: Jewell and Morehouse 1996, Table 3, 354.

ones with particularly strong party organizations. Therefore, it is not surprising that delegates in these parties were particularly likely to emphasize the tangible advantages of endorsements for candidates such as funding and volunteer efforts coming from party organizations and activists (table 8.4).

In several parties there is evidence that in 1994 party leaders, local organizations, and party activists worked vigorously and effectively for the candidate they had endorsed in the convention. Local Republican party organizations are strong in New York, most of them had supported George Pataki, and they evidently worked hard to deliver the vote for him in the primary. New York parties are dominated by the leaders of the largest local party organizations. Most of the convention members we polled said that local leaders made efforts to unite their delegates behind one candidate for governor. Pataki's only primary challenger, Richard Rosenbaum, had considerable financing but very little support from party organizations.

Local Republican party organizations are strong in Connecticut, and most of them were strongly behind John Rowland in his primary campaign. Most delegates to Connecticut conventions are experienced party activists in their cities and towns. About three-quarters of the Republican delegates held local party office. In the Connecticut Democratic party, by contrast, local party leaders in the large cities worked hard to get John Larson endorsed but failed to deliver the votes he needed to defeat Bill Curry in the primary. Curry, on the other hand, spent most of his resources on organizational efforts, worked closely with labor unions and other liberal groups, and concentrated on contacting voters who were most likely to go to the polls. Curry's success is similar to that of Mario Cuomo in 1982, who won the New York Democratic primary by putting together a coalition of labor and liberal groups that was more effective than the effort mounted by local party organizations on behalf of Edward Koch, the endorsee.

There are also state parties where the endorsement has few if any tangible advantages. The best example is the New Mexico Republican party, whose leaders and active members in 1994 had little to offer the endorsee, Dick Cheney, who lost the primary. The Republican party is not particularly well organized, and there is no tradition of party activists or local party organizations supporting the top endorsee—perhaps because New Mexico has used preprimary endorsements only intermittently.

The Colorado parties have a much longer and stronger tradition of endorsements than do those in New Mexico. But in 1994, whatever tangible advantages the Republican endorsees gained were overmatched by the resources of Bruce Benson, who did not even seek endorsement but used his personal wealth to bury them in the primary with a blitz of television advertising.

Name Recognition, Publicity, and Momentum

Almost one-third (29 percent) of the delegates polled believed that the endorsee gained an advantage simply from the fact of being endorsed ("publicity and momentum," table 8.4). They were most likely to emphasize the media attention and name recognition resulting from action by the convention. This factor was seen as particularly important for those candidates who had not been well known previously. Before the Minnesota DFL convention met, John Marty had a very low level of recognition among the Democratic electorate. The publicity he received as the endorsee may have been indispensable to his victory as the nominee. It is impossible to estimate how much the endorsement was worth, but it is plausible to argue that it accounted for Marty's narrow margin in the primary (2 percentage points, or about eight thousand votes).

When Endorsees Are in Trouble

Essentially the same factors weakened the endorsement process in some state parties in both 1982 and in 1994. When the convention failed to endorse the strongest available candidate, the endorsee was vulnerable in the primary. If the convention was controlled by delegates unrepresentative of the party or if it failed to achieve a substantial degree of unity, the endorsement process was less effective. In some state parties, the endorsement provided relatively few tangible advantages to the endorsee, or challengers were able to build a stronger organization or mount a much better financed campaign than the endorsee did.

Is there reason to believe that any of these factors that undermine the endorsee are becoming more common or more serious problems? Could such trends help explain the declining success of endorsees in primaries? In both political parties there are groups, representing either economic or ideological interests, making strong demands on the parties. In recent years that has caused deep splits in some state parties, particularly Republican ones. We may see an increasing number of cases where delegates representing such interests win a majority or large minority in a state endorsing convention, as occurred in the Minnesota Independent Republican party in 1982 and 1994. If such a convention is unrepresentative of the party electorate or is deeply divided, the endorsee may not have broad enough support to win the primary.

The value of an endorsement is depreciated if it brings with it relatively few tangible advantages. Not all state parties provide substantial resources for the endorsee, and those that do may not be keeping up with the growing cost of campaigns. Some local party organizations appear to be declining in effectiveness. The work of party activists is an important asset, but it is diminished in parties that are deeply divided over issues and candidates.

One of the purposes of endorsements is to reduce the importance of money in primary campaigns and to minimize the chances that the nomination will be captured by a wealthy outsider. The 1982 Minnesota Republican primary and the 1994 Colorado Republican primary were captured by candidates who did not even seek endorsement and easily outspent the endorsee. It is ironic the Lew Lehrman, one of the endorsees who was nominated in 1982, was a wealthy outsider who won the New York Republican endorsement by spending huge amounts to win name recognition and by threatening to spend whatever was needed to win the primary—with or without the endorsement. As the costs of campaigning grow, the risk increases that more endorsees will be overwhelmed in the primary by big spenders.

In several state parties, one important reason for the change in the success of endorsees has been a change in the norms about challenging the endorsee. Connecticut established its primary and endorsement system in 1958, and the endorsee was challenged only twice, unsuccessfully, prior to 1986. The Rhode Island primary with endorsements began in 1948, it had no gubernatorial primaries in the early years, and no endorsee lost until 1984. In Colorado only one gubernatorial endorsee was defeated, and few seriously challenged, between 1928 and 1990. Both Minnesota parties used to have strong norms discouraging challenges to the endorsee, and most endorsees who had opponents won their primaries overwhelmingly. Prior to 1982, when both parties' endorsees lost, the only defeat of an endorsee occurred in 1966, when the DFL failed to endorse the incumbent governor. In 1994 two of the candidates who challenged endorsees, in Colorado and Minnesota, were former state party chairs. Eleven of the twenty-one defeats of endorsees from 1982 through 1994 occurred in these four states—Connecticut, Rhode Island, Colorado, and Minnesota—where challenges to endorsees used to be unusual and defeats were rare.

It seems unlikely that, in any of these or other comparable state parties, the old norms about not challenging endorsees will be restored. That is one reason why the rate of endorsee success is not likely to be restored to high levels of 1960–80. Whether future endorsees are more or less successful than in recent years depends on the factors I have discussed, such as the strength of state and local parties, the frequency and depth of splits in state parties, and the role of money in primary campaigns.

If preprimary endorsements can strengthen a party and improve its chances of winning elections, we might expect to see more parties establishing endorsement systems. There have been few recent examples of such a trend, although endorsements were reestablished by the Massachusetts Democratic party prior to the 1982 election and by the California Democratic party before the 1990 election.

As Republican parties in southern states grow more competitive and have more contested primaries, we may see such efforts made in an attempt to maintain party unity and avoid divisive primaries. On several occasions Louisiana Republican leaders have endorsed statewide candidates to increase the chances of a Republican getting into the unusual nonpartisan runoff in that state. The Virginia Republican party, as well as the Democrats, have sometimes used the convention, instead of a primary, in an effort to unify the party.

Endorsee Success or Failure: Conclusions

A number of factors contribute to the success or failure of endorsees in winning the nomination. The delegates we surveyed put particular emphasis on tangible support from the party and other sources and on the publicity and momentum associated with endorsement. Our analysis suggests that several additional factors are important, particularly the political strength of the endorsee and the uniting of the party behind its endorsee.

Many of the factors that predicted success for endorsees in 1982 were repeated more than a decade later in 1994. Governors are virtually guaranteed endorsement. Strong parties that unite behind their endorsee and provide momentum and tangible support are most likely to get the endorsee nominated. But certain factors can intervene to prevent the success of an endorsee, and they are also repeats of 1982. The Minnesota Republicans continued to be split by the Christian Right, and the endorsee of this group lost in 1994, as did its endorsee in 1982. The Connecticut Democrats in 1994 repeated the experience of the New York Democrats in 1982, in which leaders of the major urban machines supported Ed Koch and helped him win the endorsement, but Mario Cuomo—as did Bill Curry in Connecticut in 1994—mobilized votes from labor, liberals, and minority interests and won the primary. The wealthy outsider Bruce Benson won in Colorado's Republican primary in 1994, and a wealthy outsider would have won in New York's Republican primary in 1982 had the party not endorsed Lew Lehrman and made him a wealthy insider.

Our data do not permit any quantitative analysis of these factors, and the nine party nominations we studied are too few to make generalizations possible. But we can illustrate the combined importance of several factors that appear most important. The first and second factors are the importance of tangible support and of publicity and momentum for the endorsee, as perceived by the delegates. The third is our judgment about the political strength of the endorsee.

In table 8.5, each endorsee is given a score depending on the proportion of delegates who stress the importance of tangible support, and also for the proportion stressing publicity and momentum. In addition, endorsees we have identified as strong are scored. The possible scores range from +3 to –1. Table 8.5 shows that most winners score +3 or +2; all the losers scored only +1 or 0.

We would have expected the endorsement process to be most successful in the five strongest parties with well established endorsing systems—those in New York, Connecticut, and Minnesota. This expectation is not met in the Minnesota IR and Connecticut Democratic parties. This difference can be explained in Minnesota by the unrepresentative character of the IR state convention, leading to the endorsement of a weak candidate and the rejection of the Republican governor. In the Connecticut Democratic party, it can be explained by the failure of the convention to achieve a compromise and avoid a primary.

TABLE 8.5.   Factors Associated with Wins and Losses of Endorsees: Tangible Support, Publicity and Momentum, and Strength of Candidate, 1994

Candidate	State Party	Score	Won or Lost
John Rowland	Connecticut Rep.	+3	Won
George Pataki	New York Rep.	+2	Won
John Marty	Minnesota DFL	+2	Won
Bruce King	New Mexico Dem.	+2	Won
Mark Roosevelt	Massachusetts Dem.	+1	Won
Allen Quist	Minnesota IR	+1	Lost
John Larsen	Connecticut Dem.	+1	Lost
Dick Cheney	New Mexico Rep.	0	Lost
Mike Bird	Colorado Rep.	0	Lost

Note: The scores are based on the following three factors—
Proportion of delegates mentioning tangible support: 35% or more, coded +1; 17% or less, coded 0.
Proportion of delegates mentioning publicity or momentum: 30% or more, coded +1; 28% or less, coded 0.
Strength of candidate: strong, coded +1; average, coded 0; weak, coded –1.

The Governor as Legislative Leader: Predictions

My study found that governors who head strong parties are able to command legislative loyalty for their programs. Governors who head weaker parties do not anticipate partisan loyalty from their legislators. They must build their own electoral and legislative organizations. Three trends may have an impact on the legislative strength of governors.

1. The first is the continuing, although abating, phenomenon of divided government. I found out several important types of party coalitions that took place under divided government in 1983, and I will review them and predict that they will continue.
2. The second is the continuing use of legislative party campaign committees and their impact on party coalition building. I found that strong legislative leaders headed strong campaign committees and could command legislative loyalty. Does this loyalty buttress or challenge gubernatorial power?
3. Term limits have just begun to have an impact on state legislatures. What impact will they have on legislative leadership and party coalition building, and how will this change affect the governor's party leadership?

The Implications of Divided Government

In recent years there has been an increase in the proportion of states where one or both legislative chambers are controlled by a party other than the governor's party. The proportion of states having such divided government has increased from 15 percent to 30 percent in the first few elections after World War II, to over 40 percent in the 1970s, and to over 50 percent by the early 1990s (Fiorina 1992, 25). In the years from 1965 through 1994, only two states did not experience divided government: Georgia and Hawaii, which have had Democratic control of both the governorship and the legislature throughout this period. Fiorina (1992, 26–28) has shown that since the 1960s, a party's control of the governorship is statistically independent from its control of the legislature.

Following the 1996 election, there was divided government in thirty-one of the forty-nine states having partisan elections for the legislature. Divided government occurred in twenty states with Republican governors, ten with Democratic governors, and one with an Independent governor (Maine). The biggest change, however, came with the gains by the Republicans in 1994 and 1996 by uniting the three branches of government to give the party unified control in a total of eighteen states. Most of these

Republican gains occurred in 1994 when five states shifted from a Democratic to a Republican governor and seven shifted from divided legislative control to Republican control of both houses. The Democrats, meanwhile, lost unified control over eight states to reduce their total to eight. While this was not a Republican sweep, it was most certainly a Republican "creep," and in the near future there may be Republican gains in even more states, particularly in the South. Some states that are now divided may become unified under Republican control, and some Democratic states may become divided.

What does divided government mean for legislative support for the governor's program? Scholars discuss two scenarios about how divided government works. The first predicts deadlock and the second compromise. Divided government in Washington has been the subject of books and many articles, both academic and journalistic (Jacobson 1990; Cox and Kernell 1991; Mayhew 1991; Sundquist 1988; C. Jones 1994). But divided government at the state level has largely been ignored. Some recent studies have been devoted to describing how frequently partisan divisions occur and analyzing or speculating about their causes (Fiorina 1992). But little attention has been paid to the consequences of divided government at the state level (Morehouse and Jewell 1992).

In my analysis of party support for the governor's program in ten legislative sessions in 1983, I found several different types of coalition building. The coalitions were dependent upon the strength of the governor's statewide party, but what I did not anticipate was that they were also dependent upon the strength of the legislative party and its leadership. In seven out of the ten states in my study, the governor's party was the legislative minority party.

The ability of the governor to get his or her program passed under conditions of divided government depends upon the strength of the statewide party as well as the cohesion of the legislative party. Under the strong legislative party model, there has been a close balance between the two parties over a period of years and some alternation in majority control; thus, in divided government the opposition party is likely to have only a modest majority. Partisanship is the most important predictor of voting on most issues, but it is noticeably lower than in states where the governor's party controls both chambers of the legislature. That is because the governor must negotiate with the opposition party and hence alienate some members of his or her own. Charles O. Jones identified two types of coalition building that take place under conditions of divided government between the president and Congress: copartisanship and bipartisanship. These types assume the strong executive–strong legislative party model. Copartisanship is the result of negotiations between the leaders of both parties, each of which have developed proposals and can commit their partisans to support them. Bipartisanship, which is a rarer type of coalition building, involves leaders of both parties in a cooperative effort from the start and involves nearly unanimous support from partisans of both (C. Jones 1994, 20–22).

In strong party states, where the legislative parties are also strong, both bipartisanship and copartisanship are likely to occur. Governor Cuomo made effort to compromise with New York senate majority leader Warren Anderson, an unusually powerful leader. The governor's budget incorporated many of the legislature's priorities and elicited broad bipartisan support. Support for the governor's program in the senate was high and was even slightly higher among Republicans than among Democrats: a clear case of bipartisanship.

In Illinois, Governor Thompson dealt with strong party leaders of both parties. The minority leader of his party in the house finally offered the major alternative to the governor's tax increase plan, which brought copartisan support, and the legislative leaders of both parties convinced enough of their flock to pass it. The governor's inability to obtain more of his partisans to support the tax increase may be laid to the need to compromise with the Democratic leaders, which alienated his fellow partisans. This is a clear case of copartisanship, where each party has a plan and the strength to commit partisans to it.

In Colorado, where the legislature was considered very powerful, the opposition Republican party was under very strong leadership. Governor Lamm, confronting a critical budget crisis, chose to negotiate with the Republican house speaker and senate president. The house speaker succeeded in forcing the governor to compromise on a number of issues, thus gaining the support of his Republican legislators for revised versions of the governor's program, which the Democrats also accepted.

California is the only state where the state parties are weak and the legislative parties are strong. In this case, Governor Deukmejian received high support from his legislative party, on average, and was opposed regularly by half the opposition, but he was able to negotiate with the strong Democratic leadership who could guarantee a winning coalition on their terms, since a two-thirds majority was required. Here copartisanship was present with the advantage on the side of the majority Democrats and their leader, Willie Brown.

The third type of situation is a weak statewide party and weak legislative parties. Partisanship has some effect on voting on the governor's program, but the effect is less strong and consistent than in strong party legislatures. A major reason for the difference may be that in the weak party model, the two legislative parties represent constituency interests that are less distinctly different. For this situation, Jones suggests another type of coalition, the cross-partisan coalition, where one party (or a faction of one party) counts on support by a faction of the other party (C. Jones 1994, 22–23).

Tennessee's Governor Alexander could not pass his Better Schools Program without the cooperation of the majority Democrats, but they were weak and divided. He was able to unite his small Republican contingent in the legislature, but he needed the votes from the Democratic majority. The governor won a significant level of cross-partisan support for his program, but a combination of a powerful education lobby and the Democratic leadership defeated the bill in the Senate Education Committee. When the resistant majority is weak, it cannot commit its members to support the governor, and its disorganization blocks his program.

Party may be less important as an explanation for support in Kansas and Oregon because they are less urbanized states in which the legislative parties do not represent such distinctly different socioeconomic interests and in which state party organizations are not traditionally strong. With less cohesive parties, the governor may have less success in winning support from members of his or her party but greater success in wooing some members of the opposition party. In Kansas, Governor Carlin received support from both parties for the severance tax, a cornerstone of his legislative program, and this cross-partisan coalition enacted most of the appropriation bills he recommended. Governor Atiyeh encountered difficulty with the legislature over his net receipts tax, which his party bucked, and a sales tax proposal, which split the majority Democrats. The appropriation bills were passed with a cross-partisan coalition in which the governor received more support from the opposition Democrats. Hence, neither Kansas nor Oregon governors seemed moved to propose bold programs because they were faced with divisions within their own parties as well as an uncertain, but necessary coalition with the opposition.

Connecticut and New York provide a recent example of the coalitions that occur as politically strong governors try to pass programs under divided government. The Republican governors of Connecticut and New York both were endorsed and nominated in 1994 with little opposition as their respective parties united behind them. Both faced houses with Democratic majorities. Copartisanship was the order of the day. In New York, the "budget brawlers bloody but smiling" (Fisher 1995) were the governor, the speaker, and the senate majority leader. Governor Pataki can claim that he delivered on his three main promises—less spending, lowered taxes, and reduced welfare—as well as a major change in the criminal justice system. The speaker held together the ninety-four fractious and ideologically diverse Democrats who comprise the New York Assembly's majority, as he concluded negotiations with the governor. In Connecticut, Governor Rowland faced the first split legislature in thirty years and managed to bargain with House Speaker Ritter so that both could claim success. The governor gave up his proposal to rescind state employees' right to bargain collectively for working conditions in exchange for a modest reduction in the income tax. The governor ceded the speaker a policy role in the budget process. Again we have an example of copartisanship, not stalemate, in two strong party states with divided government, a condition predicted by our study in 1983.

Impact of Legislative Caucus PACs and Leadership PACs

The growth of party caucus campaign committees and leadership PACs that recruit candidates and finance their legislative campaigns has been rapid since the early 1980s. There is evidence of such activity in all four of the legislative parties in twenty-two states, and one or more legislative parties in another thirteen (Jewell and Whicker 1994, 107). Until recently most legislative candidates, whether incumbents or challengers, had to organize their own campaigns and raise their own funds with little or no help from state or local party organizations or from the legislative party.

Speakers Willie Brown of California and Vern Riffe of Ohio are pioneers in large-scale fund-raising for legislative candidates. Gierzynski (1992) claims that caucus campaign committees developed because of the increased cost of campaigns, the lack of assistance from state party organizations, and the level of interparty competition. In recent years, most legislative leadership and party caucuses have assumed responsibility for raising and allocating funds for legislative races. These committees provide a number of services to candidates as well. Polling, media consultation and facilities, and mass mailings can be purchased and provided to candidates at lower cost.

These caucus PACs or campaign committees are usually composed of the legislative leaders or those appointed by them. Whatever their formal connection with the committee may be, Jewell and Whicker (1994) found that the top leadership—presiding officer or majority or minority leader—has most of the responsibility for raising funds because only these leaders have the visibility and the clout that are needed to raise large amounts of money, particularly from interest groups. However the campaign committees are formally organized, in most cases the leadership either determines or has a strong influence over the allocation of resources to legislative candidates.

A number of legislative leaders have become active in recruiting candidates to run for open seats or for seats held by the opposite party. In legislatures where the party balance is close, doing so is vitally important for both parties to hold or challenge the majority. There is an obvious link between campaign financing and recruiting because the leadership must be able to assure potential recruits that they will receive financial assistance.

What are the implications for the governor as party leader created by the recent development of legislative leadership and caucus PACs? Does this development provide the governor with a set of rivals or a set of allies in the legislature? It obviously benefits the governor as well as the legislative party if a majority is gained or enhanced. Then the house speaker, senate presiding officer, majority leaders, and chairs of important committees are of his or her own party. When the governor's party is in the minority, none of these leadership posts are filled with party loyalists, but the minority leaders have attained a power within the party that comes from their recruiting and financing efforts. They can speak for the governor in the legislature.

First, do the campaign efforts of leaders enhance their power? Jewell and Whicker's interviews (1994) indicate that leaders do expect that distribution of campaign funds to candidates will bring support in races for leadership positions. Leaders also believe that they can count on the voting loyalty of legislators they helped. Some leaders, however, say that legislators have come to expect campaign assistance as a right, not a privilege.

Second, have leadership fund-raising and campaign effort reduced the dependence of the individual legislators on the influence of interest groups and PACs? A large proportion of the funds raised by legislative leaders for campaigns comes from political action committees. These funds are redistributed to candidates greatly in need of funds (Gierzynski 1992). In this way the legislative party and its leadership act as a buffer between the interest-group PACs and the individual legislator. The leadership can take the heat from the PACs and the legislator can be loyal to the party.

Third, how does the increased influence of legislative leaders help the governor as party leader? Gierzynski (1992) claims that caucus campaign committees and leadership PACs are indisputably party organizations. Strong statewide parties bring together all elements of the party into the endorsing process including the legislative leadership as well as the local organizations. There is evidence of transfers from the state party and the governor's campaign organization to the legislative caucus PACs as well as sharing of poll information or the merging of resources for phone banks or advertising.

My judgment is that it helps a governor if the legislative leadership is strong. The governor campaigns on a platform that includes a legislative agenda. The governor needs strong leaders to help get the program enacted. That, of course, involves some negotiation, but strong leaders can expect voting loyalty on the governor's program. They can expect party voting cohesion from legislators who are grateful to the party caucus or individual leaders for campaign support. When the governor's party is in a minority, a strong minority leader can bargain effectively with the opposition. I see legislative caucus campaign committees and legislative leadership PACs as strengthening the party in the policy-making process.

The Impact of Term Limits

The adoption of term limits on legislators in many states will have major implications for legislative leadership. Beginning in 1990 with Colorado, California, and Oklahoma, term limits have been imposed on state legislatures in twenty states—nineteen by voter initiative and one by legislative action. The initiative and referendum provisions in these state constitutions opened the door to placing term-limit proposals before the voters for action. Now the field of states in which such direct citizen initiatives can be used has narrowed to three: Illinois, Mississippi, and Alaska. With these exceptions, from now on the term-limit fight to gain access to the ballot will have to be waged before those who have the most to lose. The term-limit movement may have come to an end, but the impact of term limits on the twenty states will be significant.

Of the sixteen states that endorse for governor, and hence have strong or moderately strong party systems, six will be affected by term limits: California, Colorado, Michigan, Ohio, Massachusetts, and Utah. It is in the first five of these states, where both governors and legislative leaders are strong, that the impact of term limits will be substantial. Why is that so?

Most legislatures draw their leadership from among their most experienced and senior members. The average length of service of legislative leaders in the twenty states was more than twelve years for lower houses and eleven years for senates (Hodson et al. 1995). Existing tenure norms for leaders in these term-limited states must change within the next few years. States may adopt norms (or formal rules) permitting only one term in a leadership position (Utah already has this provision). What impact will rapid turnover and less experience have on legislative leadership?

Jewell and Whicker (1994) traced the gradual growth in the tenure of legislative leaders and believe that enhanced tenure has contributed to the emergence of stronger, more effective leaders. Legislative leaders in most states play very large roles in setting agendas, controlling party caucuses, securing campaign financing, appointing and removing committee chairs and members, and hiring staff. In those legislatures where the term-limitation movement makes two-year terms as presiding officer the norm, these leaders will become almost instant lame ducks, with their effectiveness crippled. If they are elected with only two to four years of legislative service and little or no experience in the caucus or committee, they are likely to be equally ineffective.

Charles Price suggests another impact of term limits on legislative leadership. Because leaders will be able to hold office for only a few years, they may not be able to extract campaign contributions from special interests as easily as they did in the past. The diminishing ability of legislative leaders to raise large campaign war chests to give their party colleagues will weaken their hold over them (Price 1992b, 130).

Limiting legislative terms will affect the balance between the governor and the legislature. Under what conditions will there be cooperation between the two branches? Cooperation can come about only if there are incentives for it. Governors are not automatically made stronger when the legislatures they face are made weaker. I have made the point that governors have a stake in strong legislative leadership. Term limitations weaken the capacity of legislative leaders to provide cohesive majorities, and governors would have to assemble separate majorities on each issue (Malbin and Benjamin 1992).

Governors and strong parties can bridge the gap between the two branches. Governors will have to convince professional legislators who must consider their next career move that cooperation is important. State party organizations can substitute for the leadership PACs and legislative caucus PACs to provide resources to candidates as they run for the next office. Legislative leaders will become weaker after term limits and would be less inclined to build or maintain strong campaign committees. Governors can fill this gap.

The governor as party leader who provides funds for legislative campaigns can help insulate legislators from interest groups. Term limits that weaken legislative leadership PACs will leave the legislator dependent upon interest groups for campaign support. That would affect the ability of the governor to pass his or her program, as large and well organized groups that can provide assistance to legislative campaigns organize majorities against it. By collecting interest-group money and redistributing it to the legislature, the governor and the political party can provide the incentives for legislative support.

Strong Governors, Strong Parties, and Representation

This book has proved that governors backed by strong electoral parties can get strong voting support from their party's legislators. In states where the party is weak or divided, the governor will face a legislature that is also weak or hostile, and party voting loyalty is low. Thus, governors who head strong parties can get their programs passed, while weak governors and weak parties are not as successful. This is the proof that party government exists.

It was not incumbent on this research to show that the programs of the governors did indeed represent the people's needs, although I assumed that they did. The states in the study were competitive between the parties so that competition for the statehouse was keen, and voters would respond in Downsian fashion to the parties' proximities to their ideological preferences. If parties were strong, they could better represent these preferences in the governing process.

I can perform one modest test to show an association between strong governors and the policy preferences of their people. The book *Statehouse Democracy* presents convincing evidence that public opinion drives policy-making in the American states (Erikson, Wright, and McIver 1993). The association between public opinion and policy is very strong (adjusted R^2 = .68). The authors also show the association between public opinion and the opinion of policymakers. But they do not explain how policy is made. I offer evidence that political parties that have strong electoral organizations equip their governors with the strength to govern. I show how this occurs when the governors as strong party leaders present their programs to the legislature and receive support from their legislative parties. In other words, parties matter in the conversion of public preferences into public policy.

We would predict that governors represent the midpoint of public opinion in the state. They have to appeal to enough voters to get elected. Their ideological position would be similar to that of their party's electoral elite, those who seek office. Strong governors are in a stronger position to push for policies that reflect their party's promises to the electorate.

V. O. Key's hypothesis declares that it takes strong parties to enact policies that serve the needy, because such policies demand redistribution of wealth and agencies for planning and administering (Key 1950, 307). He also claims that conservative policies do not need cohesive parties because they stress less action and the dismantling of liberal initiatives. Actions to block or dismantle do not take strong parties. If this hypothesis is true, we would expect that strong parties would be associated with states that demand more liberal policies.

To test the association between public opinion, strong parties, and public policy, I used two measures from *Statehouse Democracy:* public opinion liberalism and public policy liberalism. Public opinion liberalism is a measure of the respondents' answers to questions asked on the CBS/*New York Times* surveys, 1976–88 (Erikson, Wright, and McIver 1993, chap. 2). The mean ideological identification in a state is the percentage point difference between liberals and conservatives and is labeled "opinion liberalism."

Public policy is a grand index of state policy, which Erikson Wright and McIver label "composite policy liberalism" (1993, 75–78). The index is combination of state policies on eight issues, each chosen to represent a separate aspect of state liberalism, circa 1980. Policy measures such as public educational spending, Medicaid, AFDC, consumer protection, criminal justice, legalized gambling, the Equal Rights Amendment, and tax progressivity were used.

The measure of state party strength was developed in this book's chapter 3 (table 3.1). This measure is the average primary voting strength of the state's governors over the time period 1960 through 1982. In this case, I used the six elections that predated the policy measures (circa 1980). Party strength measured this way indicates that strong parties help their gubernatorial candidates obtain the nomination, traditionally by preprimary endorsements, which often guarantee unchallenged candidates or strong primary support. Nearly every state (forty-six) had a mix of Republican and Democratic governors, with the exception of Alabama, Georgia, and Mississippi. (Nonpartisan Nebraska is excluded.)

Table 8.6 gives the correlations between party strength, public opinion, and policy liberalism. It shows that states with strong parties do not necessarily have liberal opinions ($r = .247$). But when a state does have liberal opinions, there is a high positive association between that opinion and policy ($r = .832$). Strong parties are also associated with liberal policies ($r = .411$).

Table 8.7 gives the results of this modest test boring. We are assuming that public opinion is converted by the political parties into public policy. The regression shows that party strength, whether Democratic or Republican, is associated with the ability to make this conversion. Liberal public opinion and strong parties are significantly associated with liberal policies. The reverse is that weaker parties are associated with conservative policies. This is what V. O. Key meant when he said that the "haves" benefit from political disorganization: "Organization is not always necessary to obstruct: it is essential, however, for the promotion of a sustained program in behalf of the have-nots . . ." (Key 1950, 307).

This modest test boring into the connection between parties and representation shows that the people of our states are well represented by their political leaders. When they desire a wider distribution of benefits, organized parties and strong governors matter.

TABLE 8.6. Correlations among Variables Used to
Explain State Policy Liberalism in Forty-six States

Variables	Opinion Liberalism	Party Strength	Policy Liberalism
Opinion liberalism	1.00	.247	.832
Party strength	.247	1.00	.411
Policy liberalism	.832	.411	1.00

TABLE 8.7. Regression to Explain Policy Liberalism in
Forty-six States

Variables	Beta	t-score	Significance
Opinion liberalism	.778	9.66	.001
	(0.01)		
Party strength	.219	2.717	.01
	(0.01)		
Adjusted R^2	.726		

Note: Standard errors are in parentheses.

Conclusions and Implications

This book has a wider purpose than describing the campaigning and legislative leadership of governors. It is based on my belief that political parties are basic to our survival under a humane governmental system. There is no other institution whose object is to gather the greatest number of intensities and interests in order to govern. Best able to govern are the cohesive parties because they can build these coalitions, keep their promises, and be held accountable.

Much rhetoric has been expended on the subject of party decline and the displacement of parties by media and money. Parties are hard to understand. They are vehicles for adjustment and compromise, and as such they are regarded with suspicion and distrust by those with intense interests. Nevertheless, partisanship remains stable and enduring for most adults and is still the best predictor of candidate choice. However, with an ever more educated and sophisticated electorate, there have been changes in its view of the parties and its voting behavior, and the parties have had to adjust to both of these.

Beginning in 1980, a substantial proportion of the electorate saw differences in the policy stances of the two parties. This proportion had increased since the 1950s, when there was an even balance between those who saw policy differences and those who did not. Aldrich (1995, 169–74) reports that by 1992, over 80 percent of the public saw the Republican party and its candidates as more conservative than the Democratic party and its candidates. This perception has profound implications for the parties as coalition builders, which I will explore shortly.

Not only does the electorate see the parties as distinctly different, but it is an extremely volatile electorate. Split-ticket voting has increased since the mid-1960s, making every election unsure. Students of voting behavior saw this volatility as evidence that parties were on the decline because they could no longer hold the voters' loyalty. There are indeed monumental consequences for party building since many voters have become flexible and willing to ponder short-run considerations, such as candidates and party programs (Schlesinger 1991, 192–99). There is no longer any state in which either party is incapable of winning office. The consequences of a more discriminating and volatile electorate are to make party coalition building profoundly important, and the evidence is that the parties are rising to the challenge. Both Schlesinger and Aldrich agree that the national parties have become stronger, better able to provide electoral services to candidates and officeholders, and better able to govern (Schlesinger 1991, 196–99; Aldrich 1995, 289–96).

Evidence of State Party Strength

On the state level, Cotter and his colleagues provided firm evidence that party organizational strength has been increasing in terms of the "party in service," with greater resources and professional staff. These professionals provide technical information and expertise as well as financial and in-kind resources to candidates (Cotter et al. 1984). The relationship between increased bureaucratic strength and party coalitional strength has not been tested, although the researchers found a relationship between party bureaucratic strength and party electoral strength in northern states.

In this book I have proved that the party coalitional strength of many state parties has not changed since the 1960s. In terms of endorsing candidates for nomination, the mark of a cohesive party, there has been little increase in the challenges to the endorsement since 1960 (table 8.1). Challenges average slightly over 50 percent in the most recent period, which is similar to the past. In states where the parties are not strong, and the primary determines the outcome, there are contests for the nomination about 90 percent of the time.

In terms of governing, it is important to note that state legislators support their party's governor about 78 percent of the time overall (table 7.2), but variations are also important here. In strong party states, the mean support score is 86.1 percent, and in weaker parties it is 71.1 percent. It is interesting to note that the overall governor's party support score for state legislators compares favorably with party cohesion scores for Congress (Schlesinger 1991, 186–89).

In view of the aforementioned evidence, it is clear that parties are not decomposing, as the academics and journalists have been predicting, but have been adapting to the media-driven society in which they find themselves. They have figured ways to provide needed technical information and financial resources to candidates. Some of them have built coalitions strong enough to endorse and govern.

Not all parties are strong, and the states offer "little political laboratories" to study the differences between the strong and the weak. Fifty different political systems operating within a common national framework offer a cross-sectional examination of party strength. State parties exhibit different degrees of strength, and the descriptions and the reasons for these differences made up the subject of this study.

Party Coalitional Strength

Recall that in the 1990s most of the electorate sees ideological differences between the parties. Why? Because the factions that make up the party coalitions are becoming more ideological, and both parties must accommodate these factions in order to be cohesive in the election and in the government. Ideological factions have increased because the new party activists are driven by purposive incentives. There are not as many activists these days who want patronage, jobs, or money as a reward for party work. The numbers of modern activists have increased within the parties as the jobs, contracts, and the like have diminished. No longer able to "pay" loyal supporters with material benefits, many state parties have had to absorb factions of policy-driven activists. However, these activists are not insensitive to the need for party cohesion. Many of them can understand the concept of negotiation and compromise, but they cannot be bought for money and can afford to lose now in hopes of winning concessions in the future (Schlesinger 1991, Aldrich 1995). These activists often will choose to work only for particular candidates they closely agree with rather than working in a broader range of party campaigns (Schlesinger 1991, Aldrich 1995). They are even more extreme in their demands that their party's elected officials have to tailor their actions to represent the views of activist factions.

Recent studies have shown that most persons who are active in political parties, working in campaigns and attending conventions, have strong ideological commitments. Republican party activists are more conservative than the average Republican voter, and Democratic activists are more liberal than the average Democratic voter (Erikson, Wright, and McIver

1993, chap. 5; Aldrich 1995, 171–73, 186–87). Many of the ideologically motivated party workers are also actively involved in interest groups that demand support for particular policies. Their commitment to the group is sometimes stronger than their commitment to the party. As black voters became heavily Democratic in the mid-1960s, the preferences of black activists shifted the party's center of gravity to a more liberal stance in civil rights and other issues. The Democratic party became more attractive to other liberals and less attractive to conservatives. Labor and education and pro choice factions became prominent in the Democratic party, while business, veterans, and pro life factions became active in the Republican party. In recent years both parties have been damaged by the conflicts between party activists who are advocates for pro life and pro choice positions on the abortion issue. It is up to the party leadership to moderate the conflict and hold together the divergent points of view. To the extent that the different factions have overlapping memberships, brokering is possible (Baer and Dolan 1994).

Control over the nominating of candidates is crucial to the political party if it is to remain a viable coalition. Earlier I spoke of the continued success of a third of the state parties in controlling the nomination for governor because only half of their endorsements are challenged. However, another statistic must now be mentioned. Of those contested primaries, less than half are won by the party-endorsed candidate (table 8.1). This statistic contrasts sharply with the previous time period, 1960–80, when 82 percent of the party-endorsed candidates won. Clearly the political parties, even strong parties that endorse, are facing factional strife.

The importance of policy as a motivation for activists carries a high risk for political parties. These activists have a high level of influence over the nomination of the party's candidates. They participate in the conventions that endorse candidates before the primary and they are a major source of funds and workers for primary campaigns in all parties. Because these activists are likely to have strong policy commitments, they are likely to support candidates who share these views. Such candidates may be more difficult for the party to elect if their positions diverge too widely from the moderate views held by most voters (Aldrich 1995, 187–92).

Most of the our state parties are not able to adjust and absorb the new ideological factions. They have no vehicle, such as the party convention, that can engage factions in face-to-face combat and collaboration. The primary simply registers the strength of individual candidacies and their activist supporters. There is no guarantee that a self-chosen candidate will reflect the preferences of the electorate. Primaries register the results of almost all of the nominating contests in nonendorsement states. And money largely determines who will win. My prediction is that state parties that nominate by primary only will not be able to adjust the differences between their factions, and they may be captured by a succession of factions, none of which can forge a coalition.

On the other hand, parties that endorse have the opportunity to negotiate compromises and broker coalitions. Seventy-five percent of the fifteen hundred endorsing convention delegates in the nine states surveyed in 1994 favored endorsements. Some of the toughest factional controversies, such as the Christian Right versus the regulars in the Minnesota Republican Party, are face-to-face battles. In both 1982 and 1994, the endorsed Christian Right candidate lost in the primary. But Minnesota Republican convention delegates still support the concept of endorsements, and 86 percent see tangible advantages in the endorsement process. The process may have to end in a primary challenge if the convention does not represent the mainstream of the party's supporters, but the activists still favor endorsements.

Those who support endorsements argue that the endorsement system is beneficial to party activists. It gives them a meaningful role to play in the party, specifically in the nominating process. The belief is that activists can become committed participating workers for the party. In this way, they may support a party's nominee, even if their own faction loses. They might be persuaded that moderate candidates have a higher chance of victory in the general election. Parties that endorse provide arenas where interests can work together and collaborate. Parties have to be eager to attract new workers and cannot exist if they close them out.

If preprimary endorsements can strengthen a party and make it better able to broker factions into a coalition, we might expect to see more parties establishing endorsement systems in the attempt to unify ideological activists and factions. We would expect that to happen in states where competition is increasing between the parties. The growing Republican strength in southern states has led to real GOP organizations and energized the Democratic ones, which in turn has led to closer state and legislative elections. Party organization is becoming more meaningful. Louisiana Republicans have endorsed statewide candidates on several occasions, and Virginia Republicans as well as the Democrats have sometimes used the convention, instead of a primary, in an attempt to unify the party. The Democrats, facing more Republican competition, see conventions as a way to put together a balanced ticket.

Winning a party convention requires a different kind of organizational effort, and many state parties may require this effort to unify the factions within the party. While the California Democrats decided that endorsing was too risky in 1994, they may consider endorsement now that the state has a blanket primary in which any voter can vote for any party's candidates on the primary ballot. Unifying the party may be the only way to produce an electable candidate under such bizarre uncertainty.

Governors and Party Government

What does all this mean for our governors? Governors cannot operate effectively without help from their political parties. That is true in spite of the fact that most of them are running candidate-centered campaigns with sophisticated technology: from polling, to advertising, to fund-raising. Most of them have policy-oriented policy activists working for them. Why do they need the party?

Many political party organizations are becoming stronger, not weaker. They have adapted to the new technology and have remodeled themselves to be valuable to gubernatorial candidates. The new version of the party organization does not control office seekers, as some of the traditional party urban machines were able to do. It serves their interests. It provides services such as polling, campaign seminars, advertising, and fund-raising. The more effective and extensive these services, the more important they are to ambitious candidates as they seek election and reelection.

Parties can still provide major services to gubernatorial candidates. If they can endorse candidates, who then have a 70 percent chance of receiving the nomination, they have taken a major step toward party consolidation, which benefits both the governor and the party. Parties, as durable institutions, provide cues to voters who remember them from election to election and react to their stability and message.

Finally, once the governor is elected, parties are essential in the achievement of collective choices on policy issues because they represent coalitions of interests and have basic differences on issues. They are capable of producing policy majorities. My research showed that in Minnesota and New York, states that had highly charged endorsing conventions and divisive primaries in 1982, the support for Governors Perpich and Cuomo was over 90 percent. Perhaps it is the process that involves face-to-face contact and coalition building and the collective desire to win that can anticipate party loyalty within the governing process.

In the final analysis, governors need all the help they can get in the governing process. No other institution is better able to offer that help than the political party. Strong parties build grand coalitions of people and groups, bring forth governors, and hold them accountable. In this way, the party can provide the essential linkages between governors and legislatures.

Appendix

This appendix is organized in four main sections. The first section contains a list of the people I interviewed in the course of research for this book. In the second section, I have reproduced the Gubernatorial Candidate Questionnaire used in the interviews. The third section acknowledges the panel of faculty experts who aided the project. In the fourth section, I detail the process and problems of data collection by legislative district.

List of Interviewees

Interviews with the candidates or their campaign staffers are indicated by last name and year in the text, along with page numbers to the transcripts. The transcripts are housed at the Center for Oral history at the University of Connecticut. (All dates shown here are in 1982 unless otherwise listed.)

Candidate (party)	Date	Interviewee and Position
California		
Gov. George Deukmejian (R)	6/30	Fred Karger, deputy campaign director
Mike Curb (R)	6/29	Rex Hime, director of volunteers
Tom Bradley (D)	6/30	Tom Sullivan, campaign manager
John Garamendi (D)	6/29	John Garamendi
Colorado		
Gov. Richard Lamm (D)	6/25	David Miller, speech writer
Phil Winn (R)	6/26	David Diepenbroch, campaign research
John Fuhr (R)	6/25	John Fuhr
Steve Schuck (R)	6/27	Walt Klein, campaign manager
Connecticut		
Gov. William O'Neill (D)	12/13	Gov. William O'Neill
Ernest Abate (D)	7/21	Ernest Abate
Lewis Rome (R)	7/5 & 7/16	Lewis Rome
Dick Bozzuto (R)	7/13	Dick Bozzuto
Gerald Labriola (R)	8/23	Gerald Labriola
Rusty Post (R)	7/27	Rusty Post

Illinois

Gov. Jim Thompson (R)	12/9	Bob Kjellander, top political adviser, and Phil O'Connor, campaign manager
Adlai Stevenson (D)	12/9	Adlai Stevenson

Kansas

Gov. John Carlin (D)	9/2	Gov. John Carlin
Sam Hardage (R)	9/1	Sam Hardage
Wendell Lady (R)	9/2	Keith Henley, campaign manager
Dave Owen (R)	9/3	Dave Owen

Minnesota

Lewis Wangberg (R)	6/20	Bjarnie Anderson, campaign manager
Wheelock Whitney (R)	6/19	Wheelock Whitney
Glen Sherwood (R)	6/17	Glen Sherwood
Paul Overgaard (R)	6/17	Paul Overgaard
Rudy Perpich (D)	6/7	Rudy Perpich
Walter Spannaus (D)	6/18	Walter Spannaus

New York

Mario Cuomo (D)	1/28/83	Bill Haddad, campaign manager
Ed Koch (D)	12/2	Peter Piscatelli and John LoCicero, campaign managers
Lew Lehrman (R)	12/10	Tim Carey, campaign manager
Paul Curran (R)	8/24	Paul Curran
Jim Emery (R)	7/12	George Humphreys, campaign manager
Richard Rosenbaum (R)	7/7	Richard Rosenbaum

Oregon

Gov. Victor Atiyeh (R)	6/8	Gov. Victor Atiyeh
Donald Clark (D)	6/7	Donald Clark
Ted Kulongowski (D)	6/8	Ted Kulongowski

Tennessee

Gov. Lamar Alexander (R)	8/31	Bracey Campbell, press secretary
Randy Tyree (D)	8/30	Jan Smith, campaign manager
Anna Belle Clement O'Brien (D)	8/31	Anna Belle Clement O'Brien

Texas

Gov. Bill Clements (R)	6/11	B. D. Daniels, research director
Mark White (D)	6/10	Mark White
Buddy Temple (D)	6/10	Clark Jobe, campaign treasurer
Bob Armstrong (D)	6/11	Bob Armstrong

Gubernatorial Candidate Questionnaire

Goals

1. Which of the following represented your strategy to contest the nomination?
   *(a) Winning a *majority* of the votes in the party convention in order to:
      (1) receive the endorsement
      (2) contest in the primary
      (3) other (specify)
   *(b) Winning a *minority* of the votes in the party convention in order to:
      (1) contest in the primary
      (2) bargain
      (3) other (specify)
   (c) Obtaining a winning number of the votes in the primary in order to win the nomination.
   (d) Winning a minority of the votes in the primary in order to:
      (1) bargain
      (2) compete in the runoff (Texas only)
      (3) other (specify)
   (e) Other. Explain.

Early Days

2. When did you decide to run for the nomination?
3. Whom did you first consult? Why?
4. What sort of organization did you establish? Specifically, for what reasons did you choose:
   (a) Your fund-raiser?
   (b) Your media chair?
   (c) Your campaign manager?
5. Who were the people or groups in your initial coalition? For each person or group, name their major resource. (Resources can be money, votes, information, status, ideology.) What reward do they have for

---

*Question for candidates in preprimary endorsing states only

entering? (Rewards can be sociability, future policy commitment, future jobs, money, etc.)

Person/Group   Brief Description   Resource   Reward

6. Did you have an initial advantage as the nominating campaign began?
   Strongest candidate? Explain.
   Favored by party leaders? Explain.
   Best media attention? Explain.
   Best candidate image? Explain.
   Best finance? Explain.
   Best organization? Explain.
   Best issues? Explain.
   Home region (city/county) support? Explain.
7. What probability did you have of success?
   *(a) In the party convention? What percent of the vote?
   (b) In the primary? What percent of the vote?
   (c) In the general election? What percent of the vote?
8. How much did you know about your opponents for the nomination in the early days of the campaign?

Nominating Campaign Organization

9. How did you organize your nominating campaign?
   Statewide
   Counties: Generally where?
   Localities: Generally where?
10. What areas of the state did you first count on to:
    *(a) Give you delegate votes in the convention? How many?
    (b) Support your nomination in the primary? How many votes?
11. How effective is the local party in providing campaign workers?
12. At what point in organizing your campaign did you consult the state party chair? Explain.

Factions: Coalitions

Before we talk about the progress of the campaign, I would like to ask a few questions about the factions or durable intraparty divisions in your party.

13. Is the amount of factionalism within your state party:
    (a) fairly high

(b) moderate

(c) low

(d) no factionalism at all

14. Were the factions:

(a) ideological in nature

(b) personal followings

(c) geographical

(d) regulars/reformers

(e) ins/outs

(f) urban/suburban/rural

(g) ethnic

(h) other (please specify)

15. How strong are the factions which you have identified?

16. How stable are they?

17. Do you represent a faction within your party?

18. On what is it based?

19. How strong is it?

20. How stable is it?

21. Could it provide you with the winning number of votes:

*(a) In the convention: approximately how many?

(b) In the primary: approximately how many?

22. If not, what other factions did you consider adding to your coalition? Explain.

23. Were other factional leaders opposing you for the nomination?

24. Which factions did they represent?

25. Did any of them join in a coalition against you? Explain.

*(a) Did they join in a coalition against you at the convention?

(b) Did they join in a coalition against you in the primary?

26. What faction does the state chair represent?

27. What are its resources?

28. How long has this faction been in power?

29. What other factions have held power in the party in the last 10–15 years?

30. What were their resources?

*Preprimary Endorsements

31. Did the state party support your candidacy for preprimary endorsement?

32. If you have run for governor before, did the state party back you for the preprimary endorsement in your last race(s)?

33. Can you tell me the amount of money provided you by the state party for your preprimary endorsement?
34. Who decided how much money you would receive?
35. In a preprimary fight between two or more candidates for the same nomination, do you think the state chair should become involved?
    (a) If no incumbent
    (b) If an incumbent

*Preprimary Endorsements: Continuing Strategy

36. Who were the people or groups added to your coalition as time went on? For each person or group, name their major resource. (Resources can be money, votes, information, status, ideology.) What reward do they have for entering? (Rewards can be sociability, future policy commitment, future jobs, money, etc.)

    Person/Group   Brief Description   Resource   Reward

37. Is/was your plan to arrive at the convention:
    (a) with a winning number of delegates (specify number or percent)
    (b) with a "bandwagon" effect (specify)
    (c) with a necessary minimum to contest the primary (specify)
38. Do/did you have committed delegates?
    (a) In how many localities?
    (b) How many votes?
39. If not committed, what local delegations support (have supported) you?
    (a) How many localities?
    (b) How many votes?
40. If you do/did not win the endorsement at the convention, will you contest in the primary?
41. Will the local party leaders in your coalition work to obtain votes from their districts in the primary?

Primary Contest

42. Did the state party support your candidacy for the nomination?
43. If you have run for governor before, did the state party back you for the nomination in your last race(s)?
44. Can you tell me the amount of money (to be) provided to you by the state party for your nomination?

45. Who decided how much money you should receive?
46. In a fight between two or more candidates for the same nomination, do you think the state chair should become involved?
    (a) If no incumbent
    (b) If an incumbent

Continuing Strategy

47. Who were the people or groups added to your coalition as time went on? For each person or group, name their major resource. (Resources can be money, votes, information, status, ideology.) For each resource, indicate amount or number or value. What reward do they have for entering? (Rewards can be sociability, future policy commitment, future jobs, money, etc.)

    Person/Group   Brief Description   Resource   Reward

48. Was your plan to:
    (a) Obtain a majority of the votes in the primary (specify percent)
    (b) Obtain less than a majority but still win the nomination (specify percent)
    (c) Obtain a minority for bargaining purposes (specify percent)
    (d) Other (please specify)
49. Were you able to get committed votes?
    (a) In how many localities?
    (b) Approximately how many votes?
50. If not committed, what localities did support you?
    (a) How many localities?
    (b) How many votes?
51. Do you think a divisive primary hurts a candidate's election chances?

Information Conditions

52. How accurately and by what means could you predict the strategy of your opponents:
    (a) before they declared for the nomination
    (b) after they declared for the nomination
    *(c) during the campaign for preprimary endorsement
    *(d) at the endorsing convention
53. How did this knowledge or lack of it affect your strategy?
    (a) before declaring for the nomination
    (b) after declaring for the nomination

*(c) during the campaign for preprimary endorsement
*(d) at the endorsing convention

Results of Nominating Campaign (If Known)

*54. How closely did the results of the convention match your predictions?
    If there was a disparity, how can you explain it?
55. How closely did the results of the primary match your predictions?
    If there was a disparity, how can you explain it?
56. Did the initially strongest candidate win?
57. What do the results indicate about:
    (a) the strength of the stable factions within the party
    (b) the strength of the new factions within the party
    (c) the strength of the leadership faction
    (d) the strength of your faction or coalition
    (e) the strength of personal factions
58. How do the results compare with the results of the last gubernatorial
    nominating campaign with respect to the points in question 57?

Analysis—Personal History

59. How did state finance laws influence the nominating campaign?
60. Would you change the nominating system in this state?
    (a) to make it more open (such as getting on the primary ballot by peti-
        tion, open primary, voting not limited to party members, etc.)
    (b) to make it more closed (caucus-convention, party endorsements
        stated on ballot, limit ballot access to a percentage of convention,
        closed primary, etc.)
61. What party offices have you held?
    Office   Date
62. What public (elected) offices have you held?
    Office   Date

Faculty Experts: Money versus Party Effort

The panel of faculty experts was drawn from the participants in the Gubernatorial Election and Transition Project for 1982, cosponsored by the National Governors Association and the Governors' Center at Duke University. In the event a participant was unavailable, a member of the Comparative State Politics Newsletter network was contacted. I also wish to thank Malcolm Jewell, professor emeritus of the University of Kentucky, who observed gubernatorial nominating conventions in several states in 1982 and gave me valuable information on Massachusetts and New Mexico. My own ten-state study of the 1982 gubernatorial nominations provided the information for California, Colorado, Connecticut, Illinois, Kansas, Minnesota, New York, Oregon, Tennessee, and Texas.

The faculty experts who aided this project immeasurably were: Herbert Asher, Ohio State University; Robert H. Blank, University of Idaho; Frank Bryan, University of Vermont; Janet Clark, University of Wyoming; Alan Clem, University of South Dakota; Margaret Conway, University of Maryland; Robert Darcy, Oklahoma State University; Don Driggs, University of Nevada, Reno; Robert S. Friedman, Penn State University; Bill Gormley, University of Wisconsin, Madison; Robert J. Huckshorn, Florida Atlantic University; Ruth Jones, Arizona State University; Keith Mueller, University of Nebraska; Gerald McBeath, University of Alaska; Alex N. Pattakos, University of Maine; Samuel C. Patterson, Ohio State University; Charles Press, Michigan State University; and Daniel W. Tuttle, University of Hawaii.

Data Collection by Legislative District

The Inter-university Consortium for Political and Social Research (ICPSR) at the University of Michigan has collected and made available in computer-readable form state legislative general election returns for all states and legislative primary returns in sixteen southern and border states. This primary collection includes Tennessee and Texas. Most states publish the results of the legislative primary elections, although some do not and must be asked for such data (Connecticut and New York).

The real problem with data collection involved gubernatorial election returns by legislative district. As one harassed New York elections official responded, "Who would be interested?" For the ten states in the sample, only California, Illinois, and Minnesota report gubernatorial general election data by house and senate districts, although New York gives this information by assembly district, and Texas has joined the computer age by aggregating such data since 1984. For gubernatorial primaries, only California, Minnesota, and Texas (from 1984) provide this information by legislative district. For all the other states, gubernatorial electoral data are presented by county—and in the case of New York and Connecticut, by city as well. Thus for all but two states, the gubernatorial vote had to be aggregated by legislative district. This aggregation was a long and laborious process fraught with some hazards of computation.

When there were several counties in one legislative district, there was no problem unless districts contained portions of counties. We developed a procedure to take care of this situation. The real problem occurred when there were many legislative districts within a county. We could not give all districts the same score because we knew there was wide variation among them. Usually this situation exists in counties containing large cities. In New York City, an amazing document called a calendar, published for each borough, gives state senate districts by assembly districts. Since New York presents gubernatorial election vote by assembly district, it was possible to aggregate these results to get the vote by senate district, at least for the Big Apple.

The thorniest problems were encountered in Texas and Tennessee. In Texas, eleven counties contain many state house and senate districts. Harris County, containing Houston, has eight senate and twenty-six house districts. The only way to get an accurate estimate is to ask for county totals by precinct for these counties. These the Texas secretary of state was willing to provide on microfilm, which had to be taken to a library machine. Unfortunately, the county reels did not contain all the necessary information: Dallas County had inadvertently neglected to include the gubernatorial primary returns for 1982. Once obtained in this fashion, thousands of precincts had to be aggregated and totaled by legislative district. The situation in Tennessee is much the same, with the counties containing Knoxville, Nashville, and Memphis being made up of many legislative districts with a wide range of electoral strength for governor, and hence it was necessary to add up precincts into legislative districts. No wonder researchers hesitate to acquire legislative district variables to explain legislative behavior.

The availability of socioeconomic data by legislative district determined the states selected for this part of the project. For researchers in the 1990s, Congressional Quarterly's *The Almanac of State Legislatures* gives this information for all seventy-five hundred districts in the fifty states (Lilley, DeFranco, Diefenderfer 1993). I was not so fortunate for 1980 socioeconomic data. The information was begged and bought. California provides this information, and I was fortunate enough to receive it already processed (Gerber 1991). *Almanac of Illinois Politics—1990* provides demographic information for legislative districts (Van Der Slik 1990). The state of Minnesota collects and provides population data by legislative district for a fee (Land Management Information Center). Texas also collects much socioeconomic information by legislative district. This information includes "native Texans," an item that I found intriguing but resisted (Legislative Information System).

TABLE A.1. District Averages of 1980 Socioeconomic Characteristics for Four States (by state and party)

Characteristic	California Dem.	California Rep.	Illinois Dem.	Illinois Rep.	Minnesota Dem.	Minnesota Rep.	Texas Dem.	Texas Rep.
Income								
average (in thousands)	$20.6	$24.7	$20.6	$25.5	—	—	—	—
over $25,000 (%)	—	—	—	—	29.5	33.6	24.8	43.8
Age								
under 18 (%)			29.0	29.8	28.6	29.1		
over 65 (%)	14.7	15.0	11.1	9.4	11.8	11.8		
Minorities								
black (%)	9.8	3.7	21.0	2.5			14.6	4.5
Hispanic (%)	21.7	15.4	5.8	1.9			22.8	14.7
Asian (%)	5.5	3.9	1.2	0.9				
Education								
4 yrs. college (%)	8.7	12.0			13.9	16.8		

Note: Data are not available for some states for age, minorities, or education.

References

The author's interview subjects are listed at the beginning of the appendix; most of them are from 1982. The following list of source citations is divided into two sections. The first includes books, journals, and professional papers. The second contains newspaper articles and is subdivided by state.

Books, Journals, and Professional Papers

ACIR (Advisory Commission on Intergovernmental Relations). 1986. *The Transformation of American Politics: Implications for Federalism.* Washington, D.C.: ACIR.

Aldrich, John H. 1980. *Before the Convention: Strategies and Choices in Presidential Nominating Campaigns.* Chicago: University of Chicago Press.

———. 1995. *Why Parties?* Chicago: University of Chicago Press.

Alexander, Herbert E., and Jeffrey A. Schwartz. 1993. "Laboratories for Reform: The States' Experience with Public Funding of Elections." *National Voter,* September–October, 9–11.

Appleton, Andrew M., and Daniel S. Ward. 1994. "Party Organizational Response to Electoral Change: Texas and Arkansas." *American Review of Politics* 15:191–212.

APSA (American Political Science Association) Committee on Political Parties. 1950. "Toward a More Responsible Two-Party System." *American Political Science Review* 44: Supplement.

Baer, Denise, and David Bositis. 1988. *Elite Cadres and Party Coalitions.* Westport, CT: Greenwood Press.

Baer, Denise L., and Julie A. Dolan. 1994. "Intimate Connections: Political Interests and Group Activity in State and Local Parties." *American Review of Politics* 15:257–89.

Bartels, Larry M. 1988. *Presidential Primaries and the Dynamics of Public Choice.* Princeton: Princeton University Press.

Bell, Charles G., and Charles M. Price. 1988. *California Government Today: Politics of Reform?* Chicago: Dorsey Press.

Benjamin, Gerald. 1985. "The Gubernatorial Transition in New York." In Thad Beyle, ed., *Gubernatorial Transitions: The 1982 Election.* Durham, NC: Duke University Press.

Berry, William D., and Bradley C. Canon. 1993. "Explaining the Competitiveness of Gubernatorial Primaries." *Journal of Politics* 55:454–71.

Beyle, Thad L. 1983. "The Cost of Becoming Governor." *State Government* 56:74–84.

———. 1990. "Governors." In Virginia Gray, Herbert Jacob, and Robert B. Albritton, eds., *Politics in the American States.* Glenview, IL: Scott Foresman/Little Brown.

———. 1991. "Gubernatorial Elections, 1977–1990." *Comparative State Politics* 12, no. 2: 18–21.

———. 1994. "The Governors, 1992–1993." In *The Book of the States,* vol. 30. Lexington, KY: Council of State Governments.

———, ed. 1985. *Gubernatorial Transitions: The 1982 Election.* Durham, NC: Duke University Press.

———, ed. 1986. *Re-Electing the Governor: The 1982 Elections.* Lanham, MD: University Press of America.

Black, Earl, and Merle Black. 1982. "Successful Durable Factions in Southern Politics." In Laurence W. Moreland, Tod A. Baker, and Robert P. Stead, eds., *Contemporary Southern Political Attitudes and Behavior.* New York: Praeger.

Black, Merle, and Earl Black. 1982. "The Growth of Contested Republican Primaries in the American South, 1960–1980." In Laurence W. Moreland, Tod A. Baker, and Robert P. Steed, eds., *Contemporary Southern Political Attitudes and Behavior.* New York: Praeger.

Bone, Hugh. 1986. "Moral Conservatives Control Washington State Republican Convention." *Comparative State Politics Newsletter* 7 (October): 4–5.

Bryan, Frank M. 1981. *Politics in the Rural States.* Boulder, CO: Westview Press.

Buck, Vincent. 1972. "Presidential Coattails and Congressional Loyalty." *Midwest Journal of Political Science* 16:460–72.

Burnham, Walter Dean. 1967. "Party Systems and the Political Process." In William N. Chambers and Walter Dean Burnham, eds., *The American Party Systems.* New York: Oxford University Press.

Cain, Bruce E. 1991. "Lessons from the Inside." In Gerald C. Lubenow, ed., *The 1990 Governor's Race.* Berkeley: University of California Institute of Governmental Studies Press.

Caldeira, Gregory, and Samuel C. Patterson. 1982. "Bringing Home the Votes: Electoral Outcomes in State Legislative Races." *Political Behavior* 4:33–67.

Capell, Elizabeth A. 1988. "A Freshman Succeeds in the California Legislature." Ph.D. diss., University of California, Berkeley.

Carroll, James R. 1982. "Dull Tom and Cautious Duke." *California Journal* 13 (July): 229–31.

Chertkoff, Jerome. 1966. "The Effects of Probability of Future Success on Coalition Formation." *Journal of Experimental Social Psychology* 2:265–77.

Clucas, Richard I. 1995. *The Speaker's Electoral Connection: Willie Brown and the California Assembly.* Berkeley: University of California Institute of Governmental Studies Press.

COGEL (Council on Governmental Ethics Laws). 1984–85. *Blue Book: Campaign*

Finance, Ethics, and Lobby Law. Lexington, KY: Council of State Governments.

COGEL (Council on Governmental Ethics Laws). 1993. *Blue Book: Campaign Finance, Ethics, Lobby Law and Judicial Conduct.* 9th ed. Lexington, KY: Council of State Governments.

Collie, Melissa P. 1984. "Voting Behavior in Legislatures." *Legislative Studies Quarterly* 9:3–50.

Cotter, Cornelius, James L. Gibson, John F. Bibby, and Robert J. Huckshorn. 1984. *Party Organizations in American Politics.* New York: Praeger.

Council of State Governments. 1996. *The Book of the States, 1996–1997.* Lexington, KY: Council of State Governments.

Cox, Gary W., and Samuel Kernell, eds. 1991. *The Politics of Divided Government.* Boulder, CO: Westview Press.

Cronin, Thomas E., and Robert D. Loevy. 1993. *Colorado Politics and Government.* Lincoln: University of Nebraska Press.

Cuomo, Mario M. 1984. *Diaries of Mario M. Cuomo: The Campaign for Governor.* New York: Random House.

Donovan, Beth. 1993. "Much Maligned 'Soft Money' is Precious to Both Parties." *CQ Weekly Report,* May 15, 1195–1200.

Downs, Anthony. 1957. *An Economic Theory of Democracy.* New York: Harper and Row.

Edwards, George C. III. 1978. "Presidential Electoral Performance as a Source of Presidential Power." *American Journal of Political Science* 22:152–68.

Epstein, Leon. 1986. *Political Parties in the American Mold.* Madison: University of Wisconsin.

———. 1993. "Research Directions." *American Review of Politics* 14:467–80.

Erikson, Robert S., Gerald C. Wright, and John P. McIver. 1993. *Statehouse Democracy: Public Opinion and Policy in the American States.* New York: Cambridge University Press.

Eyre, R. John, and Curtis Martin. 1967. *The Colorado Preprimary System.* Boulder: Bureau of Governmental Research and Services, University of Colorado.

Fenton, John H. 1966. *Midwest Politics.* New York: Holt, Rinehart and Winston.

Fiorina, Morris. 1992. *Divided Government.* New York: Macmillan.

Fitzgerald, Michael R., Floydette C. Cory, Stephen J. Rechichar, and Abigail S. Hudgens. 1986. "The 1982 Gubernatorial Election in Tennessee." In Thad L. Beyle, ed., *Re-electing the Governor: The 1982 Elections.* Lanham, MD: University Press of America.

Francis, Wayne. 1967. *Legislative Issues in the American States: A Comparative Analysis.* Chicago: Rand McNally.

———. 1970. "Coalitions in American State Legislatures: A Propositional Analysis." In Sven Groennings et al., eds., *The Study of Coalition Behavior.* New York: Holt, Rinehart Winston.

Francis, Wayne, and Ronald E. Weber. 1980. "Legislative Issues in the 50 States: Managing Complexity Through Classification," *Legislative Studies Quarterly* 3:407–21.

Gable, Richard W., Mark Sektnan, and Joel King. 1985. "The 1982–1983 Gubernatorial Transition in California." In Thad L. Beyle, ed., *Gubernatorial Transitions: The 1982 Election.* Durham, NC: Duke University Press.

Garand, James C. 1991. "Electoral Marginality in State Legislative Elections, 1968–1986." *Legislative Studies Quarterly* 16:7–28.

Gerber, Elizabeth. 1991. Unpublished data.

Gierzynski, Anthony. 1992. *Legislative Party Campaign Committees in the American States.* Lexington: University Press of Kentucky.

Gove, Samuel, and Louis H. Masotti. 1982. *After Daley: Chicago Politics in Transition.* Urbana: University of Illinois Press.

Gray, Virginia, and Karen Hult. 1985. "The Gubernatorial Transition in Minnesota, 1982." In Thad L. Beyle, ed., *Gubernatorial Transitions: The 1982 Election.* Durham, NC: Duke University Press.

Green, Lee S., David H. Grubbs, and Victor C. Hobday. 1982. *Government in Tennessee,* 4th ed. Knoxville: University of Tennessee Press.

Green, Paul M. 1986a. "The Democrats' Biennial Ritual:Slatemaking." *Comparative State Politics Newsletter* 7, no. 1: 7–11.

———. 1986b. "Party Politics in Illinois: Republicans v. Democrats et al." *Illinois Issues,* August–September, 10–14.

Hanson, Royce. 1989. *Tribune of the People: The Minnesota Legislature and Its Leadership.* Minneapolis: University of Minnesota Press.

Harder, Marvin A. 1986. "The Re-Election of a Governor and the Aftermath: The Case of Kansas, 1982–1983." In Thad L. Beyle, ed., *Re-electing the Governor: The 1982 Elections.* Lanham, MD: University Press of America.

Harder, Marvin A., and Carolyn Rampey. 1972. *The Kansas Legislature.* Lawrence: University Press of Kansas.

Harmel, Robert, and Keith E. Hamm. 1986. "Development of a Party Role in a No-Party Legislature." *Western Political Quarterly* 39:79–92.

Harmon, Kathryn Newcomer, and Marsha L. Brauen. 1979. "Joint Electoral Outcomes as Cues for Congressional Support of U.S. Presidents." *Legislative Studies Quarterly* 4:281–99.

Hero, Rodney. 1986. "The Lamm Landslide in Colorado: Incumbent Popularity and a Divided Opposition." In Thad L. Beyle, ed., *Re-electing the Governor: The 1982 Elections.* Lanham, MD: University Press of America.

Hevesi, Alan G. 1975. *Legislative Politics in New York State.* New York: Praeger.

Hodson, Timothy, Rich Jones, Karl Kurtz, and Gary Moncrief. 1995. "Leaders and Limits: Changing Patterns of State Legislative Leadership under Term Limits." Paper presented at the annual meeting of the Western Political Science Association, March 16–18, Portland, OR.

Jacobson, Gary. 1975. "The Impact of Broadcast Campaigning on Electoral Outcomes." *Journal of Politics* 37:769–93.

———. 1990. *The Electoral Origins of Divided Government.* Boulder, CO: Westview Press.

Jewell, Malcolm E. 1984. *Parties and Primaries: Nominating State Governors.* New York: Praeger.

———. 1985. "Political Parties, Courts, and the Nominating Process." Paper presented at the annual meeting of the Southern Political Science Association. November 7–9, Nashville, TN.

———. 1994. "The Role of Party in Nominating Gubernatorial Candidates." *American Review of Politics* 15:157–70.

Jewell, Malcolm E., and David Breaux. 1988. "The Effect of Incumbency on State Legislative Elections." *Legislative Studies Quarterly* 13:495–514.

Jewell, Malcolm E., and Sarah M. Morehouse. 1995. Preprimary Endorsements: An Asset or Liability for State Political Parties?" Paper presented at the annual meeting of the American Political Science Association, August 31–September 3, Chicago.

———. 1996. "What Are Party Endorsements Worth? A Study of Preprimary Gubernatorial Endorsements." *American Politics Quarterly* 24: 338–82.

———. 1995b. "Jewell, Malcolm E., and David M. Olson. 1982. *Political Parties and Elections in the American States.* 2d ed. Chicago: Dorsey Press.

———. 1988. *Political Parties and Elections in the American States.* 3d ed. Chicago: Dorsey Press.

Jewell, Malcolm E., and Samuel C. Patterson. 1986. *The Legislative Process in the United States.* 4th ed. New York: Random House.

Jewell, Malcolm E., and Marcia Lynn Whicker. 1994. *Legislative Leadership in the American States.* Ann Arbor: University of Michigan Press.

Jones, Charles O. 1994. *The Presidency in a Separated System.* Washington, DC: Brookings Institution.

Jones, Ruth S. 1984. "Financing State Elections." In Michael J. Malbin, ed., *Money and Politics in the United States.* Washington, DC: American Enterprise Institute for Public Policy Research.

Keenan, Boyd. 1986. "The 1982 Illinois Gubernatorial Election: Historic on Many 'Counts.'" In Thad L. Beyle, ed., *Re-electing the Governor: The 1982 Elections.* Lanham, MD: University Press of America.

Kelley, E. W. 1968. "Techniques of Studying Coalition Formation." *Midwest Journal of Political Science* 12:62–84.

Key, V. O. Jr. 1950. *Southern Politics in State and Nation.* New York: Alfred A. Knopf.

———. 1956. *American State Politics: An Introduction.* New York: Alfred A. Knopf.

———. 1964. *Politics, Parties and Pressure Groups.* 5th ed. New York: Thomas Y. Crowell.

Keynes, Edward, Richard Tobin, and Robert Danziger. 1979. "Institutional Effects on Elite Recruiting: The Case of State Nominating Systems." *American Politics Quarterly* 7:283–302.

Kunkel, Joseph A. 1987. "Organizational Effectiveness in an Era of Weakened Parties: Preprimary Endorsements in Minnesota, 1986." Paper presented at the annual meeting of the Midwest Political Science Association, April 8–11, Chicago.

Lamis, Alexander P. 1984. *The Two-Party South.* New York: Oxford University Press.

Lebedoff, David. 1969. *The 21st Ballot: A Political Party Struggle in Minnesota.* Minneapolis: University of Minnesota Press.

LeBlanc, Hugh L. 1969. "Voting in State Senates: Party and Constituency Influences." *Midwest Journal of Political Science* 13:33–57.

Lerner, Michael A. 1982. "Mike Curb's Hit Parade". *New Republic,* April 21, 10–13.

Lieberman, Joseph I. 1966. *The Power Broker.* Boston: Houghton and Mifflin.

———. 1981. *The Legacy.* Hartford: Spoonwood Press.

Lilley, William III, Laurence J. DeFranco, and William M. Diefenderfer III. 1994. *The Almanac of State Legislatures.* Washington, DC: Congressional Quarterly.

Lindblom, Charles E. 1957. "In Praise of Political Science." *World Politics* 9:240–53.

Lockard, W. Duane. 1959. *New England State Politics.* Princeton: Princeton University Press.

Logan, Andy. 1982. "Around City Hall." *New Yorker,* February 22, 104–11.

Loomis, Burdett A. 1994. *Time, Politics and Policies.* Lawrence: University Press of Kansas.

Malbin, Michael J., and Gerald Benjamin. 1992. "Legislatures after Term Limits." In Gerald Benjamin and Michael J. Malbin, eds., *Limiting Legislative Terms.* Washington, DC: Congressional Quarterly Books.

Mayhew, David R. 1986. *Placing Parties in American Politics.* Princeton, NJ: Princeton University Press.

———. 1991. *Divided We Govern: Party Control, Lawmaking and Investigations, 1946–1990.* New Haven, CT: Yale University Press.

McNitt, Andrew D. 1980. "The Effect of Preprimary Endorsement on Competition for Nominations: An Examination of Different Nominating Systems." *Journal of Politics* 42:257–66.

Meltz, David B. 1973. "Legislative Party Cohesion: A Model of the Bargaining Process in State Legislatures." *Journal of Politics* 35:649–81.

Morehouse, Sarah M. 1966. "The Governor and His Legislative Party." *American Political Science Review* 60:923–42.

———. 1973. "The State Political Party and the Policy Making Process." *American Political Science Review* 67:55–72.

———. 1980. "The Effect of Preprimary Endorsements on State Party Strength." Paper presented at the annual meeting of the American Political Science Association, August 28–31, Washington, DC.

———. 1981a. *State Politics, Parties and Policy.* New York: Holt, Rinehart and Winston.

———. 1981b. "Party Loyalty in a House Divided." Paper presented at the annual meeting of the American Political Science Association, September 3–6, New York.

———. 1986. "Connecticut: The Governor Fills His Own Shoes." In Thad L.

Beyle, ed., *Re-electing the Governor: The 1982 Elections.* Lanham, MD: University Press of America.

———. 1990. "Money versus Party Effort: Nominating for Governor." *American Journal of Political Science* 34:706–24.

———. 1992. "Legislative Party Voting for the Governor's Program." Paper presented at the annual meeting of the American Political Science Association, September 3–6, Chicago.

———. 1993. "Voting for the Governor's Program: Party versus Constituency." Paper presented at the annual meeting of the Southern Political Science Association, November 3–6, Savannah, GA.

———. 1996. "Legislative Party Voting for the Governor's Program." *Legislative Studies Quarterly* 21:359–81.

Morehouse, Sarah M., and Malcolm E. Jewell. 1992. "Divided Government and Legislative Support for the Governor's Program." Paper presented at the annual meeting of the Southern Political Science Association, November 5–7, Atlanta.

Muchmore, Lynn, and Thad L. Beyle. 1980. "The Governor as Party Leader." *State Government* 53:121–24.

Opinion Outlook. 1981. August, 7.

Parker, Joan A. 1984. *Summit and Resolution: The Illinois Tax Increase of 1983.* Springfield, IL: Sangamon State University.

Patterson, Thomas E. 1980. *The Mass Media Election: How Americans Choose Their President.* New York: Praeger.

Polsby, Nelson W., and Aaron Wildavsky. 1991. *Presidential Elections.* 8th ed. New York: Free Press.

Pomper, Gerald. 1992. *Passions and Interests.* Lawrence: University Press of Kansas.

Price, Charles. 1992a. "Political Parties Back Away from Pre-primary Endorsements." *California Journal,* April, 199–204.

———. 1992b. "The Guillotine Comes to California: Term Limit Politics in the Golden State." In Gerald Benjamin and Michael J. Malbin, eds., *Limiting Legislative Terms.* Washington, D.C.: Congressional Quarterly Press.

Ranney, Austin. 1962. *The Doctrine of Responsible Party Government.* Urbana: University of Illinois Press.

Riker, William. 1962. *The Theory of Political Coalitions.* New Haven, CT: Yale University Press.

Rose, Gary L. 1992. *Connecticut Politics at the Crossroads.* Lanham, MD: University Press of America.

Rosenthal, Alan. 1981. *Legislative Life.* Cambridge, MA: Harper and Row.

———. 1990. *Governors and Legislatures: Contending Powers.* Washington, DC: CQ Press.

Rowe, Leonard. 1961. *Preprimary Endorsements in California Politics.* Berkeley: Bureau of Public Administration, University of California.

Sabato, Larry. 1980. "Gubernatorial Politics and the New Campaign Technology." *State Government* 53:148–52.

———. 1983. *Goodbye to Goodtime Charlie.* 2d ed. Washington, DC: CQ Press.

Salzman, Ed. 1982. "Primary Analysis and Outlook for November." *California Journal* (July) 237–52.

Scarrow, Howard A. 1983. *Parties, Elections and Representation in the State of New York.* New York: New York University Press.

Schlesinger, Joseph A. 1985. "The New American Political Party." *American Political Science Review* 79:1152–69.

———. 1991. *Political Parties and the Winning of Office.* Ann Arbor: University of Michigan Press.

Schwartz, Mildred R. 1990. *The Party Network: The Robust Organization of Illinois Republicans.* Madison: University of Wisconsin Press.

Simmons, Thomas H. 1984. "Colorado." In Alan Rosenthal and Maureen Moakley, eds., *The Political Life of the American States.* New York: Praeger.

Sorauf, Frank. 1992. *Inside Campaign Finance: Myths and Realities.* New Haven, CT: Yale University Press.

Squire, Peverill. 1992. "The Theory of Legislative Institutionalization and the California Assembly." *Journal of Politics* 54:1026–54.

Stanley, Jeanie R. 1992. "Party Realignment in Texas." In Maureen Moakley, ed., *Party Realignment and State Politics.* Columbus: Ohio State University Press.

Stonecash, Jeffrey M. 1989. "Political Cleavage in Gubernatorial and Legislative Elections: Party Competition in New York, 1970–1982." *Western Political Quarterly* 42:69–81.

Sturrock, David E., Michael Margolis, John C. Green, and Dick Kimmins. 1994. "Ohio Elections and Political Parties in the 1990s." In Alexander P. Lamas, ed., *Ohio Politics.* Kent, OH: Kent State University Press.

Sundquist, James L. 1988. "Needed: A Political Theory for the New Era of Coalition Government in the United States." *Political Science Quarterly.* 103:613–35.

Tidmarch, Charles, Edward Lonergan, and John Sciortino. 1986. "Interparty Competition in the U.S. States: Legislative Elections, 1970–1978," *Legislative Studies Quarterly* 11:353–74.

Tobin, Richard J., and Edward Keynes. 1975. "Institutional Differences in the Recruitment Process: A Four-State Study." *American Journal of Political Science* 19:667–92.

Tompkins, Mark E. 1984. "The Electoral Fortunes of Gubernatorial Incumbents." *Journal of Politics* 46:520–43.

Van Der Slik, Jack. ed. 1990. *Almanac of Illinois Politics—1990.* Springfield, IL: Illinois Issues.

Van Der Slik, Jack, and Kent D. Redfield. 1989. *Lawmaking in Illinois.* Springfield, IL: Sangamon State University.

Wiggins, Charles W., Keith E. Hamm, and Howard R. Balanoff. 1985. "The 1982 Gubernatorial Transition in Texas: Bolt Cutters, Late Trains, Lame Ducks, and Bullock's Bullets." In Thad L. Beyle, ed., *Gubernatorial Transitions: The 1982 Election.* Durham, NC: Duke University Press.

Newspaper Articles, by State

California

Decker, Cathleen, and Amy Wallace. 1994. "Democrats Start Their Convention Amid Discord." *Los Angles Times,* 16 April, 1.

Colorado

Miller, Carl. 1982a. "Lamm, Dick Begin Re-election Drive." *Denver Post,* 2 May, 3B.
———. 1982b. "Awful Truth Awaits Winn." *Denver Post,* 25 June, 5B.
Westgaard, Neil. 1982. "Two Political Polls Give Strong Edge to Lamm." *Denver Post,* 20 May, 5B, 7B.
———. 1983. "Lamm, Legislators, Cooperate." *Denver Post,* 13 February, 10B.

Kansas

Ferguson, Lew. 1982. "Kansas Candidates Launch Television Advertising Blitz." *Topeka Capital-Journal,* 13 August, 1.

Minnesota

"Another Nail in Coffin." 1986. *Free Press,* 6 May, 4.
Dawson, Gary. 1982. "Wangberg Candidacy Disputed." *St. Paul Dispatch,* 11 February, 6C.
Editorial. 1982. "Glen Sherwood as Caucus Leader." *Minneapolis Star Tribune,* 6 June, 12A.
Klobuchar, Jim. 1995. "He Never Really Left the Iron Range." *Minneapolis Star Tribune,* 22 September, 1A, 7A.
Minnesota Poll. 1982. "IR Candidates for Governor Not Widely Known." *Minneapolis Tribune,* 2 May, 1A, 6A.
Salisbury, Bill. 1982a. "Sherwood's Platform Built on Bible, Believers." *St. Paul Sunday Pioneer Press,* 23 May, 1B, 15B.
———. 1982b. "Overgaard Leads After 5 Ballots." *St. Paul Pioneer Press Dispatch,* 19 June, 1A, 6A.
Salisbury, Bill, and Steven Dornfield. 1982. "Wangberg Ambitions Key to Nomination." *St. Paul Sunday Pioneer Press,* 20 June, 8A.
Spano, Wy, and D. J. Leary. 1982. "Delegates Don't Contribute; Support Moral Majority." *Politics in Minnesota,* 18 June, 2.
Sturdevant, Lori. 1982a. "Influence of Evangelical Christians Alters IR Party." *Minneapolis Star Tribune,* 9 May, 1A, 4A.
———. 1982b. "Spannaus Now Turns to Face Perpich." *Minneapolis Star Tribune,* 7 June, 1A, 4A.

——. 1982c. "Party Endorsement Assures Aid, Advice from Political Parties." *Minneapolis Star Tribune,* 30 August, 1A, 4A.

New York

Fisher, Ian. 1995. "Budget Brawlers Bloody, but Smiling." *New York Times,* 13 June, B5.
Omicinski, John. 1982. "Poll Finds Koch, Lehrman Out in Front." *Gannett Westchester Newspapers,* 16 May, 1, 10.

Oregon

Editorial. 1982. "Voter Mood Reflects the Times." *Portland Oregonian,* 20 May, B6.

Tennessee

Fletcher, Bill, and Rick Locker. 1982. "O'Brien's Campaign Bogged Down, Tyree Edging Toward Win: Experts." *Nashville Banner,* 4 August, A7.
Pigott, Mike. 1982a. "Alexander, O'Brien, Tyree Plugging Away at Election Bids." *Nashville Banner,* 27 May, D10.
——. 1982b. "Crossville Community Center Turns Down Alexander Visit." *Nashville Banner,* 3 June, C1.
Pigott, Mike, and Bill Fletcher. 1982. "Tyree Wins; Staffs Hedge on Unity." *Nashville Banner,* 6 August, 1A, 8A.

Texas

Attlesey, Sam. 1982. "Clements Kicks Off Dallas Campaign." *Dallas Morning News,* 19 April, 14A.
Blow, Steve. 1982. "East Texas Family Controls Empire." *Dallas Morning News,* 14 February, 1A, 18A.
Kinch, Sam. 1982. "Labor Panel Ducks Endorsement for Governor." *Dallas Morning News,* 12 March, 27A.
Kuempel, George. 1982. "Buying the Governor's Office." *Dallas Morning News,* 7 April, 19A.

Author Index

Advisory Commission on Intergovernmental Relations, 30, 67
Aldrich, John H., 181, 282, 283–84
Alexander, Herbert E., 71
Appleton, Andrew M., 245
Attlesey, Sam, 104
American Political Science Assocation, 6

Baer, Denise L., 28, 29, 284
Balanoff, Howard R., 109
Bartels, Larry M., 181
Bell, Charles G., 101
Benjamin, Gerald, 222, 278
Berry, William D., 20–21
Beyle, Thad L., 1, 2, 26, 79, 124, 182, 202
Bibby, John F., 29, 30, 282
Black, Earl, 20–21, 43–45
Black, Merle, 20–21, 43–45
Blow, Steve, 92
Bone, Hugh, 35
Bositis, David, 28, 29
Brauen, Marsha L., 210, 237
Breaux, David, 209
Bryan, Frank M., 41
Buck, Vincent, 210
Burnham, Walter Dean, 6

Cain, Bruce E., 50
Caldeira, Gregory, 209
Canon, Bradley C., 20–21
Capell, Elizabeth, 227
Carroll, James R., 118
Chertkoff, Jerome, 11
Clucas, Richard I., 227

Collie, Melissa, 208
Corie, Floydette, 109, 229
Council on Governmental Ethics Laws, 73
Cox, Gary W., 272
Cronin, Thomas E., 58, 225
Cuomo, Mario, 222

Danziger, Robert, 21
Dawson, Gary, 137
Decker, Cathleen, 259
DeFranco, Laurence J., 300
Diefenderfer, William M., III, 300
Dolan, Julie A., 284
Donvan, Beth, 70
Dornfield, Steven, 173
Downs, Anthony, 4, 7

Edwards, George C., III, 210
Epstein, Leon, 4
Erikson, Robert S., 6, 31, 58, 106, 114, 279–80, 283
Eyre, R. John, 59
Fenton, John H., 18
Ferguson, Lew, 112
Fiorina, Morris, 8, 271–72
Fisher, Ian, 274
Fitzgerald, Michael, R., 109, 229
Fletcher, Bill, 94, 110
Francis, Wayne, 203, 204

Garand, James C., 209
Gerber, Elizabeth, 300
Gierzynski, Anthony, 276
Gobson, James L., 29, 30, 282
Gove, Samuel, 63

313

Subject Index